ENCYCLOPAEDIA OF OPERATING SYSTEM

ENCYCLOPAEDIA
OF
OPERATING SYSTEM

[Volume—One]

By
Sudhir Kumar

ANMOL PUBLICATIONS PVT. LTD.
NEW DELHI - 110 002 (INDIA)

ANMOL PUBLICATIONS PVT. LTD.
4374/4B, Ansari Road, Daryaganj
New Delhi - 110 002
Phones: 23261597, 23278000
Visit us at: www.anmolpublications.com

Encyclopaedia of Operating System

First Edition, 2004

ISBN 81-261-1792-3 (Set)

PRINTED IN INDIA

Published by J.L. Kumar for Anmol Publications Pvt. Ltd., New Delhi and Printed at Mehra Offset Press, Delhi.

Contents

Vol. 3

Preface

Virtually, an operating system is a program that manages the computer hardware. The components of a computer system are its hardware, software and data. The operating system provides the means for the proper use of these resources in the operation of the computer system. Thus, Operating system is the heart of any computer or we can say operating system is essential part of the computer system. Similarly a course and text on operating system is an essential part of any computer-science education. This field is changing field at breathtakingly rapid rate, as computers are now prevalent in virtually every application, from games for children to the most sophisticated planning tools for governments and multinational firms. Yet the fundamental concepts remain the same and it is clear in all books of operating system.

This work is designed to meet the requirement of introductory course in operating system at the undergraduate and Postgraduate level. It provides a clear description on various concepts that are required for understanding the proper functioning of any operating system.

The hardware text required for an understanding of operating system are included in this book. For coding examples we use predominantly 'C' as well as Java, but the reader can still understand the algorithms without a thorough knowledge of these languages.

The fundamental concepts and algorithms covered in this book are based on the existing commercial operating system in use. The information gathered herein is substantially based on authoritative sources. Our aim is to present these concepts and algorithms in a general setting that is not tied to any particular operating system.

We present a large number of examples that pertain to the most popular operating systems, including Sun Microsystems, Solaris 2, Linux, MS Dos, Windows NT and Windows 2000.

Apart from these some case studies on Unix, and on windows are also included in this work. The entire information is gathered under twenty-seven chapters.

In bringing this text into a book form, I shall be grateful for Mr. J.L. Kumar, Managing Director, Anmol Publications Pvt. Ltd., New Delhi and Mr. J.K. Dawra for their valuable suggestions. Any suggestions for the improvement of the book are also welcome which will be subsequently appended in the revised edition of the book.

— S.K.

1

Introduction of Operating System

An **operating system** is a program that manages the computer hardware. It also provides a basis for application programs and acts as an intermediary between a user of a computer and the computer hardware. An amazing aspect of operating systems is how varied they are in accomplishing these tasks. Mainframe operating systems are designed primarily to optimize utilization of hardware. Personal systems are designed primarily to optimize utilization of hardware. Personal computer (PC) operating systems support complex games, business applications, and everything in between. Hand-held computer operating systems are designed to provide an environment in which a user can easily interface with the computer to execute programs. Thus, some operating systems are designed to be *convenient,* others to be *efficient,* and some others combination of the two.

To understand what operating systems are, we must first understand how they have developed. In this chapter, we trace the development of operating systems from the first hands-on systems through multiprogrammed and time-shared systems to PCs, and hand-held computers. We also discuss operating system variations, such as parallel, real-time, and embedded systems. As we move through the various stages, we see how the components of operating systems evolved as natural solutions to problems in early computer systems.

Operating System

An operating system is an important part of almost every computer systems. A computer system can be divided roughly into four components: the *hardware,* the *operating system,* the *application programs,* and the *users.*

The **hardware**—the **central processing unit (CPU), the memory,** and the **input/output (I/O) devices**—provides the basic computing resources. The **application programs**—such as word processors, spreadsheets, compilers, and web browsers—define the ways in which these resources are used to solve the computing problems of the users. The operating system controls and coordinates the use of the hardware among the various application programs for the various users.

The components of a computer system are its hardware, software, and data. The operating system provides the means for the proper use of these resources in the operation of the computer system. An operating system is similar to a *government.* Like a government, it performs no useful function by itself. It simply provides an *environment* within which other programs can do useful work. Operating systems can be explored from two viewpoints: the user and the system.

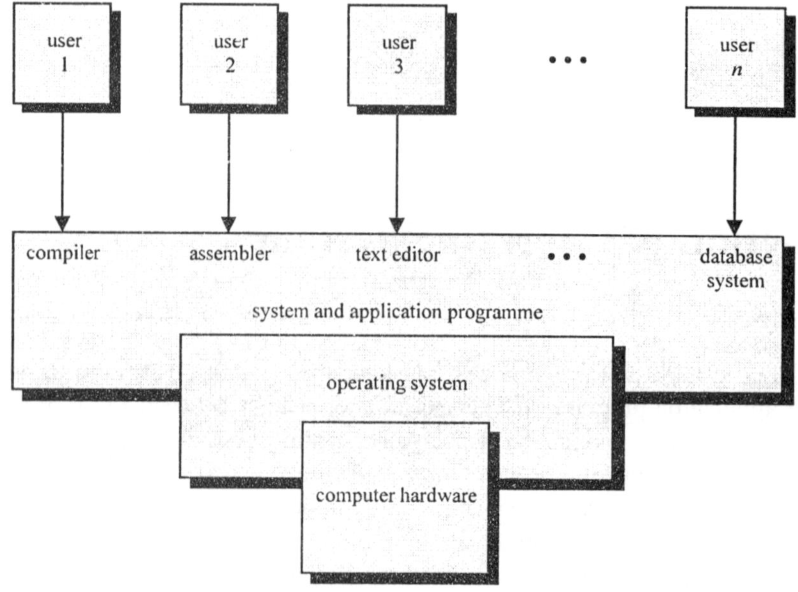

Fig. 1.1. Abstract view of the components of a computer system.

User View

The user view of the computer varies by the interface being used. Most computer users sit in front of a PC, consisting of a monitor, keyboard, mouse, and system unit. Such a system is designed for one user to monopolize its resources, to maximize the work (or play) that the user is performing. In this case, the operating system is designed mostly for **ease of use,** with some attention paid to performance, and none paid to resource utilization. Performance is important to the user, but it does not matter if most of the system is sitting idle, waiting for the slow I/O speed of the user.

Some users sit at a terminal connected to a **mainframe** or **minicomputer.** Other users are accessing the same computer through other terminals. These users share resources and may exchange information. The operating system is designed to maximize **resource utilization**—to assure that all available CPU time, memory, and I/O are used efficiently, and that no individual user takes more than her fair share.

Other users sit at **workstations,** connected to networks of other workstations and servers. These users have dedicated resources at their disposal, but they also share resources such as networking and servers—file, compute and print servers. Therefore, their operating system is designed to compromise between individual usability and resource utilization.

Recently, many varieties of hand-held computers have come into fashion. These devices are mostly stand-alone, used singly by individual users. Some are connected to networks, either directly by wire or (more often) through wireless modems. Due to power and interface limitations they perform relatively few remote operations. The operating systems are designed mostly for individual usability, but performance per amount of battery life is important as well.

Some computers have little or no user view. For example, embedded computers in home devices and automobiles may have a numeric keypad, and may turn indicator lights on or off to show status, but mostly they and their operating systems are designed to run without users intervention.

System View

From the computer's point of view, the operating system is the program that is most intimate with the hardware. We can view an operating system as a **resource allocator.** A computer system has many resources—hardware and software—that may be required to solve a problem: CPU time, memory space, file-storage space, I/O devices, and so on. The operating system acts as the manager of these resources. Facing numerous and possibly conflicting requests for resources, the operating system must decide how to allocate them to specific programs and users so that it can operate the computer system efficiently and fairly.

A slightly different view of an operating system emphasizes the need to control the various I/O devices and user programs. An operating system is a control program. A **control program** manages the execution of user programs to prevent errors and improper use of the computer. It is especially concerned with the operation and control of I/O devices.

In general, however, we have no completely adequate definition of an operating system. Operating systems exist because they are a reasonable way to solve the problem of creating a usable computing system. The fundamental goal of computer systems is to execute user programs and to make solving user problems easier. Towards this goal, computer hardware is constructed. Since bare hardware alone is not particularly easy to use, application programs are developed. These programs require certain common operation, such as those controlling the I/O devices. The common functions of controlling and allocating resources are then brought together into one piece of software: the operating system.

In addition, we have no universally accepted definition of what is part of the operating system. A simple viewpoint is that it includes everything a vendor ships when you order "the operating system." The storage (memory, disks, and tapes) requirements and features included, however, vary greatly across systems. (The storage capacity of a system is measured in gigabytes. (A kilobyte or KB is 1,024 bytes, a megabyte or MB is $1{,}024^2$ bytes, and a gigabyte or GB is $1{,}024^2$ bytes, but computer manufactures often round off these numbers and say that a megabyte is 1 million bytes, and a gigabyte is 1 billion bytes.)) Some systems take up less than 1 megabyte of space and lack even a full-screen editor, whereas others require hundreds of megabytes of space and are entirely based on graphical windowing systems. A more common definition is that the operating system is the one program running at all times on the computer (usually called the **kernel**), with all else being application programs. This last definition is the one that we generally follow. The matter of what constitutes an operating system is becoming important. In 1998, the United States Department of Justice filed suit against Microsoft, in essence claiming that Microsoft included too much functionality in its operating systems and thus prevented competition from application vendors.

System Goals

It is easier to define an operating system by what it *does* than by what it *is,* but even this can be tricky. The primary goal of some operating systems is *convenience for the user.* Operating systems exist because they are supposed to make it easier to compute with them than without them. This view is particularly clear when you look at operating systems for small PCs.

The primary goal of other operating systems is *efficient* operation of the computer system. This is the case for large, shared, multiuser systems. These systems are expensive, so it is desirable to make them as efficient as possible. These two goals—convenience and efficiency—are sometimes contradictory. In the past, efficiency was often more important than convenience (Section 1.2.1). Thus, much of operating-system theory concentrates on optimal use of computing resources. Operating systems have also evolved over time. For example UNIX started with a keyboard and printer as its interface, limiting how convenient it could be for the user. Over time, hardware changed, and UNIX was ported to new hardware with more user-friendly interfaces. Many **graphic user interfaces (GUIs)** were added, allowing UNIX to be more convenient for users while still concentrating on efficiency.

The design of an operating system is a complex task. Designers face may tradeoffs in the design and implementation, and many people are involved not only in bringing an operating system to fruition, but also constantly revising and updating it. How well and given operating system meets its design goals is open to debate, and is subjective to the different users of the operating system.

To see what operating systems are and what they do, let us consider how they have developed over the past 45 years. By tracing that evolution, we can identify the common elements of operating systems, and see how and why these systems have developed as they have.

Mainframe Systems

Mainframe computer systems were the first computers used to tackle many commercial and scientific applications. In this section, we trace the growth of mainframe systems from simple **batch systems,** where the computer runs one—and only one—application, to **time-shared systems,** which allow for user interaction with the computer systems. There are different types of operating systems which are given below.

Batch Systems

Early computers were physically enormous machines run from a console. The common input devices were card readers and tape drives. The common output devices were line printers, tape drives, and card punches. The user did not interact directly with the computer systems. Rather, the user prepared a job—which consisted of the program, the data, and some control information about the nature of the job (control cards)—and submitted it to the computer operator. The job was usually in the form of punch cards. At some later time (after minutes, hours, or days), the output appeared. The output consisted of the result of the program, as well as a dump of the final memory and register contents for debugging.

The operating system in these early computers was fairly simple. Its major task was to transfer control automatically from one job to the next. The operating system was always resident in memory.

To speed up processing, operators **batched** together jobs with similar needs and ran them through the computer as a group. Thus, the programmers would leave their programs with the operator. The operator would sort programs into batches with similar requirements and, as the computer became available, would run each batch. The output from each job would be sent back to the appropriate programmer.

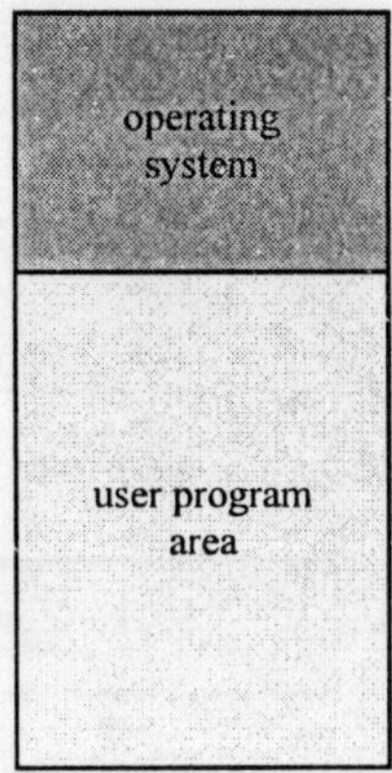

Fig. 1.2. *Memory layout for a simple batch system.*

In this execution environment, the CPU is often idle, because the speeds of the mechanical I/O devices are intrinsically slower than are those of electronic devices. Even a slow CPU works in the micro-second range, with thousands of instructions executed per second. A fast card reader, on the other hand, might read 1200 cards per minute (or 20 cards per second). Thus, the difference in speed between the CPU and its I/O devices may be three orders of magnitude or more. Over time, of course, improvements in technology and the introduction of disks resulted in faster I/O devices. However, CPU speeds increased to an even greater extent, so the problem was not only unresolved, but exacerbated.

The introduction of disk technology allowed the operating system to keep all jobs on a disk, rather than in a serial card reader. With direct access to several jobs, the operating system could perform **job scheduling,** to use resources and perform tasks efficiently.

Multiprogrammed Systems

The most important aspect of job scheduling is the ability to multiprogram. A single user cannot, in general, keep either the CPU or the I/O devices busy at all times. **Multiprogramming** increases CPU utilization by organizing jobs so that the CPU always has one to execute.

The ideas is as follows: The operating system keeps several jobs in memory simultaneously. This set of jobs is a subset of the jobs kept in the job pool—since the number of jobs that can be kept simultaneously in memory is usually much smaller than the number of jobs that can be in the job pool. The operating system picks and begins to execute one of the jobs in the memory. Eventually, the job may have to wait for some task, such as an I/O operation, to complete. In a non-multiprogrammed system, the CPU would sit idle. In a multiprogramming system, the operating system simply switches to, and executes, another job. When *that* job needs to wait, the CPU is switched to *another* job, and so on. Eventually, the first job finishes waiting and gets the CPU back. As long as at least one job needs to execute, the CPU is never idle.

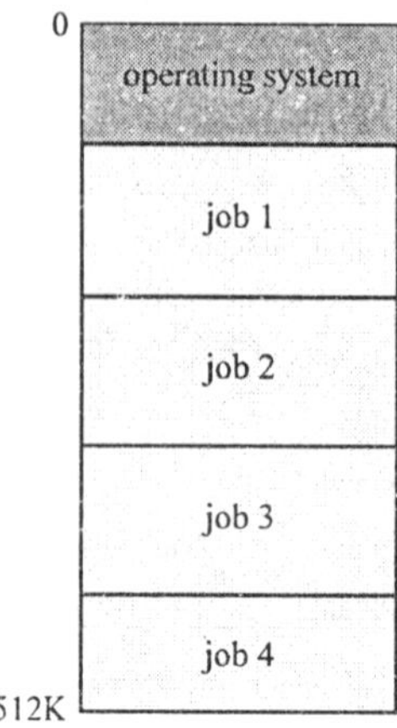

Fig. 1.3. Memory layout for a multiprogramming system.

The idea is common on other life situations. A lawyer does not work for only one client at a time. While one case is waiting to go to trial or have papers typed, the lawyer can work on another case. If she has enough clients, the lawyer will never be idle for lack of work. (Idle lawyers tend to become politicians, so there is a certain social value in keeping lawyers busy.)

Multiprogramming is the first instance where the operating system must make decision for the users. Multiprogrammed operating systems are therefore fairly sophisticated. All the jobs that enter the system are kept in the job pool. This pool consists of all processes residing on disk awaiting allocation of main memory. If several jobs are ready to be brought into memory, and if there is not enough room for all of them, then the system must choose among them. Making this decision is *job scheduling.* When the operating system selects a job from the job pool, it loads that job into memory for execution. Having several programs in memory at the same time requires some form of memory management. In addition, if several jobs are ready to run at the same time, the system must choose among them. Making this decision is *CPU scheduling.* Finally, multiple jobs running concurrently require that their ability to affect one another be limited in all phases of the operating system, including process scheduling, disk storage, and memory management. These considerations are discussed throughout the text.

Time-Sharing Systems

Multiprogrammed, batched systems provide an environment where the various system resources (for example, CPU, memory, peripheral devices) were utilized effectively, but it did not provide for user interaction with the computer system. **Time sharing** (or **multi-tasking**) is a logical extension of multiprogramming. The CPU executes multiple jobs by switching among them, but the switches occur so frequently that the users can interact with each program while it is running.

An **interactive (or hands-on) computer system** provides direct communication between the user and the system. The user gives instructions to the operating system or to a program directly, using a keyboard or a mouse, and waits for immediate results. Accordingly, the **response time** should be short—typically within 1 second or so.

A time-shared operating system allows many users to share the computer simultaneously. Since each action or command in a time-shared system tends to be short, only a little CPU time is needed for each user. As the system switches rapidly from one user to the next, each user is given the impression that the entire computer system is dedicated to her use, even though it is being shared among many users.

A time-shared operating system uses CPU scheduling and multiprogramming to provide each user with a small portion of a time-shared computer. Each user has at least one separate program in memory. A program loaded into memory and executing is commonly referred to as a **process.** When a process executes, it typically executes for only a short time before it either finishes or needs to perform I/O. I/O may be interactive; that is, output is to a display for the user and input is from a user keyboard, mouse, or other device. Since interactive I/O typically runs at "people speeds," it may take a long time to complete. Input, for example, may be bounded by the user's typing speed; seven characters per second is fast for people, but incredibly slow for computers. Rather than let the CPU sit idle when this interactive input takes place, the operating system will rapidly switch the CPU to the program of some other user.

Time-sharing operating systems are even more complex than mulitprogrammed operating systems. In both, several jobs must be kept simultaneously in memory, so the system must have memory management and protection. To obtain a reasonable response time, jobs may have to be swapped in and out of main memory to the disk that now serves as a backing store for main memory. A common method for achieving this goal is **virtual memory,** which is a technique that allows the execution of a job that may not be completely in memory. The main advantage of the virtual-memory scheme is that programs can be larger than **physical memory.** Further, it abstracts main memory into a large, uniform array of storage, separating **logical** memory as viewed by the user from physical memory. This arrangement frees programmers from concern over memory-storage limitations.

Time-sharing systems must also provide a file system. The file system resides on a collection of disks; hence, disk management must be provided. Also, time-sharing systems provide a mechanism for concurrent execution, which requires sophisticated CPU-scheduling schemes. To ensure orderly execution, the system must provide mechanisms for job synchronization and communication, and it may ensure that jobs do not get stuck in a deadlock, forever waiting for one another.

The idea of time sharing was demonstrated as early as 1960, but since time-shared systems are difficult and expensive to build, they did not become common until the early 1970s. Although some batch processing is still done, most systems today are time sharing. Accordingly, multiprogramming and time sharing are the central themes of modern operating systems, and they are the central themes of this book.

Desktop Systems

Personal computers PCs appeared in the 1970s. During their first decade, the CPUs in PCs lacked the features needed to protect an operating system from user programs. PC operating systems therefore were neither multiuser nor multitasking. However, the goals of these operating systems have changed with time; instead of maximizing CPU and peripheral utilization, the systems opt for maximizing user convenience and responsiveness. These systems include PCs running Microsoft Windows and the Apple Macintosh. The MS-DOS operating system from Microsoft has been superseded by multiple flavours of Microsoft Windows, and IBM has upgraded MS-DOS to the OS/2 multitasking system. The Apple Macintosh operating system has been ported to more advanced hardware, and now includes new features, such as virtual memory and multitasking. With the release of MacOs X, the core of the operating system is now based on Mach and FreeBSD UNIX for scalability, performances, and features, but it retains the same rich GUI. Linux, a UNIX-like operating system available for PCs, has also become popular recently.

Operating systems for these computers have benefited in several ways from the development of operating systems for mainframes. Microcomputers were immediately able to adopt some of the technology developed for larger operating systems. On the other hand, the hardware costs for microcomputers are sufficiently low that individuals have sole use of the computer, and CPU utilization is no longer a prime concern. Thus, some of the design decisions made in operating systems for mainframes may not be appropriate for smaller systems.

Other design decision still apply. For example file protection was, at first, not necessary on a personal machine. However, these computers are now often tied into other computers over local-area networks or other Internet connections. When other computers and other users can access the files on a PC, file protection again becomes a necessary feature of the operating system. The lack of such protection has made it easy for malicious programs to destroy data on system such as MS-DOS and the Macintosh operating system. These programs may be self-replicating, and may spread rapidly via **worm** or **virus** mechanisms and disrupt entire companies or even worldwide networks. Advanced time-sharing features such as protected memory and file permissions are not enough, on their own, to safeguard a system from attack. Recent security breaches have shown that time and again.

Multiprocessor Systems

Most systems to date are single-processor systems; that is, they have only one main CPU. However, **multiprocessor systems** (also known as **parallel systems** or **tightly coupled systems**) are growing in importance. Such systems have more than one processor in close communication, sharing the computer bus, the clock, and sometimes memory and peripheral devices.

Multiprocessor systems have three main advantages.

1. **Increased throughput.** By increasing the number of processors, we hope to get more work done in less time. The speed-up ratio with N processors is not N; rather, it is less than N. When multiple processors cooperate on a task, a certain amount of overhead is incurred in keeping all the parts working correctly. This overhead, plus contention for shared resources, lowers the expected gain from additional processors. Similarly, a group of N programmers working closely together does not result in N times the amount of work being accomplished.
2. **Economy of scale.** Multiprocessor systems can save more money than multiple single-processor systems, because they can share peripherals, mass storage, and power supplies. If several programs operate on the same set of data, it is cheaper to store those data on one disk

and to have all the processors share them, than to have many computers with local disks and many copies of the data.

3. **Increased reliability.** If functions can be distributed properly among several processors, then the failure of one processor will not halt the system, only slow it down. If we have ten processors and one fails, then each of the remaining nine processors must pick up a share of the work of the failed processor. Thus, the entire system runs only 10 percent slower, rather than failing altogether. This ability to continue providing service proportional to the levels of surviving hardware is called **graceful degradation.** Systems designed for graceful degradation are also called **fault tolerant.**

Continued operation in the presence of failures requires a mechanism to allow the failure to be detected, diagnosed, and, if possible, corrected. The Tandem system uses both hardware and software duplication to ensure continued operation despite faults. The system consists of two identical processors, each with its own local memory. The processors are connected by a bus. One processor is the primary and the other is the backup. Two copies are kept of each process: one on the primary processor and the other on the backup. At fixed checkpoints in the execution of the system, the state information of each job—including a copy of the memory image—is copied from the primary machine to the backup. If a failure is detected, the backup copy is activated and is restarted from the most recent checkpoint. This solution is expensive, since it involves considerable hardware duplication.

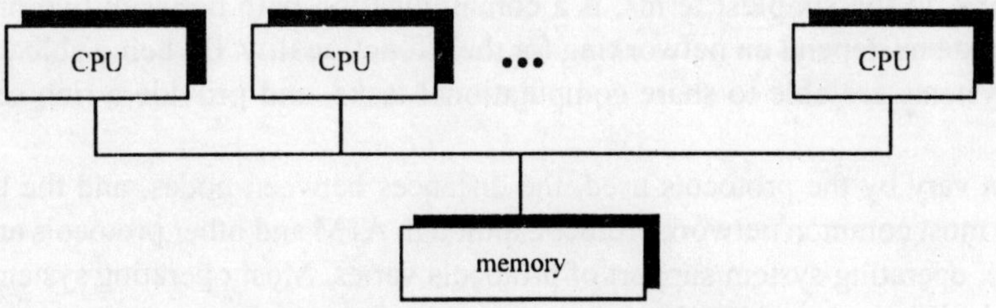

Fig 1.4. *Symmetric multiprocessing architecture.*

The most common multiple-processor systems now use **symmetric multiprocessing (SMP),** in which each processor runs an identical copy of the operating system, and these copies communicate with one another as needed. Some systems use **asymmetric multiprocessing,** in which each processor is assigned a specific task. A master processor controls the system; the other processors either look to the master for instruction or have predefined tasks. This scheme defines a master-slave relationship. The master processor schedules and allocates work to the slave processors.

SMP means that all processors are peers; no master-slave relationship exists between processors. Each processor concurrently runs a copy of the operating systems. An example of the SMP system is Encore's version of UNIX for the Multimax computer. This computer can be configured such that it employs dozens of processors, all running copies of UNIX. The benefit of this model is that many processes can run simultaneously—*N* processes can run if there are *N* CPUs—without causing a significant deterioration of performance. However, we must carefully control I/0 to ensure that the data reaches the appropriate processor. Also, since the CPUs are separate, one may be sitting idle while another is overloaded, resulting in inefficiencies. These inefficiencies can be avoided if the processors share certain data structures. A multiprocessor system of this form will allow processes and resources—such as memory—to be shared dynamically among the various processors, and can lower the variance among the processors. Such a system must be written carefully. Virtually all modern operating systems—including Windows NT, Solaris, Digital UNIX OS/2, and Linux—now provide support for SMP.

The difference between symmetric and asymmetric multiprocessing may be the result of either hardware or software. Special hardware can differentiate the multiple processors, or the software can be written to allow only one master and multiple slaves. For instance, Sun's operating system SunOS Version 4 provides asymmetric multiprocessing, whereas Version 5 (Solaris 2) is symmetric on the same hardware.

As microprocessors become less expensive and more powerful, additional operating-system functions are off-loaded to slaves processors (or **back-ends**). For example it is fairly easy to add a microprocessor with its own memory to manage disk system. The microprocessor could receive a sequence of requests form the main CPU and implement its own disk queue and scheduling algorithm. This arrangement relieves the main CPU of the overhead of disk scheduling. PCs contain a microprocessor in the keyboard to convert the keystrokes into codes to be sent to the CPU. In fact, this use of microprocessors has become so common that it is no longer considered multiprocessing.

Distributed Systems

A **network**, in the simplest terms, is a communication path between two or more systems. Distributed systems depend on networking for their functionality. By being able to communicate, distributed systems are able to share computational tasks, and provide a rich set of features to users.

Networks vary by the protocols used, the distances between nodes, and the transport media. TCP/IP is the most common network protocol, although ATM and other protocols are in widespread use. Likewise, operating-system support of protocols varies. Most operating systems support TCP/IP, including the Windows and UNIX operating systems. Some systems support proprietary protocols to suit their needs. To an operating system, a network protocol simply needs an interactive device—a network adapter, for example—with a device driver to manage it, and software to packages data in the communications protocol to send it and to unpackage it to receive it. These concepts are discussed throughout the book.

Networks are typecast based on the distances between their nodes. A **local-area network (LAN),** exists within a room, a floor, or a building. A **wide-area network (WAN),** usually exists between buildings, cities, or countries. A global company may have a WAN to connect it's offices worldwide. These networks could run on protocol or several protocols. The continuing advent of new technologies brings about new forms of networks. For example, **a metropolitan-area network (MAN),** could link buildings within a city. Blue Tooth devices communicate over a short distance of several feet, in essence creating a **small-area network.**

The media to carry networks are equally varied. They include copper wires, fiber strands, and wireless transmissions between satellites, microwave dishes, and radios. When computing devices are connected to cellular phones, they create a network. Even very short-range infrared communication can be used for networking. At a rudimentary level, whenever computers communicate they use or create a network. These network also vary by their performance and reliability.

Client-Server Systems

As PCs have become faster, more powerful, and cheaper, designers have shifted away from the centralized system architecture. Terminals connected to centralized systems are now being supplanted by PCs. Correspondingly, user-interface functionality that used to be handled directly by the centralized systems is increasingly being handled by the PCs. As a result, centralized systems today act as **server systems** to satisfy requests generated by **client systems.** The general structure of a client-server system is depicted.

Server systems can be broadly categorized as compute servers and file servers.

- **Compute-server systems** provide an interface to which client can send request to perform an action, in response to which they execute the action and send back results to the client.
- **File-server systems** provide a file-system interface where clients can create, update, read, and delete files.

Peer-to-Peer Systems

The growth of computer networks—especially the Internet and World Wide Web (WWW)—has had a profound influence on the recent development of operating systems. When PCs were introduced in the 1970s, they were designed for "personal" use and were generally considered stand-alone computers. With the beginning of widespread public use of the Internet in the 1980s for electronic mail, ftp, and gopher, many PCs became connected to computer networks. With the introduction of the Web in the mid-1990s, network connectivity became an essential component of a computer system.

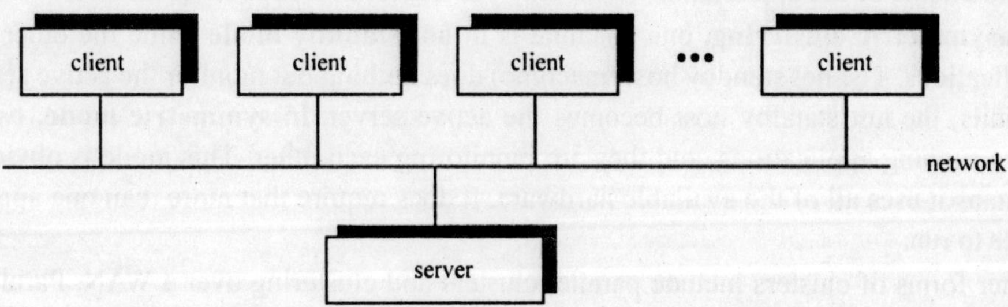

Fig. 1.5. General structure of a client-server system.

Virtually all modern PCs and workstations are capable of running a web browser for accessing **hypertext** documents on the Web. Operating systems (such as Windows, OS/2, MacOS, and UNIX) now also include the systems software (such as TCP/IP and PPP) that enables a computer to access the Internet via a local-area network or telephone connection. Several include the web browser itself, as well as electronic mail, remote login, and file-transfer clients and servers.

In contrast to the tightly coupled systems the computer networks used in these applications consist of a collection of processor that do not share memory or a clock. Instead, each processor has its own local memory. The processors communicate with one another through various communication lines, such as high-speed buses or telephone lines. These systems are usually referred to as **loosely coupled systems** (or **distributed systems**).

Some operating systems have taken the concept of networks and distributed systems further than the notion of providing network connectivity. A **network operating system** is an operating system that provides features such as file sharing across the network, and that includes a communication scheme that allows different processes on different computers to exchange messages. A computer running a network operating system acts autonomously from all other computers on the network, although it is aware of the network and is able to communicate with other networked computers. A distributed operating system is a less autonomous environment: The different operating systems communicate closely enough to provide the illusion that only a single operating system controls the network.

Clustered Systems

Like parallel systems, **clustered systems** gather together multiple CPUs to accomplish computational work. Clustered systems differ from parallel systems, however, in that they are composed of two or more individual systems coupled together. The definition of the term *clustered* is not concrete; many commercial packages wrestle with what a clustered system is, and why one form is better than another. The generally accepted definition is that clustered computers share storage and are closely linked via LAN networking.

Clustering is usually performed to provide **high availability.** A layer of cluster software runs on the cluster nodes. Each node can monitor one or more of the others (over the LAN). If the monitored machine fails, the monitoring machine can take ownership of its storage, and restart the application(s) that were running on the failed machine. The filed machine can remain down, but the users and clients of the application would only see a brief interruption of service.

In **asymmetric clustering,** one machine is in **hot standby mode** while the other is running the applications. The hot standby host (machine) does nothing but monitor the active server. If that server fails, the hot standby host becomes the active server. In **symmetric mode,** two or more hosts are running applications, and they are monitoring each other. This mode is obviously more efficient, as it uses all of the available hardware. It does require that more than one application be available to run.

Other forms of clusters include parallel clusters and clustering over a WAN. Parallel clusters allow multiple hosts to access the same data on the shared storage. Because most operating systems lack support for this simultaneous data access by multiple hosts, parallel clusters are usually accomplished by special versions of software and special releases of applications. For example, Oracle Parallel Server is a version of Oracle's database that has been designed to run on parallel clusters. Each machine runs Oracle, and a layer of software tracks access to the shared disk. Each machine has full access to all data in the database.

In spite of improvements in distributed computing, most systems do not offer general-purpose distributed file systems. Therefore, most clusters do not allow shared access to data on the disk. For this, distributed file systems must provide access control and locking to the files to ensure no conflicting operations occur. This type of service is commonly known as a **distributed lock manager (DLM)**. Work is ongoing for general-purpose distributed file systems, with vendors like Sun Microsystems announcing roadmaps for delivery of a DLM within the operating system.

Cluster technology is rapidly changing. Cluster directions include global clusters, in which the machines could be anywhere in the world (or anywhere a WAN reaches). Such projects are still the subject of research and development.

Clustered system use and features should expand greatly as **storage-area networks (SANs)**, become prevalent. SANs allow easy attachment of multiple hosts to multiple storage units. Current clusters are usually limited to two or four hosts due to the complexity of connecting the hosts to shared storage.

Real-Time Systems

Another form of a special-purpose operating system is the **real-time system.** A real-time system is used when rigid time requirements have been placed on the operation of a processor or the flow of data; thus, it is often used as a control device in a dedicated application. Sensors bring data to the computer. The computer must analyze the data and possibly adjust controls to modify the sensor inputs. Systems that control scientific experiments, medical imaging systems, industrial control systems, and certain display systems are real-time systems. Some automobile-engine fuel-injection systems, home-appliance controllers, and weapon systems are also real-time systems.

A real-time system has well-defined, fixed times constraints. Processing *must* be done within the defined constraints, or the system will fail. For instance, it would not do for a robot arm to be instructed to halt *after* it had smashed into the car it was building. A real-time system functions correctly only if it returns the correct result within its time constraints. Contrast this requirement to a time-sharing system, where it is desirable (but not mandatory) to respond quickly, or to a batch system, which may have no time constraints at all.

Real-time systems come in two flavours: hard and soft. A **hard real-time system** guarantees that critical tasks be completed on time. This goal requires that all delays in the system be bounded, from the retrieval of stored data to the time that it takes the operating system to finish any request made of it. Such times constraints dictate the facilities that are available in hard real-time systems. Secondary storage of any sort is usually limited or missing, with data instead being stored in short-term memory or in read-only memory (ROM). ROM is located on non-volatile storage devices that retain their contents even in the case of electric outage; most other types of memory are volatile. Most advanced operating-system features are absent too, since they tend to separate the user from the hardware, and that separation results in uncertainty about the amount of time an operation will take. For instance, virtual memory is almost never found on real-time systems. Therefore, hard real-time systems conflict with the operation of time-sharing systems, and the two cannot be mixed. Since none of the existing general-purpose operating systems support hard real-time functionality, we do not concern ourselves with this type of system in this text.

A less restrictive type of real-time systems is a **soft real-time system,** where a critical real-time task gets priority over other tasks, and retains that priority until it completes. As in hard real-time systems, the operating-system kernel delays need to be bounded: A real-time task cannot be kept waiting indefinitely for the kernel to run it. Soft real time is an achievable goal that can be mixed with other types of systems. Soft real-time systems, however, have more limited utility than hard real-time systems. Given their lack of deadline support, they are risky to use for industrial control and robotics. They are useful, however in several areas, including multimedia, virtual reality, and advanced scientific projects—such as undersea exploration and planetary rovers. These systems need advanced operating-system features that cannot be supported by hard real-time systems. Because of the expanded uses for soft real-time functionality, it is finding its way into most current operating systems, including major versions of UNIX.

We consider the scheduling facility needed to implement soft real-time functionality in an operating system. We describe the design of memory management for real-time computing. Finally, we describe the real-time components of the Windows 2000 operating system.

Hand-held Systems

Handheld systems include **personal digital assistants (PDAs),** such as *Palm-Pilots* or cellular telephones with connectivity to a network such as the Internet. Developers of hand-held systems and applications face many challenges, most of which are due to the limited size of such devices. For example, a PDA is typically about 5 inches in height and 3 inches in width, and it weighs less than one-half pound. Due to this limited size, most hand-held devices have a small amount of memory, include slow processors, and feature small display screens. We will take a look now at each of these limitations.

Many hand-held devices have between 512KB and 8MB of memory. (Contrast this with a typical PC or workstation, which may have several hundred megabytes of memory!) As a result, the operating system and applications must manage memory efficiently. This includes returning all allocated memory back to the memory manager once the memory is no longer being used. We will explore virtual memory, which allows developers to write programs that behave as if the system has more memory than may be physically available. Currently, many hand-held devices do not use virtual memory techniques, thus forcing program developers to work within the confines of limited physical memory.

A second issue of concern to developers of hand-held devices is the speed of the processor used in the device. Processors for most hand-held devices often run at a fraction of the speed of a processor in a PC. Faster processors require more power. To include a faster processor in a hand-held device would require a larger battery that would have to be replaced (or recharged) more frequently. To minimize the size of most hand-held devices, smaller, slower processors which consume less power are typically used. Therefore, the operating system and applications must be designed not to tax the processor.

The last issue confronting program designers for hand-held devices is the small display screens typically available. Whereas a monitor for a home computer may measure up to 21 inches, the display for a hand-held device is often no more than 3 inches square. Familiar tasks, such as reading e-mail or browsing web pages, must be condensed onto smaller displays. One approach for displaying the content in web pages is **web clipping,** where only a small subset of a web page is delivered and displayed on the hand-held device.

Some hand-held devices may use wireless technology, such as BlueTooth, allowing remote access to e-mail and web browsing. Cellular telephones with connectivity to the **internet fall** into this category. However, many PDAs currently do not provide wireless access. To download data to these devices, typically one first downloads the data to a PC or workstation, and then downloads the data to the PDA. Some PDAs allow data to be directly copied from one device to another using an infrared link. Generally, the limitations in the functionality of PDAs are balanced by their convenience and portability. Their use continues to expand as network connections become more available and other options, such as cameras and MP3 players, expand their utility.

Feature Migration

Overall, an examination of operating system for main frames and microcomputers shows that features once available only on mainframes have been adopted by microcomputers. The same concepts are appropriate for the various classes of computers: mainframes, minicomputers, microcomputers, and hand-held. Many of the concepts will be covered later in this book. However, to start understanding modern operating systems, you need to realize the theme of feature migration and to recognize the long history of many operating-system features.

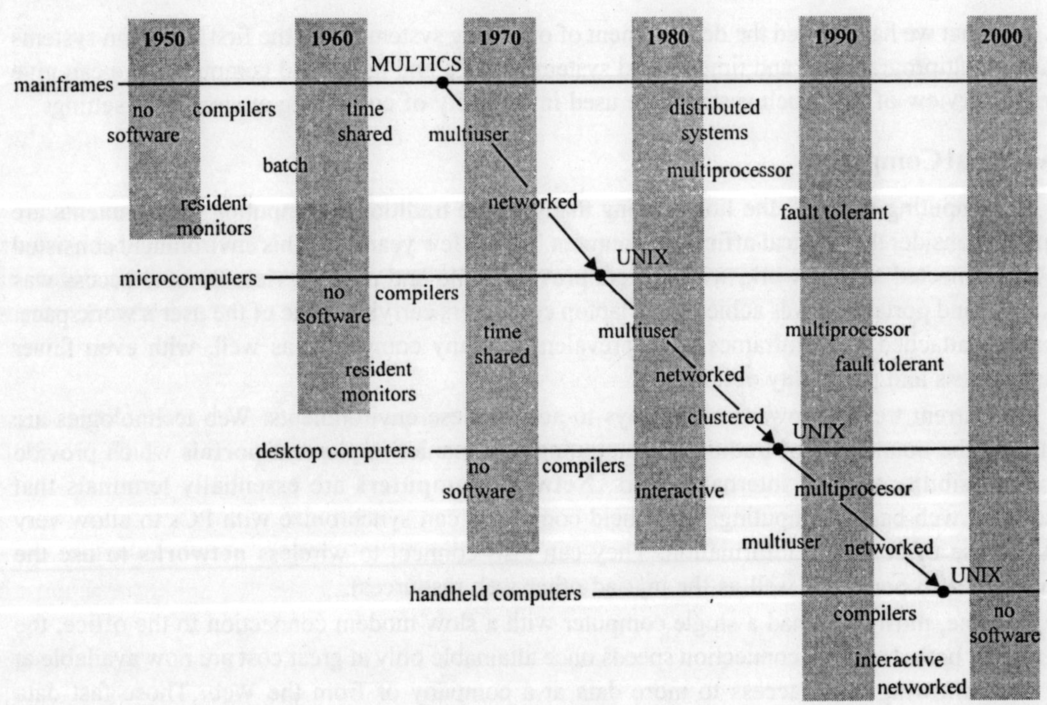

Fig 1.6. Migration of operating-system concepts and features.

A good example of this movement occurred with the MULTIplexed Information and Computing Services (MULTICS) operating systems. MULTICS was developed from 1965 to 1970 at the Massachusetts Institute of Technology (MIT) as a computing **utility.** It ran on a large, complex mainframe computer (the GE 645). Many of the ideas that were developed for MULTICS were subsequently used at Bell Laboratories (one of the original partners in the development of MULTICS) in the design of UNIX. The UNIX operating system was designed circa 1970 for a PDP-11 minicomputer. Around 1980, the features of UNIX became the basis for UNIX-like operating systems on microcomputer systems, and they are being included in more recent operating systems such as Microsoft Windows NT, IBM OS/2, and the Macintosh operating system. Thus, the features developed for a large mainframe system have moved to microcomputers over time.

At the same time as features of large operating systems were being scaled down to fit PCs, more powerful, faster, and more sophisticated hardware systems were being developed. The **personal workstation** is a large PC—for example, the Sun SPARCstation, the HP/Apollo, the IBM RS/6000, and the Intel Pentium class system running Windows NT or a UNIX derivative. Many universities and businesses have large numbers of workstations tied together with local-area networks. As PCs gain more sophisticated hardware and software, the line dividing the two categories—mainframes and microcomputers—is blurring.

Computing Environments

Now that we have traced the development of operating systems from the first hands-on systems through multiprogrammed and time-shared systems to PCs and hand-held computers, we can give a brief overview of how such systems are used in a variety of computing environment settings.

Traditional Computing

As computing matures, the lines among many of the traditional computing environments are blurring. Consider the "typical office environment." Just a few years ago, this environment consisted of PCs connected to a network, with servers providing file and print service. Remote access was awkward, and portability was achieved by laptop computers carrying some of the user's workspace. Terminals attached to mainframes were prevalent at many companies as well, with even fewer remote access and portability options.

The current trend is toward more ways to access these environments. Web technologies are stretching the boundaries of traditional computing. Companies implement **portals** which provide web accessibility to their internal servers. **Network computers** are essentially terminals that understand web-based computing. Hand-held computers can synchronize with PCs to allow very portable use of company information. They can also connect to wireless **networks** to use the company's web portal (as well as the myriad other web resources).

At home, most users had a single computer with a slow modem connection to the office, the Internet, or both. Network connection speeds once attainable only at great cost are now available at low cost, allowing more access to more data at a company or from the Web. Those fast data connections are allowing home computers to serve up web pages and to contain their own networks with printers, client PCs, and servers. Some homes even have **firewalls** to protect these home environments from security breaches.

Web-Based Computing

The Web has become ubiquitous, leading to more access by a wider variety of devices than was dreamt about a few years ago. PCs are still the most prevalent access devices, with workstations (high-end graphics-oriented PCs), hand-held PDAs, and even cell phones also providing access.

Web computing has increased the emphasis on networking. Devices that were not previously networked now have wired or wireless access. Devices that were not previously networked now have faster network connectivity, either by improved networking technology, optimized network implementation code, or both.

The implementation of web-based computing has given rise to new categories of devices, such as **load balancers** which distribute network connections among a pool of similar servers. Operating systems like Windows 95, which acted as web clients, have evolved into Windows ME and Windows 2000, which can act as web servers as well as clients. Generally, the Web has increased the complexity of devices as their users require them to be web-enabled.

Embedded Computing

Embedded computers are the most prevalent form of computers in existence. They run embedded real-time operating systems. These devices are found everywhere, from car engines and manufacturing robots to VCRs and microwave ovens. They tend to have very specific tasks. The systems they run on are usually primitive, lacking advanced features, such as virtual memory, and even disks. Thus, the operating systems provide limited features. They usually have little or no user interface, preferring to spend their time monitoring and managing hardware devices, such as automobile engines and robotic arms.

As an example, consider the afore mentioned firewalls and load balancers. Some are general-purpose computers, running standard operating systems—such as UNIX—with special-purpose applications loaded to implement the functionality. Others are hardware devices with a special-purpose operating system embedded within, providing just the functionality desired.

The use of embedded systems continues to expand. The power of those devices, both as standalone units and as members of networks and the Web, is sure to increase as well. Entire houses can be computerized, so that a central computer—either a general-purpose computer or an embedded systems—can control heating and lighting, alarm systems, and even coffee makers. Web access can let a home-owner tell the house to heat up before he arrives home. Someday, the refrigerator may call the grocery store when it notices the milk is gone.

Summary

Operating systems have been developed over the past 45 years for two main purposes. First, the operating system attempts to schedule computational activities to ensure good performance of the computing systems. Second, it provides a convenient environment of the development and execution of programs. Initially, computer systems were used from the front console. Software such as assemblers, loaders, linkers, and compilers improved the convenience of programming the system, but also required substantial set-up time. To reduce the set-up time, facilities hired operators and batched similar jobs.

Batch systems allowed automatic job sequencing by a resident operating system and greatly improved the overall utilization of the computer. The computer no longer had to wait for human operation. CPU utilization was still low, however, because of the slow speed of the I/O devices relative to that of the CPU. Off-line operation of slow devices provided a means to use multiple reader-to-tape and tape-to-printer systems for one CPU.

To improve the overall performance of the computer system, developers introduced the concept of multiprogramming, so that several jobs could be kept in memory at one time. The CPU is switched back and forth among them to increase CPU utilization and to decrease the total time needed to execute the jobs.

Multiprogramming also allows time sharing. Time-shared operating systems allow many users (from one to several hundred) to use a computer system interactively at the same time.

PCs are microcomputers; they are considerably smaller and less expensive than mainframe systems. Operating systems for these computers have benefitted from the development of operating systems, for mainframes in several ways. However, since an individual has sole use of the computer, CPU utilization is no longer a prime concern. Hence, some of the design decisions made for mainframe operating systems may not be appropriate for these smaller systems. Other design decisions, such as those for security, are appropriate for both small and large systems, as PCs can now be connected to other computers and users through networks and the Web.

Parallel systems have more than one CPU in close communications; the CPUs share the computer bus, and sometimes share memory and peripheral devices. Such systems can provide increased throughput and enhanced reliability. Distributed systems allow sharing of resources on geographically dispersed hosts. Clustered systems, allow multiple machines to perform commutations on data contained on shared storage, and let computing continue in the case of failures of some subset of cluster members.

A hard real-time system is often used as a control device in a dedicated application. A hard real-time operating system has well-defined, fixed time constraints. Processing *must* be done within the defined constraints, or the system will fail. Soft real-time systems have less stringent timing constraints, and do not support deadline scheduling.

Recently, the influence of the Internet and the World Wide Web has encouraged the development of modern operating systems that include web browsers and networking and communication software as integral features.

We have shown the logical progression of operating-system development, driven by inclusion of features in the CPU hardware needed for advanced functionality. This trend can be seen today in the evolution of PCs, with inexpensive hardware being improved sufficiently to allow, in turn, improved characteristics.

2

Computer-System Structures

Introduction of Computer System Structures

We need to have a general knowledge of the structure of a computer system before we can explore the details of system operation. In this chapter, we look at several disparate parts of this structure to round out our background knowledge. This chapter is mostly concerned with computer-system architecture, so you can skim or skip it if you already understand the concepts. The first topics covered here include system startup, I/O, and storage.

The operating system must also ensure the correct operation of the computer system. To ensure that user programs will not interfere with the proper operation of the system, the hardware must provide appropriate mechanisms to ensure correct behavior. Later in this chapter, we describe the basic computer architecture that makes it possible to write a functional operating system. We conclude with a network architecture overview.

Computer-System Operation

A modern, general-purpose computer system consists of a CPU and a number of device controllers that are connected through a common bus that provides access to shared memory. Each device controller is in charge of a specific type of device (for example, disk drives, audio devices, and video displays). The CPU and the device controller can execute concurrently, competing for memory cycles. To ensure orderly access to the shared memory, a memory controller is provided whose function is to synchronize access to the memory.

For a computer to start running—for instance, when it is powered up or rebooted —it needs to have an initial program to run. This initial program, or **bootstrap program,** tends to be simple. Typically, it is stored in read-only memory (ROM) such as firmware or EEPROM within the computer hardware. It initializes all aspects of the system, from CPU registers to device controllers to memory contents. The bootstrap program must know how to load the operating system and to start executing that system. To accomplish this goal, the bootstrap program must locate and load into memory the operating-system kernel. The operating system then starts executing the first process, such as "init" and waits for some event to occur.

The occurrence of an event is usually signaled by an **interrupt** from either the hardware or the software. Hardware may trigger an interrupt at any time by sending a signal to the CPU, usually by way of the system bus. Software may trigger an interrupt by executing a special operation called a **system call** (also called a **monitor call**).

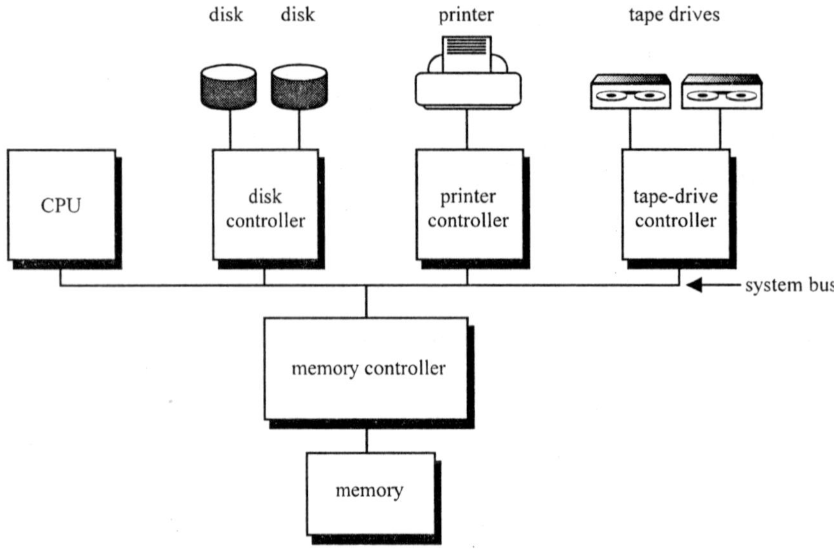

Fig. 2.1. A modern computer system.

Modern operating systems are **interrupt driven.** If there are no processes to execute, no I/O devices to service, and no users to whom to respond, an operating system will sit quietly, waiting for something to happen. Events are almost always signaled by the occurrence of an interrupt or a trap. A **trap** (or an **exception**) is a software-generated interrupt caused either by an error (for example, division by zero or invalid memory access) or by a specific request from a user program that an operating-system service be performed. The interrupt-driven nature of an operating system defines that system's general structure. For each type of interrupt, separate segments of code in the operating system determine what action should be taken. An interrupt service routine is provided that is responsible for dealing with the interrupt.

When the CPU is interrupted, it stops what it is doing and immediately transfers execution to a fixed location. The fixed location usually contains the starting address where the service routine for the interrupt is located. The interrupt service routine executes; on completion, the CPU resumes the interrupted computation.

Interrupts are an important part of a computer architecture. Each computer design has its own interrupt mechanism, but several functions are common. The interrupt must transfer control to the appropriate interrupt service routine. The straightforward method for handling this transfer would be to invoke a generic routine to examine the interrupt information; the routine, in turn, would call the interrupt-specific handler. However, interrupts must be handled quickly, and given that only a predefined number of interrupts is possible, a table of pointers to interrupt routines can be used instead. The interrupt routine is then called indirectly through the table, with no intermediate routine needed. Generally, the table of pointers is stored in low memory (the first 100 or so locations). These locations hold the addresses of the interrupt service routines for the various devices. This array, or **interrupt vector**, of addresses is then indexed by a unique device number, given with the interrupt request, to provide the address of the interrupt service routine for the interrupting device. Operating systems as different as MS-DOS and UNIX dispatch interrupts in this manner.

The interrupt architecture must also save the address of the interrupted instruction. Many old designs simply stored the interrupt address in a fixed location or in a location indexed by the device number. More recent architectures store the return address on the system stack. If the interrupt routine needs to modify the processor state—for instance, by modifying register values—it must explicitly save the current state and then restore that state before returning. After the interrupt is serviced, the saved return address is loaded into the program counter, and the interrupted computation resumes as though the interrupt had not occurred.

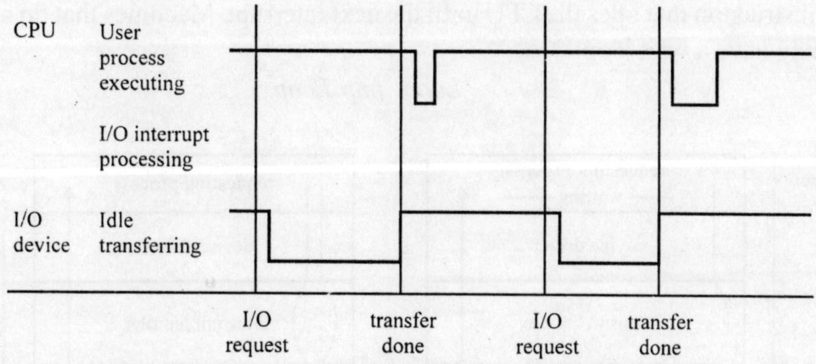

***Fig 2.2.** Interrupt time line for a single process doing output.*

A system call is invoked in a variety of ways, depending on the functionality provided by the underlying processor. In all forms, it is the method used by a process to request action by the operating system. A system call usually takes the form of a trap to a specific location in the interrupt vector. This trap can be executed by a generic trap instruction, although some systems (such as the MIPS R2000 family) have a specific syscall instruction.

I/O Structure

A general-purpose computer system consists of a CPU and multiple device controllers that are connected through a common bus. Each device controller is in charge of a specific type of device. Depending on the controller, there may be more than one attached device. For instance, the **small computer-system interface (SCSI)** controller can have seven or more devices attached to it. A device controller maintains some local buffer storage and a set of special-purpose registers. The device controller is responsible for moving the data between the peripheral devices that it controls and its local buffer storage. The size of the local buffer within a device controller varies from one controller to another, depending on the particular device being controlled. For example, the size of the buffer of a disk controller is the same as or a multiple of the size of the smallest addressable portion of a disk, called a sector, which is usually 512 bytes.

I/O Interrupts

To start an I/O operation, the CPU loads the appropriate registers within the device controller. The device controller, in turn, examines the contents of these registers to determine what action to take. For example, if it finds a read request, the controller will start the transfer of data from the device to its local buffer. Once the transfer of data is complete, the device controller informs the CPU that it has finished its operation. It accomplishes this communication by triggering an interrupt.

This situation will occur, in general, as the result of a user process requesting I/O. Once the I/O is started, two courses of action are possible. In the simplest case, the I/O is started; then, at I/O completion, control is returned to the user process. This case is known as **synchronous** I/O. The other possibility, called **asynchronous** I/O, returns control to the user program without waiting for the I/O to complete. The I/O then can continue while other system operations occur.

Waiting for I/O completion may be accomplished in one of two ways. Some computers have a special wait instruction that idles the CPU until the next interrupt. Machines that do not have such an instruction may have a wait loop:

Loop; jmp Loop

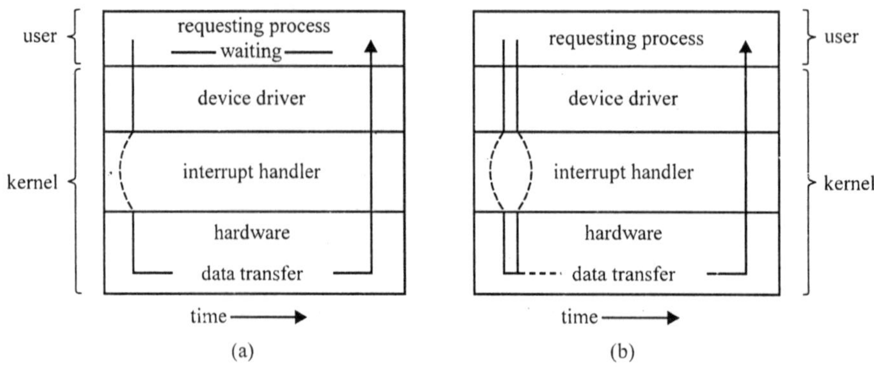

Fig. 2.3. *Two I/O methods: (a) synchronous, and (b) asynchronous.*

This tight loop simply continues until an interrupt occurs, transferring control to another part of the operating system. Such a loop might also need to poll any I/O devices that do not support the interrupt structure; instead, these devices simply set a flag in one of their registers and expect the operating system to notice that flag.

If the CPU always waits for I/O completion, at most one I/O request is outstanding at a time. Thus, whenever an I/O interrupt occurs, the operating system knows exactly which device is interrupting. On the other hand, this approach excludes concurrent I/O operations to several devices, and also excludes the possibility of overlapping useful computation with I/O.

A better alternative is to start the I/O and then to continue processing other operating-system or user program code. A system call is then needed to allow the user program to wait for I/O completion, if desired. If no user programs are ready to run, and the operating system has no other work to do, we still require the wait instruction or idle loop, as before. We also need to be able to keep track of many I/O requests at the same time. For this purpose, the operating system uses a table containing an entry for each I/O device: **the device-status table.** Each table entry indicates the device's type, address, and state (not functioning, idle, or busy). If the device is busy with a request, the type of request and other parameters will be stored in the table entry for that device. Since it is possible for other processes to issue requests to the same device, the operating system will also maintain a wait queue—a list of waiting requests—for each I/O device.

An I/O device interrupts when it needs service. When an interrupt occurs, the operating system first determines which I/O device caused the interrupt. It then indexes into the I/O device table to determine the status of that device, and modifies the table entry to reflect the occurrence of the interrupt. For most devices, an interrupt signals completion of an I/O request. If there are additional requests waiting in the queue for this device, the operating system starts processing the next request.

Finally, control is returned from the I/O interrupt. If a process was waiting for this request to complete (as recorded in the device-status table), we can now return control to it. Otherwise, we return to whatever we were doing before the I/O interrupt: to the execution of the user program (the program started an I/O operation and that operation has now finished, but the program has not yet waited for the operation to complete) or to the wait loop (the program started two or more I/O operations and is waiting for a particular one to finish, but this interrupt was from one of the other operations). In a time-sharing system, the operating system could switch to another ready-to-run process.

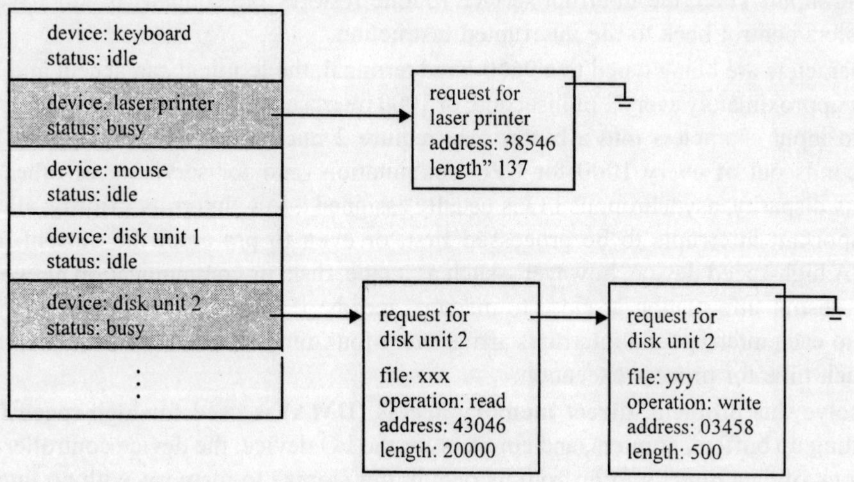

Fig. 2.4. Device-status table.

The schemes used by specific input devices may vary from this one. Many interactive systems allow users of type ahead—to enter data before the data are requested—on the keyboard. In this case, interrupts may occur, signaling the arrival of characters from the terminal, while the device-status block indicates that no program has requested input from this device. If type ahead is to be allowed, then a buffer must be provided to store the type ahead characters until some program wants them. In general, we may need a buffer for each input device.

The main advantage of asynchronous I/O is increased system efficiency. While I/O is taking place, the system CPU can be used for processing or starting I/Os to other devices. Because I/O can be slow compared to processor speed, the system makes efficient use of its facilities. We describe another mechanism for improving system performance.

DMA Structure

In a simple terminal-input driver, when a line is to be read from the terminal, the first character typed is sent to the computer. When that character is received, the asynchronous-communication (or serial-port) device to which the terminal line is connected interrupts the CPU. When the interrupt request from the terminal arrives, the CPU is about to execute some instruction. (If the CPU is in the middle of executing an instruction, the interrupt is normally held pending the completion of instruction execution.) The address of this interrupted instruction is saved, and control is transferred to the interrupt service routine for the appropriate device.

The interrupt service routine saves the contents of any CPU registers that it will need to use. It checks for any error conditions that might have resulted from the most recent input operation. It then takes the character from the device, and stores that character in a buffer. The interrupt routine must also adjust pointer and counter variables, to be sure that the next input character will be stored at the next location in the buffer. The interrupt routine next sets a flag in memory indicating to the other parts of the operating system that new input has been received. The other parts are responsible for processing the data in the buffer, and for transferring the characters to the program that is requesting input. Then, the interrupt service routine restores the contents of any saved registers, and transfers control back to the interrupted instruction.

If characters are being typed to a 9600-baud terminal, the terminal can accept and transfer one character approximately every 1 millisecond, or 1000 microseconds. A well-written interrupt service routine to input characters into a buffer may require 2 microseconds per character, leaving 998 microseconds out of every 1000 for CPU computation (and for servicing of other interrupts). Given this disparity, asynchronous I/O is usually assigned a low interrupt priority, allowing other, more important interrupts to be processed first, or even to pre-empt the current interrupt for another. A high-speed device, however—such as a tape, disk, or communication network—may be able to transmit information at close to memory speeds; if the CPU needs two microseconds to respond to each interrupt and interrupts arrive every four microseconds, for example, that does not leave much time for process execution.

To solve this problem, **direct memory access (DMA)** is used for high-speed I/O devices. After setting up buffers, pointers, and counters for the I/O device, the device controller transfers an entire block of data directly to or from its own buffer storage to memory, with no intervention by the CPU. Only one interrupt is generated per block, rather than the one interrupt per byte (or word) generated for low-speed devices.

The basic operation of the CPU is the same. A user program, or the operating system itself, may request data transfer. The operation system finds a buffer (an empty buffer for input, or a full buffer for output) from a pool of buffers for the transfer. (A buffer is typically 128 to 4,096 bytes, depending on the device type.) Next, a portion of the operating system called a **device driver** sets the DMA controller registers to use appropriate source and destination addresses, and transfer length. The DMA controller is then instructed to start the I/O operation. While the DMA controller is performing the data transfer, the CPU is free to perform other tasks. Since the memory generally can transfer only one word at a time, the DMA controller "steals" memory cycles from the CPU. This cycle stealing can slow down the CPU execution while a DMA transfer is in progress. The DMA controller interrupts the CPU when the transfer has been completed.

Storage Structure (RAM & DRAM)

Computer programs must be in main memory (also called **random-access memory or RAM)** to be executed. Main memory is the only large storage area (millions to billions of bytes) that the processor can access directly. It is implemented in a semiconductor technology called **dynamic random-access memory (DRAM),** which forms an array of memory words. Each word has its own address. Interaction is achieved through a sequence of load or store instructions to specific memory addresses. The load instruction moves a word from main memory to an internal register within the CPU, whereas the store instruction moves the content of a register to main memory. Aside from explicit loads and stores, the CPU automatically loads instructions from main memory for execution.

A typical instruction—execution cycle, as executed on a system with a **von Neumann** architecture, will first fetch an instruction from memory and will store that instruction in the **instruction register**. The instruction is then decoded and may cause operands to be fetched from memory and stored in some internal register. After the instruction on the operands has been executed, the result may be stored back in memory. Notice that the memory unit sees only a stream of memory addresses; it does not know how they are generated (by the instruction counter, indexing, indirection, literal addresses, and so on) or what they are for (instructions or data). Accordingly, we can ignore *how* a memory address is generated by a program. We are interested only in the sequence of memory addresses generated by the running program.

Ideally, we want the programs and data to reside in main memory permanently. This arrangement is not possible for the following two reasons:

1. Main memory is usually too small to store all needed programs and data permanently.
2. Main memory is a *volatile* storage device that loses its contents when power is turned off or otherwise lost.

Thus, most computer systems provide **secondary storage** as an extension of main memory. The main requirement for secondary storage is that it be able to hold large quantities of data permanently.

The most common secondary-storage device is a magnetic disk, which provides storage of both programs and data. Most programs (web browsers, compilers, word processors, spreadsheets, and so on) are stored on a disk until they are loaded into memory. Many programs then use the disk as both a source and a destination of the information for their processing. Hence, the proper management of disk storage is of central importance to a computer system.

In a larger sense, however, the storage structure that we have described—consisting of registers, main memory, and magnetic disks—is only one of many possible storage systems. There are also cache memory, CD-ROM, magnetic tapes, and so on. Each storage system provides the basic functions of storing a datum, and of holding that datum until it is retrieved at a later time. The main differences among the various storage systems lie in speed, cost, size, and volatility. We described main memory, magnetic disks, and magnetic tapes, because they illustrate the general properties of all important, commercially-available storage devices. We discussed the specific properties of any particular devices, such as floppy disks, hard disks, CD-ROMs, and DVDs.

Main Memory of Computer

Main memory and the registers built into the processor itself are the only storage that the CPU access directly. There are machine instructions that take memory addresses as arguments, but none that take disk addresses. Therefore, any instructions in execution, and any data being used by the instructions, must be in one of these direct-access storage devices. If the data are not in memory, they must be moved there before the CPU can operate on them.

In the case of I/O, each I/O controller includes registers to hold commands and the data being transferred. Usually, special I/O instructions allow data transfers between these registers and system memory. To allow more convenient access to I/O devices, many computer architectures provide **memory-mapped** I/O. In this case, ranges of memory addresses are set aside, and are mapped to the device registers. Reads and writes to these memory addressed cause the data to be transferred to and from the device registers. This method is appropriate for devices that have fast response times, such as video controllers. In the IBM PC, each location on the screen is mapped to a memory location. Displaying text on the screen is almost as easy as writing the text into the appropriate memory-mapped locations.

Memory-mapped I/O is also convenient for other devices, such as the serial and parallel ports used to connect modems and printers to a computer. The CPU transfers data through these kinds of devices by reading and writing a few device registers, called an I/O **port.** To send out a long string of bytes through a memory-mapped serial port, the CPU writes one data byte to the data register, then sets a bit in the control register to signal that the byte is available. The device takes the data byte, and then clears the bit in the control register to signal that it is ready for the next byte. Then, the CPU can transfer the next byte. If the CPU uses polling to watch the control bit, constantly looping to see whether the device is ready, this method of operation is called **programmed I/O (PIO).** If the CPU does not poll the control bit, but instead receives an interrupt when the device is ready for the next byte, the data transfer is said to be **interrupt driven.**

Registers that are built into the CPU are generally accessible within one cycle of the CPU clock. Most CPUs can decode instructions and perform simple operations on register contents at the rate of one or more operations per clock tick. The same cannot be said of main memory, which is accessed via a transaction on the memory bus. Memory access may take many cycles of the CPU clock to complete, in which case the processor normally needs to **stall**, since it does not have the data required to complete the instruction that it is executing. This situation is intolerable because of the frequency of memory accesses. The remedy is to add fast memory between thee CPU and main memory. A memory buffer used to accommodate a speed differential, called a **cache**.

Magnetic Disks

Magnetic disks provide the bulk of secondary storage for modern computer systems. Conceptually, disks are relatively simple. Each disk **platter** has a flat circular shape, like a CD. Common platter diameters range from 1.8 to 5.25 inches. The two surfaces of a platter are covered with a magnetic material. We store information by recording it magnetically on the platters.

A read-write head "flies" just above each surface of every platter. The heads are attached to a **disk arm,** which moves all the heads as a unit. The surface of a platter is logically divided into circular **tracks,** which are subdivided into **sectors.** The set of tracks that are at one arm position form a **cylinder.** There may be thousands of concentric cylinders in a disk drive, and each track may contain hundreds of sectors. The storage capacity of common disk drives is measured in gigabytes.

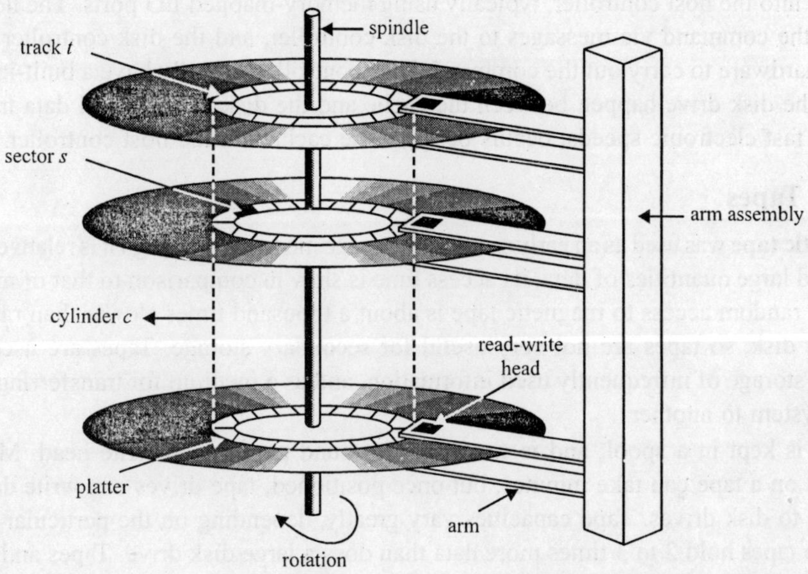

Fig. 2.5. Moving-head disk mechanism.

When the disk is in use, a drive motor spins it at high speed., Most drives rotate 60 to 200 times per second. Disk speed has two parts. The **transfer rate** is the rate at which data flows between the drive and the computer. The **positioning time**, sometimes called the **random-access time,** consists of the time to move the disk arm to the desired cylinder, called the **seek time,** and the time for the desired sector to rotate to the disk head, called the **rotational latency**. Typical disks can transfer several megabytes of data per second, and they have seek times and rotational latencies of several milliseconds.

Because the disk head flies on an extremely thin (measured in microns) cushion of air, there is a danger of the head making contact with the disk surface. Although the disk platters are coated with a thin protective layer, sometimes the head will damage the magnetic surface. This accident is called a **head crash.** A head crash normally cannot be repaired; the entire disk must be replaced.

A disk can be **removable,** allowing different disks to be mounted as needed. Removable magnetic disks generally consist of one platter, held in a plastic case to prevent damage while not in the disk drive. **Floppy disks** are inexpensive removable magnetic disks that have a soft plastic case containing a flexible platter. The head of a floppy-disk drive generally sits directly on the disk surface, so the drive is designed to rotate more slowly than a hard-disk drive to reduce the wear on the disk surface. The storage capacity of a floppy disk is typically only 1 MB or so. Removable disks are available that work much like normal hard disks and have capacities measured in gigabytes.

A disk drive is attached to a computer by a set of wires called an **I/O bus.** Several kinds of buses are available, including **enhanced integrated drive electronics (EIDE), advanced technology attachment (ATA),** and SCSI buses. The data transfers on a bus are carried out by special electronic processors called **controllers**. The host controller is the controller at the computer end of the bus. A **disk controller** is built into each disk drive. To perform a disk I/O operation, the computer places a command into the host controller, typically using memory-mapped I/O ports. The host controller then sends the command via messages to the disk controller, and the disk controller operates the disk-drive hardware to carry out the command. Disk controllers usually have a built-in cache. Data transfer at the disk drive happen between the cache and the disk surface, and data transfer to the host, at the fast electronic speeds, occurs between the cache and the host controller.

Magnetic Tapes

Magnetic tape was used as an early secondary-storage medium. Although it is relatively permanent and can hold large quantities of data, its access time is slow in comparison to that of main memory. In addition, random access to magnetic tape is about a thousand times slower than random access to magnetic disk, so tapes are not very useful for secondary storage. Tapes are used mainly for backup, for storage of infrequently used information, and as a medium for transferring information from one system to another.

A tape is kept in a spool, and is wound or rewound past a read-write head. Moving to the correct spot on a tape can take minutes, but once positioned, tape drives can write data at speeds comparable to disk drives. Tape capacities vary greatly, depending on the particular kind of tape drive. Some tapes hold 2 to 3 times more data than does a large disk drive. Tapes and their drivers are usually categorized by width, including 4, 8, and 19 millimeters, 1/4 and 1/2 inch.

Storage Hierarchy

The wide variety of storage systems in a computer system can be organized in a hierarchy according to speed and cost. The higher levels are expensive, but they are fast. As we move down the hierarchy, the cost per bit generally decreased, whereas the access time generally increases. This trade-off is reasonable; if a given storage system were both faster and less expensive than another—other properties being the same—then there would be no reason to use the slower, more expensive memory. In fact, many early storage devices, including paper tape and core memories, are relegated to museums now that magnetic tape and **semiconductor memory** have become faster and cheaper. The top three levels of memory may be constructed using semiconductor memory.

In addition to having differing speed and cost, the various storage systems are either volatile or nonvolatile. **Volatile storage** loses its contents when the power to the device is removed. In the absence of expensive battery and generator backup systems, data must be written to **nonvolatile storage** for safekeeping. In the hierarchy the storage systems above the electronic disk are volatile, whereas those below are nonvolatile. An **electronic disk** can be designed to be either volatile or nonvolatile. During normal operation, the electronic disk stores data in a large DRAM array, which is volatile. But many electronic-disk devices contain a hidden magnetic hard disk and a battery for backup power. If external power is interrupted the electronic disk controller copies the data from RAM to the magnetic disk. When external power is restored, the controller copies the data back into the RAM.

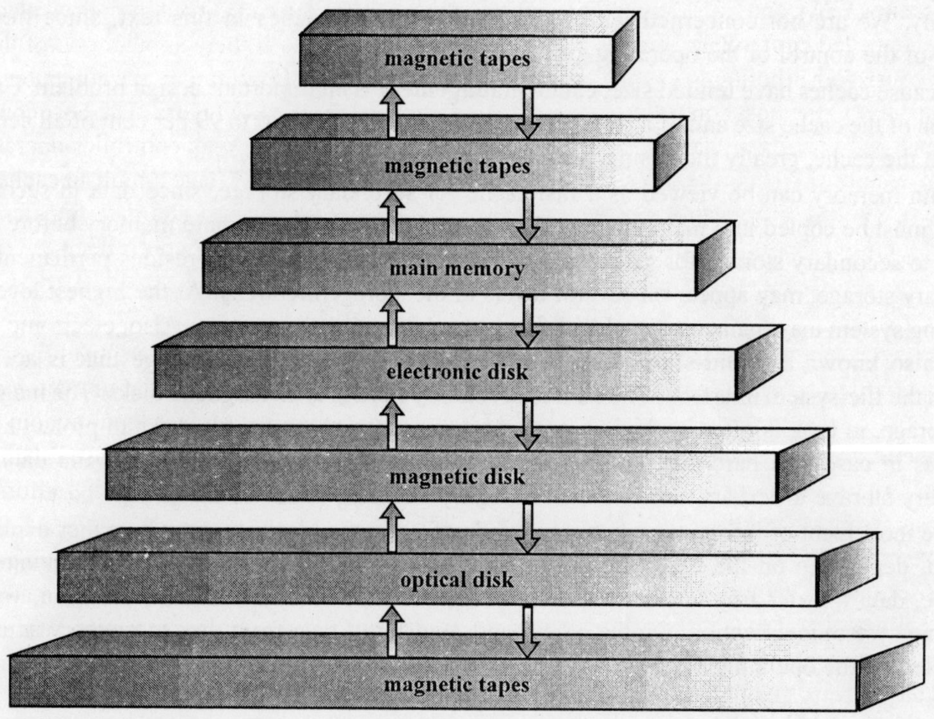

Fig. 2.6. Storage-device hierarchy.

The design of a complete memory system must balance all these factors: It uses only as much expensive memory as necessary while providing as much inexpensive, nonvolatile memory as possible. Caches can be installed to improve performance where a large access-time or transfer-rate disparity exists between two components.

Caching

Caching is an important principle of computer systems. Information is normally kept in some storage system (such as main memory). As it is used, it is copied into a faster storage system—the cache—on a temporary basis. When we need a particular piece of information, we first check whether it is in the cache. If it is, we use the information directly from the cache; if it is not, we use the information from the main storage system, putting a copy in the cache under the assumption that we will need it again soon.

In addition, internal programmable registers, such as index registers, provide a high-speed cache for main memory. The programmer (or compiler) implements the register-allocation and register-replacement algorithms to decide which information to keep in registers and which to keep in main memory. There are also caches that are implemented totally in hardware. For instance, most systems have an instruction cache to hold the next instructions expected to be executed. Without this cache, the CPU would have to wait several cycles while an instruction is fetched from main memory. For similar reasons, most systems have one or more high-speed data caches in the memory hierarchy. We are not concerned with these hardware-only caches in this text, since they are outside of the control of the operating system.

Because caches have limited size, **cache management** is an important design problem. Careful selection of the cache size and of a replacement policy can result in 80 to 99 per cent of all accesses being in the cache, greatly increasing performance.

Main memory can be viewed as a fast cache for secondary storage, since data in secondary storage must be copied into main memory for use, and data must be in main memory before being moved to secondary storage for safekeeping. The file-system data, which resides permanently on secondary storage, may appear on several levels in the storage hierarchy. At the highest level, the operating system may maintain a cache of file-system data in main memory. Also, electronic RAM disks (also known as **solid-state disks**) may be used for high-speed storage that is accessed through the file-system interface. The bulk of secondary storage is on magnetic disks. The magnetic-disk storage, in turn, is often backed up onto magnetic tapes or removable disks to protect against data loss in case of a hard-disk failure. Some systems automatically archive old file data from secondary storage to tertiary storage, such as tape jukeboxes, to lower the storage cost.

The movement of information between levels of a storage hierarchy may be either explicit or implicit, depending on the hardware design and the controlling operating-system software. For instance, data transfer from cache to CPU and registers is usually a hardware function, with no operating-system intervention. On the other hand, transfer of data from disk to memory is usually controlled by the operating system.

Coherency and Consistency

In a hierarchical storage structure, the same data may appear in different levels of the storage system. For example, suppose that an integer *A* is located in file *B* that is to be incremented by 1, and file *B* resides on magnetic disk. The increment operation proceeds by first issuing an I/O operation to copy the disk block on which *A* resides to main memory. This operation is followed by copying *A* to the cache and to an internal register. Thus, the copy of *A* appears in several places: on the magnetic disk, in main memory, in the cache, and in an internal register. Once the increment takes place in the internal register, the value of *A* differs in the various storage systems. The value of *A* becomes the same only after the new value of *A* is written from the internal register back to the magnetic disk.

In a computing environment where only one process executes at a time, this arrangement poses no difficulties, since an access to the integer *A* will always be to the copy at the highest level of the hierarchy. However, in a multitasking environment, where the CPU is switched back and forth among various processes, extreme care must be taken to ensure that, if several processes wish to access A, then each of these processes will obtain the most recently updated value of *A*.

The situation becomes more complicated in a multiprocessor environment where, in addition to maintaining internal register, each of the CPUs also contains a local cache. In such an environment, a copy of A may exist simultaneously in several caches. Since the various CPUs can all execute concurrently, we must make sure that an update to the value of A in one cache is immediately reflected in all other caches where A resides. This situation is called **cache coherency,** and it is usually a hardware problem (handled below the operating-system level).

In a distributed environment, the situation becomes even more complex. In such an environment, several copies (or replicas) of the same file can be kept on different computers that are distributed in space. Since the various replicas may be accessed and updated concurrently, we must ensure that, when a replica is updated in one place, all other replicas are brought up-to-date as soon as possible. There are various ways to achieve this guarantee.

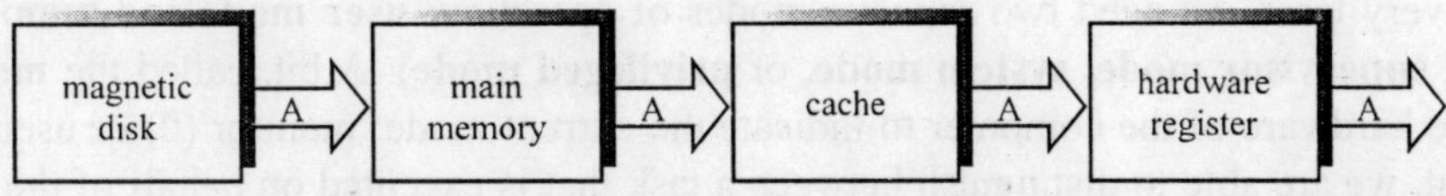

Fig. 2.7. Migration of integer A from disk to register.

Hardware Protection

Early computer system were single-user programmer-operated systems. When the programmers operated the computer from the console, they had complete control over the system. As operating systems developed, however, this control was given to the operating system. Early operating systems were called **resident monitors**, and starting with the **resident monitor,** the operating system began to perform many of the functions, especially I/O, for which the programmer had previously been responsible.

In addition, to improve system utilization, the operating system began to *share* system resources among several programs simultaneously. With spooling, one program might have been executing while I/O occurred for other processes; the disk simultaneously held data for many processes. Multiprogramming put several programs in memory at the same time.

This sharing both improved utilization and increased problem. When the system was run without sharing, an error in a program could cause problems for only the one program that was running. With sharing, many processes could be adversely affected by a bug in one program.

For example, consider the simple batch operating system, which provides nothing more than automatic job sequencing. If a program gets stuck in a loop reading input cards, the program will read through all its data and, unless something stops it, will continue reading the cards of the next job, and the next, and so on. This loop could prevent the correct operation of many jobs.

Without protection against these sorts of errors, either the computer must execute only one process at a time, or all output must be suspect. A properly designed operating system must ensure that an incorrect (or malicious) program cannot cause other programs to execute incorrectly.

Many programming errors are detected by the hardware. These errors are normally handled by the operating system. If a user program fails in some way—such as by making an attempt either to execute an illegal instruction, or to access memory that is not in the user's address space—then the hardware will trap to the operating system. The trap transfers control through the interrupt vector to the operating system, just like an interrupt. Whenever a program error occurs, the operation system must abnormally terminate the program. This situation is handled by the same code as is a user-requested abnormal termination. An appropriate error message is given, and the memory of the program may be dumped. The memory dump is usually written to a file so that the user or programmer can examine it, and perhaps can correct and restart the program.

Dual-Mode Operation

To ensure proper operation, we must protect the operating system and all other programs and their data from any malfunctioning program. Protection is needed for any shared resource. The approach taken by many operating systems provides hardware support that allows us to differentiate among various modes of execution.

At the very least, we need two separate modes of operation: **user mode** and **monitor mode** (also called **supervisor mode, system mode,** or **privileged mode**). A bit, called the **mode bit,** is added to the hardware of the computer to indicate the current mode: monitor (0) or user (1). With the mode bit, we are able to distinguish between a task that is executed on behalf of the operating system, and one that is executed on behalf of the user. As we shall see, this architectural enhancement is useful for many other aspects of system operation.

At system boot time, the hardware starts in monitor mode. The operating system is then loaded, and starts user processes in user mode. Whenever a trap or interrupt occurs, the hardware switches from user mode to monitor mode (that is, changes the state of the mode bit to 0.) Thus, whenever the operating system gains control of the computer, it is in monitor mode. The system always switches to user mode (by setting the mode bit to 1) before passing control to a user program.

The dual mode of operation provides us with the means for protecting the operating system from errant users, and errant users from one another. We accomplish this protection by designating some of the machine instructions that may cause harm as **privileged instructions.** The hardware allows privileged instructions to be executed only in monitor mode. If an attempt is made to execute a privileged instruction in user mode, the hardware does not execute the instruction, but rather treats the instruction as illegal and traps it to the operating system.

The concept of privileged instructions also provides us with the means for the user to interact with the operating system by asking the system to perform some designated tasks that only the operating system should do. Each such request is invoked by the user executing a privileged instruction. Such a request is known as a system call (also called a monitor call or an operating-system function call).

When a system call is executed, it is treated by the hardware as a software interrupt. Control passes through the interrupt vector to a service routine in the operating system, and the mode bit is set to monitor mode. The system-call service routine is a part of the operating system. The monitor examines the interrupting instruction to determine what system call has occurred; a parameter indicates what type of service the user program is requesting. Additional information needed for the request may be passed in registers, on the stack, or in memory (with pointers to the memory locations passed in registers). The monitor verifies that the parameters are correct and legal, executes the request, and returns control to the instruction following the system call.

The lack of a hardware-supported dual mode can cause serious shortcomings in an operating system. For instance, MS-DOS was written for the Intel 8088 architecture, which has no mode bit, and therefore, no dual mode. A user program running away can wipe out the operating system by writing over it with data, and multiple programs are able to write to a device at the same time, with possibly disastrous results. More recent and advanced versions of the Intel CPU, such as the Pentium, do provide dual-mode operation. As a result, more recent operating systems, such as Microsoft Windows 2000 and IBM OS/2, take advantage of this feature and provide greater protection for the operating system.

I/O Protection

A user program may disrupt the normal operation of the system by issuing illegal I/O instructions, by accessing memory locations within the operating system itself, or by refusing to relinquish the CPU. We can use various mechanisms to ensure that such disruptions cannot take place in the system.

To prevent users from performing illegal I/O, we define all I/O instructions to be privileged instructions. Thus, users cannot issue I/O instructions directly; they must do it through the operating system. For I/O protection to be complete, we must be sure that a user program can never gain control of the computer in monitor mode. If it could, I/O protection could be compromised.

Consider a computer executing in user mode. It will switch to monitor mode whenever an interrupt or trap occurs, jumping to the address determined from the interrupt vector. If a user program, as part of its execution, stores a new address in the interrupt vector, this new address could overwrite the previous address with an address in the user program. Then, when a corresponding trap or interrupt occurred, the hardware would switch to monitor mode, and would transfer control through the (modified) interrupt vector to the user program. The user program could gain control of the computer in monitor mode. In fact, user programs could gain control of the computer in monitor mode in many other ways. In addition, new bugs are discovered every day that can be exploited to bypass system protections.

Thus, to do I/O, a user program executes a system call to request that the operating system perform I/O on its behalf. The operating system, executing in monitor mode, checks that the request is valid, and (if the request is valid) does the I/O requested. The operating system then returns to the user.

Memory Protection

To ensure correct operation, we must protect the interrupt vector from modification by a user program. In addition, we must also protect the interrupt-service routines in the operating system from modification. Even if the user did not gain unauthorized control of the computer, modifying the interrupt service routines would probably disrupt the proper operation of the computer system and of its spooling and buffering.

We see then that we must provide memory protection at least for the interrupt vector and the interrupt-service routines of the operating system. In general, we want to protect operating system from access by user programs, and, in addition, to protect user programs from one another. This protection must be provided by the hardware. It can be implemented in several ways, as here, we outline one such possible implementation.

To separate each program's memory space, we need the ability to determine the range of legal addresses that the program may access, and to protect the memory outside that space. We can provide this protection by using two registers, usually a base and a limit. The **base register** holds the smallest legal physical memory address; the **limit register** contains the size of the range. For example, if the base register holds 300040 and limit register is 120900, then the program can legally access all addresses from 300040 through 420940 inclusive.

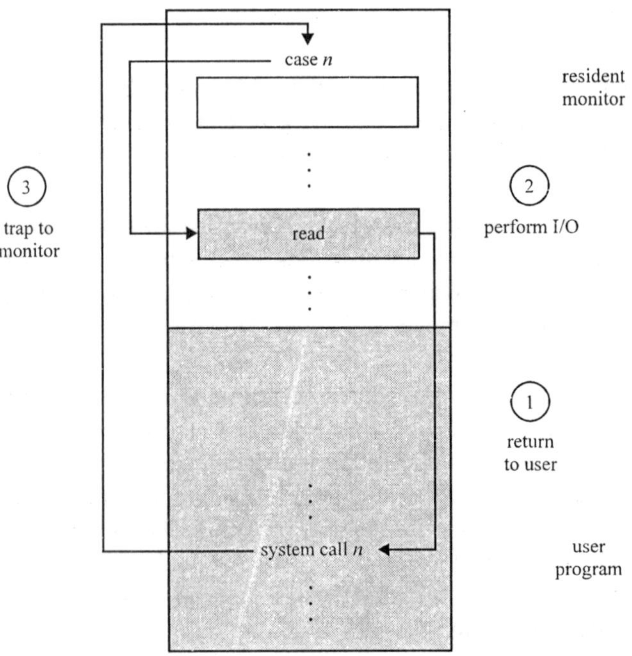

Fig.2.8. Use of a system call to perform I/O.

This protection is accomplished by the CPU hardware comparing *every* address generated in user mode with the registers. Any attempt by a program executing in user mode to access monitor memory or other users, memory results in a trap to the monitor, which treats the attempt as a fatal error. This scheme prevents the user program from (accidentally or deliberately) modifying the code or data structures of either the operating system or other users.

The base and limit registers can be loaded by only the operating system, which uses a special privileged instruction. Since privileged instructions can be executed in only monitor mode, and since only the operating system executes in monitor mode, only the operating system can load the base and limit registers. This scheme allows the monitor to change the value of the registers, but prevents user programs from changing the registers' contents.

CPU Protection

In addition to protecting I/O and memory, we must ensure that the operating system maintains control. We must prevent a user program from getting stuck in an infinite loop or not calling system services, and never returning control to the operating system. To accomplish this goal, we can use a **timer.** A timer can be set to interrupt the computer after a specified period. The period may be fixed (for example, 1/60 second) or variable (for example, from 1 millisecond to 1 second). A **variable timer** is generally implemented by a fixed-rate clock and a counter. The operating system sets the counter. Every time the clock ticks, the counter is decremented. When the counter reaches 0, an interrupt occurs. For instance, a 10-bit counter with a 1-millisecond clock allows interrupts at intervals from 1 millisecond to 1,024 milliseconds, in steps of 1 millisecond.

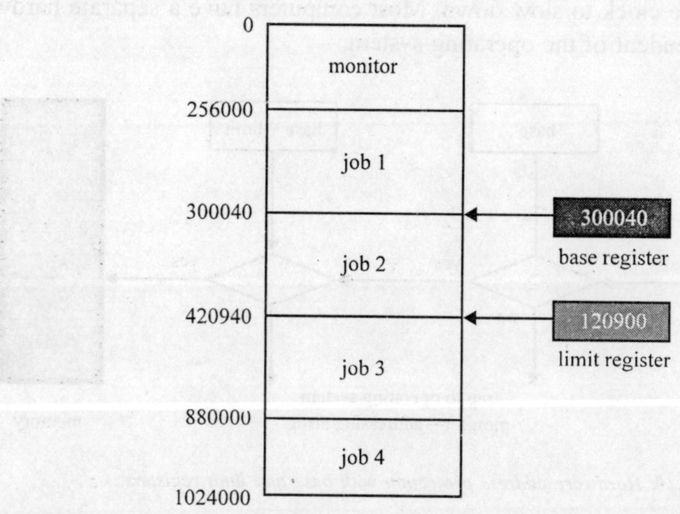

Fig. 2.9. *A base and a limit register define a logical address space.*

Before turning over control to the user, the operating system ensures that the timer is set to interrupt. If the timer interrupts, control transfers automatically to the operating system, which may treat the interrupt as a fatal error or may give the program more time. Clearly, instructions that modify the operation of the timer are privileged.

Thus, we can use the timer to prevent a user program from running too long. A simple technique is to initialize a counter with the amount of time that a program is allowed to run. A program with a 7-minute time limit, for example, would have its counter initialized to 420. Every second, the timer interrupts and the counter is decremented by 1. As long as the counter is positive, control is returned to the user program. When the counter becomes negative, the operating system terminates the program for exceeding the assigned time limit.

A more common use of a timer is to implement time sharing. In the most straightforward case, the timer could be set to interrupt every *N* milliseconds, where *N* is the **time slice** that each user is allowed to execute before the next user gets control of the CPU. The operating system is invoked at the end of each time slice to perform various housekeeping tasks, such as adding the value *N* to the record that specifies (for accounting purposes) the amount of time the user program has executed thus far. The operating system also saves registers, internal variables, and buffers, and changes several other parameters to prepare for the next program to run. This procedure is known as a **context switch.** Following a context switch, the next program continues with its execution from the point at which it left off (when its pervious time slice ran out).

Another use of the timer is to compute the current time. A timer interrupts signals the passage of some period, allowing the operating system to compute the current time in reference to some initial time. If we have interrupts every 1 second, and we have had 1427 interrupts since we were told that it was 1:00 P.M., then we can compute that the current time is 1:23:47 P.M. Some computers determine the current time in this manner, but the calculations must be done carefully for the time to be kept accurately, since the interrupt-processing time (and other times when interrupts are disabled) tends to cause the software clock to slow down. Most computers have a separate hardware time-of-day clock that is independent of the operating system.

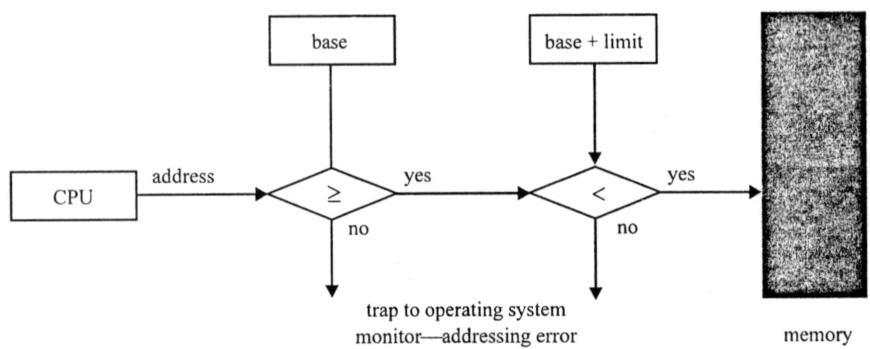

Fig. 2.10. *Hardware address protection with base and limit registers.*

Network Structure

There are basically two types of networks: **local-area networks (LAN)** and **wide-area networks (WAN).** The main difference between the two is the way in which they are geographically distributed. Local-area networks are composed of processors that are distributed over small geographical areas (such as a single building or a number of adjacent buildings). Wide-area networks, on the other hand, are composed of a number of autonomous processors that are distributed over a large geographical area (such as the United States). These differences imply major variations in the speed and reliability of the communications network, and they are reflected in the distributed operating-system design.

Local-Area Networks

Local-area networks emerged in the early 1970s, as a substitute for large main frame computer systems. For many enterprises, it is more economical to have a number of small computers, each with its own self-contained applications, rather than a single large system. Because each small computer is likely to need a full complement of peripheral devices (such as disks and printers), it was a natural step to connect these small systems into a network.

LANs are usually designed to cover a small geographical area (such as a single building, or a few adjacent buildings) and are generally used in an office environment. All the sites in such systems are close to one another, so the communication links tend to have a higher speed and lower error rate than do their counterparts in wide-area networks. High-quality (expensive) cables are needed to attain this higher speed and reliability. It is also possible to use the cable exclusively for data network traffic. Over longer distances, the cost of using high-quality cable is enormous, and the exclusive use of the cable tends to be prohibitive.

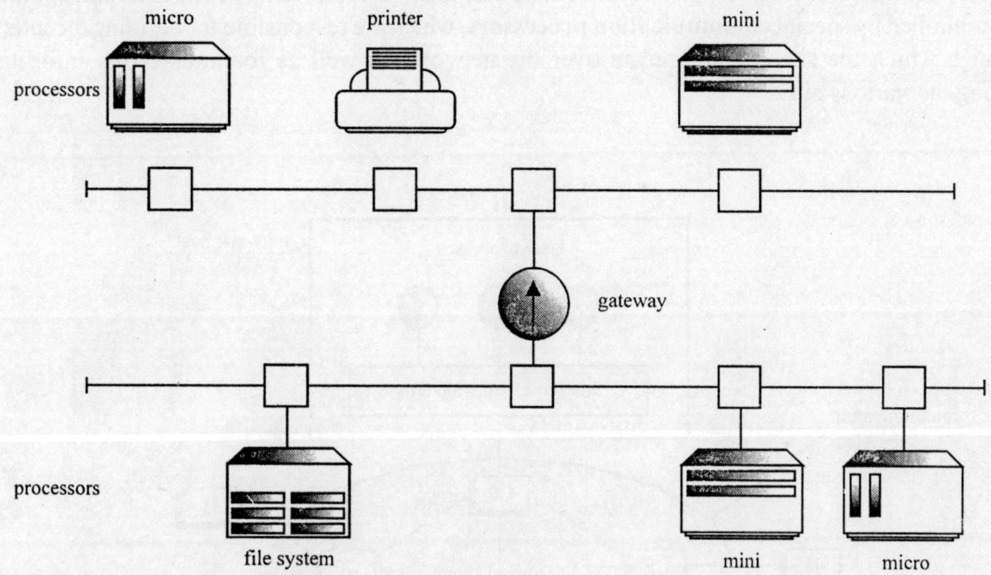

Fig. 2.11. Local-area network.

The most common links in a local-area network are twisted pair and fiber optic cabling. The most common configurations are multi-access bus, ring, and star networks. Communication speeds range from 1 megabit per second, for networks such as AppleTalk, infrared, and the new Bluetooth local radio network, to 1 gigabit per second for gigabit-Ethernet. Ten megabits per second is most common, and is the speed of **10BaseT Ethernet. 100BaseT Ethernet** requires a higher-quality cable but runs at 100 megabits per second, and is becoming common. Also growing is the use of optical-fiber-based FDDI networking. The FDDI network is token-based and runs at over 100 megabits per second.

A typical LAN may consist of a number of different computers (from mainframes to laptops or PDAs), various shared peripheral devices (such as laser printers or magnetic-tape drives), and one or more gateways (specialized processors) that provide access to other networks. An Ethernet scheme is commonly used to construct LANs. An Ethernet network has no central controller, because it is a multiaccess bus, so new hosts can be added easily to the network.

Wide-Area Networks

Wide-area networks emerged in the late 1960s, mainly as an academic research project to provide efficient communication among sites, allowing hardware and software to be shared conveniently and economically by a wide community of users. The first WAN to be designed and developed was the *Arpanet.* Begun in 1968, the Arpanet has grown from a four-site experimental network to a worldwide network of networks, the Internet, comprising millions of computer system.

Because the sites in a WAN are physically distributed over a large geographical area, the communication links are, by default, relatively slow and unreliable. Typical links are telephone lines, leased (dedicated data) lines, microwave links, and satellite channels. These communication links are controlled by special **communication processors,** which are responsible for defining the interface through which the sites communicate over the network, as well as for transferring information among the various sites.

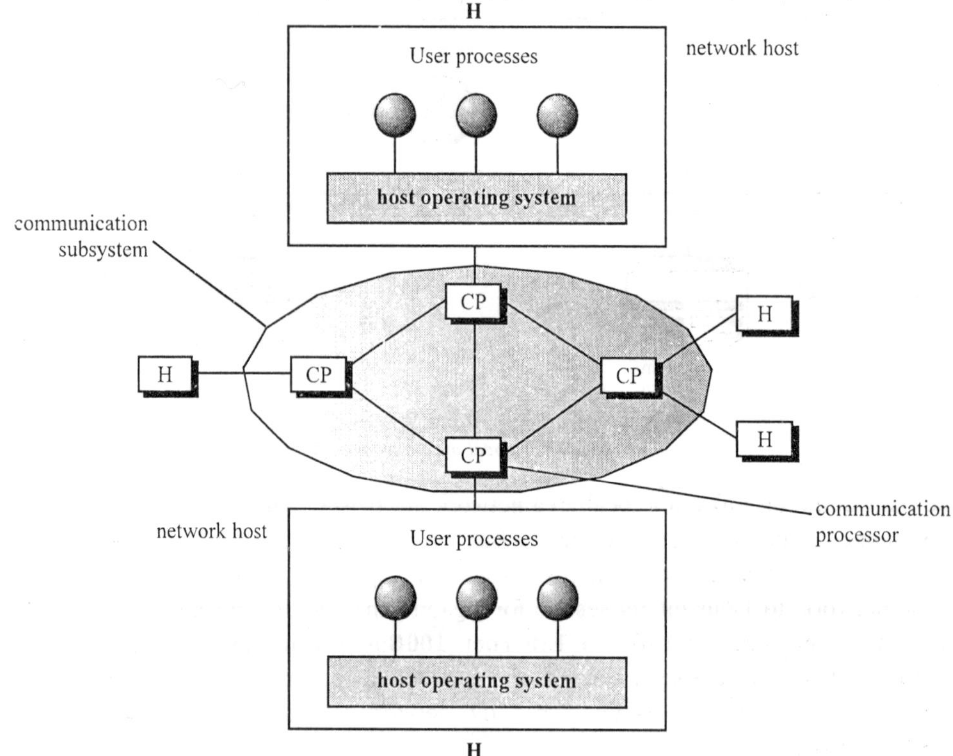

Fig. 2.12. Communication processors in a wide-area network.

For example, the Internet WAN provides the ability for hosts at geographically separated sites to communicate with one another. The host computers typically differ from one another in type, speed, word length, operating system, and so on. Hosts are generally on LANs, which are in turn, connected to the Internet via regional networks. The regional networks, such as NSFnet in the northeast United States, are interlinked with **routers** to form the worldwide network. Connections between networks frequently use a telephone-system service called T1, which provides a transfer rate of 1.544 megabits per second over a leased line. For sites requiring faster Internet access, T1s are collected into multiple-T1 units that work in parallel to provide more throughput. For instance, a T3 is composed of 28 T1 connections and has a transfer rate of 45 megabits per second. The routers control the path each message takes through the net. This routing may be either dynamic, to increase communications efficiency, or static, to reduce security risks or to allow communication charges to be computed.

Other WANs in operation use standard telephone lines as their primary means of communication. **Modems** are devices that accept digital data from the computer side and convert it to the analog signals that the telephone system uses. A modem at the destination site converts the analog signal back to digital and the destination receives the data. The UNIX news network, UUCP, allows systems to communicate with each other at predetermined times, via modems, to exchange messages. The messages are then routed to other nearby systems and in this way either are propagated to all hosts on the network (public messages) or are transferred to their destination (private messages). WANs are generally slower than LANs; their transmission rates range from 1,200 bits per second to over 1 megabit per second. UUCP has been superseded by PPP, the Point-to-Point Protocol. PPP functions over modem connections, allowing home computers to be fully connected to the Internet.

Summary

Multiprogramming and time-sharing systems improve performance by overlapping CPU and I/O operations on a single machine. Such an overlap requires that data transfer between the CPU and an I/O device be handled either by polled or interrupt-driven access to an I/O port, or by a DMA data transfer.

For a computer to do its job of executing programs, the programs must be in main memory. Main memory is the only large storage area that the processor can access directly. It is an array of words or bytes, ranging in size from hundred of thousands to hundreds of millions. Each word has its own address. The main memory is a volatile storage device that loses its contents when power is turned off or lost. Most computer systems provide secondary storage as an extension of main memory. The main requirement of secondary storage is to be able to hold large quantities of data permanently. The most common secondary-storage device is a magnetic disk, which provides storage of both programs and data. A magnetic disk is a nonvolatile storage device that also provides random access. Magnetic tapes are used mainly for backup, for storage of infrequently used information, and as a medium for transferring information from one system to another.

The wide variety of storage systems in a computer system can be organized in a hierarchy according to their speed and cost. The higher levels are expensive, but they are fast. As we move down the hierarchy, the cost per bit generally decreases, whereas the access time generally increases.

The operating system must ensure correct operation of the computer system. To prevent user programs from interfering with the proper operation of the system, the hardware has two modes: user mode and monitor mode. Various instructions (such as I/O instructions and halt instructions) are privileged, and can be executed in only monitor mode. The memory in which the operating system resides must also be protected from modification by the user. A timer prevents infinite loops. These facilities (dual mode, privileged instructions, memory protection, timer interrupt) are basic building blocks used by operating systems to achieve correct operation.

LANs and WANs are the two basic types of networks. Usually connected by expensive twisted-pair or fiber-optic cabling, LAN allows processors distributed over a small geographical area to communicate. Connected by telephone lines, leased lines, microwave links, or satellite channels, WANs allow processors distributed over a larger geographical area to communicate. LANs typically transmit more than 100 megabits per second, whereas slower WANs transmit from 1,200 bits per second to more than 1 megabit per second.

3

Operating-System Structures

Introduction to Operating System Structures

An operating system provides the environment within which programs are executed. Internally, operating systems vary greatly in their makeup, being organized along many different lines. The design of a new operating system is a major task. The goals of the system must be well defined before the design begins. The type of system desired is the basis for choices among various algorithms and strategies.

An operating system may be viewed from several vantage points. One is by examining the services that it provides. Another is by looking at the interface that it makes available to users and programmers. A third is by disassembling the system into its components and their interconnections. In this chapter, we explore all three aspects of operating systems, showing the viewpoints of users, programmers, and operating-system designers. We consider what services an operating system provides, how they are provided, and what the various methodologies are for designing such systems.

System Components

We can create a system as large and complex as an operating system only by partitioning it into smaller pieces. Each piece should be a well-delineated portion of the system, with carefully defined inputs, outputs, and functions. Obviously, not all systems have the same structure. However, many modern systems share the goal of supporting the system components.

Process Management

A program does nothing unless its instructions are executed by a CPU. A **process** can be thought of as a program in execution, but its definition will broaden as we explore it further. A time-shared user program such as a compiler is a process. A word-processing program being run by an individual user on a PC is a process. A system task, such as sending output to a printer, is also a process. For now, you can consider a process to be a job or a time-shared program, but later you will learn that the concept is more general. We can provide systems calls that allow processes to create subprocesses to execute concurrently.

A process needs certain resources—including CPU time, memory, files, and I/O devices—to accomplish its task. These resources are either given to the process when it is created, or allocated to it while it is running. In addition to the various physical and logical resources that a process obtains when it is created, various initialization data (or input) may be passed along. For example, consider a process whose function is to display the status of a file on the screen of a terminal. The process will be given as an input the name of the file, and will execute the appropriate instructions and system calls to obtain and display on the terminal the desired information. When the process terminates, the operating system will reclaim any reusable resources.

We emphasize that a program by itself is not a process; a program is a *passive* entity, such as the contents of a file stored on disk, whereas a process is an *active* entity, with a **program counter** specifying the next instruction to execute. The execution of a process must be sequential. The CPU executes one instruction of the process after another, until the process completes. Further, at any time, at most one instruction is executed on behalf of the process. Thus, although two processes may be associated with the same program, they are nevertheless considered two separate execution sequences. It is common to have a program that spawns many processes as it runs.

A process is the unit of work in a system. Such a system consists of a collection of processes, some of which are operating-system processes (those that execute system code) and the rest of which are user processes (those that execute user code). All these processes can potentially execute concurrently, by multiplexing the CPU among them.

The operating system is responsible for the following activities in connection with process management:

- Creating and deleting both user and system processes
- Suspending and resuming processes
- Providing mechanisms for process synchronization
- Providing mechanisms for process communication
- Providing mechanisms for deadlock handling

Main-Memory Management

The main memory is central to the operation of a modern computer system. Main memory is a large array of words or bytes, ranging in size from hundreds of thousands to billions. Each word or byte has its own address. Main memory is a repository of quickly accessible data shared by the CPU and I/O devices. The central processor reads instructions from main memory during the instruction-fetch cycle, and it both reads and writes data from main memory during the data-fetch cycle. The I/O operations implemented via DMA also read and write data in main memory. The main memory is generally the only large storage device that the CPU is able to address and access directly. For example, for the CPU to process data from disk, those data must first be transferred to main memory by CPU-generated I/O calls. Equivalently, instructions must be in memory for the CPU to execute them.

For a program to be executed, it must be mapped to absolute addresses and loaded into memory. As the program executes, it accesses program instructions and data from memory by generating these absolute addresses. Eventually, the program terminates, its memory space is declared available, and the next program can be loaded and executed.

To improve both the utilization of the CPU and the speed of the computer's response to its users, we must keep several programs in memory. Many different memory-management schemes are available, and the effectiveness of the different algorithms depends on the particular situation. Selection of a memory-management scheme for a specific system depends on many factors—especially on the *hardware* design of the system. Each algorithm requires its own hardware support.

The operating system is responsible for the following activities in connection with memory management:

- Keeping track of which parts of memory are currently being used and by whom
- Deciding which processes are to be loaded into memory when memory space becomes available
- Allocating and de-allocating memory space as needed

File Management

File management is one of the most visible components of an operating system. Computers can store information on several different types of physical media. Magnetic tape, magnetic disk, and optical disk are the most common media. Each of these media has its own characteristics and physical organization. Each medium is controlled by a device, such as a disk drive or tape drive, that also has unique characteristics. These properties include access speed, capacity, data-transfer rate, and access method (sequential or random).

For convenient use of the computer system, the operating system provides a uniform logical view of information storage. The operating system abstracts from the physical properties of its storage devices to define a logical storage unit, the file. The operating system maps files onto physical media, and accesses these files via the storage devices.

A **file** is a collection of related information defined by its creator. Commonly, files represent programs (both source and object forms) and data. Data files may be numeric, alphabetic, or alphanumeric. Files may be free-form (for example, text files), or may be formatted rigidly (for example, fixed fields). A file consists of a sequence of bits, bytes, lines, or records whose meanings are defined by their creators. The concept of a file is an extremely general one.

The operating system implements the abstract concept of a file by managing mass storage media, such as disks and tapes, and the devices that control them. Also, files are normally organized into directories to ease their use. Finally, when multiple users have access to files, we may want to control by whom and in what ways (for example, read, write, append) files may be accessed.

The operating system is responsible for the following activities in connection with file management:

- Creating and deleting files
- Creating and deleting directories
- Supporting primitives for manipulating files and directories
- Mapping files onto secondary storage
- Backing up files on stable (nonvolatile) storage media

I/O-System Management

One of the purposes of an operating system is to hide the peculiarities of specific hardware devices from the user. For example, in UNIX, the peculiarities of I/O devices are hidden from the bulk of the operating system itself by the I/O **subsystem.** The I/O subsystem consists of:

- A memory-management component that includes buffering, caching, and spooling
- A general device-driver interface
- Drivers for specific hardware devices

Only the device driver knows the peculiarities of the specific device to which it is assigned.

Secondary-Storage Management

The main purpose of a computer system is to execute programs. These programs, with the data they access, must be in main memory, or **primary storage,** during execution. Because main memory is too small to accommodate all data and programs, and because the data that it holds are lost when power is lost, the computer system must provide **secondary storage** to back up main memory. Most modern computer systems use disks as the principal on-line storage medium, for both programs and data. Most programs—including compilers, assemblers, sort routines, editors, and formatters—are stored on a disk until loaded into memory, and then use the disk as both the source and destination of their processing. Hence, the proper management of disk storage is of central importance to a computer system.

The operating system is responsible for the following activities in connection with disk management:

- Free-space management
- Storage allocation
- Disk scheduling

Because secondary storage is used frequently, it must be used efficiently. The entire speed of operation of a computer may hinge on the speeds of the disk subsystem and of the algorithms that manipulate that subsystem.

Networking

A **distributed system** is a collection of processors that do not share memory, peripheral devices, or a clock. Instead, each processor has its own local memory and clock, and the processors communicate with one another through various communication lines, such as high-speed buses or networks. The processors in a distributed system vary in size and function. They may include small microprocessors, workstations, minicomputers, and large, general-purpose computer systems.

The processors in the system are connected through a **communication network,** which can be configured in a number of different ways. The network may be fully or partially connected. The communication-network design must consider message routing and connection strategies, and the problems of contention and security.

A distributed system collects physically separate, possibly heterogeneous, systems into a single coherent system, providing the user with access to the various resources that the system maintains. Access to a shared resource allows computation speedup, increased functionality, increased data availability, and enhanced reliability. Operating systems usually generalize network access as a form of file access, with the details of networking being contained in the network interface's device driver. The protocols that create a distributed system can have a great effect on that system's utility and popularity. The innovation of the World Wide Web was to create a new access method for information sharing. It improved on the existing **file-transfer protocol (FTP)** and **network file-system (NFS)** protocol by removing the need for a user to log in before she is allowed to use a remote resource. It defined a new protocol, **hypertext transfer protocol (http),** for use in communication between a web server and a web browser. A web browser then just needs to send a request for information to a remote machine's web server, and the information (text, graphics, links to other information) is returned. This increase in convenience fostered huge growth in the use of http and of the Web in general.

Protection System

If a computer system has multiple users and allows the concurrent execution of multiple processes, then the various processes must be protected from one another's activities. For that purpose, mechanisms ensure that the files, memory segments, CPU, and other resources can be operated on by only those processes that have gained proper authorization from the operating system.

For example, memory-addressing hardware ensures that a process can execute only within its own address space. The timer ensures that no process can gain control of the CPU without eventually relinquishing control. Device control registers are not accessible to users, so that the integrity of the various peripheral devices is protected.

Protection is any mechanism for controlling the access of programs, processes, or users to the resources defined by a computer system. This mechanism must provide means for specification of the controls to be imposed and means for enforcement.

Protection can improve reliability by detecting latent errors at the interfaces between component subsystems. Early detection of interface errors can often prevent contamination of a healthy subsystem by another subsystem that is malfunctioning. An unprotected resource cannot defend against use (or misuse) by an unauthorized or incompetent user. A protection-oriented system provides a means to distinguish between authorized and unauthorized usage.

Command-Interpreter System

One of the most important systems programs for an operating system is the **command interpreter**, which is the interface between the user and the operating system. Some operating systems include the command interpreter in the kernel. Other operating systems, such as MS-DOS and UNIX, treat the command interpreter as a special program that is running when a job is initiated, or when a user first logs on (on time-sharing systems).

Many commands are given to the operating system by **control statements.** When a new job is started in a batch system, or when a user logs on to a time-shared system, a program that reads and interprets control statements is executed automatically. This program is sometimes called the **control-card interpreter** or the **command-line interpreter,** and is often known as the shell. Its function is simple: To get the next command statement and execute it.

Operating systems are frequently differentiated in the area of the shell, with a user-friendly command interpreter making the system more agreeable to some users. One style of user-friendly interface is the mouse-based window-and-menu system used in the Macintosh and in Microsoft Windows. The mouse is moved to position the mouse pointer on images, or icons, on the screen that represent programs, files, and system functions. Depending on the mouse pointer's location, clicking a button on the mouse can invoke a program, select a file or directory—known as a **folder**—or pull down a menu that contains commands. More powerful, complex, and difficult-to-learn shells are appreciated by other users. In some of these shells, commands are typed on a keyboard and displayed on a screen or printing terminal, with the enter (or return) key signaling that a command is complete and is ready to be executed. The MS-DOS and UNIX shells operate in this way.

Operating-System Services

An operating system provides an environment for the execution of programs. It provides certain services to programs and to the users of those programs. The specific services provided, of course, differ from one operating system to another, but we can identify common classes. These operating-system services are provided for the convenience of the programmer, to make the programming task easier.

- **Program execution:** The system must be able to load a program into memory and to run that program. The program must be able to end its execution, either normally or abnormally (indicating error).
- **I/O operations:** A running program may require I/O. This I/O may involve a file or an I/O device. For specific devices, special functions may be desired (such as to rewind a tape drive, or to blank a CRT screen). For efficiency and protection, users usually cannot control I/O devices directly. Therefore, the operating system must provide a means to do I/O.
- **File-system manipulation:** The file system is of particular interest. Obviously, programs need to read and write files. Programs also need to create and delete files by name.
- **Communications:** In many circumstances, one process needs to exchange information with another process. Such communication can occur in two major ways. The first takes place between processes that are executing on the same computer; the second takes place between processes that are executing on different computer systems that are tied together by a computer network. Communications may be implemented via **shared memory,** or by the technique of **message passing,** in which packets of information are moved between processes by the operating system.
- **Error detection:** The operating system constantly needs to be aware of possible errors. Errors may occur in the CPU and memory hardware (such as a memory error or a power failure), in I/O devices (such as a parity error on tape, a connection failure on a network, or lack of paper in the printer) and in the user program (such as an arithmetic overflow, an attempt to access and illegal memory location, or a too-great use of CPU time). For each type of error, the operating system should take the appropriate action to ensure correct and consistent computing.

  In addition, another set of operating-system functions exists not for helping the user, but for ensuring the efficient operation of the system itself. Systems with multiple users can gain efficiency by sharing the computer resources among the users.
- **Resource allocation:** When multiple users are logged on the system or multiple jobs are running at the same time, resources must be allocated to each of them. Many different types of resources are managed by the operating system. Some (such as CPU cycles, main memory, and file storage) may have special allocation code, whereas others (such as I/O devices) may have much more general request and release code. For instance, in determining how best to use the CPU, operating systems have CPU-scheduling routines that take into account the speed of the CPU, the jobs that must be executed, the number of registers available, and other

factors. There might also be routines to allocate a tape drive for use by a job. One such routine locates an unused tape drive and marks an internal table to record the drive's new user. Another routine is used to clear that table. These routines may also allocate plotters, modems, and other peripheral devices.

- **Accounting:** We want to keep track of which users use how many and which kinds of computer resources. This record keeping may be used for accounting (so that users can be billed) or simply for accumulating usage statistics. Usage statistics may be a valuable tool for researchers who wish to reconfigure the system to improve computing services.
- **Protection:** The owners of information stored in a multiuser computer system may want to control use of that information. When several disjointed processes execute concurrently, it should not be possible for one process to interface with the others, or with the operating system itself. Protection involves ensuring that all access to system resources is controlled.
- **Security** of the system from outsiders is also important. Such security starts with each user having to authenticate himself to the system, usually by means of a password, to be allowed access to the resources. It extends to defending external I/O devices, including modems and network adapters, from invalid access attempts, and to recording all such connections for detection of break-ins. If a system is to be protected and secure, precautions must be instituted throughout it. A chain is only as strong as its weakest link.

System Calls

System calls provide the interface between a process and the operating system. These calls are generally available as assembly-language instructions, and they are usually listed in the various manuals used by the assembly-language programmers.

Certain systems allow system calls to be made directly from a higher-level language program, in which case the calls normally resemble predefined function or subroutine calls. They may generate a call to special run-time routine that makes the system calls, or the system call may be generated directly in-line.

Several languages—such as C, C++, and Perl—have been defined to replace assembly language for systems programming. These languages allow system calls to be made directly. For example, UNIX system calls may be invoked directly from a C or C++ program. System calls for modern Microsoft Windows platforms are part of the Win32 **application programmer interface (API),** which is available for use by all the compilers written for Microsoft Windows.

As an example of how system calls are used, consider writing a simple program to read data from one file and to copy them to another file. The first input that the program will need is the names of the two files: the input file and the output file. These names can be specified in many ways, depending on the operating-system design. One approach is for the program to ask the user for the names of the two files. In an interactive system, this approach will require a sequence of system calls, first to write a prompting message on the screen, and then to read from the keyboard the characters that define the two files. On mouse-based window-and-menu systems, a menu of file names is usually displayed in a window. The user can then use the mouse to select the source name, and a similar window can be opened for the destination name to be specified.

Once the two file names are obtained, the program must open the input file and create the output file. Each of these operations requires another system call and may encounter possible error conditions. When the program tries to open the input file, it may find that no file of that name exists or that the file is protected against access. In these cases, the program should print a message on the console (another sequence of system calls), and then terminate abnormally (another system call). If the input file exists, then we must create a new output file. We may find an output file with the same name. This situation may cause the program to abort (a system call), or we may delete the existing file (another system call) and create a new one(another system call). In an interactive system, another option is to ask the user (a sequence of system calls to output the prompting message and to read the response from the keyboard) whether to replace the existing file or to abort the program.

Now that both files are set up, we enter a loop that reads from the input file (a system call) and writes to the output file (another system call). Each read and write must return status information regarding various possible error conditions. On input, the program may find that the end of the file has been reached, or that a hardware failure occurred in the read (such as a parity error). On output, various errors may occur, depending on the output device (such as no more disk space, physical end of tape, printer out of paper).

Finally, after the entire file is copied, the program may close both files (another system call), write a message to the console (more system calls), and finally terminate normally (the final system call). As we can see, even simple programs may make heavy use of the operating system.

Most users never see this level of detail, however. The run-time support system (the set of functions built into libraries included with a compiler) for most programming languages provides a much simpler interface. For example, the count statement in C++ is probably compiled into a call to a run-time support routine that issues the necessary system calls, checks for errors, and finally returns to the user program. Thus, most of the details of the operating-system interface are hidden from the programmer by the compiler and by the run-time support package.

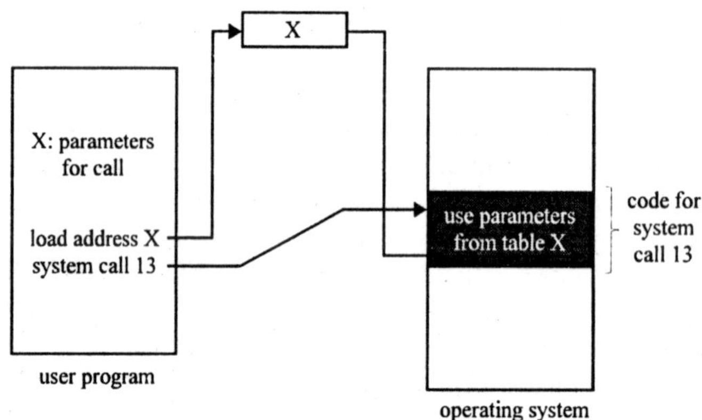

Fig. 3.1. Passing of parameters as a table.

System calls occur in different ways, depending on the computer in use. Often, more information is required than simply the identity of the desired system call. The exact type and amount of information vary according to the particular operating system and call. For example, to get input, we may need to specify the file or device to use as the source, and the address and length of the memory buffer into which the input should be read. Of course, the device of file and length may be implicit in the call.

Three general methods are used to pass parameters to the operating system. The simplest approach is to pass the parameters in *registers.* In some cases, however, there may be more parameters than registers. In these cases, the parameters are generally stored in a *block* or table in memory, and the address of the block is passed as a parameter in a register. This is the approach taken by Linux. Parameters can also be placed, or *pushed,* onto the *stack* by the program, and *popped off* the stack by the operating system. Some operating systems prefer the block or stack methods, because those approaches do not limit the number or length of parameters being passed.

System calls can be grouped roughly into five major categories: **process control, file management, device management, information maintenance,** and **communications.** We discuss briefly the types of system calls that may be provided by an operating system. Most of these system calls support, or are supported by, concepts and functions that are discussed in later chapters.

Process Control

A running program needs to be able to halt its execution either normally (end) or abnormally (abort). If a system call is made to terminate the currently running program abnormally, or if the program runs into a problem and causes an error trap, a dump of memory is sometimes taken and an error message generated. The dump is written to disk and may be examined by a **debugger** to determine the cause of the problem. Under either normal or abnormal circumstances, the operating system must transfer control to the command interpreter. The command interpreter then reads the next command. In an interactive system, the command interpreter simply continues with the next command; it is assumed that the user will issue an appropriate command to respond to any error. In a batch system, the command interpreter usually terminates the entire job and continues with the next job. Some systems allow control cards to indicate special recovery actions in case an error occurs. If the program discovers an error in its input and wants to terminate abnormally, it may also want to define an error level. More severe errors can be indicated by a higher-level error parameter. It is then possible to combine normal and abnormal termination by defining a normal termination as error at level 0. The command interpreter or a following program can use this error level to determine the next action automatically.

- Process control
  - end, abort
  - load, execute
  - create process, terminate process
  - get process attributes, set process attributes
  - wait for time
  - wait event, signal event
  - allocate and free memory
- File management
  - create file, delete file
  - open, close

- read, write, reposition
- get file attributes, set file attributes

- Device management
  - request device, release device
  - read, write, reposition
  - get device attributes, set device attributes
  - logically attach or detach devices
- Information maintenance
  - get time or date, set time or date
  - get system data, set system data
  - get process, file, or device attributes
  - set process, file, or device attributes
- Communications
  - create, delete communication connection
  - send, receive messages
  - transfer status information
  - attach or detach remote devices

Fig. 3.2. Types of system calls.

A process or job executing one program may want to load and execute another program. This feature allows the command interpreter to execute a program as directed by, for example, a user command, the click of a mouse, or a batch command. An interesting question is where to return control when the loaded program terminates. This question is related to the problem of whether the existing program is lost, saved, or allowed to continue execution concurrently with the new program.

If control returns to the existing program when the new program terminates, we must save the memory image of the existing program, thus, we have effectively created a mechanism for one program to call another program. If both programs continue concurrently, we have created a new job or process to be multiprogrammed. Often, system calls exists specifically for this purpose (create process or submit job).

If we create a new job or process, or perhaps even a set of jobs or processes, we should be able to control its execution. This control requires the ability to determine and reset the attributes of a job or process, including the job's priority, its maximum allowable execution time, and so on (get process attributes and set process attributes). We may also want to terminate a job or process that we created (terminate process) if we find that it is incorrect or is no longer needed.

Having created new jobs or processes, we may need to wait for them to finish their execution. We may want to wait for a certain amount of time (wait time); more likely, we may want to wait for a specific event to occur (wait event). The jobs or processes should then signal when that event has occurred (signal event). System calls of this type, deal with the coordination of concurrent processes.

Another set of system calls is helpful in debugging a program. Many systems provide system calls to dump memory. This provision is useful for debugging. A program trace lists each instruction as it is executed; it is provided by fewer systems. Even microprocessors provide a CPU mode known as single step, in which a trap is executed by the CPU after every instruction. The trap is usually caught by a debugger, which is a system program designed to aid the programmer in finding and correcting bugs.

Many operating systems provide a time profile of a program. It indicates the amount of time that the program executes at a particular location or set of locations. A time profile requires either a tracing facility or regular timer interrupts. At every occurrence of the timer interrupt, the value of the program counter is recorded. With sufficiently frequent timer interrupts, a statistical picture of the time spent on various parts of the program can be obtained.

Process and job control have so many facets and variations that we shall use examples to clarify these concepts. The MS-DOS operating system is an example of a single-tasking system, which has a command interpreter that is invoked when the computer is started. Because MS-DOS is single-tasking it uses a simple method to run a program and does not create a new process. It loads the program into memory, writing over most of itself to give the program as much memory as possible. It then sets the instruction pointer to the first instruction of the program. The program then runs and either an error causes a trap, or the program executes a system call to terminate. In either case, the error code is saved in the system memory for later use. Following this action, the small portion of the command interpreter that was not overwritten resumes execution. Its first task is to reload the rest of the command interpreter from disk. Once this task is accomplished, the command interpreter makes the previous error code available to the user or to the next program.

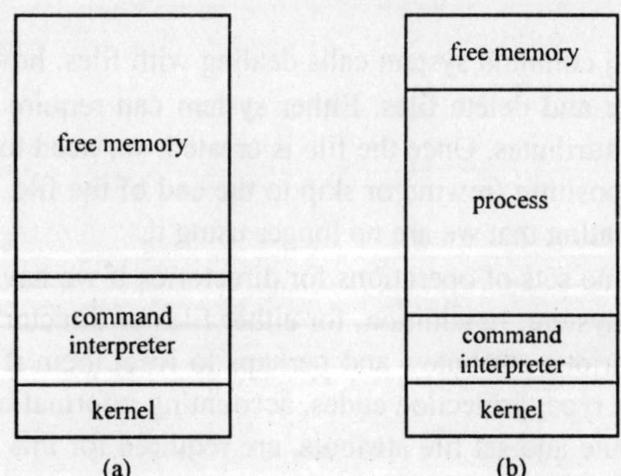

Fig. 3.3. *MS-DOS execution. (a) At system startup. (b) Running a program.*

FreeBSD is an example of a multitasking system. When a user logs on to the system, the shell (or command interpreter) of the user's choice is run. This shell is similar to the MS-DOS shell in that it accepts commands and executes programs that the user requests. However, since FreeBSD is a multitasking system, the command interpreter may continue running while another program is executed. To start a new process, the shell executes a fork system call. The selected program is then executed. Depending on the way the command is issued, the shell then either waits for the process to finish, or runs the process "in the background." In the latter case, the shell immediately requests another command. When a process is running in the background, it cannot receive input directly from the keyboard, because the shell is using this resource. I/O is therefore done through files, or through a window-and-menu interface. Meanwhile, the user is free to ask the shell to run other programs, to monitor the progress of the running process, to change that program's priority, and so on. When the process is done, it executes an exit system call to terminate, returning to the invoking process a status code of 0, or a nonzero error code. This status (or error) code is then available to the shell or other programs.

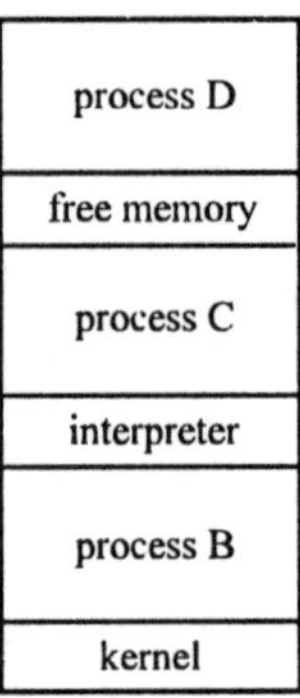

Fig. 3.4. UNIX running multiple programs.

File Management

We can identify several common system calls dealing with files, however.

We first need to create and delete files. Either system can require the name of the file and perhaps some of the file's attributes. Once the file is created, we need to open it and to use it. We may also read, write, or reposition (rewind or skip to the end of the file, for example). Finally, we need to close the file, indicating that we are no longer using it.

We may need these same sets of operations for directories if we have a directory structure for organizing files in the file system. In addition, for either files or directories, we need to be able to determine the values of various attributes, and perhaps to reset them if necessary. File attributes include the file name, a file type, protection codes, accounting information, and so on. At least two system calls, get file attribute and set file attribute, are required for this function. Some operating systems provide many more calls.

Device Management

A program, as it is running, may need additional resources to proceed. Additional resources may be more memory, tape drives, access to files, and so on. If the resources are available, they can be granted, and control can be returned to the user program, otherwise, the program will have to wait until sufficient resources are available.

Files can be thought of as abstract or virtual devices. Thus, many of the system calls for files are also needed for devices. If the system has multiple users, however, we must first request the device, to ensure exclusive use of it. After we are finished with the device, we must release it. These functions are similar to the open and close system calls for files.

Once the device has been requested (and allocated to us), we can read, write, and (possibly) reposition the device, just as we can with ordinary files. In fact, the similarity between I/O devices and files is so great that many operating systems, including UNIX and MS-DOS, merge the two into a combined **file-device structure.** In this case, I/O devices are identified by special file names.

Information Maintenance

Many system calls exist simply for the purpose of transferring information between the user program and the operating system. For example, most systems have a system call to return the current time and date. Other system calls may return information about the system, such as the number of current users, the version number of the operating system, the amount of free memory or disk space, and so on.

In addition, the operating system keeps information about all its processes, and there are system calls to access this information. Generally, there are also calls to reset the process information (get process attributes and set process attributes).

Communication

There are two common models of communication. In the **message-passing model**, information is exchanged through an interprocess-communication facility provided by the operating system. Before communication can take place, a connection must be opened. The name of the other communicator must be known, be it another process on the same CPU, or a process on another computer connected by a communications network. Each computer in a network has a host name, such as an IP name, by which it is commonly known. Similarly, each process has a **process name,** which is translated into an equivalent identifier by which the operating system can refer to it. To get hostid and get processid system calls do this translation. These identifiers are then passed to the general-purpose open and close calls provided by the file system, or to specific open connection and close connection system calls, depending on the system's model of communications. The recipient process usually must give its permission for communication to take place with an accept connection call. Most processes that will be receiving connections are special-purpose **daemons**—systems programs provided for that purpose. They execute a wait for connection call and are awakened when a connection is made. The source of the communication, known as the *client,* and the receiving daemon, known as a *server,* then exchange messages by read message and write message system calls. The close connection call terminates the communication.

In the **shared-memory model,** processes use map memory system calls to gain access to regions of memory owned by other processes. Recall that, normally, the operating system tries to prevent one process from accessing another process memory. Shared memory requires that several processes agree to remove this restriction. They may then exchange information by reading and writing data in these shared areas. The form of the data and the location are determined by these processes and are not under the operating system's control. The processes are also responsible for ensuring that they are not writing to the same location simultaneously. We will also look at a variation of the process model—**threads**—that shares memory by default.

Both of these methods are common in operating systems, and some systems even implement both. Message passing is useful when smaller numbers of data need to be exchanged, because no conflict needs to be avoided. It is also easier to implement than is shared memory for intercomputer communication. Shared memory allows maximum speed and convenience of communication, as it can be done at memory speeds when within a computer. Problems exist, however in the areas of protection and synchronization.

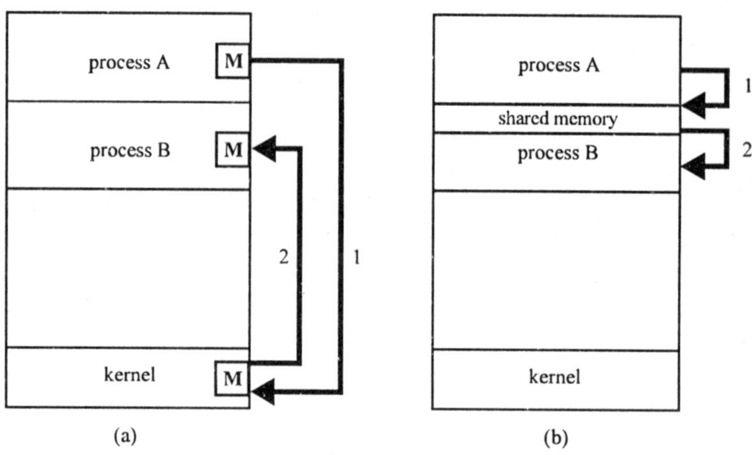

Fig. 3.5. Communication models. (a) Msg passing. (b) Shared memory.

System Programs

Another aspect of a modern system is the collection of system programs. Recall Figure 1.1, which depicted the logical computer hierarchy. At the lower level is hardware. Next is the operating system, then the system program and finally the application programs. System programs provide a convenient environment for program development and execution. Some of them are simply user interfaces to system calls; others are considerably more complex. They can be divided into these categories:

- **File management:** These programs create, delete, copy, rename, print, dump, list, and generally manipulate files and directories.
- **Status information:** Some programs simply ask the system for the date, time, amount of available memory or disk space, number of users, or similar status information. That information is then formatted, and is printed to the terminal or other output device or file.
- **File modification:** Several text editors may be available to create and modify the content of files stored on disk or tape.
- **Programming-language support:** Compilers, assemblers, and interpreters for common programming languages (such as C, C++, Java, Visual Basic, and PERL) are often provided to the user with the operating system. Some of these programs are now priced and provided separately.
- **Program loading and execution:** Once a program is assembled or compiled, it must be loaded into memory to be executed. The system may provide absolute loaders, relocatable

loaders, linkage editors, and overlay loaders. Debugging systems for either higher-level languages or machine language are also needed.

- **Communications:** These programs provide the mechanism for creating, virtual connections among processes, users, and different computer systems. They allow users to send messages to one another's screens, to browse web pages, to send electronic-mail messages, to log in remotely, or to transfer files from one machine to another.

Most operating systems are supplied with programs that solve common problems, or perform common operations. Such programs include web browsers, word processors and text formatters, spreadsheets, database systems, compiler compilers, plotting and statistical-analysis packages, and games. These programs are known as **system utilities** or **application programs.**

Perhaps the most important system program for an operating system is the command interpreter, the main function of which is to get and execute the next user-specified command.

Many of the commands given at this level manipulate files: create, delete, list, print, copy, execute, and so on. These commands can be implemented in two general ways. In one approach, the command interpreter itself contains the code to execute the command. For example, a command to delete a file may cause the command interpreter to jump to a section of its code that sets up the parameters and makes the appropriate system call. In this case, the number of commands that can be given determines the size of the command interpreter, since each command requires its own implementing code.

An alternative approach—used by UNIX, among other operating systems—implements most commands by system programs. In this case, the command interpreter does not understand the command in any way; it merely uses the command to identify a file to be loaded into memory and executed. Thus, the UNIX command to delete a file

```
rm G
```

would search for a file called rm, load the file into memory, and execute it with the parameter G. The function associated with the rm command would be defined completely by the code in the file rm. In this way, programmers can add new commands to the system easily by creating new files with the proper names. The command-interpreter program, which can be small, does not have to be changed for new commands to be added.

This approach to the design of a command interpreter has problems. First, because the code to execute a command is a separate system program, the operating system must provide a mechanism for passing parameters from the command interpreter to the system program. This task can often be clumsy, because the command interpreter and the system program may not be in memory at the same time, and the parameter list can be extensive. Also, it is slower to load a program and to execute it than simply to jump to another section of code within the current program.

Another problem is that the interpretation of the parameters is left up to the programmer of the system program. Thus, parameters may be provided inconsistently across programs that appear similar to the user, but were written at different times by different programmers.

The view of the operating system seen by most users is thus defined by the system programs, rather than by the actual system calls. Think of using a PC. When your computer is running the Microsoft Windows operating system, you might see a command-line MS-DOS shell, or the graphical window-and-menu interface. Both use the same set of system calls, but the system calls look different and act in different ways. Consequently, your view may be substantially removed from the actual system structure. The design of a useful and friendly user interface is therefore not a direct function of the operating system. In this book, we shall concentrate on the fundamental problems of providing adequate service to user programs. From the point of view of the operating system, we do not distinguish between user programs and system programs.

System Structure

A system as large and complex as a modern operating system must be engineered carefully if it is to function properly and be modified easily. A common approach is to partition the task into small components, rather than have one monolithic system. Each of these modules should be a well-defined portion of the system, with carefully defined inputs, outputs, and function. We have already discussed briefly the common components of operating systems. In this section, we discuss the way these components are interconnected and melded into a kernel.

Simple Structure

Many commercial systems do not have a well-defined structure. Frequently, such operating systems started as small, simple, and limited systems, and then grew beyond their original scope. MS-DOS is an example of such a system. It was originally designed and implemented by a few people who had no idea that it would become so popular. It was written to provide the most functionality in the least space (because of the limited hardware on which it ran), so it was not divided into modules carefully.

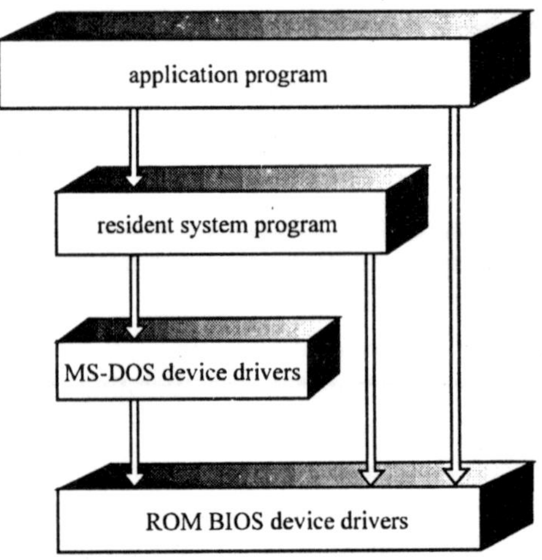

Fig. 3.6. MS-DOS layer structure.

UNIX is another system that was initially limited by hardware functionality. It consists of two separable parts: the kernel and the system programs. The kernel is further separated into a series of interfaces and device drivers, which were added and expanded over the years as UNIX evolved. We can view the traditional UNIX operating system as being layered as shown in Figure 3.7. Everything below the system-call interface and above the physical hardware is the kernel. The kernel provides the file system, CPU scheduling, memory management, and other operating-system functions through system calls. Taken in sum, that is an enormous amount of functionality to be combined into one level. This makes UNIX difficult to enhance, as changes in one section could adversely affect other areas.

System calls define the API to UNIX; the set of system programs commonly available defines the user interface. The programmer and user interfaces define the context that the kernel must support.

New versions of UNIX are designed to use more advanced hardware. Given proper hardware support, operating systems may be broken into pieces that are smaller and more appropriate than are those allowed by the original MS-DOS or UNIX systems. The operating system can then retain much greater control over the computer and over the applications that make use of that computer. Implementers have more freedom to make changes to the inner workings of the system and in the creation of modular operating systems. Under the top-down approach, the overall functionality and features are determined and are separated into components. This separation allows programmers to hide information; they are therefore free to implement the low-level routines as they see fit, provided that the external interface of the routine stays unchanged and that the routine itself performs the advertised task.

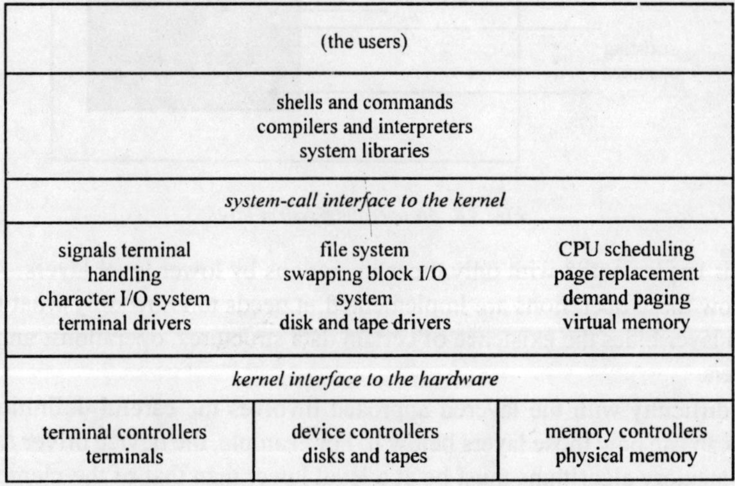

Fig. 3.7. UNIX system structure.

Layered Approach

The modularization of a system can be done in many ways. One method is the **layered approach,** in which the operating system is broken up into a number of layers (or levels), each built on top of lower layers. The bottom layer (layer 0) is the hardware; the highest (layer N) is the user interface.

An operating-system layer is an implementation of an abstract object that is the encapsulation of data, and of the operations that can manipulate those data. A typical operating-system layer—say layer M. It consists of data structures and a set of routines that can be invoked by higher-level layers. Layer M, in turn, can invoke operations on lower-level layers.

The main advantage of the layered approach is **modularity.** The layers are selected such that each uses functions (or operations) and services of only lower-level layers. This approach simplifies debugging and system verification. The first layer can be debugged without any concern for the rest of the system, because, by definition, it uses only the basic hardware (which is assumed correct) to implement its functions. Once the first layer is debugged, its correct functioning can be assumed while the second layer is debugged, and so on. If an error is found during the debugging of a particular layer, the error must be on that layer, because the layers below it are already debugged. Thus, the design and implementation of the system are simplified when the system is broken down into layers.

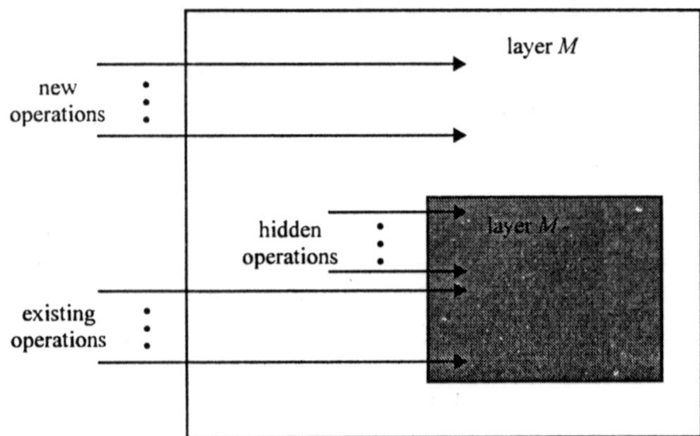

Fig. 3.8. An operating-system layer.

Each layer is implemented with only those operations by lower-level layers. A layer does not need to know how these operations are implemented; it needs to know only what these operations do. Hence, each layer hides the existence of certain data structures, operations, and hardware from higher-level layers.

The major difficulty with the layered approach involves the careful definition of the layers, because a layer can use only those layers below it. For example, the device driver for the disk space used by virtual-memory algorithms must be at a level lower than that of the memory-management routines, because memory management requires the ability to use the disk space.

Other requirements may not be so obvious. The backing-store driver would normally be above the CPU scheduler, because the driver may need to wait for I/O and the CPU can be rescheduled during this time. However, on a large system, the CPU scheduler may have more information about all the active processes than can fit in memory. Therefore, this information may need to be swapped in and out of memory, requiring the backing-store driver routine to be below the CPU scheduler.

A final problem with layered implementations is that they tend to be less efficient than other types. For instance, when a user program executes an I/O operation, it executes a system call that is trapped to the I/O layer, which calls the memory-management layer, which in turn calls the CPU-scheduling layer, which is then passed to the hardware. At each layer, the parameters may be modified, data may need to be passed, and so on. Each layer adds overhead to the system call; the net result is a system call that takes longer than does one on a nonlayered system.

These limitations have caused a small backlash against layering in recent years. Fewer layers with more functionality are being designed, providing most of the advantages of modularized code while avoiding the difficult problems of layer definition and interaction. For instance, OS/2 is a descendant of MS-DOS that adds multitasking and dual-mode operation, as well as other new features. Because of this added complexity and the more powerful hardware for which OS/2 was designed, the system was implemented in a more layered fashion. Compare the MS-DOS structure from both the system-design and implementation standpoints, OS/2 has the advantage. For instance, direct user access to low-level facilities is not allowed, providing the operating system with more control over the hardware and more knowledge of which resources each user program is using.

As a further example, consider the history of Windows NT. The first release had a highly layer-oriented organization; however, it delivered low performance compared to that of Windows 95. Windows NT 4.0 partially redressed the performance problem by moving layers from user space to kernel space and more closely integrating them.

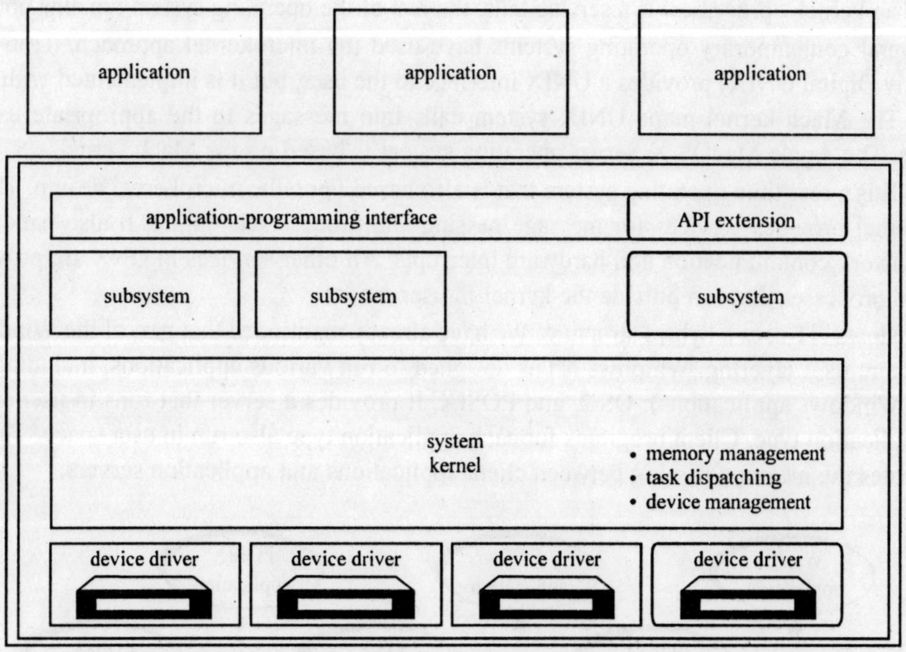

***Fig. 3.9.** OS/2 layer structure.*

Microkernels

As the UNIX operating system expanded, the kernel became large and difficult to manage. In the mid-1980s, researches at Carnegie Mellon University developed an operating system called

Mach that modularizes the kernel using the **microkernel** approach. This method structures the operating system by removing all nonessential components from the kernel, and implementing them as system- and user-level programs. The result is a smaller kernel. There is little consensus regarding which services should remain in the kernel and which should be implemented in user space. In general, however, microkernels typically provide minimal process and memory management, in addition to a communication facility.

The main function of the microkernel is to provide a communication facility between the client program and the various services that are also running in user space. Communication is provided by message passing. For example, if the client program wishes to access a file, it must interact with the file server. The client program and the service never interact directly. Rather, they communicate indirectly by exchanging messages with the microkernel.

The benefits of the microkernel approach include the ease of extending the operating system. All new services are added to user space and consequently do not require modification of the kernel. When the kernel does have to be modified, the changes tend to be fewer, because the microkernel is a smaller kernel. The resulting operating system is easier to port from one hardware design to another. The microkernel also provides more security and reliability, since most services are running as user—rather than kernel—processes. If a service fails, the rest of the operating system remains untouched.

Several contemporary operating systems have used the microkernel approach. Tru64 UNIX (formerly Digital UNIX) provides a UNIX interface to the user, but it is implemented with a Mach kernel. The Mach kernel maps UNIX system calls into messages to the appropriate user-level services. The Apple MacOS X Server operating system is based on the Mach kernel.

QNX is a real-time operating system that is also based upon the microkernel design. The QNX microkernel provides services for message passing and process scheduling. It also handles low-level network communication and hardware interrupts. All other services in QNX are provided by standard processes that run outside the kernel in user mode.

Windows NT uses a hybrid structure. We have already mentioned that part of the Windows NT architecture uses layering. Windows NT is designed to run various applications, including Win32 (native Windows applications), OS/2, and POSIX. It provides a server that runs in user space for each application type. Client programs for each application type also run in user space. The kernel coordinates the message passing between client applications and application servers.

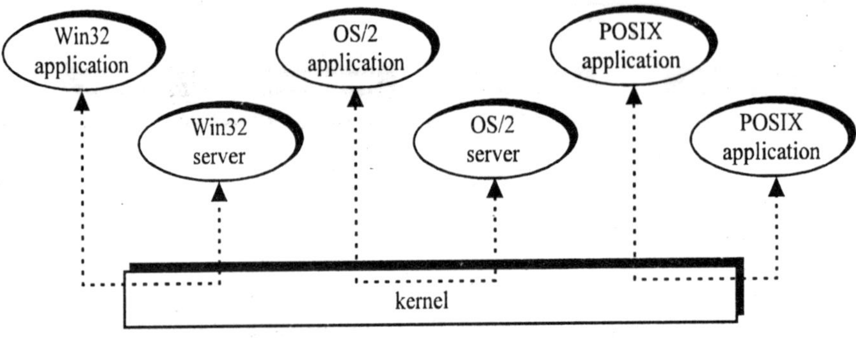

Fig. 3.10. Windows NT client-server structure.

Virtual Machines

Conceptually, a computer system is made up of layers. The hardware is the lowest level in all such systems. The kernel running at the next level uses the hardware instructions to create a set of system calls for use by outer layers. The system programs above the kernel are therefore able to use either system calls or hardware instructions, and in some ways these programs do not differentiate between these two. Thus, although they are accessed differently, they both provide functionality that the program can use to create even more advanced functions. System programs, in turn, treat the hardware and the system calls as though they were both at the same level.

Some systems carry this scheme a step further by allowing the system programs to be called easily by the application programs. As before, although the system programs are at a level higher than that of the other routines, the application programs may view everything under them in the hierarchy as though the latter were part of the machine itself. This layered approach is taken to its logical conclusion in the concept of a **virtual machine.** The VM operating system for IBM systems is the best example of the virtual-machine concept, because IBM pioneered the work in this area.

By using CPU scheduling and virtual-memory techniques, an operating system can create the illusion that a process has its own processor with its own (virtual) memory. Of course, normally, the process has additional features, such as system calls and a file system, that are not provided by the bare hardware. The virtual-machine approach, on the other hand, does not provide any additional functionality, but rather provides an interface that is *identical* to the underlying bare hardware. Each process is provided with a (virtual) copy of the underlying computer.

The physical computer shares resources to create the virtual machines. CPU scheduling can share out the CPU to create the appearance that users have their own processors. Spooling and a file system can provide virtual card readers and virtual line printers. A normal user time-sharing terminal provides the function of the virtual-machine operator's console.

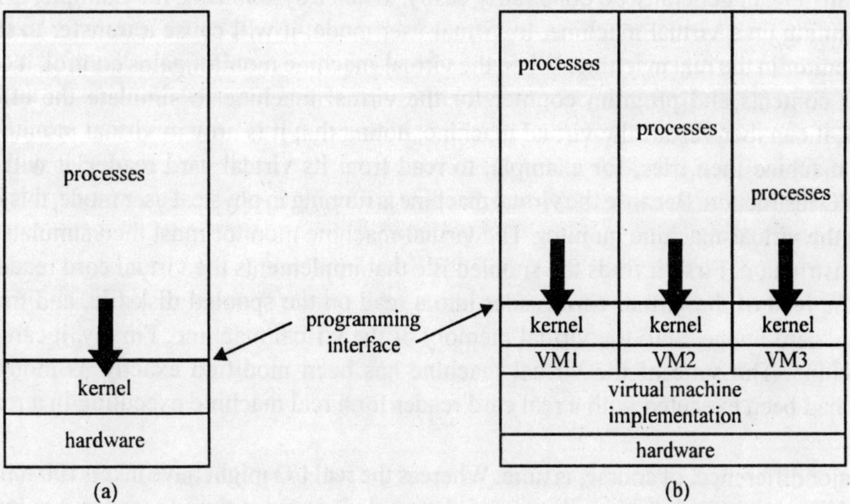

Fig. 3.11. System models. (a) Nonvirtual machine. (b) Virtual machine.

A major difficulty with the virtual-machine approach involves disk systems. Suppose that the physical machine has three disk drives but wants to support seven virtual machines. Clearly, it cannot allocate a disk drive to each virtual machine. Remember that the virtual-machine software itself will need substantial disk space to provide virtual memory. The solution is to provide virtual disks, which are identical in all respects except size—termed *minidisks* in IBM's VM operating system. The system implements each minidisk by allocating as many tracks on the physical disks as the minidisk needs. Obviously, the sum of the sizes of all minidisks must be smaller than the size of the physical disk space available.

Users thus are given their own virtual machines. They can then run any of the operating systems or software packages that are available on the underlying machine. For the IBM VM system, a user normally runs CMS—a single-user interactive operating system. The virtual-machine software is concerned with multiprogramming multiple virtual machines onto a physical machine, but it does not need to consider any user-support software. This arrangement may provide a useful partitioning into two smaller pieces of the problem of designing a multiuser interactive system.

Implementation

Although the virtual-machine concept is useful, it is difficult to implement. Much work is required to provide and *exact* duplicate of the underlying machine. Remember that the underlying machine has two modes: user mode and monitor mode. The virtual-machine software can run in monitor mode, since it is the operating system. The virtual machine itself can execute in only user mode. Just as the physical machine has two modes, however, so must the virtual machine. Consequently, we must have a virtual user mode and a virtual monitor mode, both of which run in a physical user mode. Those actions that cause a transfer from user mode to monitor mode on a real machine (such as a system call or an attempt to execute a privileged instruction) must also cause a transfer from virtual user mode to virtual monitor mode on a virtual machine.

This transfer can generally be done fairly easily. When a system call, for example, is made by a program running on a virtual machine, in virtual user mode, it will cause a transfer to the virtual-machine monitor in the real machine. When the virtual-machine monitor gains control, it can change the register contents and program counter for the virtual machine to simulate the effect of the system call. It can then restart the virtual machine, noting that it is now in virtual monitor mode. If the virtual machine then tries, for example, to read from its virtual card reader, it will execute a privileged I/O instruction. Because the virtual machine is running in physical user mode, this instruction will trap to the virtual-machine monitor. The virtual-machine monitor must then simulate the effect of the I/O instruction. First, it finds the spooled file that implements the virtual card reader. Then, it translates the read of the virtual card reader into a read on the spooled disk file, and transfers the next virtual "card image" into the virtual memory of the virtual machine. Finally, it can restart the virtual machine. The state of the virtual machine has been modified exactly as though the I/O instruction had been executed with a real card reader for a real machine executing in a real monitor mode.

The major difference, of course, is time. Whereas the real I/O might have taken 100 milliseconds, the virtual I/O might take less time (because it is spooled) or more time (because it is interpreted). In addition, the CPU is the virtual being multiprogrammed among many virtual machines, further slowing down the virtual machines in unpredictable ways. In the extreme case, it may be necessary to simulate all instructions to provide a true virtual machine. VM works for IBM machines because normal instructions for the virtual machines can execute directly on the hardware. Only the privileged instructions (needed mainly for I/O) must be simulated and hence execute more slowly.

Benefits

There are two primary advantages to using virtual machines. First, by completely protecting system resources, the virtual machine provides a robust level of security. Second, the virtual machine allows system development to be done without disrupting normal system operation.

Each virtual machine is completely isolated from all other virtual machines, so we have no security problems as the various system resources are completely protected. For example, untrusted applications downloaded from the Internet could be run within a separate virtual machine. A disadvantage of this environment is that there is no *direct* sharing of resources. Two approaches to provide sharing have been implemented. First, it is possible to share a minidisk. This scheme is modeled after a physical shared disk, but is implemented by software. With this technique, files can be shared. Second, it is possible to define a network of virtual machines, each of which can send information over the virtual communications network. Again, the network is modeled after physical communication networks, but it is implemented in software.

Such a virtual-machine system is a perfect vehicle for operating-systems research and development. Normally, changing an operating system is a difficult task. Because operating systems are large and complex programs, a change in one part may cause obscure bugs in some other part. The power of the operating system makes this situation particularly dangerous. Because the operating system executes in monitor mode, a wrong change in a pointer could cause an error that would destroy the entire file system. Thus, it is necessary to test all changes to the operating system carefully.

The operating system, however, runs on and controls the entire machine. Therefore, the current system must be stopped and taken out of use while changes are made and tested. This period is commonly called **system-development time.** Since it makes the system unavailable to users, system-development time is often scheduled late at night or on weekends, when system load is low.

A virtual-machine system can eliminate much of this problem. System programmers are given their own virtual machine, and system development is done on the virtual machine instead of on the actual physical machine. Normal system operation seldom needs to be disrupted for system development. Despite these advantages, little improvement on the technique had been made until recently.

Virtual machines are increasing in popularity as a means of solving system compatibility problems. For instance, thousands of applications are available for Microsoft Windows on Intel CPU-based systems. Computer vendors such as Sun Microsystems use other, faster processors, but would like their customers to be able to run these Windows applications. The solution is to create a virtual Intel machine on top of the native processor. A Windows program is run in this environment, and its Intel instructions are translated into the native instruction set. Microsoft Windows is also run in this virtual machine, so the program can make its system calls as usual. The net result is a program that appears to be running on an Intel-based system but is really executing on a different processor. If the processor is sufficiently fast, the Windows program will run quickly, even though every instruction is being translated into several native instructions for execution. Similarly, the PowerPC-based

Apple Macintosh includes a Motorola 68000 virtual machine to allow execution of binary codes that were written for the older 68000-based Macintosh. Unfortunately, the more complex the machine being emulated, the more difficult it is to build an accurate virtual machine, and the slower that virtual machine runs.

A more recent example can be shown with the growth of the Linux operating system. Virtual machines now exist that allow Windows applications to run on Linux-based computers. The virtual machine runs both the Windows application and the Windows operating system.

One of the key features of Java is that it runs on a virtual machine, thereby allowing a Java program to run on any computer system that has a Java virtual machine.

Java

Java is a very popular object-oriented language introduced by Sun Microsystems in late 1995. In addition to a language specification and a large API library, Java also provides a specification for a **Java virtual machine (JVM).**

Java objects are specified with the class construct; a Java program consists of one or more classes. For each Java class, the Java compiler produces an architecture-neutral **bytecode** output (.class) file that will run on any implementation of the JVM.

The JVM is a specification for an abstract computer. The JVM consists of a **class loader,** a **class verifier,** and a Java interpreter that executes the architecture-neutral bytecodes. The class loader loads .class files from both the Java program and the Java API for execution by the Java interpreter. After a class is loaded, the verifier checks that the class file is valid Java bytecode and does not overflow or underflow the stack. It also ensures that the bytecode does not perform pointer arithmetic, which could potentially provide illegal memory access. If the class passes verification, it is run by the Java interpreter. The JVM also automatically manages memory by performing **garbage collection**—the practice of reclaiming memory from objects no longer in use and returning it to the system. Much research focuses on garbage collection algorithms for increasing the performance of Java programs in the virtual machine.

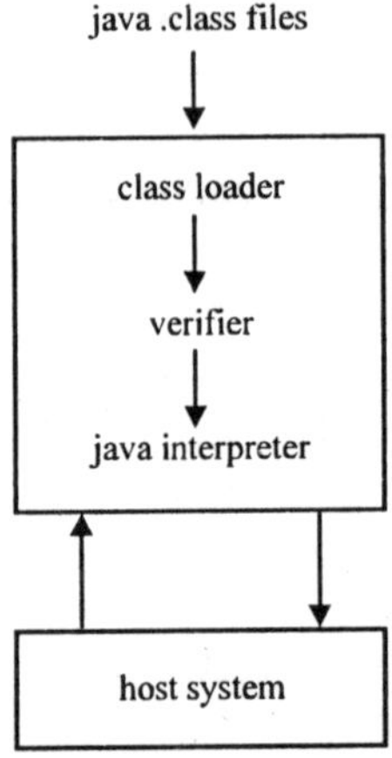

Fig. 3.12. The Java virtual machine.

The Java interpreter may be a software module that interprets the bytecodes one at a time, or it may be a **just-in-time (JIT)** compiler that turns the architecture-neutral bytecodes into native machine language for the host computer. Most implementations of the JVM use a JIT compiler for enhanced performance. In other instances, the interpreter may be implemented in hardware that executes Java bytecodes natively.

The JVM makes it possible to develop programs that are architecture neutral and portable. The implementation of the JVM is specific for each system—such as Windows or UNIX—and it abstracts the system in a standard way to the Java program, providing a clean, architecture-neutral interface. This interface allows a .class file to run on any system that has implemented the JVM according to the specification.

Java takes advantage of the complete environment that a virtual machine implements. Its virtual-machine design provides a secure, efficient, object-oriented, portable, and architecture-neutral platform on which to run Java programs.

System Design and Implementation

In this section, we discuss problems we face when designing and implementing a system. No complete solutions to the design problems exist, but some approaches have been successful.

Design Goals

The first problem in designing a system is to define the goals and specifications of the system. At the highest level, the design of the system will be affected by the choice of hardware and type of system: batch, time shared, single user, multiuser, distributed, real time, or general purpose.

Beyond this highest design level, the requirements may be much harder to specify. The requirements can be divided into two basic groups: *user* goals and *system* goals.

Users desire certain obvious properties in a system: The system should be convenient and easy to use, easy to learn, reliable, safe, and fast. Of course, these specifications are not particularly useful in the system design, since there is no general agreement on how to achieve these goals.

A similar set of requirements can be defined by those people who must design, create, maintain, and operate the system: The operating system should be easy to design, implement, and maintain; it should be flexible, reliable, error free, and efficient. Again, these requirements are vague and have no general solution.

4

Processes

Introduction to Processes

All modern computers can do several things at the same time. While running a user program, a computer can also be reading from a disk and outputting text to a screen or printer. In a multiprogramming system, the CPU also switches from program to program, running each for tens or hundreds of milliseconds. While, strictly speaking, at any instant of time, the CPU is running only one program, in the course of 1 second, it may work on several programs, thus giving the users the illusion of parallelism. Sometimes people speak of **pseudoparallelism** to mean this rapid switching back and forth of the CPU between program to contrast it with the true hardware parallelism of **multiprocessor** systems (which have two or more CPUs sharing the same physical memory). Keeping track of multiple, parallel activities is hard for people to do. Therefore, operating system designers over the years have evolved a model (sequential processes) that makes parallelism easier to deal with. That model and its users are the subject of this chapter.

The Process Model

In this model, all the runnable software on the computer, often including the operating system, is organized into a number of **sequential processes**, or just **processes** for short. A process is just an executing program including the current values of the program counter, registers, and variables. Conceptually, each process has its own virtual CPU. In reality, of course, the real CPU switches back and forth from process to process, but to understand the system, it is much easier to think about a collection of processes running in (pseudo) parallel, than to try to keep track of how the CPU switches from program to program. This rapid switching back and forth is called **multiprogramming**, as we saw in the previous chapter.

In Fig. 4.1 (a) we see a computer multiprogramming four programs in memory. In Fig. 4.1 (b) we see four processes, each with its own flow of control (i.e., its own program counter), and each one running independently of the other ones. In Fig. 4.1 (c) we see that viewed over a long enough time interval, all the processes have made progress, but at any given instant only one process is actually running.

With the CPU switching back and forth among the processes, the rate at which a process performs its computation will not be uniform, and probably not even reproducible if the same processes are run again. Thus, processes must not be programmed with built-in assumptions about timing. Consider, for example, an I/O process that starts a streamer tape to restore backed up files, executes an idle loop 10,000 times to let it get up to speed, and then issues a command to read the first record. If the CPU decides to switch to another process during the idle loop, the tape process might not run again until after the first record was already past the read head. When a process has critical real-time requirements like this that is, particular events *must* occur within a specified number of milliseconds, special measures must be taken to ensure that they do occur. Normally, however, most processes are not affected by the underlying multiprogramming of the CPU or the relative speeds of different processes.

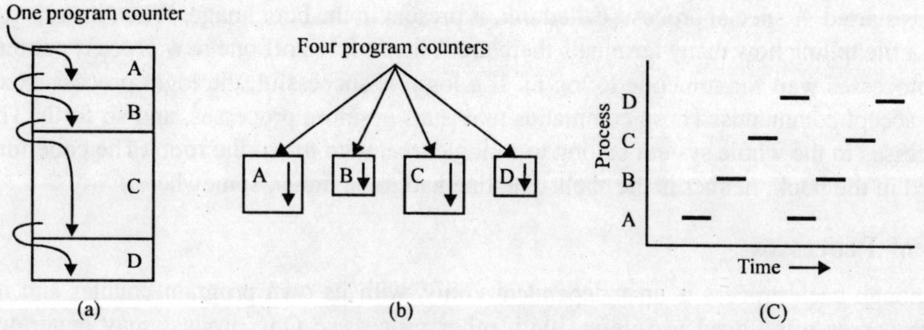

Fig. 4.1. (a) Multiprogramming of four programs. (b) Conceptual model of four independent, sequential processes. (c) Only one program is active at any instant.

The difference between a process and a program is subtle, but crucial. An analogy may help make this point clearer. Consider a culinary-minded computer scientist who is baking a birthday cake for his daughter. He has a birthday cake recipe and a kitchen well-stocked with the necessary input: flour, eggs, sugar, extract of vanilla, and so on. In this analogy, the recipe is the program (i.e., an algorithm expressed in some suitable notation), the computer scientist is the processor (CPU), and the cake ingredients are the input data. The process is the activity consisting of our baker reading the recipe, fetching the ingredient, and baking the cake.

Now imagine that the computer scientist's son comes running is crying, saying that he has been stung by a bee. The computer scientist records where he was in the recipe (the state of the current process is saved), gets out a first aid book, and begins following the directions in it. Here we see the processor being switched from one process (baking) to a higher priority process (administering medical care), each having a different program (recipe vs. first aid book). When the bee sting has been taken care of, the computer scientist goes back to his cake, continuing at the point where he left off.

The key idea here is that a process is an activity of some kind. It has a program, input, output, and a state. A single processor may be shared among several processes, with some scheduling algorithm being used to determine when to stop work on one process and service a different one.

The Hierarchies of Processes

Operating systems that support the process concepts must provide some way to create all the processes needed. In very simple systems, or in systems designed for running only a single application (e.g., controlling a device in real time), it may be possible to have all the processes that will ever be needed be present when the system comes up. In most systems, however, some way is needed to create and destroy processes as needed during operation. In MINIX, processes are created by the FORK system call, which creates an identical copy of the calling process. The child process can also execute FORK, so it is possible to get a whole tree of processes. In other operating systems, system calls exist to create a process, load its memory, and start it running. Whatever the exact nature of the system call, processes need a way to create other processes. Note that each process has one parent but zero, one, two, or more children.

As a simple example of how process trees are used, let us look at how MINIX initializes itself when it is started. A special process, called *init*, is present in the boot image. When it starts running, it reads a file telling how many terminals there are. Then it forks off one new process per terminal. These processes wait for someone to log in. If a login is successful, the login process executes a shell to accept commands. These commands may start up more processes, and so forth. Thus, all the processes in the whole system belong to a single tree, with *init* at the root. (The code for *init* is not listed in the book; neither is the shell. The line had to be drawn somewhere.)

States of Processes

Although each process is an independent entity, with its own program counter and internal state, processes often need to interact with other processes. One process may generate some output that another process uses as input. In the shell command

cat chapter1 chapter2 chapter3 | grep tree

the first process, running *cat*, concatenates and outputs three files. The second process, running *grep*, selects all lines containing the word "tree." Depending on the relative speeds of the two processes (which depends on both the relative complexity of the programs and how much CPU time each one has had), it may happen that *grep* is ready to run, but there is no input waiting for it. It must then **block** until some input is available.

When a process blocks, it does so because logically it cannot continue, typically because it is waiting for input that is not yet available. It is also possible for a process that is conceptually ready and able to run to be stopped because the operating system has decided to allocate the CPU to another process for a while. These two conditions are completely different. In the first case, the suspension is inherent in the problem (you cannot process the user's command line until it has been typed). In the second case, it is technicality of the system (not enough CPUs to give each process its own private processor). In Fig. 4.2 we see a state diagram showing the three states a process may be in:

1. Running (actually using the CPU at that instant).
2. Ready (runnable; temporarily stopped to let another process run).
3. Blocked (unable to run until some external event happens).

Logically, the first two states are similar. In both cases the process is willing to run, only in the second one, there is temporarily no CPU available for it. The third state is different from the first two in that the process cannot run, even if the CPU has nothing else to do.

Four transitions are possible among these three states, as shown. Transition 1 occurs when a process discovers that it cannot continue. In some systems the process must execute a system call,

BLOCK, to get into blocked state. In other systems, including MINIX, when a process reads from a pipe or special file (e.g., a terminal) and there is no input available, the process is automatically blocked.

Transitions 2 and 3 are caused by the process scheduler, a part of the operating system, without the process even knowing about them. Transition 2 occurs when the scheduler decides that the running process has run long enough, and it is time to let another process have some CPU time. Transition 3 occurs when all the other processes have had their fair share and it is time for the first process to get the CPU to run again. The subject of scheduling, that is, deciding which process should run when and for how long, is an important one; we will look at it later in this chapter. Many algorithms have been devised to try to balance the competing demands of efficiency for the system as a whole and fairness to individual processes.

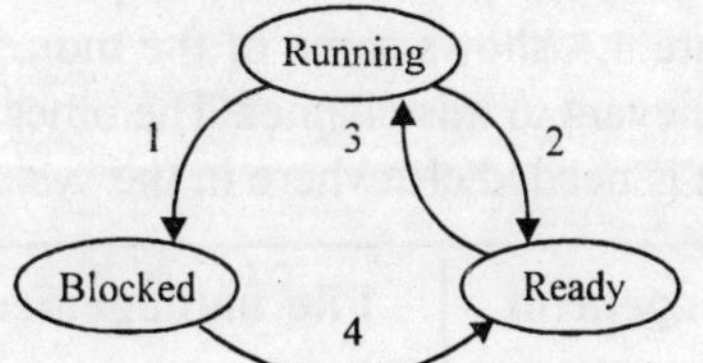

1. Process blocks for input
2. Scheduler picks another process
3. Scheduler picks this process
4. Input becomes available

Fig. 4.2. A process can be in running, blocked, or ready state. Transitions between these states are as shown.

Transition 4 occurs when the external event for which a process was waiting (such as the arrival of some input) happens. If no other process is running at that instant, transition 3 will be triggered immediately, and the process will start running. Otherwise it may have to wait in *ready* state for a little while until the CPU is available.

Using the process model, it becomes much easier to think about what is going on inside the system. Some of the processes run programs that carry out commands typed in by a user. Other processes are part of the system and handle tasks such as carrying out requests for file services or managing the details of running a disk or a tape drive. When a disk interrupt occurs, the system makes a decision to stop running the current process and run the disk process, which was blocked waiting for that interrupt. Thus, instead of thinking about interrupts, we can think about user processes, disk processes, terminal processes, and so on, which block they are waiting for something to happen. When the disk block has been read or the character typed, the process waiting for it is unblocked and is eligible to run again.

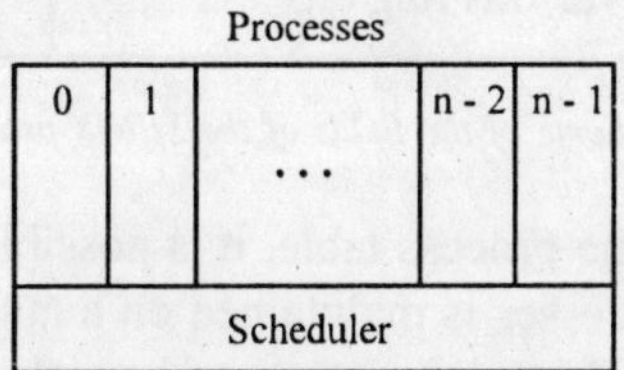

Fig. 4.3. The lowest layer of a process-structured operating system handles interrupts and scheduling. Above that layer are sequential processes.

Here the lowest level of the operating system is the scheduler, with a variety of processes on top of it. All the interrupt handling and details of actually starting and stopping processes are hidden away in the scheduler, which is actually quite small. The rest of the operating system is nicely structured in process form.

Implementation of Processes

To implement the process model, the operating system maintains a table (an array of structures), called the **process table**, with one entry per process. This entry contains information about the process state, its program counter, stack pointer, memory allocation, the status of its open files, its accounting and scheduling information, and everything else about the process that must be saved when the process is switched from *running* to *ready* state so that it can be restarted later as if it had never been stopped.

In MINIX the process management, memory management, and the file management are each handled by separate modules within the system, so the process table is partitioned, with each module maintaining the fields that it needs. Figure 4.4 shows some of the more important fields. The fields in the first column are the only ones relevant to this chapter. The other two columns are provided just to give an idea of what information is needed elsewhere in the system.

Process management	Memory management	File management
Registers	Pointer to text segment	UMASK mask
Program counter	Pointer to data segment	Root directory
Program status word	Pointer to bss segment	Working directory
Stack pointer	Exit status	File descriptors
Process state	Signal status	Effective uid
Time when process started	Process id	Effective gid
CPU time used	Parent process	System call parameters
Children's CPU time	Process group	Various flag bits
Time of next alarm	Real uid	
Message queue pointers	Effective	
Pending signal bits	Real gid	
Process id	Effective gid	
Various flag bits	Bit maps for signals	
	Various flag bits	

Fig. 4.4. Some of the fields of the MINIX process table.

Now that we have looked at the process table, it is possible to explain a little more about the illusion of multiple sequential processes is maintained on a machine with one CPU and many I/O devices. What follows is technically a description of how the "scheduler" of Fig. 4.3 works in MINIX but most modern operating systems works essentially the same way. Associated with each I/O device class (e.g., floppy disks, hard disks, timers, terminals) is a location near the bottom of memory called the **interrupt vector**. It contains the address of the interrupt service procedure. Suppose that user process 3 is running when a disk interrupt occurs. The program counter, program status word, and possibly one or more registers are pushed onto the (current) stack by the interrupt hardware. The computer then jumps to the address specified in the disk interrupt vector. That is all the hardware does. From here on, it is up to the software.

The interrupt service procedure starts out by saving all the registers in the process table entry for the current process. The current process number and a pointer to its entry are kept in global variables so they can be found quickly. Then the information deposited by the interrupt is removed from the stack, and the stack pointer is set to a temporary stack used by the process handler. Actions such as saving the registers and setting the stack pointer cannot even be expressed in C, so they are performed by a small assembly language routine. When this routine is finished, it calls a C procedure to do the rest of the work.

Interprocess communication in MINIX is via messages, so the next step is to build a message to be sent to the disk process, which will be blocked waiting for it. The message says that an interrupt occurred, to distinguish it from messages from user processes requesting disk blocks to be read and things like that. The state of the disk process is now changed from *blocked* to *ready* and the scheduler is called. In MINIX, different processes have different priorities, to give better service to I/O device handlers than to user processes. If the disk process is now the highest priority runnable process, it will be schedule to run. If the process that was interrupted is just as important or more so, then it will be scheduled to run again, and the disk process will have to wait a little while.

Either way, the C procedure called by the assembly language interrupt code now returns, and assembly language code loads up the registers and memory map for the now-current process and starts it running. Interrupt handling and scheduling are summarized in Fig. 4.5. It is worth noting that the details vary slightly from system to system.

1. Hardware stacks program counter, etc.
2. Hardware loads new program counter from interrupt vector.
3. Assembly language procedure saves registers.
4. Assembly language procedure sets up new stack.
5. C interrupt service runs (typically reads and buffers input).
6. Scheduler marks waiting task as ready.
7. Scheduler decides which process is to run next.
8. C procedure returns to the assembly code.
9. Assembly language procedure starts up new current process.

Fig. 4.5. *Skeleton of what the lowest level of the operating system does when an interrupt occurs.*

Threads

In a traditional process, of the type we have just studied, there is a single thread of control and a single program counter in each process. However, in some modern operating system support is provided for multiple threads of control within a process. These threads of control are usually just called **threads,** or occasionally **lightweight processes.**

In Fig 4.6 (a) we see three traditional processes. Each process has its own address space and a single thread of control. In contrasts in Fig. 4.6 (b) we see a single process with three threads of control. Although in both cases we have three threads, in Fig 4.6 (a) each of them operates in a different address space, whereas in Fig. 4.6 (b) all three of them share the same address space.

As an example of where multiple threads might be used, consider a file server process. It receives requests to read and write files and sends back the requested data or accepts updated data. To improve performance, the server maintains a cache of recently used files in memory, reading from the cache and writing to the cache when possible.

This situation lends itself well to the model of Fig. 4.6 (b). When a request comes in, it is handed to a thread for processing. If that thread blocks part way through waiting for a disk transfer, other threads are still able to run, so the server can keep processing new requests even while disk I/O is taking place. The model of Fig 4.6 (a) is not suitable, because it is essential that all file server threads access the same cache, and the three threads of Fig. 4.6(a) do not share the same address space and thus cannot share the same memory cache.

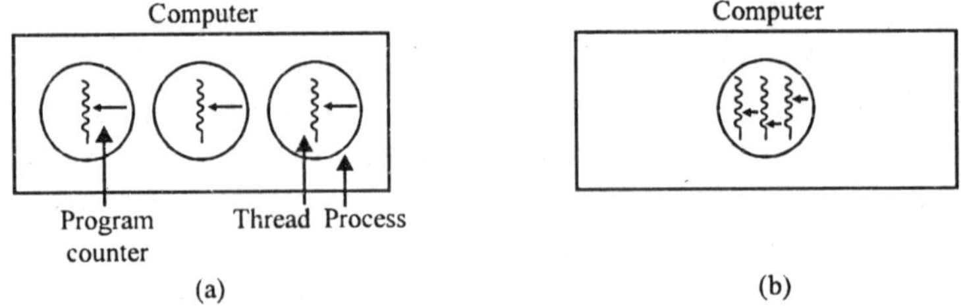

Fig. 4.6. (a) Three processes each with one threads. (b) One process with three threads.

Another example of where threads are useful is in browsers for the World Wide Web, such as Netscape and Mosaic. Many Web pages contain multiple small images. For each image on a Web page, the browser must set up a separate connection to the page's home site and request the image. A great deal of time is wasted establishing and releasing all these connections. By having multiple threads within the browser, many images can be requested at the same time, greatly speeding up performance in most cases, since with small images, the setup time is the limiting factor, not the speed of the transmission line.

When multiple threads are present in the same address space, a few of the fields of Fig. 4.4 are not per process, but per thread, so a separate thread table is needed, with one entry per thread. Among the per-thread items are the program counter, registers, and state. The program counter is needed because threads, like processes, can be suspended and resumed. The registers are needed because when threads are suspended, their registers must be saved. Finally, threads, like processes, can be in *running, ready,* or *blocked* state.

In some systems, the operating system is not aware of the threads. In other words, they are managed entirely in user space. When a thread is about to block, for example, it chooses and starts its successor before stopping. Several user-level thread packages are in common use, including the POSIX **P-threads** and Mach **C-thread** packages.

In some systems, the operating system is aware of the existence of multiple threads per process, so when a thread blocks, the operating system chooses the next one to run, either from the same process or a different one. To do scheduling, the kernel must have a thread table that lists all the threads in the system, analogous to the process table.

Although these two alternatives may seem equivalent, they differ considerably in performance. Switching threads is much faster when thread management is done in user space than when a kernel call is needed. This fact argues strongly for doing thread management in user space. On the other hand, when threads are managed entirely in user space and one thread blocks.

No matter whether threads are managed by the kernel or in user space, they introduce a raft of problems that must be solved and which change the programming model appreciably. To start with, consider the effects of the FORK system call. If the parent process has multiple threads, should the child also have them? If not, the process may not function properly, since all of them may be essential.

Another class of problems is related to the fact that threads share many data structures. What happens if one thread closes a file while another one is still reading from it? Suppose that one thread notices that there is too little memory and starts allocating more memory. Then, part way through, a thread switch occurs, and the new thread also notices that there is too little memory and also starts allocating more memory. Does the allocation happen once or twice? In nearly all systems that were not designed with thread in mind, the libraries (such as the memory allocation procedure) are not reentrant, and will crash if a second call is made while the first one is still active.

Another problem relates to error reporting. In UNIX, after a system call, the status of the call is put into a global variable, *errno*. What happens if a thread makes a system call, and before it is able to read *errno*, another thread makes a system call, wiping out the original value?

Next, consider signals. Some signals are logically thread specific, whereas others are not. For example, if a thread calls ALARMS, it makes sense for the resulting signal to go to the thread that made the call. When the kernel is aware of threads, it can usually make sure the right threads get the signal. When the kernel is not aware of threads, somehow the threads package must keep track of alarms. An additional complication for the user-level threads exists when (as in UNIX) a process may only have one alarm at a time pending and several threads call ALARM independently.

Other signals, such as keyboard interrupt, are not thread specific. Who should catch them? One designated thread? All the thread? A newly created thread? All these solutions have problems. Furthermore, what happens if one thread changes the signal handlers without telling other threads?

One last problem introduced by threads is stack management. In many systems, when stack overflow occurs, the kernel just provides more stack, automatically. When a process has multiple threads, it must also have multiple stacks. If the kernel is not aware of all these stacks, it cannot grow them automatically upon stack fault. In fact, it may not even realize that a memory fault is related to stack growth.

These problems are certainly not insurmountable, but they do show that just introducing threads into an existing system without a fairly substantial system redesign is not going to work at all. The semantics of system calls have to be redefined and libraries have to be rewritten, at the very least. And all of these things must be done in such a way as to remain backward compatible with existing programs for the limiting case of a process with only one thread.

Interprocess Communication Technique

Processes frequently need to communicate with other processes. For example, in a shell pipeline, the output of the first process must be passed to the second process, and so on down the line. Thus there is a need for communication between processes, preferably in a well-structured way not using interrupts. In the following sections we will look at some of the issues related to this **Interprocess Communication** or **IPC**.

Very briefly, there are three issues here. The first was alluded to above: how one process can pass information to another. The second has to do with making sure two or more processes do not get into each other's way when engaging in critical activities (suppose two processes each try to grab the last 100K of memory). The third concerns proper sequencing when dependencies are present: if process *A* produces data and process *B* prints it, *B* has to wait until *A* has produced some data before starting to print. We will examine all three of these issues starting in the next section.

Race Conditions

In some operating systems, processes that are working together may share some common storage that each one can read and write. The shared storage may be in main memory or it may be a shared file; the location of the shared memory does not change the nature of the communication or the problems that arise. To see how interprocess communication works in practice, let us consider a simple but common example, a print spooler. When a process wants to print a file, it enters the file name in a special **spooler directory**. Another process, the **printer daemon**, periodically checks to see if there are any files to be printed, and if there are it prints them and then removes their names from the directory.

Imagine that our spooler directory has a large (potentially infinite) number of slots, numbered 0, 1, 2, ..., each one capable of holding a file name. Also imagine that there are two shared variables, *out*, which points to the next file to be printed, and *in*, which points to the next free slot in the directory. These two variables might well be kept on a two-word file available to all processes. At a certain instant, slots 0 to 3 are empty (the files have already been printed) and slots 4 to 6 are full (with the names of files queued for printing). More or less simultaneously, processes *A* and *B* decide they want to queue a file for printing. This situation is shown in Fig 4.7.

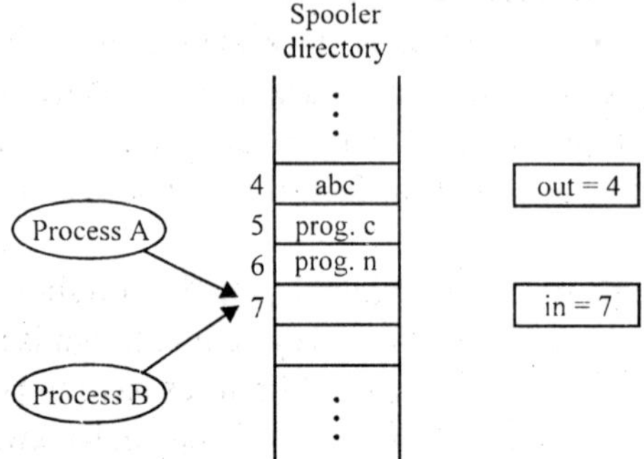

Fig. 4.7. Two processes want to access shared memory at the same time.

In jurisdictions where Murphy's law is applicable, the following might happen. Process *A* reads *in* and stores the value, 7, in a local variable called *next_free_slot*. Just then a clock interrupt occurs and the CPU decides that process *A* has run long enough, so it switches to process *B*. Process *B* also reads *in*, and also gets a 7, so it stores the name of its file in slot 7 and updates *in* to be an 8. Then it goes off and does other things.

Eventually, process *A* runs again, starting from the place it left off. It looks at *next_free_slot*, finds a 7 there, and writes its file name in slot 7, erasing the name that process *B* just put there. Then it computes *next_free_slot* + 1, which is 8, and sets *in* to 8. The spooler directory is now internally consistent, so the printer daemon will not notice anything wrong, but process *B* will never get any output. Situations like this, where two or more processes are reading or writing some shared data and the final result depends on who runs precisely when, are called **race conditions**. Debugging programs containing race conditions is no fun at all. The results of most test runs are fine, but once in a rare while something weird and unexplained happens.

Critical Sections

How do we avoid race conditions? The key to preventing trouble here and in many other situations involving shared memory, shared files, and shared everything else is to find some way to prohibit more than one process from reading and writing the shared data at the same time. Put in other words, what we need is **mutual exclusion**—some way making sure that if one process is using a shared variable or file, the other processes will be excluded from doing the same thing. The difficulty above occurred because process *B* started using one of the shared variables before process *A* was finished with it. The choice of appropriate primitive operations for achieving mutual exclusion is a major design issue in any operating system, and a subject that we will examine in great detail in the following sections.

The problem of avoiding race conditions can also be formulated in an abstract way. Part of the time, a process is busy doing internal computations and other things that do not lead to race conditions. However, sometimes a process may be accessing shared memory or files, or doing other critical things can lead to races. That part of the program where the shared memory is accessed is called the **critical region** or **critical section**. If we could arrange matters such that no two processes were ever in their critical regions at the same time, we could avoid race conditions.

Although this requirement avoids race conditions, this is not sufficient for having parallel processes cooperate correctly and efficiently using shared data. We need four conditions to hold to have a good solution:

1. No two processes may be simultaneously inside their critical regions.
2. No assumptions may be made about speeds or the number of CPUs.
3. No process running outside its critical region may block other processes.
4. No process should have to wait forever to enter its critical region.

Mutual Exclusion with Busy Waiting

In this section we will examine various proposals for achieving mutual exclusion, so that while one process is busy updating shared memory in its critical region, no other process will enter *its* critical region and cause trouble.

Disabling of Interrupts

The simplest solution is to have each process disable all interrupts just after entering its critical region and re-enable them just before leaving it. With interrupts disabled, no clock interrupts can occur. The CPU is only switched from process to process as a result of clock or other interrupts, after all, and with interrupts turned off the CPU will not be switched to another process. Thus, once a process has disabled interrupts, it can examine and update the shared memory without fear that any other process will intervene.

This approach is generally unattractive because it is unwise to give user processes the power to turn off interrupts. Suppose that one of them did it, and never turned them on again? That could be the end of the system. Furthermore, if the system is a multiprocessor, with two or more CPUs, disabling interrupts affects only the CPU that executed the disable instruction. The other ones will continue running and can access the shared memory.

On the other hand, it is frequently convenient for the kernel itself to disable interrupts for a few instructions while it is updating variables or lists. If an interrupt occurred while the list of ready processes, for example, was in an inconsistent state, race conditions could occur. The conclusion is: disabling interrupts is often a useful technique within the operating system itself but is not appropriate as a general mutual exclusion mechanism for user processes.

Lock Variables (Software Solution)

As a second attempt, let us look for a software solution. Consider having a single, shared, (lock) variable, initially 0. When a process wants to enter its critical region, it first tests the lock. If the lock is 0, the process sets it to 1 and enters the critical region. If the lock is already 1, the process just waits until it becomes 0. Thus, a 0 means that no process is in its critical region, and a 1 means that some process is in its critical region.

Unfortunately, this idea contains exactly the same fatal flaw that we saw in the spooler directory. Suppose that one process read the lock and sees that it is 0. Before it can set the lock to 1, another process is scheduled, runs, and sets the lock to 1. When the first process runs again, it will also set the lock to 1, and two processes will be in their critical regions at the same time.

Now you might think that we could get around this problem by first reading out the lock value, then checking it again just before storing into it, but that really does not help. The race now occurs if the second process modifies the lock just after first process has finished its second check.

Strict Alternation (Real Time Operating System)

A third approach to the mutual exclusion problem is shown in Fig. 4.8. This program fragment, like nearly all the others in this book, is written C. C was chosen here because real operating systems are commonly written in C (or occasionally C++), but hardly ever in languages like Modula 2 or Pascal.

In Fig 4.8, the integer variable *turn*, initially 0, keeps track of whose turn it is to enter the critical region and examine or update the shared memory. Initially, process 0 inspects *turn*, finds it to be 0, and enters its critical region. Process 1 also finds it to be 0 and therefore sits in a tight loop continually testing *turn* to see when it becomes 1. Continuously testing a variable until some value appears is called **busy waiting**. It should usually be avoided, since it wastes CPU time. Only when there is a reasonable expectation that the wait will be short is busy waiting used.

When process 0 leaves the critical region, it sets *turn* to 1, to allow process 1 to enter its critical region. Suppose that process 1 finishes its critical region quickly, so both processes are in their noncritical regions, with *turn* set to 0. Now process 0 executes its whole loop quickly, coming back to its noncritical region with *turn* set to 1. At this point, process 0 finishes its noncritical region and goes back to the top of its loop. Unfortunately, it is not permitted to enter its critical region now, because *turn* is 1 and process 1 is busy with its noncritical region. Put differently, taking turns is not a good idea when one of the processes is much slower than the other.

```
while (TRUE) {
  while (turn !=0) /* wait */ ;
  critical_region();
  turn = 1;
  noncritical_region();
}

        (a)
```

```
while (TRUE) {
  while (turn !=1) /* wait */ ;
  critical_region();
  turn = 0;
  noncritical_region();
}

        (b)
```

Fig. 4.8. *A proposed solution to the critical region problem.*

This situation violates condition 3 set out above: process 0 is being blocked by a process not in its critical region. Going back to the spooler directory discussed above, if we now associate the critical region with reading and writing the spooler directory, process 0 would not be allowed to print another file because process 1 was doing something else.

If fact, this solution requires that the two processes strictly alternate in entering their critical regions, for example, in spooling files. Neither one would be permitted to spool two in a row. While this algorithm does avoid all races, it is not really a serious candidate as a solution because it violates condition 3.

Peterson's Solution

By combining the idea of taking turns with the idea of lock variables and warning variables, a Dutch mathematician, T. Dekker, was the first one to devise a software solution to the mutual exclusion problem that does not require strict alteration.

In 1981, G.L. Peterson discovered a much simpler way to achieve mutual exclusion, thus rendering Dekker's solution obsolete. Peterson's algorithm is shown in Fig 4.9. This algorithm consists of two procedures written in ANSI C, which means that function prototypes should be supplied for all the functions defined and used. However, to save space, we will not show the prototypes in this or subsequent examples.

Before using the shared variables (i.e., before entering its critical region), each process calls *enter_region* with its own process number, 0 or 1, as parameter. This call will cause it to wait, if need be, until it is safe to enter. After it has finished with the shared variables, the process calls *leave_region* to indicate that it is done and to allow the other process to enter, if it so desires.

Let us see how this solution works. Initially neither process is in its critical region. Now process 0 calls *enter_region*. It indicates its interest by setting its array element and sets *turn* to 0. Since process 1 is not interested, *enter_region* returns immediately. If process 1 now calls *enter_region*, it will hang there until *interested*[0] goes to *FALSE*, an event that only happens when process 0 calls *leave_region* to exit the critical region.

```
#define FALSE   0
#define TRUE    1
```

```
#define N       2                     /* number of processes */
int turn;                             /* whose turn is it? */
int interested[N]                     /* all values initially 0 (FALSE) */

void enter_region(int process);       /* process is 0 or 1 */
{
 int other;                           /( number of the other process */

 other = 1 - process;                 /* the opposite of process */
 interested[process] = TRUE           /* show that you are insterested */
 turn = process;                      /* set flag */
 while (turn==process && intersted[other] == TRUE) /* null statement */
}
void leave_region(int process)        /* process: who is leaving */
{
 interested[process] = FALSE;         /indicate departure from critical region */
```

Fig. 4.9. Peterson's solution for achieving mutual exclusion.

Now consider the case that both processes call *enter_region* almost simultaneously. Both will srore their process number in *turn*. Whichever store is done last is the one that couns; the first one is lost. Suppose that process 1 stores last, so *turn* is 1. When both processes come to the while statement, process 0 executes it zero times and enters its critical region. Process 1 loops and does not enter its critical region.

The TSL Instruction

Now let us look at a proposal that requires a little help from the hardware. Many computers, especially those designed with multiple processors in mind, have an instruction TEST AND SET LOCK (TSL) that works as follows. It reads the contents of the memory word into a register and then stores a nonzero value at that memory address. The operations of reading the word and storing into it are guaranteed to be indivisible—no other processor can access the memory word until the instruction is finished. the CPU executing the TSL instruction locks the memory bust to prohibit other CPUs from accessing memory until it is done.

How can this instruction be used to prevent two processes from simultaneously entering their critical regions? The solution is given in Fig. 4.10. There a four-instruction subroutine in a fictitious (but typical) assembly language is shown. The first instruction copies the old value of *lock* to the register and then sets *lock* to 1. Then the old value is compared with 0. If it is nonzero, the lock was already set, so the program just goes back to the beginning and sets it again. Sooner or later it will become 0 (when the process currently in its critical region is done with its critical region), and the subroutine returns, with the lock set. Clearing the lock is simple. The program just stores a 0 in *lock*. No special instructions are needed.

```
enter_region:
        tsl register,lock       | copy lock to register and set lock to 1
        cmp register,#0         | was lock zero?
```

```
        jne enter_region     | if it was non zero, lock was set, so loop
        ret                  | return to caller; critical region entered

leave_region:
        move lock,#0         | store a 0 in lock
        ret                  | return to caller
```

Fig. 4.10. Setting and clearing locks using TSL.

One solution to the critical region problem is now straightforward. Before entering its critical region, a process calls *enter_region*, which does busy waiting until the lock is free; then it acquires the lock and returns. After the critical region the process calls *leave_region*, which stores a 0 in *lock*. As with all solutions based on critical regions, the processes must call *enter_region* and *leave_region* at the correct times for the method to work. If a process cheats, the mutual exclusion will fail.

Sleep and Wakeup

Both Peterson's solution and the solution using TSL are correct, but both have the defect of requiring busy waiting. In essence, what these solutions do is this: when a process wants to enter its critical region, it checks to see if the entry is allowed. If it is not, the process just sits in a tight loop waiting until it is.

Not only does this approach waste CPU time, but it can also have unexpected effects. Consider a computer with two processes, *H*, with high priority and *L*, with low priority. The scheduling rules are such that *H* is run whenever it is in ready state. At a certain moment, with *L* in its critical region, *H* becomes ready to run (e.g., an I/O operation completes). *H* now begins busy waiting, but since *L* is never scheduled while *H* is running, *L* never gets the chance to leave its critical region, so *H* loops forever. This situation is sometimes referred to as the **priority inversion problem**.

Now let us look at some interprocess communication primitives that block instead of wasting CPU time when they are not allowed to enter their critical regions. One of the simplest is the pair SLEEP and WAKEUP. SLEEP is a system call that causes the caller to block, that is, be suspended until another process wakes it up. The WAKEUP call has one parameter, the process to be awakened. Alternatively, both SLEEP and WAKEUP each have one parameter, a memory address used to match up SLEEP_s with WAKEUP_s.

The Procedure-Consumer Problem (Bounded Buffer Problem)

As an example of how these primitives can be used, let us consider the **producer-consumer** problem (also known as the **bounded buffer** problem). Two processes share a common, fixed-size buffer. One of them, the producer puts information into the buffer, and the other one, the consumer, takes it out. (It is also possible to generalize the problem to have *m* producers and *n* consumers, but we will only consider the case of one producer and one consumer because this assumption simplifies the solutions).

Trouble arises when the producer wants to put a new item in the buffer, but it is already full. The solution is for the producer to go to sleep, to be awakened when the consumer has removed one or more items. Similarly, if the consumer wants to remove an item from the buffer and sees that the buffer is empty, it goes to sleep until the producer puts something in the buffer and wakes it up.

This approach sounds simple enough, but it leads to the same kinds of race conditions we saw earlier with the spooler directory. To keep track of the number of items in the buffer, we will need a variable, *count*. If the maximum number of items the buffer can hold is *N*, the producer's code will first test to see if *count* is *N*. If it is, the producer will go to sleep; if it is not, the producer will add an item and increment *count*.

The consumer's code is similar: first test *count* to see if it is 0. If it is, go to sleep; if it is nonzero, remove an item and decrement the counter. Each of the processes also tests to see if the other should be sleeping, and if not, wakes it up. The code for both producer and consumer is shown in Fig. 4.11.

To express system calls such as SLEEP and WAKEUP in C, we will show them as calls to library routines. They are not part of the standard C library but presumable would be available on any system that actually has these system calls. The procedures *enter_item* and *remove_item*, which are not shown, handle the book-keeping of putting items into the buffer and taking items out of the buffer.

```
#define N 100                        /* number of slots in the buffer */
int count = 0;                       /* number of items in the buffer */

void producer(void)
{
  while (TRUE) {                     /* repeat forever */
        produce_item();              /* generate next item */
        if (count == N) sleep ();    /* if buffer is full, go to sleep */
        enter_item();                /* put item in buffer */
        count = count + 1;           /* increment count of items in buffer */
        if (count == 1)              /* was buffer empty? */
        wakeup(consumer)
   }
}

void consumer(void)
{
  while (TRUE) {                     /* repeat forever */
        if (count = = 0) sleep ();   /* if buffer is empty, got to sleep */
        remove_item();               /* take item out of buffer */
        count = count - 1;           /* decrement count of items in buffer */
        if (count = = N-1)           /* was buffer full? */
        wakeup(producer);
        consume_item();              /* print item */
   }
}
```

Fig. 4.11. The producer-consumer problem with a fatal race condition.

Now let us get back to the race condition. It can occur because access to *count* is unconstrained. The following situation could possibly occur. The buffer is empty and the consumer has just read *count* to see if it is 0. At that instant, the scheduler decides to stop running the consumer temporarily and start running the producer. The producer enters an item in the buffer, increments *count*, and notices that it is now 1. Reasoning that *count* was just 0, and thus the consumer must be sleeping, the producer calls *wakeup* to wake the consumer up.

The essence of the problem here is that a wakeup sent to a process that is not (yet) sleeping is lost. If it were not lost, everything would work. A quick fix is to modify the rules to add a **wakeup waiting bit** to the picture. When a wakeup is sent to process that is still awake, this bit is set. Later, when the process tries to go to sleep, if the wakeup waiting bit is on, it will be turned off, but the process will stay awake. The wakeup waiting bit is a piggy bank for wakeup signals.

While the wakeup waiting bit saves the day in this simple example, it is easy to construct examples with three or more processes in which one wakeup waiting bit is insufficient. We could make another patch, and add a second wakeup waiting bit, or may be 8 or 32 of them, but in principle the problem is still there.

Semaphores

This was the situation in 1965, when E. W. Dijkstra (1965) suggested using an integer variable to count the number of wakeups saved for future use. In his proposal, a new variable type, called a **semaphore**, was introduced. A semaphore could have the value 0, indicating that no wakeups were saved, or more positive value if one or more wakeups were pending.

Dijkstra proposed having two operations, DOWN and UP (generalizations of SLEEP and WAKEUP, respectively). The DOWN operation on a semaphore checks to see if the value is greater than 0. If so, it decrements the value (i.e., uses up one stored wakeup) and just continues. If the value is 0, the process is put to sleep without completing the DOWN for the moment. Checking the value, changing it, and possibly going to sleep is all done as a single, indivisible, **atomic action**. It is guaranteed that once a semaphore operation has started, no other process can access the semaphore until the operation has completed or blocked. This atomicity is absolutely essential to solving synchronization problems and avoiding race conditions.

The UP operation increments the value of the semaphore addressed. If one or more processes were sleeping on that semaphore, unable to complete an earlier DOWN operation, one of them is chosen by the system (e.g., at random) and is allowed to complete its DOWN. Thus, after an UP on a semaphore with processes sleeping on it, the semaphore will still be 0, but there will be one fewer process sleeping on it. The operation of incrementing the semaphore and waking up one process is also indivisible. No process ever blocks doing an UP, just as no process ever blocks doing a WAKEUP in the earlier model.

As an aside, in Dijkstra's original paper, he used the names P and V instead of DOWN and UP, respectively, but since these have no mnemonic significance to people who do not speak Dutch (and only marginal significance to those who do), we will use the terms DOWN and UP instead. These were first introduced in Algol 68.

Solving the Producer-Consumer Problem through Semaphores Techniques

Semaphores solve the lost-wakeup problem, as shown in Fig 4.12. It is essential that they be implemented in an indivisible way. The normal way is to implement UP and DOWN as system calls, with the operating system briefly disabling all interrupts while it is testing the semaphore, updating it, and putting the process to sleep, if necessary. As all these actions take only a few instructions, no harm is done in disabling interrupts. If multiple CPUs are being used, each semaphore should be protected by a lock variable, with the TSL instruction used to make sure that only one CPU at a time examines the semaphore. Be sure you understand that using TSL to prevent several CPUs from accessing the semaphore at the same time is quite different from busy waiting by the producer or consumer waiting for the other to empty or fill the buffer. The semaphore operation will only take a few microseconds, whereas the producer or consumer might take arbitrarily long.

```
#define N 100                         /* number of slots in the buffer */
typedef int semaphore;                /* semaphore are a special kind of int */
semaphore mutex = 1;                  /* controls assess to critical region */
semaphore empty = N;                  /* count empty buffer slots */
semaphore full = 0;                   /* counts full buffer slots */

void producer(void)
{
  int item;

  while (TRUE) {                      /* TRUE is the constant 1 */
    produce_item(&item);              /* generate something to put in buffer */
    down(&empty);                     /*decrement empty count */
    down(&mutex);                     /* enter critical region */
    enter_item(item);                 /* put new item in buffer */
    up(&mutex);                       /* leave critical region */
    up(&full);                        /* increment count of full slots */
  }
}

void consumer(void)
{
  int item;

  while (TRUE) {                      /* infinite loop */
    down(&full);                      /*decrement full count */
    down(&mutes);                     /* enter critical region */
    remove_item(&item);               /* take item from buffer */
    up(&mutex);                       /* leave critical region */
```

(Contd.)

```
    up(&empty);                  /* increment count of empty slots */
    consume_item(item);          /* do something with the item */
  }
}
```

Fig. 4.12. *The producer-consumer problem using semaphores.*

This solution uses three semaphores: one called *full* for counting the number of slots that are full, one called *empty* for counting the number of slots that are empty, and one called *mutex* to make sure the producer and consumer do not access the buffer at the same time. *Full* is initially 0, *empty* is initially equal to the number of slots in the buffer, and *mutex* is initially 1. Semaphores that are initialized to 1 and used by two or more processes to ensure that only one of them can enter its critical region at the same time are called **binary semaphores**. If each process does a DOWN just before entering its critical region and an UP just after leaving it, mutual exclusion is guaranteed.

Now that we have a good interprocess communication primitive at our disposal, let us go back and look at the interrupt sequence of Fig 4.5 again. In a system using semaphores, the natural way to hide interrupts is to have a semaphore, initially set to 0, associated with each I/O device. Just after starting an I/O device, the managing process does a DOWN on the associated semaphore, thus blocking immediately. When the interrupt comes in, the interrupt handler then does an UP on the associated semaphore, which makes the relevant process ready to run again. In this model, step 6 in Fig. 4.5 consists of doing an UP on the device's semaphore, so that in step 7 the scheduler will be able to run the device manager. Of course, if several processes are now ready, the scheduler may choose to run an even more important process next. We will look at how scheduling is done later in this chapter.

In the example of Fig 4.12, we have actually used semaphores in two different ways. This difference is important enough to make explicit. The *mutex* semaphore is used for mutual exclusion. It is designed to guarantee that only one process at a time will be reading or writing the buffer and the associated variables. This mutual exclusion is required to prevent chaos.

The other use of semaphores is for **synchronization**. The *full* and *empty* semaphores are needed to guarantee that certain event sequences do or do not occur. In this case, they ensure that the producer stops running when the buffer is full, and the consumer stops running when it is empty. This use is different from mutual exclusion.

Although semaphores have been around for more than a quarter of a century, people are still doing research about their use.

Monitors

With semaphores interprocess communication looks easy, right? Forget it. Look closely at the order of the DOWN_s before entering or removing items from the buffer in Fig. 4.12. Suppose that the two DOWN_s in the producer's code were reversed in order, so *mutex* was decremented before *empty* instead of after it. If the buffer were completely full, the producer would block, with *mutex* set to 0. Consequently, the next time the consumer tried to access the buffer, it would do a DOWN on *mutex*, now 0, and block too. Both processes would stay blocked forever and no more work would ever be done. This unfortunate situation is called a **deadlock.**

This problem is pointed out to show how careful you must be when using semaphores. One subtle error and everything comes to a grinding halt. It is like programming in assembly language, only worse, because the errors are race conditions, deadlocks, and other forms of unpredictable and irreproducible behavior.

To make it easier to write correct programs, Hoare (1974) and Brinch Hansen (1975) proposed a higher level synchronization primitive called a **monitor**. Their proposals differed slightly, as described below. A monitor is a collection of procedures, variables, and data structures that are all grouped together in a special kind of module or package. Processes may call the procedures in a monitor whenever they want to, but they cannot directly access the monitor's internal data structures from procedures declared outside the monitor. Figure 4.13 illustrates a monitor written in an imaginary language, pidgin Pascal.

```
monitor example
  integer i;
  condition c;

  procedure producer(x);
   .
   .
   .
  end;

  procedure consumer(x);
   .
   .
   .
  end;
end monitor;
```

Fig. 4.13. A monitor.

Monitors have an important property that makes them useful for achieving mutual exclusion: only one process can be active in a monitor at any instant. Monitors are a programming language construct, so the compiler knows they are special and can handle calls to monitor procedures differently from other procedure calls. Typically, when a process calls a monitor procedure, the first few instructions of the procedures will check to see if any other process is currently active within the monitor. If so, the calling process will be suspended until the other process has left the monitor. If no other process is using the monitor, the calling process may enter.

It is up to the compiler to implement the mutual exclusion on monitor entries but a common way is to use a binary semaphore. Because the compiler, not the programmer, is arranging for the mutual exclusion, it is much less likely that something will go wrong. In any event, the person writing the monitor does not have to be aware of how the compiler arranges for mutual exclusion. It is sufficient to know that by turning all the critical regions into monitor procedures, no two processes will ever execute their critical regions at the same time.

Although monitors provide an easy way to achieve mutual exclusion, as we have seen above, that is not enough. We also need a way for processes to block when they cannot proceed. In the producer-consumer problem, it is easy enough to put all the tests for buffer-full and buffer-empty in monitor procedures, but how should the producer block when it finds the buffer full?

The solution lies in the introduction of **condition variables**, along with two operations on them, WAIT and SIGNAL. When a monitor procedure discovers that it cannot continue (e.g., the producer finds the buffer full), it does a WAIT on some condition variable, say, *full*. This action causes the calling process to block. It also allows another process that had been previously prohibited from entering the monitor to enter now.

Condition variables are not counters. They do not accumulate signals for later use the way semaphores do. Thus if a condition variable is signaled with no one waiting on it, the signal is lost. The WAIT must come before the SIGNAL. This rule makes the implementation much simpler. In practice it is not a problem because it is easy to keep track of the state of each process with variables, if need be. A process that might otherwise do a SIGNAL can see that this operation is not necessary by looking at the variables.

A skeleton of the producer-consumer problem with monitors is given in Fig. 4.14 in pidgin Pascal.

You may be thinking that the operation WAIT and SIGNAL look similar to SLEEP and WAKEUP, which we saw earlier had fatal race conditions. They *are* very similar, but with one crucial difference: SLEEP and WAKEUP failed because while one process was trying to go to sleep, the other one was trying to wake it up. With monitors, that cannot happen. The automatic mutual exclusion on monitor procedures guarantees that if, say, the producer inside a monitor procedure discovers that the buffer is full, it will be able to complete the WAIT operation without having to worry about the possibility that the scheduler may switch to the consumer just before the WAIT completes. The consumer will not even be let into the monitor at all until the WAIT is finished and the producer has been marked as no longer runnable.

```
monitor ProducerConsumer
  condition full, empty;
  integer count;

  procedure enter;
  begin
    if count = N then wait (full);
    enter_item;
    count := count + 1;
    if count =1then signal (empty)
  end:

  procedure remove;
  begin
    if count = 0 then wait (empty)
```

(Contd.)

```
      remove_item;
      count := count - 1;
      if count = N -1 then signal (full)
    end;
    count := 0;
end monitor;

procedure producer;
begin
    while true do
    begin
      produce_item;
      ProducerConsumer.enter
    end
end;

procedure consumer;
begin
    while true do
    begin
      ProducerConsumer. remove;
      consume_item
    end
end;
```

Fig. 4.14. An outline of the producer-consumer problem with monitors. Only one monitor procedure at a time is active. The buffer has N slots.

By making the mutual exclusion of critical regions automatic, monitors make parallel programming much less error-prone than with semaphores. Still, they too have some drawbacks. It is not for nothing that Fig 4.14 is written in a strange kind of pidgin Pascal rather than in C, as are the other examples in this book. As we said earlier, monitors are a programming language concept. The compiler must recognize them and arrange for the mutual exclusion somehow. C, Pascal, and most other languages do not have monitors, so it is unreasonable to expect their compilers to enforce any mutual exclusion rules. In fact, how could the compiler even know which procedures were in monitors and which were not?

These same languages do not have semaphores either, but adding semaphores is easy: All you need to do is add two short assembly code routines to the library to issue the UP and DOWN system calls. The compilers do not even have to know that they exist. Of course, the operating systems have to know about the semaphores, but at least if you have a semaphore-based operating system, you can still write the user programs for it in C or C++ (or even BASIC if you are masochistic enough). With monitors, you need a language that has them built in. A few languages, such as Concurrent Euclid have them, but they are rare.

Another problem with monitors, and also with semaphores, is that they were designed for solving the mutual exclusion problem on one or more CPUs that all have access to a common memory. By putting the semaphores in the shared memory and protecting them with TSL instructions, we can avoid races. When we go to a distributed system consisting of multiple CPUs, each with its own private memory, connected by a local area network, these primitives become inapplicable. The conclusion is that semaphores are too low level and monitors are not usable except in a few programming languages. Also, none of the primitives provide for information exchange between machines. Something else is needed.

Message Passing

That something else is **message passing**. This method of interprocess communication uses two primitives SEND and RECEIVE, which, like semaphores and unlike monitors, are system calls rather than language constructs. As such, they can easily be put into library procedures such as

send(destination, &message);

and

receive(source, &message);

The former call sends a message to a given destination and the latter one receives a message from a given source (or from *ANY*, if the receiver does not care). If no message is available, the receiver could block until one arrives. Alternatively, it could return immediately with an error code.

Design Issues for Message Passing Systems

Message passing systems have many challenging problems and designs issues that do not arise with semaphore or monitors, especially if the communicating processes are on different machines connected by a network. For example, messages can be lost by the network. To guard against lost messages, the sender and receiver can agree that as soon as a message has been received, the receiver will send back a special **acknowledgement** message. If the sender has not received the acknowledgement within a certain time interval, it retransmits the message.

Now consider what happens if the message itself is received correctly, but the acknowledgement is lost. The sender will retransmit the message, so the receiver will get it twice. It is essential that the receiver can distinguish a new message from the retransmission of an old one. Usually, this problem is solved by putting consecutive sequence numbers in each original message. If the receiver gets a message bearing the same sequence number as the previous message, it knows that the message is a duplicate that can be ignored.

Message systems also have to deal with the question of how processes are named, so that the process specified in a SEND or RECEIVE call is unambiguous. **Authentication** is also an issue in message systems: how can the client tell that he is communicating with the real file server, and not with an imposter?

At the other end of the spectrum, there are also design issues that are important when the sender and receiver are on the same machine. One of these is performance. Copying messages from one process to another is always slower than doing a semaphore operation or entering a monitor. Much work has gone into making message passing efficient. Cheriton, for example, has suggested limiting message size to what will fit in the machine's registers, and then doing message passing using the registers.

The Producer-Consumer Problem with Message Passing

Now let us see how the producer consumer problem can be solved with message passing and no shared memory. A solution is given in Fig. 4.15. We assume that all messages are the same size and that messages sent but not yet received are buffered automatically by the operating system. In this solution, a total of *N* messages is used, analogous to the *N* slots in shared memory buffer. The consumer starts out by sending *N* empty messages to the producer. Whenever the producer has an item to give to the consumer, it takes an empty message and sends back a full one. In this way, the total number of messages in the system remains constant in time, so they can be stored in a given amount of memory known in advance.

If the producer works faster than the consumer, all the messages will end up full, waiting for the consumer; the producer will be blocked, waiting for an empty to come back. If the consumer works faster, then the reverse happens: all the messages will be empties waiting for the producer to fill them up; the consumer will be blocked, waiting for a full message.

```
#define N 100                           /* number of slots in the buffer */
void producer(void)
{
  int item;
  message m;                            /* message buffer */

  while (TRUE) {
    produce_item(&item);                /* generate something to put in buffer */
    receive(consumer, &m);              /* wait for an empty to arrive */
    build_message(&m, item);            /* construct a message to send */
    send(consumer, &m);                 /* send item the consumer */
  }
}

void consumer(void)
{
  int item, i;
  message m;
  for (i = 0; i < N; i++)               /* send N empties */
  send(producer, &m);

  while (TRUE) {
    receive(producer, &m);              /* get message containing item */
    extract_item(&m, &item);            /* extract item from message */
    send(producer, &m);                 /* send back empty reply */
```

(Contd.)

```
        consume_item(item);              /* do something with the item */.
    }
}
```

Fig. 4.15. The producer-consumer problem with N messages.

Many variants are possible with message passing. For starters, let us look at how messages are addressed. One way is to assign each process a unique address and have messages addressed to processes. A different way is to invent a new data structure, called a **mailbox**. A mailbox is a place to buffer a certain number of messages, typically specified when the mailbox is created. When mailboxes are used, the address parameters in the SEND and RECEIVE calls are mailboxes, not processes. When a process tries to send to a mailbox that is full, it is suspended until a message is removed from that mailbox, making room for a new one.

For the producer-consumer problem, both the producer and consumer would create mailboxes large enough to hold *N* messages. The producer would send messages containing data to the consumer's mailbox, and the consumer would send empty messages to the producer's mailbox. When mailboxes are used, the buffering mechanism is clear; the destination mailbox holds messages that have been sent to the destination process but have not yet been accepted.

The other extreme from having mailboxes is to eliminate all buffering. When this approach is followed, if the SEND is done before the RECEIVE, the sending process is blocked until the RECEIVE happens, at which time the message can be copied directly from the sender to the receiver, with no intermediate buffering. Similarly, if the RECEIVE is done first, the receiver is blocked until a SEND happens. This strategy is often known as a rendezvous. It is easier to implement than a buffered message scheme but is less flexible since the sender and receiver are forced to run in lockstep.

Classical IPC Problems

The operating systems literature is full of interesting problems that have been widely discussed and analyzed. In the following sections we will examine three of the better-known problems.

The Dining Philosophers Problem

In 1965, Dijkstra posed and solved a synchronization problem he called the **dining philosophers problem**. Since that time, everyone inventing yet another synchronization primitive has felt obligated to demonstrate how wonderful the new primitive is by showing how elegantly it solves the dining philosophers problem. The problem can be stated quite simply as follows. Five philosophers are seated around a circular table. Each philosopher has a plate of spaghetti. The spaghetti is so slippery that a philosopher needs two forks to eat it. Between each pair of plates is one fork. The layout of the table is illustrated in Fig. 4.16.

The life of philosopher consists of alternate periods of eating and thinking. (This is something of an abstraction, even for philosophers, but the other activities are irrelevant here.) When a philosopher gets hungry, she tries to acquire her left and right fork, one at a time, in either order. If successful in acquiring two forks, she eats for a while, then puts down the forks and continues to think. The key question is: Can you write a program for each philosopher that does what it is supposed to do and never gets stuck? (it has been pointed out that the two-fork requirement is somewhat artificial;

perhaps we should switch from Italian to Chinese food, substituting rice for spaghetti and chopsticks for forks.)

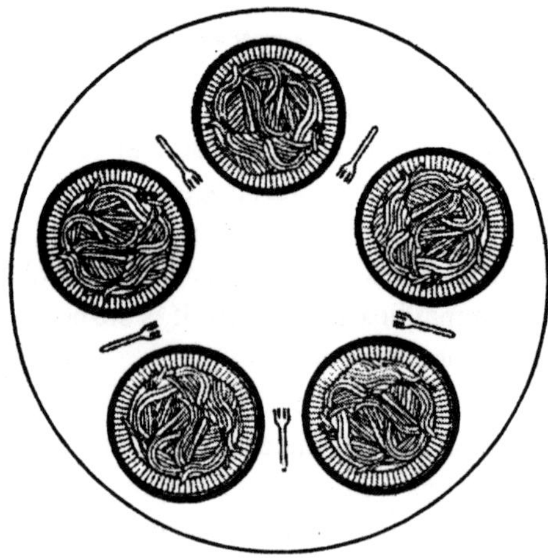

Fig. 4.16. Lunch time in the Philosophy Department.

Figure 4.17 shows the obvious solution. The producer *take_fork* waits until the specified fork is available and then seizes it. Unfortunately, the obvious solution is wrong. Suppose that all five philosophers take their left forks simultaneously. None will be able to take their right forks, and there will be a deadlock.

We could modify the program so that after taking the left fork, the program checks to see if the right fork is available. If it is not, the philosopher puts down the left one, waits for some time, and then repeats the whole process. This proposal too, fails, although for a different reason. With a little bit of bad luck, all the philosophers could start the algorithm simultaneously, picking up their left forks, seeing that their right forks were not available, putting down their left forks, waiting, picking up their left forks again simultaneously, and so on, forever. A situation like this, in which all the programs continue to run indefinitely but fail to make any progress is called **starvation.** (It is called starvation even when the problem does not occur in an Italian or a Chinese restaurant.)

Now you might think, "If the philosophers would just wait a random time instead of the same time after failing to acquire the right-hand fork, the chance that everything would continue in lockstep for even an hour is very small." This observation is true, but in some applications one would prefer a solution that always works and cannot fail due to an unlikely series of random numbers. (Think about safety control in a nuclear power plant.)

```
#define N 5                    /* number of philosophers */

void philosopher(int i)        /* i: philosopher number, from 0 to 4 */
{
  while (TRUE) {
```

(Contd.)

```
    think();                   /* philosopher is thinking */
    take_fork(i);              /* take left fork */
    take_fork((i +1) % N);     /* take right fork; % is modulo operator */
    eat();                     /* yum-yum, spaghetti */
    put_fork(i);               /* put left fork back on the table */
    put_fork((i+1) %N);        /* put right fork back on the table */
  }
}
```

Fig. 4.17. A nonsolution to the dining philosophers problem.

One improvement to Fig. 4.17 that has no deadlock and no starvation is to protect the five statements following the call to *think* by a binary semaphore. Before starting to acquire forks, a philosopher would do a DOWN on *mutex*. After replacing the forks, she would do an UP on *mutex*. From a theoretical viewpoint, this solution is adequate. From a practical one, it has a performance bug; only one philosopher can be eating at any instant. With five forks available, we should be able to allow two philosophers to eat at the same time.

The solution presented in Fig. 4.18, is correct and also allows the maximum parallelism for an arbitrary number of philosophers. It uses an array, *state*, to keep track of whether a philosopher is eating, thinking, or hungry (trying to acquire forks). A philosopher may move only into eating state if neither neighbour is eating. Philosopher *i*'s neighbours are defined by the macros *LEFT* and *RIGHT*. In other words, if *i* is 2, *LEFT* is 1 and *RIGHT* is 3.

```
#define N 5                    /* number of philosphers */
#define LEFT (i-1)% N          /* number of i's left neighbour */
#define RIGHT (i+1)% N         /* number of i's right neighbour */
#define THINKING 0             /* philospher is thinking */
#define HUNGRY 1               /* philospher is flying to get forks */
#define EATING 2               /* philospher is eating */

typedef int semaphore;         /* semaphores are a special kind of int */
int state[N];                  /* array to keep track of everyone's state
*/
semaphore mutex = 1;           /* mutual exclusion for critical regions */
semaphore s[N];                /* one semaphore per philospher */

void philospher(int i)         /* i: philospher number, from 0 to N-1 */
{
  while (TRUE) {               /* repeat forever */
    think();                   /* philospher is thinking */
    take_forks(i);             /* acquire two forks or block */
    eat();                     /* yum-yum, spaghetti */
    put_forks(i);              /* put both forks back on table */
  }
}
```

(Contd.)

```
void take_forks(int i)          /* i: philospher number, from 0 to N-1 */
{
    down(&mutex);               /* enter critical region */
    state[i] = HUNGRY;          /* record fact that philospher i is hungry */
    test(i);                    /* try to acquire 2 forks */
    up(&mutex);                 /* exit critical region */
    down(&s[i]);                /* block if forks were not acquired */
}

void put_forks(i)               /* i: philospher number, from 0 to N-1 */
{   down(&mutex);               /* enter critical region */
    state[i] = THINKING;        /* philospher has finished eating */
    test(LEFT);                 /* see if left neighbour can now eat */
    test(Right);                /* see if right neighbour can now eat */
    up(&mutex);                 /* exit critical region */
}

void test(i)                    /* i: philospher number, from  0 to N-1 */
{
    if (state[i] = = HUNGRY && state [LEFT] != EATING && state [RIGHT] !=
        EATING) {
        state[i] = EATING;
        up(&s[i]);
    }
}
```

Fig. 4.18. *A Solution to the dining philospher's problem.*

The Readers and Writers Problem

The dining philosophers problem is useful for modeling processes that are competing for exclusive access to a limited number of resources, such as I/O devices. Another famous problem is the readers and writers problem which models access to a database. Imagine, for example, an airline reservation system, with many competing processes wishing to read and write it. It is acceptable to have multiple processes reading the database at the same time, but if one process is updating (writing) the database, no other processes may have access to the database, not even readers. The question is how do you program the readers and writers? One solution is shown in Fig. 4.19.

In this solution, the first reader to get access to the database does a DOWN on the semaphore *db*. Subsequent readers merely increment a counter, *rc*. As readers leave, they decrement the counter and the last one out does an UP on the semaphore, allowing a blocked writer, if there is one, to get in.

The solution presented here implicitly contains a subtle decision that is worth commenting on. Suppose that while a reader is using the database, another reader comes along. Since having two readers at the same time is not a problem the second reader is admitted. A third and subsequent reader can also be admitted if they come along.

```
typedef int semaphore;               /* use your imagination */
semaphore mutex = 1;                 /* controls access to 'rc' */
semaphore db = 1;                    /* controls access to the data base */
int rc = 0;                          /* # of processes reading or wanting tp */
void reader(void)
{
    while (TRUE) {                   /* repeat forever */
        down(&mutex);                /* get exclusive access to 'rc' */
        rc = rc + 1;                 /* one reader more now */
        if (rc == 1) down(&db);      /* if this is the first reader ... */
        up(&mutex);                  /* release exclusive access to 'rc' */
        read_data_base();            /* access the data */
        down(&mutex);                /* get exclusive access to 'rc' */
        rc = rc - 1;                 /* one reader fewer now */
        if (rc = = 0) up(&db);       /* if this is the last reader ... */
        up(&mutex);                  /* release exclusive access to 'rc' */
        use_data_read();             /* noncritical rgion */
    }
}

void writer(void)
{
    while (TRUE) {                   /* repeat forever */
        think_up_data();             /* noncritical region */
        down(&db);                   /* get exclusive access */
        write_data_base();           /* update the data */
        up(&db);                     /* release exclusive access */
    }
}
```

Fig. 4.19. A solution to the readers and writers problem.

To prevent this situation, the program could be written slightly differently: when a reader arrives and a writer is waiting, the reader is suspended behind the writer instead of being admitted immediately. In this way, a writer has to wait for readers that were active when it arrived to finish but does not have to wait for readers that came along after it. The disadvantage of this solution is that it achieves less concurrency and thus lower performance. Courtois et al. present a solution that gives priority to writers. For details, we prefer you to the paper.

The Sleeping Barber Problem

Another classical IPC problem takes place in a barber shop. The barber shop has one barber, one barber chair, and n chairs for waiting customers, if any, to sit on. If there are no customers present, the barber sits down in the barber chair and falls asleep, as illustrated in Fig. 4.20. When a customer arrives, he has to wake up the sleeping barber. If additional customers arrive while the barber is cutting a customer's hair, they either sit down (if there are empty chairs) or leave the shop (if all chairs are full). The problem is to program the barber and the customers without getting into race consitions.

Our solution uses three semaphores: *customers*, which counts waiting customers (excluding the customer in the barber chair, who is not waiting), *barbers*, the number of barbers who are idle, waiting for customers (0 or 1), and *mutex*, which is used for mutual exclusion. We also need a variable, *waiting*, which also counts the waiting customers. It is essentially a copy of *customers*. The reason for having *waiting* is that there is no way to read the current value of a semaphore. In this solution, a customer entering the shop has to count the number of waiting customers. If it is less than the number of chairs, he stay; otherwise, he leaves.

Our solution is shown in Fig. 4.21. When the barber shows up for work in the morning, he executes the procedure *barber*, causing him to block on the semaphore *customers* until somebody arrives. He then goes to sleep as shown in Fig. 4.20.

Fig. 4.20. The sleeping barber.

When a customer arrives, he executes *customer*, starting by acquiring *mutex* to enter a critical region. If another customer enters shortly thereafter, the second one will not be able to do anything until the first one has released *mutex*. The customer then checks to see if the number of waiting customer is less than the number of chairs. If not, he releases *mutex* and leaves without a haircut.

If there is an available chair, the customer increments the integer variable, *waiting*. Then he does an UP on the semaphore *customer*, thus waking up the barber. At this point, the customer and barbers are both awake. When the customer releases *mutex*, the barber grabs it, does some housekeeping, and begins the haircut.

```
#define CHAIRS 5                      /* # chairs for waiting customers */
typedef int semaphore;                /* use your imagination */
semaphore customers = 0;              /* # of customers waiting for service */
semaphore barbers = 0;                /* # of barbers waiting for customers */
semaphores mutex = 1;                 /* for mutual exclusion */
int waiting = 0;                      /* customers are waiting (not being cut) */

void barber(void)
{
   while (TRUE) {
      down(customers);                /* go to sleep if # of customer is 0 */
      down(mutex);                    /* acquire access to 'waiting' */
      waiting = waiting - 1;          /* decrement count of waiting customers */
      up(barbers);                    /* one barber is now ready to cut hair    */
      up(mutex);                      /* release 'waiting' */
      cut_hair();                     /* cut hair (outside critical region) */
   }
}

void customer(void)
{
   down(mutex);                       /* enter critical region */
   if (waiting < CHAIRS) {            /* if there are no free chairs, leave */
      waiting = waiting + 1;          /* increment count of waiting customers */
      up(customers);                  /* wake up barber if necessary */
      up(mutex);                      /* release access to 'waiting' */
      down(barbers);                  /* go to sleep if # of free barbers is 0 */
      get_haircut();                  /* be seated and be serviced */
   } else {
      up(mutex);                      /* shop is full; do not wait */
   }
}
```

Fig. 4.21. A solution to the sleeping barber problem.

When the haircut is over, the customer exits the procedure and leaves the shop. Unlike our earlier examples, there is no loop for the customer because each one gets only one haircut. The barber loops, however, to try to get the next customer. If one is present, another haircut is given. If not, the barber goes to sleep.

As an aside, it is worth pointing out that although the readers and writers and sleeping barber problems do not involve data transfer, they still belong to the area of IPC because they involve synchronization between multiple processes.

Process Scheduling

In the examples of the previous sections, we have often had situations in which two or more processes (e.g., producer and consumer) were logically runnable. When more than one process is runnable, the operating system must decide which one to run first. The part of the operating system that makes this decision is called the **scheduler**; the algorithm it uses is called the **scheduling algorithm**.

Back in the old days of batch systems with input in the form of card images on a magnetic tape, the scheduling algorithm was simple; just run the next job on the tape. With timesharing systems, the scheduling algorithm is more complex, as there are often multiple users waiting for service, and there may be one or more batch streams as well (e.g., at an insurance company, for processing claims). Even on personal computers, there may be several user-initiated processes competing for the CPU, not to mention background jobs, such as network or electronic mail daemons sending or receiving e-mail.

Before looking at specific algorithms, we should think about what the scheduler is trying to achieve. After all, the scheduler is concerned with deciding on policy, not providing a mechanism. Various criteria come to mind as to what constitutes a good scheduling algorithm. Some of the possibilities include:

1. Fairness—make sure each process gets its fair share of the CPU.
2. Efficiency—keep the CPU busy 100 percent of the time.
3. Response time—minimize response time for interactive users.
4. Turnaround—minimize the time batch users must wait for output.
5. Throughput—maximize the number of jobs processed per hour.

A little thought will show that some of these goals are contradictory. To minimize response time for interactive users, the scheduler should not run any batch jobs at all (except may be between 3 A.M. and 6 A.M., when all the interactive users are snug in their beds). The batch users probably will not like this algorithm, however; it violates criterion 4. It can be shown (Kleinrock, 1975) that any scheduling algorithm that favors some class of jobs hurts another class of jobs. The amount of CPU time available is finite, after all. To give one user more you have to give another user less. Such is life.

A complication that schedulers have to deal with is that every process is unique and unpredictable. Some spend a lot of time waiting for file I/O, while others would use the CPU for hours at a time if given the chance. When the scheduler starts running some process, it never knows for sure how long it will be until that process blocks, either for I/O, or on a semaphore, or for some other reason. To make sure that no process runs too long, nearly all computers have an electronic timer or clock built in, which causes an interrupt periodically. A frequency of 50 or 60 times a second (called 50 or 60 **Hertz** and abbreviated **Hz**) is common, but on many computers the operating system can set the timer frequency to anything it wants. At each clock interrupt, the operating system gets to run and decide whether the currently running process should be allowed to be continue, or whether it has had enough CPU time for the moment and should be suspended to give another process the CPU.

The strategy of following processes that are logically runnable to be temporarily suspended is called **preemptive scheduling**, and is in contrast to the **run to completion** method of the early batch systems. Run to completion is also called **nonpreemptive scheduling**. As we have seen throughout this chapter, a process can be suspended at an arbitrary instant, without warning, so another process can be run. This leads to race conditions and necessitates semaphores, monitors, messages, or some other sophisticated method for preventing them. On the other hand, a policy of letting a process run as long as it wanted to would mean that some process computing π to a billion places could deny service to all other processes indefinitely.

Thus although nonpreemptive scheduling algorithms are simple and easy to implement, they are usually not suitable for general-purpose systems with multiple competing users. On the other hand, for a dedicated system, such as a database server, it may well be reasonable for the master process to start a child process working on a request and let it run until it completes or blocks. The difference from the general-purpose system is that all processes in the database system are under the control of a single master, which knows what each child is going to do and about how long it will take.

Round Robin Scheduling

Now let us look at some specific scheduling algorithms. One of the oldest simplest, fairest, and most widely used algorithms is **round robin**. Each process is assigned a time interval, called its **quantum**, which it is allowed to run. If the process is still running at the end of the quantum, the CPU is preempted and given to another process. If the process has blocked or finished before the quantum has elapsed, the CPU switching is done when the process blocks, of course and robin is easy to implement. All the scheduler needs to do is maintain a list of runnable processes, as shown in Fig 4.22(a). When the process uses up its quantum, it is put on the end of the list, as shown in Fig. 2.22(b).

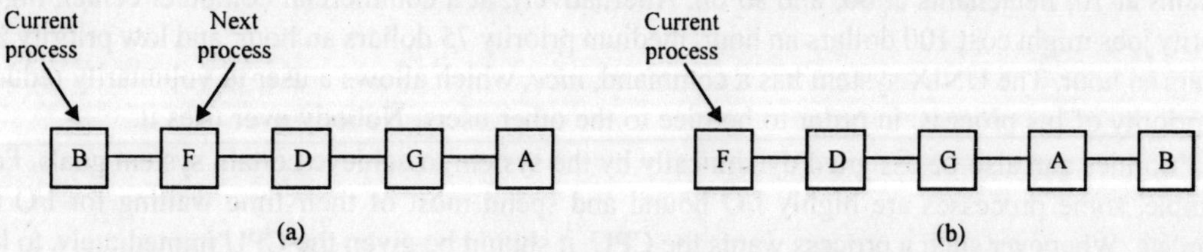

Fig. 4.22. Round robin scheduling. (a) The list of runnable processes. (b) The list of runnable processes after B *uses up its quantum.*

The only interesting issue with round robin is the length of the quantum. Switching from one process to another requires a certain amount of time for doing the administration—saving and loading registers and memory maps, updating various tables and lists, etc. Suppose that this **process switch** or **context switch**, as it is sometimes called, takes 5 msec. Also suppose that the quantum is set at 20 msec. With these parameters, after doing 20 msec of useful work, the CPU will have to spend 5 msec on process switching. Twenty percent of the CPU time will be wasted on administrative overhead.

To improve the CPU efficiency, we could set the quantum to, say, 500 msec. Now the wasted time is less than 1 percent. But consider what happens on a timesharing system if ten interactive users hit the carriage return key at roughly the same time. Ten processes will be put on the list of runnable processes. If the CPU is idle, the first one will start immediately, the second one may not start until about ½ sec later, and so on. The unlucky last one may have to wait 5 sec before getting a chance, assuming all the others use their full quanta. Most users will perceive a 5-sec response to a short command as terrible. The same problem can occur on a personal computer that supports multiprogramming.

The conclusion can be formulated as follows: setting the quantum too short causes too many process switches and lowers the CPU efficiency, but setting it too long may cause poor response to short interactive requests. A quantum around 100 msec is often a reasonable compromise.

Priority Scheduling

Round robin scheduling makes the implicit assumption that all processes are equally important. Frequently, the people who own and operate multiuser computers have different ideas on that subject. At a university, the pecking order may be deans first, then professors, secretaries, janitors, and finally students. The need to take external factors into account leads to **priority scheduling**. The basic idea is straightforward: each process is assigned a priority, and the runnable process with the highest priority is allowed to run.

To prevent high-priority processes from running indefinitely, the scheduler may decrease the priority of the currently running process at each clock tick (i.e., at each clock interrupt). If this action causes its priority to drop below that of the next highest process, a process switch occurs. Alternatively, each process may be assigned a maximum quantum that it is allowed to hold the CPU continuously. When this quantum is used up, the next highest priority process is given a chance to run.

Priorities can be assigned to processes statically or dynamically. On a military computer, processes started by generals might begin at priority 100, processes started by colonels at 90, majors at 80, captains at 70, lieutenants at 60, and so on. Alternatively, at a commercial computer center, high-priority jobs might cost 100 dollars an hour, medium priority 75 dollars an hour, and low priority 50 dollars an hour. The UNIX system has a command, *nice*, which allows a user to voluntarily reduce the priority of his process, in order to be nice to the other users. Nobody ever uses it.

Priorities can also be assigned dynamically by the system to achieve certain system goals. For example, some processes are highly I/O bound and spend most of their time waiting for I/O to complete. Whenever such a process wants the CPU, it should be given the CPU immediately, to let it start its next I/O request, which can then proceed in parallel with another process actually computing. Making the I/O bound process wait a long time for the CPU will just mean having it around occupying memory for an unnecessarily long time. A simple algorithm for giving good service to I/O bound processes is to set the priority to $1/f$, where f is the fraction of the last quantum that a process used. A process that used only 2 msec of its 100 msec quantum would get priority 50, while a process that ran 50 msec before blocking would get priority 2, and a process that used the whole quantum would get priority 1.

It is often convenient to group processes into priority classes and use priority scheduling among the classes but round-robin scheduling within each class. Fig. 4.23 shows a system with four priority classes. The scheduling algorithm is as follows: as long as there are runnable processes in priority class 4, just run each one for one quantum, round-robin fashion, and never bother with lower priority classes. If priority class 4 is empty, then run the class 3 processes round robin. If classes 4 and 3 are both empty, then run class 2 round, robin and so on. If priorities are not adjusted occasionally, lower priority classes may all starve to death.

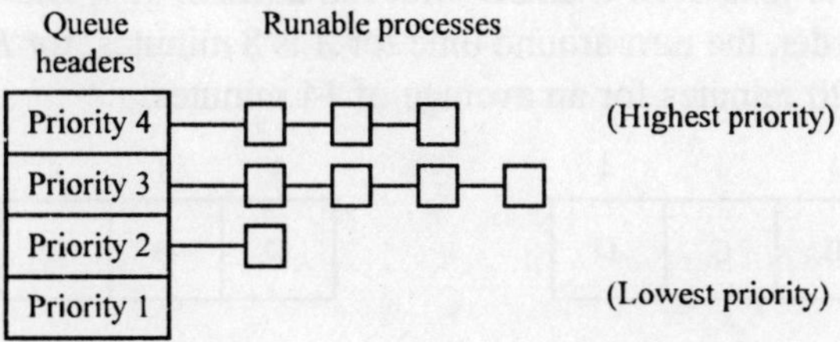

Fig. 4.23. A scheduling algorithm with four priority classes.

Multiple Queues

One of the earliest priority schedulers was in CTSS. CTSS had the problem that process switching was very slow because the 7094 could hold only one process in memory. Each switch meant swapping the current process to disk and reading in a new one from disk. The CTSS designers quickly realized that it was more efficient to give CPU-bound processes a large quantum once in a while, rather than giving them small quanta frequently (to reduce swapping). On the other hand, giving all processes a large quantum would mean poor response time, as we have already seen. Their solution was to set up priority classes. Processes in the highest class were run for one quantum. Processes in the next highest class were run for two quanta. Processes in the next class were run for four quanta, and so on. Whenever a process used up all the quanta allocated to it, it was moved down one class.

The following policy was adopted to prevent a process that needed to run for a long time when it first started but became interactive later, from being punished forever. Whenever a carriage return was typed at a terminal, the process belonging to that terminal was moved to the highest priority class, on the assumption that it was about to become interactive. One fine day some user with a heavily CPU-bound process discovered that just sitting at the terminal and typing carriage returns at random every few seconds did wonders for his response time. He told all his friends. Moral of the story: getting it right in practice is much harder than getting it right in principle.

Many other algorithms have been used for assigning processes to priority classes. For example, the influential XDS 940 system, built at Berkeley, had four priority classes, called terminal, I/O, short quantum, and long quantum. When a process that was waiting for terminal input was finally awakened, it went into the highest priority class (terminal). When a process waiting for a disk block became ready, it went into the second class. When a process was still running when its quantum ran out, it was initially placed in the third class. However, if a process used up its quantum too many times in a row without blocking for terminal or other I/O, it was moved down to the bottom queue. Many other systems use something to favor interactive users and processes over background ones.

Shortest Job First (SJF)

Most of the above algorithms were designed for interactive systems. Now let us look at one that is especially appropriate for batch jobs for which the run times are known in advance. In an insurance company, for example, people can predict quite accurately how long it will take to run a batch of 1000 claims, since similar work is done every day. When several equally important jobs are sitting in the input queue waiting to be started, the scheduler should use **shortest job first**. Look at Fig. 4.24. Here we find four jobs *A*, *B*, *C* and *D* with run times 8, 4, 4, and 4 minutes, respectively. By running them in that order, the turn-around time for *A* is 8 minutes, for *B* is 12 minutes, for *C* is 16 minutes, and for *D* is 20 minutes for an average of 14 minutes.

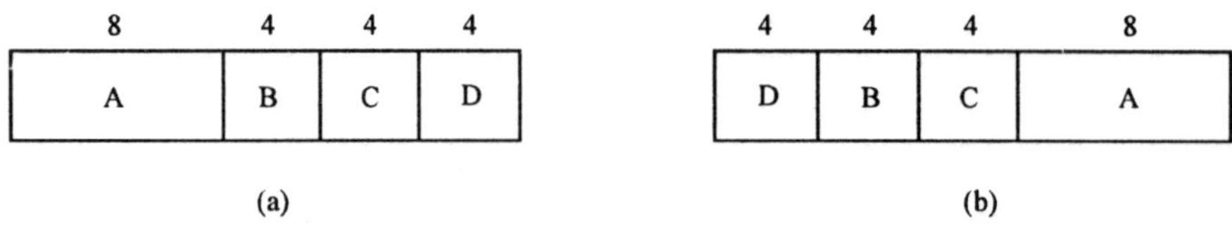

Fig. 4.24. An example of shortest job first scheduling.

Now let us consider running these four jobs using shortest job first, as shown in Fig 4.24(b). The turn-around times are now 4, 8, 12, and 20 minutes for an average of 11 minutes. Shortest job first is probably optimal. Consider the case of four jobs, with run times of *a*, *b*, *c*, and *d*, respectively. The first job finishes at time *a*, the second finishes at time $a + b$, and so on. The mean turn-around times is $(4a + 3b + 2c + d)/4$. It is clear that *a* contributes more to the average than the other times, so it should be the shortest job, with *b* next, then *c* and finally *d* as the longest as it effects only its own turn-around time. The same argument applies equally well to any number of jobs.

Because shortest job first always produces the minimum average response time, it would be nice if it could be used for interactive processes as well. To a certain extent, it can be. Interactive processes generally follow the pattern of wait for command, execute command, wait for command, and so on. If we regard the execution of each command as a separate "job," then we could minimize overall response time by running the shortest one first. The only problem is figuring out which of the currently runnable processes is the shortest one.

One approach is to make estimates based on past behavior and run the process with the shortest estimated running time. Suppose that the estimated time per command for some terminal is T_0. Now suppose its next run is measured to be T_1. We could update our estimate by taking a weighted sum of these two numbers, that is $aT_0 + (1 - a)T_1$. Through the choice of *a* we can decide to have the estimation process forget old runs quickly, or remember them for a long time. With $a = 1/2$, we get successive estimates of

$$T_0,\ T_0/2 + T_1/3,\ T_0/4 + T_1/4 + T_2/2,\ T_0/8 + T_1/8 + T_2/4 + T_3/2$$

After three new runs, the weight of T_0 in the new estimates has dropped to 1/8.
The technique of estimating the next value in a series by taking the weighted average of the current measured value and the previous estimate is sometimes called **ageing**. It is applicable to many situations where a prediction must be made based on previous values. Ageing is especially easy to implement when $a = 1/2$. All that is needed is to add the new value to the current estimate and divide the sum by 2 (by shifting it right 1 bit).

It is worth pointing out that the shortest job first algorithm is only optimal when all the jobs are available simultaneously. As a counter-example, consider five jobs, *A* through *E*, with run times of 2, 4, 1, 1, and 1, respectively. Their arrival times are 0, 0, 3, 3, and 3.

Guaranteed Scheduling

A completely different approach to scheduling is to make real promises to the user about performance and then live up to them. One promise that is realistic to make and easy to live up to is this: If there are *n* users logged in while you are working, you will receive about 1/*n* of the CPU power. Similarly, on a single-user system with *n* processes running, all things being equal, each one should get 1/*n* of the CPU cycles.

To make good on this promise, the system must keep track of how much CPU each process has had since its creation. It then computes the amount of CPU each one is entitled to, namely the time since creation divided by *n*. Since the amount of CPU time each process has actually had is also known, it is straightforward to compute the ratio of actual CPU had to CPU time entitled. A ratio of 0.5 means that a process has only had half of what it should have had, and a ratio of 2.0 means that a process has had twice as much as it was entitled to. The algorithm is then to run the process with the lowest ratio until its ratio has moved above its closest competitor.

Lottery Scheduling

While making promises to the users and the living up to them is a fine idea, it is difficult to implement. However, another algorithm can be used to give similarly predictable results with a much simpler implementation. It is called **lottery scheduling** (Waldspurger and Weihl, 1994).

The basic idea is to give processes lottery tickets for various system resources, such as CPU time. Whenever a scheduling decision has to be made, a lottery ticket is chosen at random, and the process holding that ticket gets the resource. When applied to CPU scheduling, the system might hold a lottery 50 times a second, with each winner getting 20 msec of CPU time as a prize.

To paraphrase George Orwell: " All processes are equal, but some processes are more equal." More important processes can be given extra tickets, to increase their odds of winning. If there are 100 tickets outstanding, and one process holds 20 of them, it will have a 20 percent chance of winning each lottery. In the long run, it will get about 20 percent of the CPU. In contrast to a priority scheduler, where it is very hard to state what having a priority of 40 actually means, here the rule is clear: a process holding a fraction *f* of the tickets will get about a fraction *f* of the resource in question.

Cooperating processes may exchange tickets if they wish. For example, when a client process sends a message to a server process and then blocks, it may give all of its tickets to the server, to increase the chance of the server running next. When the server is finished, it returns the tickets so the client can run again. In fact, in the absence of clients, servers need no ticket at all.

Lottery scheduling can be used to solve problems that are difficult to handle with other methods. One example is a video server in which several processes are feeding video streams to their clients, but at different frame rates. Suppose that the processes need frames at 10, 20, and 25 frames/sec. By allocating these processes 10, 20, and 25 tickets, respectively, they will automatically divide the CPU in the correct proportion.

Real-Time Scheduling

A **real-time** system is one in which time plays an essential role. Typically, one or more physical devices external to the computer generate stimuli, and the computer must react appropriately to them within a fixed amount of time. For example, the computer in a compact disc player gets the bits as they come off the drive and must convert them into music within a very tight time interval. If the calculation takes too long, the music will sound peculiar. Other real-time systems are patient monitoring in a hospital intensive-care unit, the autopilot in an aircraft, and safety control in a nuclear reactor. In all these cases, having the right answer but having it too late is often just as bad as not having it at all.

Real-time systems are generally categorized as **hard real time**, meaning there are absolute deadlines that must be met, or else, and **soft real time**, meaning that missing an occasional deadline is tolerable. In both cases, real-time behavior is achieved by dividing the program into a number of processes, each of whose behavior is predictable and known in advance. These processes are generally short lived and can run to completion in under a second. When an external event is detected, it is the job of the scheduler to schedule the processes in such a way as that all deadlines are met.

The events that a real-time system may have to respond to can be further categorized as **periodic** (occurring at regular intervals) or **aperiodic** (occurring unpredictably). A system may have to respond to multiple periodic event streams. Depending on how much time event requires for processing, it may not even be possible to handle them all. For example, if there are m periodic events and event i occurs with period P_i and requires C_i seconds of CPU time to handle each event, then the load can only be handled if

$$\sum_{i=1}^{m} \frac{C_i}{P_i} \leq 1$$

A real-time system that meets this criteria is said to be **schedulable**.

As an example, consider a soft real-time system with three periodic events, with periods of 100, 200, and 500 msec. respectively. If these events require 50, 30, and 100 msec of CPU time per event, respectively, the system is schedulable because $0.5 + 0.15 + 0.2 < 1$. If a fourth event with a period of 1 sec is added, the system will remain schedulable as long as this event does not need more than 150 msec of CPU time per event. Implicit in this calculation is the assumption that the context-switching overhead is so small that it can be ignored.

Real-time scheduling algorithms can be dynamic or static. The former make their scheduling decisions at run time; the latter make them before the system starts running. Let us briefly consider a few of the dynamic real-time scheduling algorithms. The classic algorithm is the **rate monotonic algorithm**. In advance, it assigns to each process a priority proportional to the frequency of occurrence of its triggering event. For example, a process to run every 20 msec gets priority 50 and a process to run every 100 msec gets priority 10. At run time, the scheduler always runs the highest priority ready process, pre-empting the running process if need be. Liu and Layland proved that this algorithm is optimal.

Another popular real-time scheduling algorithm is **earliest deadline first**. Whenever an event is detected, its process is added to the list of ready processes. The list is kept sorted by deadline, which for a periodic event is the next occurrence of the event. The algorithm runs the first process on the list, the one with the closest deadline.

A third algorithm first computes for each process the amount of time it has to spare, called its **laxity**. If a process requires 200 msec and must be finished in 250 msec, its laxity is 50 msec. The algorithm, called **least laxity**, chooses the process with the smallest amount of time to spare.

While in theory it is possible to turn a general-purpose operating system into a real-time system by using one of these scheduling algorithms, in practice the context-switching overhead of general-purpose systems is so large that real-time performance can only be achieved for applications with easy time constraints. As a consequence, most real-time work uses special real-time operating systems that have certain important properties. Typically these include a small size, fast interrupt time, rapid context switch, short interval during which interrupts are disabled, and the ability to manage multiple timers in the millisecond or microsecond range.

Two-Level Scheduling

Up until now we have more or less assumed that all runnable processes are in main memory. If insufficient main memory is available, some of the runnable processes will have to be kept on the disk, in whole or in part. This situation has major implications for scheduling, since the process switching time to bring in and run a process from disk is orders of magnitude more than switching to a process already in main memory.

A more practical way of dealing with swapped out processes is to use a two-level scheduler. Some subset of runnable processes is first loaded into main memory, as shown in Fig. 4.25(a). The scheduler then restricts itself to only choosing processes from this subset for a while. Periodically, a higher-level scheduler is invoked to remove processes that have been in memory long enough and to load processes that have been on disk too long. Once the change has been made, as in Fig. 4.25(b), the lower-level scheduler again restricts itself to only running processes that are actually in memory. Thus, the lower-level scheduler is concerned with making a choice among the runnable processes that are in memory at that moment, while the higher-level scheduler is concerned with shuttling processes back and forth between memory and disk.

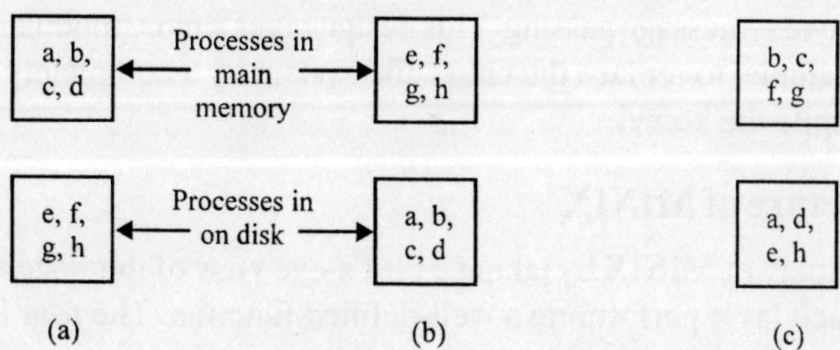

Fig. 4.25. A two-level scheduler must move processes between disk and memory and also choose processes to run from among those in memory. Three different instants of time are represented by (a), (b), and (c).

Among the criteria that the higher-level scheduler could use to make its decisions are the following ones:

1. How long has it been since the process was swapped in or out?
2. How much CPU time has the process had recently?
3. How big is the process? (Small ones do not get in the way.)
4. How high is the priority of the process?

Again here we could use round-robin, priority scheduling, or any of various other methods. The two schedulers may or may not use the same algorithm.

Policy versus Mechanism

Up until now, we have tacitly assumed that all the processes in the system belong to different users and are thus competing for the CPU. While this is often true, sometimes it happens that one process has many children running under its control. For example, a database management system process may have many children. Each child might be working on a different request, or each one might have some specific function to perform (query parsing, disk access, etc.). It is entirely possible that the main process has an excellent idea of which of its children are the most important (or time critical) and which the least. Unfortunately, none of the schedulers discussed above accept any input from user processes about scheduling decisions. As a result, the scheduler rarely makes the best choice.

The solution to this problem is to separate the **scheduling mechanism** from the **scheduling policy**. What this means is that the scheduling algorithm is parameterized in some way, but the parameters can be filled in by user processes. Let us consider the data base example again. Suppose that the kernel uses a priority scheduling algorithm but provides a system call by which a process can set (and change) the priorities of its children. In this way the parent can control in detail how its children are scheduled, even though it itself does not do the scheduling. Here the mechanism is in the kernel but the policy is set by a user process.

Overview of Processes in MINIX

Having completed our study of the principles of process management, interprocess communication, and scheduling, we can now take a look at how they are applied in MINIX. Unlike UNIX, whose kernel is monolithic program not split up into modules, MINIX itself is a collection of processes that communicate with each other and with user processes using a single interprocess communication primitive—message passing. This design gives a more modular and flexible structure, making it easy, for example, to replace the entire file system by a completely different one, without having even to recompile the kernel.

The Internal Structure of MINIX

Let us begin our study of MINIX by taking a bird's-eye view of the system. MINIX is structured in four layers, with each layer performing a well-defined function. The four layers are illustrated in Fig. 4.26.

The bottom layer catches all interrupts and traps, does scheduling, and provides higher layers with a model of independent sequential processes that communicate using messages. The code in this layer has two major functions. The first is catching the traps and interrupts, saving and restoring registers, scheduling, and the general nuts and bolts of actually making the process abstraction provided to the higher layers work. The second is handling the mechanics of messages; checking for legal destinations, locating send and receive buffers in physical memory, and copying bytes from sender to receiver. That part of the layer dealing with the lowest level of interrupt handling is written in assembly language. The rest of the layer and all of the higher layers, are written in C.

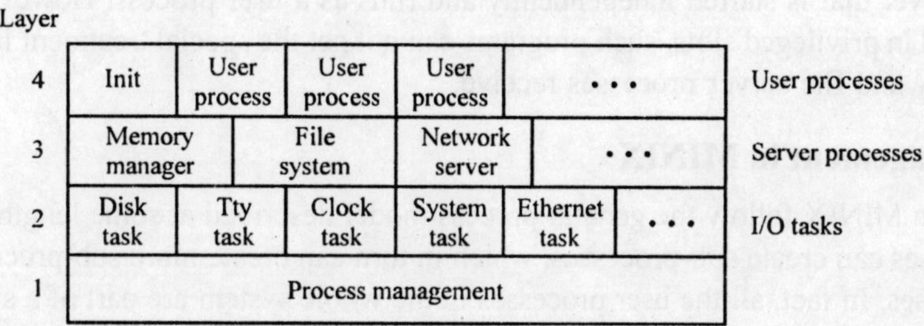

Fig. 4.26. MINIX is structured in four layers.

Layer 2 contains the I/O processes, one per device type. To distinguish them from ordinary user processes, we will call them **tasks**, but the difference between tasks and processes are minimal. In many systems the I/O tasks are called **device drivers**; we will use the terms "task" and "device driver" interchangeably. A task is needed for each device type, including disk, printers, terminals, network interfaces, and clocks. If other I/O devices are present, a task is needed for each one of those, too. One task, the system task, is a little different, since it does not correspond to any I/O device. We will discuss the tasks in the next chapter.

All of the tasks in layer 2 and all the code in layer 1 are linked together into a single binary program called the **kernel**. Some of the tasks share common subroutine, but otherwise they are independent from one another, are scheduled independently, and communicate using messages. Intel processors starting with the 286 assign one of four levels of privileges to each process. Although the tasks and the kernel are compiled together, when the kernel and the interrupt handlers are executing, they are accorded more privileges than the tasks. Thus the true kernel code can access any part of memory and any processors register—essentially, the kernel can execute any instruction using data from anywhere in the system. Tasks cannot execute all machine level instruction, nor can they access all CPU registers or all parts of memory. They can, however, access memory regions belonging to less-privileged processes, in order to perform I/O for them. One task, the system task, does not do I/O in the normal sense but exists in order to provide services, such as copying between different memory regions, for processes which are not allowed to do such things for themselves. On machines which do not provide different privilege levels, such as older Intel processors, these restrictions cannot be enforced, of course.

Layer 3 contains processes that provide useful services to the user processes. These server processes run at a less privileged level than the kernel and tasks and cannot access I/O ports directly. They also cannot access memory outside the segments allotted to them. The **memory manager** (MM) carries out all the MINIX system called that involve memory management, such as FORK, EXEC, and BRK. The **file system** (FS) carries out all the file system calls, such as READ, MOUNT, and CHDIR.

Finally, layer 4 contains all the user processes—shells, editors, compilers, and user-written *a.out* programs. A running system usually has some processes that are started when the system is booted and which run forever. For example, a **daemon** is a background process that executes periodically or always waits for some event, such as packet arrival from a network. In a sense a daemon is a server that is started independently and runs as a user process. However, unlike true servers installed in privileged slots, such programs can not get the special treatment from the kernel that the memory and file server processes receive.

Process Management in MINIX

Processes in MINIX follow the general process model described at some length earlier in this chapter. Processes can create sub-processes, which in turn can create more sub-processes, yielding a tree of processes. In fact, all the user processes in the whole system are part of a single tree with *init* at the root.

How does this situation come about? When the computer is turned on, the hardware reads the first sector of the first track of the boot disk into memory and executes the code it finds there. The details vary depending upon whether the boot disk is a diskette or a hard disk. On a diskette this sector contains the **bootstrap** program. It is very small, since it has to fit in one sector. The MINIX bootstrap loads a larger program, *boot*, which then loads the operating system itself.

In contrast, hard disks require an intermediate step. A hard disk is divided into **partitions**, and the first sector of a hard disk contains a small program and the disk's **partition table.** Collectively these are called the **master boot record**. The program part is executed to read the partition table and to select the active partition. The active partition has a bootstrap on its first sector, which is then loaded and executed to find and start a copy of *boot* in the partition, exactly as is done when booting from a diskette.

During its initialization phase, the kernel starts the tasks, and then the memory manager, the file system, and any other servers that run in layer 3. When all these have run and initialized themselves, they will block, waiting for something to do. When all tasks and servers are blocked, *init*, the first user process, will be executed. It is already in memory, but it could, of course, have been loaded from the disk as a separate program since everything else is working by the time it is started. However, since *init* is started only this one time and is never reloaded from the disk, it is easiest just to include it in the system image file with the kernel, tasks, and servers.

Init starts out by reading the file */etc/ttytab*, which lists all potential terminal devices. Those devices that can be used as login terminals (in the standard distribution, just the console) have an entry in the *getty* field of */etc/ttytab*, and *init* forks off a child process for each such terminal. Normally, each child executes */usr/bin/getty* which prints a message, then waits for a name to be typed. Then */user/bin/login* is called with the name as its argument. If a particular terminal requires special treatment (e.g., a dial-up line) */etc/ttytab* can specify a command (such as */usr/bin/sty*) to be executed to initialize the line before running *getty*.

After a successful login, */bin/login* executes the user's shell (specified in the */etc/passwd* file, and normally */bin/sh* or */usr/bin/ash*). The shell waits for commands to be types and then forks off a new process for each command. In this way, the shells are the children of *init*, the user processes are the grandchildren of *init*, and all the user processes in the system are part of a single tree.

The two principal MINIX system calls for process management are FORK and EXEC. FORK is the only way to create a new process. EXEC allows a process to execute a specified program. When a program is executed, it is allocated a portion of memory whose size is specified in the program file's header. It keeps this amount of memory throughout its execution, although the distribution among data segment, stack segment, and unused can vary as the process runs.

All the information about a process is kept in the process table, which is divided up among the kernel, memory manager, and file system, with each one having those fields that it needs. When a new process comes into existence (by FORK), or an old process terminates, the memory manager first updates its part of the process table and then sends messages to the file system and kernel telling them to do likewise.

Interprocess Communication in MINIX

Three primitives are provided for sending and receiving messages. They are called by the C library procedures

send(dest, &message);

to send a message to process *dest*,

receive(source, &message);

to receive a message from process *source* (or ANY), and

send_rec(src_dst, &message);

to send a message and wait for a reply from the same process. The second parameter in each call is the local address of the message data. The message passing mechanism in the kernel copies the message from the sender to the receiver. The reply (for *send_rec*) overwrites the original message. In principle this kernel mechanism could be replaced by a function which copies messages over a network to a corresponding function on another machine, to implement a distributed system. In practice this would be complicated somewhat by the fact that message contents are sometimes pointers to large data structures, and a distributed system would also have to provide for copying the data itself over the network.

Each process or task can send and receive messages from processes and tasks in its own layer, and from those in the layer directly below it. User processes may not communicate directly with the I/O tasks. The system enforces this restriction.

When a process (which also includes the tasks as a special case) sends a message to a process that is not currently waiting for a message, the sender blocks until the destination does a RECEIVE. In other words, MINIX uses the rendezvous method to avoid the problems of buffering sent, but not yet received, messages. Although less flexible than a scheme with buffering, it turns out to be adequate for this system, and much simpler because no buffer management is needed.

Process Scheduling in MINIX

The interrupt system is what keeps a multiprogramming operating system going. Processes block when they make requests for input, allowing other processes to execute. When input becomes available, the current running process is interrupted by the disk, keyboard, or other hardware. The clock also generates interrupts that are used to make sure a running user process that has not requested input eventually relinquishes the CPU, to give other processes their chance to run. It is the job of the lowest layer of MINIX to hide these interrupts by turning them into messages. As far as processes (and tasks) are concerned, when an I/O device completes an operation it sends a message to some process, waking it up and making it runnable.

Each time a process is interrupted, whether from a conventional I/O device or from the clock, there is an opportunity to redetermine which process is most deserving of an opportunity to run. Of course, this must be done whenever a process terminates, as well, but in a system like MINIX interruptions due to I/O operations or the clock occurs more frequently than process termination. The MINIX scheduler uses a multilevel queueing system with three levels, corresponding to layers 2, 3, and 4 in Fig. 2.26. Within the task and server levels processes run until they block, but user processes are scheduled using round robin. Tasks have the highest priority, the memory manager and file server are next, and user processes are last.

At each clock tick, a check is made to see if the current process is a user process that has run more than 100 msec. If it is, the scheduler is called to see if another user process is waiting for the CPU. If one is found, the current process is moved to the end of its scheduling queue, and the process now at the head is run. Tasks, the memory manager, and the file system are never pre-empted by the clock, no matter how long they have been running.

Implementation of Processes in MINIX

We are now moving closer to looking at the actual code, so a few words about the notation we will use are in order. The terms "procedure," "function," and "routine" will be used interchangeably. Names of variables, procedures, and files will be written in italics, as in *rw_flag*. When a variable, procedure, or file name starts a sentence, it will be capitalized, but the actual names all begin with lower case letters. System calls will be in small caps, for example, READ.

The book and the software, both of which are continuously evolving, did not "go to press" on the same day, so there may be minor discrepancies between the references to the code, the printed listing, and the CD-ROM version. Such differences generally only affect a line or two, however. The source code printed in the book has also been simplified by eliminating code used to compile options that are not discussed in the book.

Organization of the MINIX Source Code

Logically, the source code is organized as two directories. The full paths to these directories on a standard MINIX system are */usr/include/* and */usr/src/* (a trailing "/ " in a path name indicates that it refers to a directory). The actual location of the directories may vary from system to system, but normally the structure of the directories below the topmost level will be the same on any system. We will refer to these directories as *include/* and *src/* in the text.

The *include/* directory contains a number of POSIX standard header files. In addition, it has three sub-directories:

1. *sys/* – this subdirectory contains additional POSIX headers.
2. *minix/* – includes header files used by the operating system.
3. *ibm/* – includes header files with IBM PC-specific definitions.

To support extensions to MINIX and programs that run in the MINIX environment, other files and sub-directories are also present in *include/*as provided on the CD-ROM or over the Internet. For instance, the *include/net/* directory and its subdirectory *include/net/gen/* support network extensions. However, in this text only the files needed to compile the basic MINIX system are printed and discussed.

The *src/* directory contains three important sub-directories containing the operating system source code:

1. *kernel/* –layers 1 and 2 (processes, messages, and drivers).
2. *mm/* – the code for the memory manager.
3. *fs/* – the code for the file system.

There are three other source code directories that are not printed or discussed in the text, but which are essential to producing a working system:

1. *src/lib/* – source code for library procedures (e.g., open, read).
2. *src/tools/* – source code for the init program, used to start MINIX.
3. *src/boot/* – the code for booting and installing MINIX.

The standard distribution of MINIX includes several more source directories. An operating system exists, of course, to support commands (programs) that will run on it, so there is a large *src/commands/* directory with source code for the utility programs (e.g., *cat*, *cp*, *date, ls*, *pwd*). Since MINIX is an educational operating system, meant to be modified, there is a *src/test/*directory with programs designed to test thoroughly a newly compiled MINIX system. Finally, the */src/inet/* directory includes source code for recompiling MINIX with network support.

For convenience we will usually refer to simple file names when it will be clear from that the context what the complete path name is. It should be note, however, that some file names appear in more than open directory. For instance, there are several files named *const.h* in which constants relevant to a particular part of the system are defined. The files in a particular directory will be discussed together, so there should not be any confusion. The files are listed in Appendix A in the order they are discussed in the text, to make it easier to follow along. Acquisition of a couple of bookmarks might be of use at this point.

Also worth noting is that Appendix B contains an alphabetical list of all files described in Appendix A, and Appendix C contains a list of where to find the definitions of macros, global variables, and procedures used in MINIX.

The code for layers 1 and 2 is contained in the directory *src/kernel/*. In this chapter we will study the files in this directory which support process management, the lowest layer of the MINIX structure we saw in Fig. 4.26. This layer includes functions which handle system initialization, interrupts, message passing and process scheduling. We will look at the rest of the files in this directory, which support the various tasks, the second layer in Fig. 4.26.

When the MINIX is compiled, all the source code files in *src/kernel/*, *src/mm/*, and *src/fs/* are compiled to object files. All the object files in *src/kernel/* are linked to form a single executable program, *kernel*. The object files in *src/mm/* are also linked together to form a single executable program, *mm*. The same holds for *fs*. Extensions can be added by adding additional servers, for instance network support is added by modifying *include/minix/config.h* to enable compilation of the files in *src/inet/* to form *inet*. Another executable program, *init*, is built in *src/tools/*. The program *installboot* (whose source is in *src/boot/*) adds names to each of these programs, pads each one out so that its length is a multiple of the disk sector size (to make it easier to load the parts independently), and concatenated them onto a single file. This new file is the binary of the operating system and can be copied onto the root directory or the */minix/* directory of a floppy disk or hard disk partition.

Later, the boot monitor programs can load and execute the operating system. Figure 4.27 shows the layout of memory after the concatenated programs are separated and loaded. Details, of course, depend upon the system configuration. The example in the figure is for a MINIX system configured to take advantage of a computer equipped with several megabytes of memory. This makes it possible to allocate a large number of file system buffer, but the resulting large file system does not fit in the lower range of memory, below 640K. If the number of buffers is reduced drastically it is possible to make that the entire system fit into less than 640K of memory, with room for a few user processes as well.

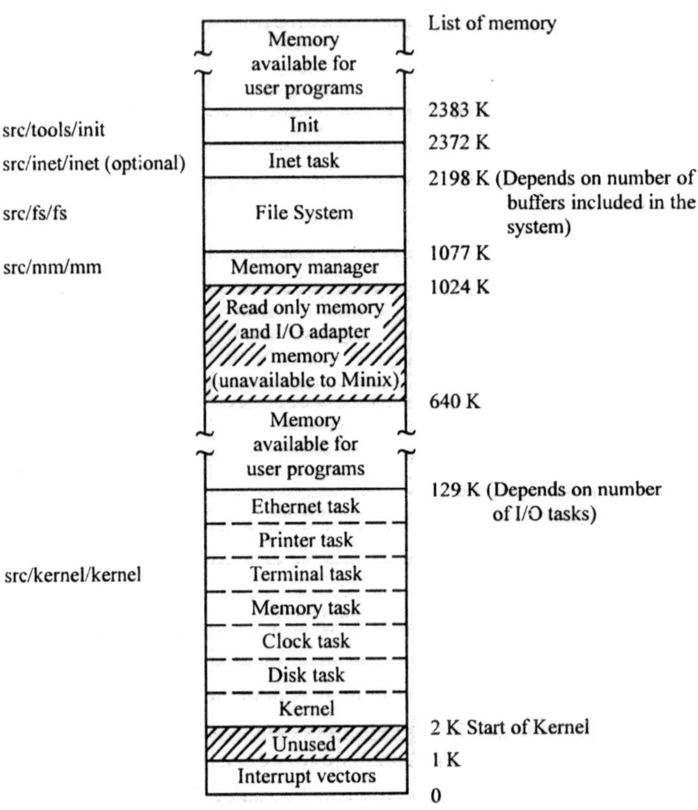

Fig. 4.27. Memory layout after MINIX has been loaded from the disk into memory. The four (or five, with network support) independently compiled and linked parts are clearly distinct. The sizes are approximate, depending on the configuration.

It is important to realize that MINIX consists of three or more totally independent programs that communicate only by passing messages. A procedure called *panic* in *src/fs/* does not conflict with a procedure called *panic* in *src/mm/* because they ultimately are linked into different executable files. The only procedures that the three pieces of the operating system have in common are a few of the library routines in *lib/*. This modular structure makes it very easy to modify, say, the file system, without having these changes affect the memory manager. It also makes it straightforward to remove the file system altogether and to put it on a different machine as a file server, communicating with user machines by sending messages over a network.

As another example of the modularity of MINIX, compiling the system with or without network support makes absolutely no difference to the memory manager or the file system and affects the kernel only because the Ethernet task is compiled there, along with support for other I/O devices. When enabled, the network server is integrated into the MINIX system as a server with the same level of priority as the memory manager or the file server. Its operation can involve the transfer of large quantities of data very rapidly, and this requires higher priority than a user process would receive. Except for the Ethernet task, however, network functions could be performed by user level processes. Network functions are not traditional operating system functions, and detailed discussion of the network code is beyond the scope of this book. In succeeding sections and chapters the discussion will be based on a MINIX system compiled without network support.

The Common Header Files

The directory *include/* and its sub-directories contain a collection of files defining constants, macros, and type. The POSIX standard requires many of these definitions and specifies in which files of the main *include/* directory and its sub-directory *include/sys/*each required definition is to be found. The files in these directories are **header** or **include files**, identified by the suffix *.h*, and used to means of #include statements in C source files. These statements are a feature of the C language. Include files make maintenance of a large system easier.

The first headers to be considered are truly general purpose ones, so much as that they are not referenced directly by any of the C language source files for the MINIX system. Rather, they are themselves included in other header files, the master headers *src/kernel/kernel.h*, *src/mm/mm.h*, and *src/fs/fs.h* for each of the three main parts of the MINIX system, which in turn are included in every compilation. Each master header is tailored to the needs of the corresponding part of the MINIX system, but each one starts with a section like the one shown in Fig. 4.28. The master headers will be discussed again in other sections of the book. This preview is to emphasize that headers from several directories are used together. In this section and the next one we will mention each of the files referenced in Fig. 4.28.

```
#include <minix/config.h>          /* MUST be first */
#include <ansi.h>                  /* MUST be second */
#include <sys/types.h>
#include <minix/const.h>
#include <minix/type.h>
#include <limits.h>
#include <errno.h>
#include <minix/syslib.h>
```

Fig. 4.28. Part of a master header which ensures inclusion of header files needed by all C source files.

Let us start with the first header in *include/*, *ansi.h* (line 0000). This is the second header that is processed whenever any part of the MINIX system is compiled; only *include/minix/config.h* is processed earlier. The purpose of *ansi.h* is to test whether the compiler meets the requirements of Standard C, as defined by the International Organization for Standards. Standard C is also called ANSI C, since the standard was originally developed by the American National Standards Institute before gaining international recognition. A Standard C compiler defines several macros that can be tested in programs being compiled. _ _*STDC*_ _ is such a macro, and it is defined by a standard compiler to have a value of 1, just as if the C preprocessor had read a line like

#define _ _*STDC*_ _ 1

The compiler distributed with current versions of MINIX conforms to Standard C, but older versions of MINIX were developed before the adoption of the standards and it is still possible to compile MINIX with a classic (Kernighan & Ritchie) C compiler. It is intended that MINIX should be easy to port to new machines, and allowing older compilers is part of this. At lines 0023 to 0025 the statement

#define _ANSI

is processed if a Standard C compiler is in use. *Ansi.h* defines several macros in different ways, depending upon whether the *_ANSI* macro is defined.

The most important macro in this file is *_PROTOTYPE*. This macro allows us to write function prototypes in the form

_PROTOTYPE (return-type function-name, (argument-type argument, ...))

and have this transformed by the C preprocessor into

return-type function-name(argument-type, argument, ...)

if the compiler is an ANSI Standard C compiler, or

return-type function-name()

if the compiler is an old-fashioned (i.e. Kernighan & Ritchie) compiler.

Before we leave *ansi.h* let us mention one more feature. The entire file is enclosed between lines that read

#ifndef _ANSI_H
and
#endif

On the line immediately following the #ifndef *_ANSI_H* itself is defined. A header file should be included only once in a compilation; this construction ensures that the contents of the file will be ignored if it is included multiple times. We will see this technique used in all the header files in the *include/* directory.

The second file in *include/* that is indirectly included in every MINIX source file is the *limits.h* header (line 0100). This file defines many basic sizes, both language types such as the number of bits in an integer, as well as operating system limits such as the length of a file name. *Errno.h* (line 0200), is also included by all the master headers. It contains the error numbers that are returned are user programs in the global variable *errno* when a system call fails. *Errno* is also used to identify some internal errors, such as trying to send a message to a nonexistent task. The error numbers are negative to mark them as error codes within MINIX system, but they must be made positive before being returned to user programs. The trick that is used is that each error code is defined in a line like

```
#define EPERM (_SIGN 1)
```

(line 0236). The master header for each part of the opening system defines the macro *_SYSTEM*, but *_SYSTEM* is never defined when a user program is compiled. If *_SYSTEM* is defined, then *SIGN* is defined as "–"; otherwise it is given a null definition.

The next group of files to be considered are not included in all the master headers, but are nevertheless used in many source file in all parts of the MINIX system. The most important is *unistd.h* (line 0400). This header defines many constants, most of which are required by POSIX. In addition, it includes prototypes for many C functions, including all those used to access MINIX system calls. Another widely used file is *string.h* (line 0600), which provides prototypes for many C functions used for string manipulation. The header *signal.h* (line 0700) defines the standard signal names. It also contains prototypes for some signal-related functions. As we will see later, signal handling involves all parts of MINIX.

Fcntl.h (line 0900) symbolically defines many parameters used in file control operations. For instance, it allows one to use the macro *O_RDONLY* instead of the numeric value 0 as a parameter to an *open* call. Although this file is referenced most by the file system, its definitions are also needed in a number of places in the kernel and the memory manager.

The remaining files in *include/* are not as widely used as the ones already mentioned. *Stdlib.h* (line 1000) defines types, macros, and function prototypes that are likely to needed in the compilation of all but the most simple of C programs. It is one of the most frequently used headers in compiling user programs, although within the MINIX system source it is referenced by only a few files in the kernel.

The console and terminal interface of an operating system is complex, because many different types of hardware have to interact with the operating system and user programs in a standardized way. The *termios.h* (line 1100) header defines constant, macros, and function prototypes used for control of terminal-type I/O devices. The most important structure is the *termios* structure. It contains flags to signal various modes of operation, variables to set input and output transmissions speeds, and an array to hold special characters, such as the *INTR* and *KILL* characters. This structure is required by POSIX, as are many of the macros and function prototypes defined in this file.

However, as all-encompassing as the POSIX standard is meant to be, it does not provide everything one might want, and the last part of file, from line 1241 onward, provide extensions to POSIX. Some of these are of obvious value, such as extensions to define standard baud rates of 57,600 baud and higher, and support for terminal display screen windows. The POSIX standard does not forbid extensions, as no reasonable standard can ever be all-inclusive. But when writing a program in the MINIX environment which is intended to be portable to other environments, some caution is required to avoid the use of definitions specific to MINIX. This is easy to do. In this file and other files that define MINIX-specific extensions the use of the extensions is controlled by an

```
#ifdef _MINIX
```

statement. If *_MINIX* is not defined, the compiler will not even see the MINIX extensions.

The last file we will consider in *include/* is *a.out.h* (line 1400), a header which defines the format of the files in which executable programs are stored on disk, including the header structure used to start a file executing and the symbol table structure produced by the compiler. It is referenced only by the file system.

Now let us go on to the sub-directory *includes/sys/*. As shown in Fig. 4.28, the master header for the main parts of the MINIX system all include *sys/types.h* (line 1600) immediately after reading *ansi.h*. This header defines many data types used by MINIX. Errors that could arise from misunderstanding which fundamental data types are used in particular situation can be avoided by using the definitions provided here. Fig. 4.29 shows the way the sizes, in bits, of a few types defined in this file differ when compiled for 16-bit or 32-bit processors. Note that all type names end with "_t". This is just a convention; it is a requirement of the POSIX standard. This is an example of a **reserved suffix**, and it should not be used as suffix of any name which is *not* a type name.

Type	16-Bit minix	32-Bit minix
gid_t	8	8
dev_t	16	16
pid_t	16	32
ino_t	16	32

Fig. 4.29. The size, in bits, of some types on 16-bit and 32-bit systems.

Although it is not so widely used that it is included in the master header for each section, *sys/ioctl.h* (line 100) defines many macros used for device control operations. It also contains the prototype for the IOCTL system call. This call is not directly invoked by programmers in many cases, since the POSIX-define functions prototyped in *include/termios.h* have replaced many uses of the old *ioctl* library function for dealing with terminals, consoles, and similar devices. Nevertheless, it is still necessary. In fact, the POSIX functions for control of terminal devices are converted into IOCTL system calls by the library. Also, there are an ever-increasing number of devices, all of which need various kinds of control, which can be interfaced with a modern computer system. For instance, near the end of this file there are several operation codes defined that begin with *DSPIO*, for controlling a digital signal processor. Indeed, the main difference between MINIX as described in this book and other versions is that for purpose of the book we describe a MINIX with relatively few input/output devices. Many others, such as network interfaces, CD-ROM drives, and sound cards, can be added; control codes for all of these are defined as macros in this file.

The MINIX Header Files

We will start with the *minix/* directory. In the previous section, it was noted that *config.h* is included in the master header for all parts of the MINIX system, and is thus the first file actually processed by the compiler. On many occasions, when difference in hardware or the operating system is intended to be used require changes in the configuration of MINIX, editing this file and recompiling the system is all that must be done. The user-settable parameters are all in the first part of the file. The first of these is the *MACHINE* parameter, which can take values such as *IBM_PC*, *SUN_4*, *MACINTOSH*, or other values, depending on the type of machine for which MINIX is being compiled. Most of the code for MINIX is independent of the type of machine, but an operating system always has some system-dependent code. In the few places in this book where we discuss code that is written differently for different systems we will use as our examples code for IBM PC-type machines with advanced processor chips that sue 32-bit words. We will refer to all of these as Intel 32-bit processors. MINIX can also be compiled for older IBM PCs with a 16-bit word size, and the machine-dependent parts of MINIX must be coded differently for these machines. On a PC, the compiler itself determines the machine type for which MINIX will be compiled. The standard PC MINIX compiler is the Amsterdam Compiler Kit (ACK) compiler. It identifies itself by defining, in addition to the *__STDC__* macro, the *__ACK__* macro. It also defines a macro *_EM_WSIZE* which is the word size (in bytes) for its target machine. In lines 2626 to 2628 a macro *_WORD_SIZE* is assigned the value of *_EM_WSIZE*. Further along in the file and at various places in the other MINIX source files these definitions are used. For example, the lines 2647 to 2650 begin with the test

```
#if (MACHINE == IBM_PC && _WORD_SIZE == 4)
```

and define a size for the file system's buffer cache on 32-bit systems.

Other definitions in *config.h* allow customization for other needs in a particular installation. For instance, there is a section that allows various types of device drivers to be included when the MINIX kernel is compiled. This is likely to be the most often edited part of the MINIX source code. This section starts out with:

```
#define ENABLE_NETWORKING 0
#define ENABLE_AT_WINI 1
#define ENABLE_BIOS_WINI 0
```

By changing the 0 in the first line to 1 we can compile a MINIX kernel for a machine that needs network support. By defining ***ENABLE_AT_WIN1*** as 0 and ***ENABLE_BIOS_WIN1*** as 1, we can eliminate the AT-type (i.e., IDE) hard disk driver code and use the PC BIOS for hard disk support.

The next file is *const.h*, which illustrates another common use of header files. Here we find a variety of constant definitions that are not likely to be changed when compiling a new kernel but that are used in a number of places. Defining them here helps to prevent errors that could be hard to track down if inconsistent definitions were made in multiple places. There are other files names *const.h* in the MINIX source tree, but they are for more limited use. Definitions that are used only in the kernel are included in *src/kernel/const.h*. Definitions that are used only in the file system are included in *src/fs/const.h*. The memory manager uses *src/mm/const.h* for its local definitions. Only those definitions that are used in more than one part of the MINIX system are included in *include/minix/const.h*.

```
EXTERN int who;
```

If the variable were declared just as

```
int who;
```

and included in two or more files, some linker would complain about a multiply defined variable. Furthermore, the C reference manual (Kernighan and Ritchie, 1988) explicitly forbids this construction.

To avoid this problem, it is necessary to have the declaration read

```
extern int who;
```

in all places but one. Using *EXTERN* prevents this problem by having it expand into *extern* everywhere that *const.h* is included, except following an explicit redefinition of *EXTERN* as the null string. This is done in each part of MINIX by putting global definition in a special file called *glo.h*, for instance, *src/kernel/glo.h*, which is indirectly included in every compilation. Within each *glo.h* there is a sequence

```
#ifdef _TABLE
#undef EXTERN
#define EXTERN
#endif
```

and in the *table.c* files of each part of MINIX there is a line

```
#define _TABLE
```

preceding the #include section. Thus when the header files are included and expanded as part of the compilation of *table.c*, *extern* is not inserted anywhere (because *EXTERN* is defined as the null string within *table.c*) and storage for the global variables is reserved only in one place, in the object file *table.o*.

If you are new to C programming and do not quite understand what is going on here, fear not; the details are really not important. Multiple inclusion of header files can cause problems for some linkers because it can lead to multiple declarations for included variables. The *EXTERN* business is simply a way to make MINIX more portable so it can be linked on machines whose linkers do not accept multiply defined variables.

PRIVATE is defined as a synonym for *static*. Procedures and data that are not referenced outside the file in which they are declared are always declared as *PRIVATE* to prevent their names from being visible outside the file in which they are declared. As a general rule, all variables and procedures should be declared with as local a scope as possible. *PUBLIC* is defined as the null string. Thus, the declaration

```
PUBLIC void free_zone(Dev_t dev, zone_t numb)
```

comes out of the C preprocessor as

```
void free_zone(Dev_t dev, zone_t numb)
```

which, according to the C scope rules, means that the name *free_zone* is exported from the file and can be used in other files. *PRIVATE* and *PUBLIC* are not necessary but are attempts to undo the damage caused by the C scope rules (the default is that names are exported outside the file; it should be just the reverse).

The rest of *const.h* defines numerical constants used throughout the system. A section of *const.h* is devoted to machine or configuration-dependent definitions. For instance, throughout the source code the basic unit of memory size is the click. The size of a click depends upon the processor architecture, and alternatives for Intel, Motorola 68000, and Sun SPARC architectures are defined on lines 2957 to 2965. This file also contains the macros *MAX* and *MIN*, so we can say

```
z = MAX (x, y);
```

to assign the larger of x and y to z.

Type.h is another file that is included in every compilation by means of the master headers. It contains a number of key type definitions, along with related numerical values. The most important definition in this file is *message* on lines 3135 to 3146. While we could have defined *message* to be an array of some number of bytes, it is better programming practice to have it be a structure containing a union of the various message types that are possible. Six message formats, *mess_1* through *mess_6*, are defined. A message is a structure containing a field *m_source*, telling who sent the message, a field *m_type*, telling what the message type is (e.g., GET_TIME to the clock task) and the data fields. The six message types are shown in Fig. 4.30. In the figure the first and second message types seem identical, as do the fourth and sixth types. This is true for MINIX as implemented on an Intel CPU with a 32-bit word size, but would not be the case on a machine where *ints*, *longs* and pointers were different sizes. Defining six distinct formats makes it easier to recompile for a different architecture.

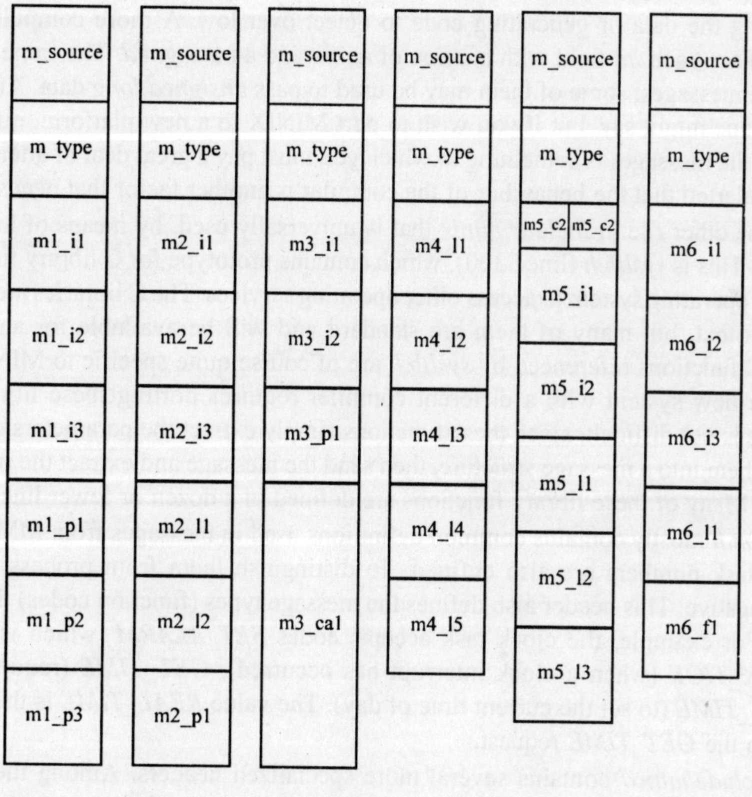

m_source	m_source	m_source	m_source	m_source	m_source
m_type	m_type	m_type	m_type	m_type	m_type
m1_i1	m2_i1	m3_i1	m4_l1	m5_c2 m5_c2	m6_i1
m1_i2	m2_i2	m3_i2	m4_l2	m5_i1	m6_i2
m1_i3	m2_i3	m3_p1	m4_l3	m5_i2	m6_i3
m1_p1	m2_l1	m3_ca1	m4_l4	m5_l1	m6_l1
m1_p2	m2_l2		m4_l5	m5_l2	m6_f1
m1_p3	m2_p1			m5_l3	

Fig 4.30. ***The six message types used in*** **MINIX.** ***The sizes of message elements will vary, depending upon the architecture of the machine; this diagram illustrates sizes on a machine with 32-bit pointers, such as the Pentium (Pro).***

When it is necessary to send a message containing, say, three integers and three pointers (or three integers and two pointers), then the first format in Fig. 4.30 is the one to use. The same applies to the other formats. How does one assign a value to the first integer in the first format? Suppose that the message is called *x*. Then *x.m_u* refers to the union portion of the message struct. To refer to the first of the six alternatives in the union, we use *x.m_u.m_m1*. Finally, to get at the first integer in this struct we say *x.m_u.m_m1.m1i1*. This is quite a mouthful, so somewhat shorter field names are defined as macros after the definition of message itself. Thus *x.m1_i1* can be used instead of *x.m_u.m_m1.m1i1*. The short names all have the form of the letter m, the format number, an underscore, one or two letters indicating whether the field is an integer, pointer, long, character, character array, or function, and a sequence number of distinguish multiple instances of the same type within a message.

As an aside, while discussing message formats, this is a good place to note that an operating system and its compiler often have an "understanding" about things like the layout of structures, and this can make the implementor's life easier. In MINIX the *int* fields in messages are sometimes used to hold *unsigned* data types. In some cases this could cause overflow, but the code was written using the knowledge that the MINIX compiler copies *unsigned* types to *inst* and *vice versa* without changing the data or generating code to detect overflow. A more compulsive approach would be to replace each *int* field with a *union* of an *int* and an *unsigned.* The same applies to the *long* field in the messages; some of them may be used to pass *unsigned long* data. Are we cheating here? Perhaps, one might say, but if you wish to port MINIX to a new platform, quite clearly the exact format of the messages is something to which you must pay a great deal of attention, and now you have been alerted that the behaviour of the compiler is another factor that needs attention.

There is one other file in *include/minix* that is universally used, by means of inclusion in the master headers. This is *syslib.h* (line 3300), which contains prototype for C library functions called from within the operating system to access other operating services. The C libraries are not discussed in detail in this text, but many of them are standard and will be available for any C compiler. However, the C functions referenced by *syslib.h* are of course quite specific to MINIX and a port of MINIX to a new system with a different compiler requires porting these library functions. Fortunately this is not difficult, since these functions simply extract the parameters of the function call and insert them into a message structure, then send the message and extract the results from the reply message. Many of these library functions are defined in a dozen or fewer lines of C code.

The file *com.h* mostly contains common definitions used in messages from MM and FS to the I/O task. The task numbers are also defined. To distinguish them from process numbers, task numbers are negative. This header also defines the message types (function codes) that can be sent to each task. For example, the clock task accepts codes *SET_ALARM* (which is used to set a timer), *CLOCK_TICK* (when a clock interrupt has occurred), *GET_TIME* (request for the real time), and *SET_TIME* (to set the current time of day). The value *REAL_TIME* is the message type for the reply to the *GET_TIME* request.

Finally, *include/minix/* contains several more specialized headers. Among these are *boot.h*, which are used by both the kernel and file system to define devices and to access parameters passed to the system by the *boot* program. Another example is *keymap.h*, which defines the structures used to implement specialized keyboard layouts for the character sets needed for different languages. It is also needed by programs which generate and load these tables. Some files here, like *partition.h*, are used only by the kernel, and not by the file system or the memory manager. In an implementation with support for additional I/O devices there are more header files like this, supporting other devices.

Their placement in this directory needs explanation. Ideally all user programs would access devices only through the operating system, and files like this would be placed in *src/kernel/*. However, the realities of system management require that there be some, user commands that access system-level structures, such as commands to make disk partitions. It is to support such utility programs that such specialized header files are placed in the *include/* directory tree.

The last specialized header directory we will consider, *include/ibm/*, contains two files which provide definitions related to the IBM PC family of computers. One of these is *diskparm.h*, which is needed by the floppy disk task. Although this task is included in the standard version of MINIX, its source code is not discussed in detail in this text, since it is so similar to the hard disk task. The other file in this directory is *partition.h*, which defines disk partition tables and related constants as used on **IBM** compatible systems. These are placed here to facilitate porting MINIX to another hardware platform. For different hardware *include/ibm/partition.h* would have to be replaced, presumably with a *partition.h* in another appropriately named directory, but the structure defined in the file *include/minix/partition.h* is internal to MINIX and should remain unchanged in a MINIX hosted on a different hardware platform.

Process Data Structures and Header Files

Now let us dive in and see what the code in *src/kernel/* looks like. In the previous two sections we structured our discussion around an excerpt from a typical master header; we will look first at the real master header for the kernel, *kernel.h*. It begins by defining three macros. The first, *_POSIX_SOURCE* is a **feature test macro** defined by the POSIX standard itself. All such macros are required to begin with the underscore character, "_". The effect of defining the *_POSIX_SOURCE* macro is to ensure that all symbols required by the standard and any that are explicitly permitted, but not required, will be visible, while hiding any additional symbols that are unofficial extensions to POSIX. We have already mentioned the next two definitions: the *_MINIX* macro overrides the effect of *_POSIX_SOURCE* for extensions defined by MINIX, and *_SYSTEM* can be tested wherever it is important to do something differently when compiling system code, as opposed to user code, such as changing the sign of error codes. *Kernel.h* then includes other header files from *include/* and its sub-directories *include/sys/*and *include/minix/*, including all those referred to in Fig 4.28. We have discussed all of these files in the previous two sections. Finally; four more headers from the local directory, *src/kernel/*, are included.

This is a good place to point out for newcomers to the C language how file names are quoted in a #include statement. Every C compiler has a default directory in which it looks for include files. Usually, this is */usr/include/*, as it is in a standard MINIX system. When the name of a file to be included is quoted between less-than and greater-than symbols ("<...>") the compiler searches for the file in the default include directory or in a specified sub-directory of the default directory. When the name is quoted between ordinary quote characters (" ``...`` ") the file is searched for first in the current directory (or a specified sub-directory) and then, if not found there, in the default directory.

Kernel.h makes it possible to guarantee that all source files share a large number of important definitions by writing the single line

#include "kernel.h"

in each of the other kernel source files. Since the order of inclusion of header files is sometimes important, *kernel.h* also ensures that this ordering is done correctly. Once and forever. This carries to a higher level the "get it right once, then forget the details" technique embodied in the header file concept. There are similar master header in the source directories for the file system and the memory manager.

Now let us proceed to look at the four local header files included in *kernel.h* just as we have files *const.h* and *type.h* in the common header directory *include/minix/*, we also have files *const.h* and *type.h* in the kernel source directory, *src/kernel/*. The files in *include/minix/* are placed there because they are needed by many parts of the system, including programs that run under the control of the system. The files in *src/kernel/*provide definitions needed only for compilation of the kernel. The FS and MM source directories also contain *const.h* and *type.h* files to define constants and types needed only for those parts of the system. The other two files included in the master header, *proto.h* and *glo.h*, have no counterparts in the main *include/* directories, but we will find that they, too, have counterparts used in compiling the file system and the memory manager.

Const.h contains a number of machine-dependent values, that is, values that apply to the Intel CPU chips, but that are likely to be different when MINIX is compiled for different hardware. These values are enclosed between

#if (CHIP = = INTEL)

and

#endif

statements to bracket them.

When compiling MINIX for one of the Intel chips the macros *CHIP* and *INTEL* are defined and set equal in *include/minix/config.h*, and thus the machine-dependent code will be compiled. When MINIX was ported to a system based on the Motorola 68000, the people doing the port added section of code bracketed by

#if (CHIP = = M68000)

and

#endif

and made appropriate changes in *include/minix/config.h* so a line reading

#define CHIP M68000

would be effective. In this way, MINIX can deal with constants and code that are specific to one system. This construction does not especially enhance readability, so it should be used as little as possible. In fact, in the interest of readability, we have removed many sections of machine-dependent code for 68000 and other processors from the version of the code printed in this text. The code distributed on the CD-ROM and via the Internet retains the code for other platforms.

A few of the definitions in *const.h* deserve special mention. Some of these are machine dependent, such as important interrupt vectors and field values used for resetting the interrupt controller chip after each interrupt. Each task within the kernel has its own stack, but while handling interrupts a special stack of size *K_STACK_BYTES*, defined here on line 4304, is used. This is also defined within the machine-dependent section, since a different architecture could require more or less stack space.

Other definitions are machine-independent, but needed by many parts of the kernel codes. For instance, the MINIX scheduler has *NQ* (3) priority queues, named *TASK_Q* (highest priority), *SERVER_Q* (middle priority), and *USER_Q* (lowest priority). The names are used to make the source code understandable, but the numeric values defined by these macros are actually compiled into the executable program. Finally, the last line of *const.h* defines *printf* as a macro which will evaluate as *printk*. This allows the kernel to print messages, such as error messages, on the console using a procedure defined within kernel. This bypasses the usual mechanism, which requires passing messages from the kernel to the file system, and then from the file system to the printer task. During a system failure this might not work. We will see calls to *printf*, alias *printk*, in a kernel procedure called *panic*, which, as you might expect, is invoked when fatal errors are detected.

The file *type.h* defines several prototypes and structures used in any implementation of MINIX. The *tasktab* structure defines the structure of an element of the *tasktab* array and the *memory* structure defines the two quantities that uniquely specify an area of memory. This is a good place to mention some concepts used in referring to memory. A *click* is the basic unit of measurement of memory; in MINIX for Intel processor a click is 256 bytes. Memory is measured as *phys_clicks*, which can be used by the kernel to access any memory element anywhere in the system, or as *vir_clicks*, used by processes other than the kernel. A *vir_clicks* memory reference is always with respect to the base of a segment of memory assigned to a particular process, and the kernel often has to make translations between the two. The inconvenience of this is offset by the fact that a process can do all its own memory references in *vir_clicks*. One might suppose that the same unit could be used to specify the size of either type of memory, but there is an advantage to using *vir_clicks* to specify the size of a unit of memory allocated to a process, since when this unit is used a check is done to be sure that no memory is accessed outside of what has been specifically assigned to the current process. This is a major feature of the **protected mode** of modern Intel processors, such as the Pentium and Pentium Pro. Its absence in the early 8086 and 8088 processors caused some headaches in the design of earlier versions of MINIX.

Type.h also contains several machine-dependent type definitions, such as the *port_t segm_t*, and *reg_t* types used on Intel processors, used, respectively, to address I/O ports, memory segments, and CPU registers.

Structures, too, may be machine-dependent. The *stackframe_s* structure, which defines how the machine registers are saved on the stack, is defined for Intel processors. This structure is extremely important—it is used to save and restore the internal state of the CPU whenever a process is put into or taken out of the "running" state. Defining it in a form that can be efficiently read or written by assembly language code reduces the time required for a context switch. *Segdesc_s* is another structure related to the architecture of Intel processors. It is part of the protection mechanism that keeps processes from accessing memory regions outside those assigned to them.

To illustrate differences between platforms a few definitions for the Motorola 68000 family of processors were retained in this file. The Intel processor family includes some models with 16-bit registers and others with 32-bit registers, so the basic *reg_t* type is *unsigned* for the Intel architecture. For Motorola processors *reg_t* is defined as the *u32_t* type. These processors also need a *stackframe_s* structure, but the layout is different, to make the assembly code operations that use it as fast as possible. The Motorola architecture has no need at all for the *port_t* and *segm_t* types, or for the *segdesc_s* structure. There are also several structures defined for the Motorola architecture that have no Intel counterparts.

The next file, *proto.h* (line 4700), is the longest header file we will see. Prototypes of all functions that must be known outside of the file in which they are defined are in this file. All are written using the *_PROTOTYPE* macro discussed in the previous section, and thus the MINIX kernel can be compiled either with a classic C compiler, such as the original MINIX. C compiler, or a modern ANSI Standard C compiler, such as the one which is part of the MINIX Version 2 distribution. A number of these prototypes are system-dependent, including interrupt and exception handlers and functions that are written in assembly language. Prototypes of functions needed by drivers not discussed in this text are not shown. Conditional code for Motorola processors has also been deleted from this and the remaining files we will discuss.

The last of the kernel headers included in the master header is *glo.h*. Here we find the kernel's global variables. The purpose of the macro *EXTERN* was described in the discussion of *include/minix/const.h*. It normally expands into *extern*. Note that many definitions in *glo.h* are preceded by this macro. *EXTERN* is forced to be undefined when this file is included in *table.c*, where the macro *_TABLE* is defined. Including *glo.h* in other C source files makes the variables in *table.c* known to the other modules in the kernel. *Held_head* and *held_tail* are pointers to a queue of pending interrupts. *Proc_ptr* points to the process table entry for the current process. When a system call or interrupt occurs, it tells where to store the registers and processor state. *Sig_procs* counts the number of processes that have signals pending that have not yet been sent to the memory manager for processing. A few items in *glo.h* are defined with *extern* instead of *EXTERN*. These include *sizes*, an array filled in by the boot monitor, the task table, *tasktab*, and the task stack, *t_stack*. The last two are **initialized variables**, a feature of the C language. The use of *EXTERN* macro is not compatible with C-style initialization, since a variable can only be initialized once.

Each task has its own stack with *t_stack*. During interrupt handling, the kernel uses a separate stack, but it is not declared here, since it is only accessed by the assembly language level routine that handles interrupt processing, and does not need to be known globally.

There are two more kernel header files that are widely used, although not so much that they are included in *kernel.h*. The first of these is *proc.h*, which defines a process table entry as a struct *proc*. Later on in the same file, it defines the process table itself as an array of such structs, *proc[NR_TASKS + NR_PROCS]*. In the C language this reuse of a name is permitted. The macro *NR_TASKS* is defined in *include/minix/const.h* and *NR_PROCS* is defined in *include/minix/config.h*. Together these set the size of the process table. *NR_PROCS* can be changed to create a system capable of handling a larger number of users. Because the process table is accessed frequently, and calculating an address in an array requires slow multiplication operations, an array of pointers to the process table elements, *pproc_addr*, is used to allow speedy access.

Each table entry contains storage for the process' registers, stack pointer, state, memory map, stack limit, process id, accounting, alarm time, and message information. The first part of each process table entry is a *stackframe_s* structure. A process is put into execution by loading its stack pointer with the address of its process table entry and popping all the CPU register from this structure. When a process cannot complete a SEND because the destination is not waiting, the sender is put onto a queue pointed to by the destination's *p_callerq* field. That way, when the destination finally does a RECEIVE, it is easy to find all the processes waiting to send to it. The *p_sendlink* field is used to link the members of the queue together.

When a process does a RECEIVE and there is no message waiting for it, it blocks and the number of the process it wants to RECEIVE from is stored in *p_getfrom*. The address of the message buffer is stored in *p_messbuf*. The last three fields in each process table slot are *p_nextready*, *p_pending*, and *p_pendcount*. The first is of these used to link processes together on the scheduler queues, and the second is a bit map used to keep track of signals that have not yet been passed to the memory manager (because the memory manager is not waiting for a message). The last field is a count of these signals.

The flag bits in *p_flags* define the state of each table entry. If any of the bits is set, the process cannot be run. The various flags are defined. If the slot is not in use, *P_SLOT_FREE* is set. After a FORK, *NO_MAP* is set to prevent the child process from running until its memory map has been set up. *SENDING* and *RECEIVING* indicate that the process is blocked trying to send or receive a message. *PENDING* and *SIG_PENDING* indicate that signals have been received, and *P_STOP* provides support for tracing, during debugging.

The macro *proc_addr* is provided because it is not possible to have negative subscripts in C. Logically, the array *proc* should go from *–NR_TASKS* to+*NR_PROCS*. Unfortunately, in C it must start at 0, so *proc*[0] refers to the most negative task, and so forth. To make it easier to keep track of which slots goes with which process, we can write

rp = proc_addr(*n*);

to assign to *rp* the address of the process slot for process n, either positive or negative.

Bill_ptr points to the process being charged for the CPU. When a user process calls the file system, and the file system is running, *proc_ptr* (in *glo.h*) points to the file system process. However, *bill_ptr* will point to the user making the call, since CPU time used by the file system is charged as system time to the caller.

The two arrays *rdy_head* and *rdy_tail* are used to maintain the scheduling queues. The first process on, for example, the task queue is pointed to by *rdy_head*[*TASK_Q*].

Another header that is included in a number of different source files is *protect.h*. Almost everything in this file deals with architecture details of the Intel processors that support protected mode (the 80286, 80386, 80486, Pentium and Pentium Pro). A detailed description of these chips is beyond the scope of this book. Suffice it to say that they contain internal registers that point to **descriptor tables** in memory. Descriptor tables define how system resources are used and prevent process from accessing memory assigned to other processes. In addition the processor architecture provides for four **privilege levels**, of which MINIX takes advantage of three. The most central parts of the kernel, the parts that run during interrupts and that switch processes, run with *INTR_PRIVILEGE*. There is no part of memory or register in the CPU that cannot be accessed by a process with this privilege level. The task run at *TASK_PRIVILEGE* level, which allows them to access I/O but not to use instructions that modify special registers, like those that point to descriptor tables. Servers and user processes run at *USER_PRIVILEGE* level. Processes executing at this level are unable to execute certain instructions, for instance those that access I/O ports, change memory assignments, or change privilege levels themselves. The concept of privilege levels will be familiar to those who are familiar with the architecture of modern CPUs, but those who have learned computer architecture through study of the assembly language of low-end microprocessors may not have encountered such restrictions.

There are several other header files in the kernel directory, but we will mention only two more here. First, there is *sconst.h*, which contains constants used by assembler code. These are all offsets into the *stackframe_s* structure portion of a process table entry, expressed in a form usable by the assembler. Since assembler code is not processed by the C compiler, it is simpler to have such definitions in a separate file. Also, since these defintions are all machine dependent, isolating them here simplifies the process of porting MINIX to another processor which will need a different version of *sconst.h*. Note that many offsets are expressed as the previous value plus *W*. This allows the same file to serve for compiling a 16-bit or 32-bit version of MINIX.

There is a potential problem here. Header files are supposed to allow one to provide a single correct set of definitions and then proceed to use them in many places without devoting a lot of further attention to the details. Obviously, duplicate definitions, like those in *sconst.h*, violate that principle. This is a special case, of course, but as such, special attention is required if changes are made either to this file or to *proc.h*, to ensure the two files are consistent.

The final header we will mention here is *assert.h*. The POSIX standard requires the availability of an *assert* function, which can be used to make a run-time test and abort a program, printing a message. In fact, POSIX requires that an *assert.h* header be provided in the *include/* directory, and one is provided there. So why is there another version here? The answer is that when something goes wrong in a user process, the operating system can be counted upon to provide services such as printing a message to the console. But if something goes wrong in the kernel itself, the normal system resources cannot be counted upon. The kernel thus provides its own routines to handle *assert* and print messages, independently of the versions in the normal system library.

There are a few header files in *kernel/* we have not discussed yet. They support the I/O tasks and will be described in the next chapter where they are relevant. Before passing on to the executable code, however, let us look at *table.c*, whose compiled object file will contain all the kernel data structures. We have already seen many of these data structures defined, in *glo.h* and *proc.h*. The macro *_TABLE* is defined, immediately before the #include statements. As explained earlier, this definition causes *EXTERN* to become deined as the null string, and storage space to be allocated for all the data declarations preceded by *EXTERN*. In addition to the structures in *glo.h* and *proc.h*, storage for a few global variables used by the terminal task, defined in *tty.h*, is also allocated here.

In addition to the variables declared in header files there are two other places where global data storage is allocated. Some definitions are made directly in *table.c*. Stack space is allocated for each task. For each optional task the corresponding *ENABLE_XXX* macro (defined in the file *include/minix/config.h*) is used to calculate the stack size. Thus no space is allocated for a task that is not enabled. Following this, the various *ENABLE_XXX* macros are used to determine whether each optional task will be represented in the *tasktab* array, composed of *tasktab* structures, as declared earlier in *src/kernel/type.h*. There is an element for each process that is started during system initialization, whether task, server, or user process (i.e., *init*). The array index implicitly maps between task numbers and the associated startup procedures. *Tasktab* also specifies the stack space needed for each process and provides an identification string for each process. It has been put here rather than in a header file because the trick with *EXTERN* used to prevent multiple declarations does not work with initialized variables; that is, you may not say extern int $x = 3$;

anywhere. The previous definitions of stack size also permit allocation of stack space for all the tasks.

Despite trying to isolate all users-settable configuration information in *include/minix/config.h*, an error is possible in matching the size of the *tasktab* array to *NR_TASKS*. At the end of *table.c* a test is made for this error, using a little trick. The array *dummy_tasktab* is declared here in such a way that its size will be impossible and will trigger a compiler error if a mistake has been made. Since the dummy array is declared as *extern*, no space is allocated for it here (or anywhere). Since it is not referenced anywhere else in the code, this will not bother the compiler.

The other place where global storage is allocated is at the end of the assembly language file *mpx386.s*. This allocation, at the label *_sizes*, puts a magic number (to identify a valid MINIX kernel) at the very beginning of the kernel's data segment. Additional space is allocated here by the .space pseudoinstruction. Reservation of storage in this way by the assembly language program makes it possible to force the *_sizes* array to be physically located at the beginning of the kernel's data segment, making it easy to program *boot* to put the data in the right place. The boot monitor reads the magic number and, if it is correct, overwrites it to initialize the *_sizes* array with the sizes of different parts of the MINIX system. The kernel uses these data during initialization. At startup time, as far as the kernel is concerned, this is an initialized data area. However, the data the kernel eventually finds there are not available at compilation time. They are patched in by the boot monitor just before the kernel is started. This is all somewhat unusual normally one does not need to write programs that know about the internal structure of other programs. But the period of time after power is applied, but before the operating system is running, is nothing if not unusual and requires unusual techniques.

Bootstrapping MINIX

It is almost time to start looking at the executable code. But before we do that let us take a few moments to understand how MINIX is loaded into memory. It is, of course, loaded from a disk. Figure 4.31 shows how diskettes and partitioned disks are laid out.

When the system is started, the hardware (actually, a program in ROM) reads the first sector of the boot disk and executes the code found there. On an Unpartitioned MINIX diskette the first sector is a bootblock which loads the boot program, as in Fig. 4.31(a). Hard disks are partitioned, and the program on the first sector reads the partition table, which is also in the first sector, and loads and executes the first sector of the active partition, as shown in Fig 4.31 (b). (Normally one and only one partition is marked active). A MINIX partition has the same structure as an unpartitioned MINIX diskette, with a bootblock that loads the boot program.

The actual situation can be a little more complicated than the figure shows, because a partition may contain sub-partitions. In this case the first sector of the partition will be another master boot record containing the partition table for the sub-partitions. Eventually, however, control will be passed to a boot sector, the first sector on a device that is not further sub-divided. On a diskette the first sector is always a boot sector. MINIX does allow a form of partitioning of a diskette, but only the first partition may be booted; there is no separate master boot record, and subpartitions are not possible. This makes it possible for partitioned and nonpartitioned diskettes to be mounted in exactly the same way. The main use for a partitioned floppy disk is that it provides a convenient way to divide an installation disk into a root image to be copied to a RAM disk and a mounted portion that can be dismounted when no longer needed, in order to free the diskette drive for continuing the installation process.

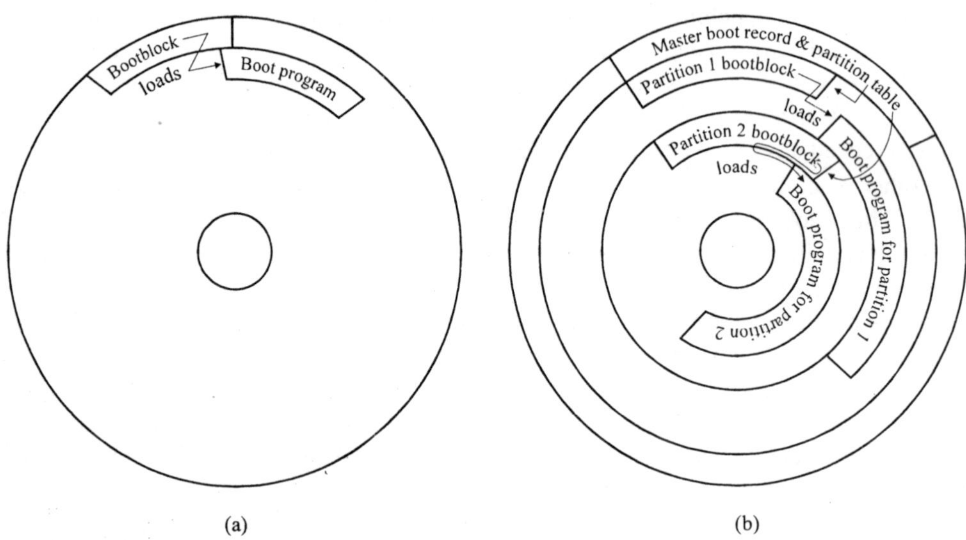

***Fig. 4.31.**Disk structures used for bootstrapping. (a) Unpartitioned disk. The first sector is the bootblock. (b) Partitioned disk. The first sector is the master boot record.*

The MINIX boot sector is modified at the time it is written to the disk by patching in the sector numbers needed to find a program called *boot* on its partition or sub-partition. This patching is necessary because previous to loading the operating system there is no way to use the directory and file names to find a file. A special program called *installboot* is used to do the patching and writing of the boot sector. *Boot* is the secondary loader for MINIX. It can do more than just load the operating system however, as it is a **monitor program** that allows the user to change, set, and save various parameters. *Boot* looks in the second sector of its partition to find a set of parameters to use. MINIX, like standard UNIX, reserves the first 1K block of every disk device as a **bootblock**, but only one 512-byte sector is loaded by the ROM boot loader or the master boot sector, so 512 bytes are available for saving settings. These control the boot operation, and are also passed to the operating system itself. The default settings present a menu with one choice, to start MINIX, but the setting can be modified to present a more complex menu allowing other operating systems to be started (by loading and executing boot sectors from other partitions), or to start MINIX with various options. The default settings can also be modified to bypass the menu and start MINIX immediately.

Boot is not a part of the operating system, but it is smart enough to use the file system data structures to find the actual operating system image. By default, *boot* looks for a file called */minix*, or, if there is a */minix/* directory, for the newest file within it, but the boot parameters can be changed to look for a file with any name. This degree of flexibility is unusual, and most operating systems have a predefined file name for the system image. But, MINIX is an unusual operating system that encourages users to modify it and create experimental new versions. Prudence demands that users who do this should have a way to select multiple versions, in order to be able to return to the last version that worked correctly when an experiment fails.

The MINIX image loaded by *boot* is nothing more than a concatenation of the individual files produced by the compiler when the kernel, memory manager, file system, and *init* programs are compiled. Each of these includes a short header of the type defined in *include/a.out.h*, and from the information in the header of each part, *boot* determines how much space to reserve for uninitialized data after loading the executable code and the initialized data for each part, so the next part can be loaded at the proper address. The *_sizes* array mentioned in the previous section also receives a copy of this information so the kernel itself can have access to the locations and sizes of all the modules loaded by *boot*. The regions of memory available for loading the bootsector, *boot* itself, and MINIX will depend upon the hardware. Also, some machine architectures may require adjustment of internal addresses within executable code to correct them for the actual address where a program is loaded. The segmented architecture of Intel processors makes this unnecessary. Since details of the loading process differ with machine type, and *boot* is not itself part of the operating system, we will not discuss it further here. The important thing is that by one means or another the operating system is loaded into memory. Once the loading is complete, control passes to the executable code of the kernel.

As an aside, we should mention that operating systems are not universally loaded from local disks. **Diskless workstations** may load their operating systems from a remote disk, over a network connection. This requires network software in ROM, of course. Although details vary from what we have described here, the elements of the process are likely to be similar. The ROM code must be just smart enough to get an executable file over the net that can then obtain the complete operating system. If MINIX were loaded this way, very little would need to be changed in the initialization process that occurs once the operating system code is loaded into memory. It would, of course, need a network server and a modified file system that could access files via the network.

System Initialization

MINIX for IBM PC-type machines can be compiled in 16-bit mode if compatibility with older processor chips is required, or in 32-bit mode for better performance on 80386+ processors. The same C source code is used and the compiler generates the appropriate output depending upon whether the compiler itself is the 16-bit or 32-bit version of the compiler. A macro defined by the compiler itself determines the definition of the *_WORD_SIZE* macro in *include/minix/config.h*. The first part of MINIX to execute is written in assembly language, and different source code files must be used for the 16-bit or 32-bit compiler. The 32-bit version of the initialization code is in *mpx386.s*. The alternative, for 16-bit systems, is in *mpx88.s*. Both of these also include assembly language support for other low-level kernel operations. The selection is made automatically in *mpx.s*. This file is so short that the entire file can be presented in Fig. 4.32.

```
#include <minix/config.h>
#if_ WORD_SIZE = = 2
#include "mpx88.s"
#else
```

(Contd.)

```
#include "mpx386.s"
#endif
```

***Fig. 4.32.**How alternative assembly language source files are selected.*

Since this is our first look at executable code, let us start with a few words about how we will do this throughout the book. The multiple source file used in compiling a large C program can be hard to follow. In general, we will keep discussions confined to a single file at a time, and we will go in order through the files. We will start with the entry point for each part of the MINIX system, and we will follow the main line of execution. When a call to a supporting function is encountered, we will say a few words about the purpose of the call, but normally we will not go into a detailed description of the internals of the function at that point, leaving that until we arrive at the definition of the called function. Important subordinate functions are usually defined in the same file in which they are called, following the higher-level calling functions, but small or general-purpose functions are sometimes collected in separate files. Also, an attempt has been made to put machine-dependent code in separate files from machine-independent code to facilitate portability to other platforms. A substantial amount of effort has been made to organize the code, and, in fact, many files were rewritten in the course of writing this text in order to organize them better for the reader. But a large program has many branches, and sometimes understanding a main function requires reading the functions it calls, so having a few slips of paper to use as bookmarks and deviating from our order of discussion to look at things in a different order may be helpful at times.

Having laid out our intended way of organizing the discussion of the code, we must start off by immediately justifying a major exception. The startup of MINIX involves several transfers of control between the assembly language routines in *mpx386.s* and routines written in C and found in the files *start.c* and *main.c*. We will describe these routines in the order that they are executed, even though that involves jumping from one file to another.

Once the bootstrap process has loaded the operating system into memory, control is transferred to the label *MINIX*. The first instruction is a jump over a few bytes of data; this includes the boot monitor flags used by the boot monitor to identify various characteristics of the kernel, most importantly, whether it is a 16-bit or 32-bit system. The boot monitor always starts in 16-bit mode, but switches the CPU to 32-bit mode if necessary. This happens before control passes to *MINIX*. The monitor also sets up a stack. There is a substantial amount of work to be done by the assembly language code, setting up a stack frame to provide the proper environment for code compiled by the C compiler, copying tables used by the processor to define memory segments, and setting up various processor registers. As soon as this work is complete, the initialization process continues by calling the C function *cstart*. Note that it is referred to as *_cstart* in the assembly language code. This is because all functions compiled by the C compiler have an underscore prepended to their names in the symbol tables, and the linker looks for such names when separately compiled modules are linked. Since the assembler does not add underscores, the writer of an assembly language program must explicitly add one in order for the linker to be able to find a corresponding name in the object file compiled by the C compiler. *Cstart* calls another routine to initialize the **Global Descriptor Table,** the central data structure used by Intel 32-bit processors to oversee memory protection, and the **Interrupt Descriptor Table**, used to select the code to be executed for each possible interrupt type. Upon returning from *cstart* the lgdt and lidt instructions make these tables effective by loading the dedicated registers by which they are addresses. The following instruction, jmpf CS_SELECTOR:csinit

looks at first glance like a no-operation, since it transfers control to exactly where control would be if there were a series of nop instructions in its place. But this is an important part of the initialization process. This jump forces use of the structures just initialized. After some more manipulation of the processor registers, *MINIX* terminates with a jump (not a call) to the kernel's *main* entry point (in *main.c*). At this point the initialization code in *mpx386.s* is complete. The rest of the file contains code to start or restart a task or process, interrupt handlers, and other support routines that had to be written in assembly language for efficiency. We will return to these in the next section.

We will now look at the top-level C initialization functions. The general strategy is to do as much as possible using high-level C code. There are already two versions of the *mpx* code, as we have seen, and anything that can be off-loaded to C code eliminates two chunks of assembler code. Almost the first thing done by *cstart* is to set up the CPU's protection mechanism and the interrupt tables, by calling *prot_init*. Then it does such things as copying the boot parameters to the kernel's part of memory and converting them into numeric values. It also determines the type of video display, size of memory, machine type, processor operating mode (real or protected), and whether a return to the boot monitor is possible. All information is stored in appropriate global variables, for access when needed by any part of the kernel code.

Main, completes initialization and then starts normal execution of the system. It configures the interrupt control hardware by calling *intr_init*. This is done here because it cannot be done until the machine type is known, and the procedure is in a separate file because it is so dependent upon the hardware. The parameter (1) in the call tells *intr_init* that it is initializing for MINIX. With a parameter (0) it can be called to reinitialize the hardware to the original state. The call to *intr_init* also takes two steps to insure that any interrupts that occur before initialization is complete have no effect. First a byte is written to each interrupt controller chip that inhibits response to external input. Then all entries in the table used to access device-specific interrupts handler are filled in with the address of a routine that will harmlessly print a message if a spurious interrupt is received. Later these table entries will be replaced, one by one, with pointers to the handlers routines, as each of the I/O tasks runs its own initialization routine. Each task then will reset a bit in the interrupt controller chip to enable its own interrupt input.

Mem_init is called next. It initializes and array that defines the location and size of each chunk of memory available in the system. As with the initialization of the interrupt hardware, the details are hardware-dependent and isolation of *mem_init* as a function in a separate file keeps *main* itself free of code that is not portable to different hardware.

The largest part of *main*'s code is devoted to setup of the process table, so that when the first tasks and processes are scheduled, their memory maps and registers will be set correctly. All slots in the process table are marked as free, and the *pproc_addr* array that speeds access to the process table is initialized by the loop

(pproc_addr + NR_TASKS)[*t*] = *rp*;

could just as well have been defined as

pproc_addr[*t* + NR_TASKS] = *rp*;

because in the C language *a*[*i*] is just another way writing *(*a* + *i*). So it does not make much difference if you add a constant to *a* or to *i*. Some C compilers generate slightly better code if you add a constant to the array instead of the index.

Initializes the process table with the necessary information to run the tasks, servers, and *init*. All of these processes must be present at startup time and none of them will terminate during normal operation. At the start of the loop, *rp* is assigned the address of a process table entry. Since *rp* is a pointer to a structure, the elements of the structure can be accessed using notation like *rp –>p_name*, as is done. This notation is used extensively in the MINIX source code.

The tasks, of course, are all compiled into the same file as the kernel, and the information about their stack requirements is in the *tasktab* array defined in *table.c*. Since tasks are compiled into the kernel and can call code and access data located anywhere in the kernel's space, the size of an individual task is not meaningful, and the size field for each of them is filled with the sizes for the kernel itself. The array *sizes* contains the text and data sizes in clicks of the kernel, memory manager, file system, and *init*. This information is patched into the kernel's data area by *boot* before the kernel starts executing and appears to the kernel as if the compiler had provided it. The first two elements of *sizes* are the kernel's text and data sizes; the next two are the memory manager's, and so on. If any of the four programs does not use separate I and D space, the text size is 0 and the text and data are lumped together as data. Assigning *sizeindex* a value of zero for each of the tasks assures that the zeroth element of *sizes* will be accessed for all of the tasks. The assignment to *sizeindex* gives each of the servers and *init* its own index into *sizes*.

The design of the original IBM PC placed read-only memory at the top of the usable range of memory, which is limited to 1 MB on an 8088 CPU. Modern PC-compatible machines always have more memory than the original PC, but for compatibility they still have read-only memory at the same addresses as the older machines. Thus, the read-write memory is discontinuous, with a block of ROM between the lower 640 KB and the upper range above 1 MB. The boot monitor loads the servers and *init* into the memory range above the ROM if possible. This is primarily for the benefit of the file system, so a very large block cache can be used without bumping into the read-only memory. The conditional code ensures that this use of the high memory area is recorded in the process table.

Two entries in the process table correspond to processes that do not need to be scheduled in the ordinary way. These are the *IDLE* and *HARDWARE* processes. *IDLE* is a do-nothing loop that is executed when there is nothing else ready to run, and the *HARDWARE* process exists for book keeping purpose—it is credited with the time used while servicing an interrupt. All other processes are put on the appropriate queues by the code. The function called, *lock_ready*, sets a lock variable, *switching*, before modifying the queues and then removes the lock when the queue has been modified. The locking and unlocking are not required at this point, when nothing is running yet, but this is the standard method, and there is no point in creating extra code to be used just once.

The last step in initializing each slot in the process table is to call *alloc_segments*. This procedure is part of the system task, but of course no tasks are running yet, and it is called as an ordinary procedure. It is a machine-dependent routine that sets into the proper fields the locations, sizes, and permission levels for the memory segments used by each process. For older Intel processors that do not support protected mode, it defines only the segment locations. It would have to be rewritten to handle a processor type with a different method of allocating memory.

Once the process table is initialized for all the tasks, the servers, and *init*, the system is almost ready to roll. The variable *bill_ptr* tells which process gets billed for processor time; it needs to have an initial value set, and *IDLE* is an appropriate choice. Later on it may be changed by the next function called, *lock_pick_proc*. All of the tasks are now ready to run and *bill_prt* will be changed when a user process runs. *Lock_pick_proc*'s other job is to make the variable *proc_ptr* point to the entry in the process table for the next process to be run. This selection is made by examining the task, server, and user process queues, in that order. In this case, the result is to point *proc_ptr* to the entry point for the console task, which is always the first one to be started.

Finally, *main* has run its course. In many C programs *main* is a loop, but in the MINIX kernel its job is done once the initialization is complete. The call to *restart* starts the first task. Control will never return to *main*.

Restart is an assembly language routine in *mpx386.s*. In fact, *restart is* not a complete function; it is an intermediate entry point in a larger procedure. We will discuss it in detail in the next section; for now we will just say that–*restart* causes a context switch, so the process pointed to by *proc_ptr* will run. When *_restart* has executed for the first time we can say that MINIX is running—it is executing a process. *_Restart* is executed again and again as tasks, servers, and user processes are given their opportunities to run and then are suspended, either to wait for input or to give other processes their turns.

The task queued first (the one using slot 0 of the process table, that is, the one with the most negative number) is always the console task, so other tasks can use it to report progress or problems as they start. It runs until it blocks trying to receive a message. Then the next task will run until it, too, blocks trying to receive a message. Eventually, all the tasks will be blocked, so the memory manager and file system can run. Upon running for the first time, each of these will do some initialization, but both of them will eventually block, also. Finally *init* will fork off a *getty* process for each terminal. These processes will block until input is typed at some internal, at which point the first user can log in.

We have now traced the startup of MINIX through three files, two written in C and one in assembly language. The assembly language file, *mpx386.s*, containing additional code is used in handling interrupts, which we will look at in the next section. However, before we go on let us wrap up with a brief description of the remaining routines in the two C files. The other procedures in *start.c* are *k–atoi* (line 6594), which coverts a string to an integer, and *k–getenv* which is used to find entries in the kernel's environment, which is a copy of the boot parameters. These are both simplified versions of standard library functions which are rewritten here in order to keep the kernel simple. The only remaining procedure in *main.c* is *panic*. It is called when the system has discovered a condition that makes it impossible to continue. Typical panic conditions are a critical disk block unreadable, an inconsistent internal state being detected, or one part of the system calling another part with invalid parameters. The calls to *printf* here are actually calls to the kernel routine *printk*, so the kernel can print on the console even if normal interprocess communication is disrupted.

Interrupt Handling in MINIX

The details of interrupt hardware are system dependent, but any system must have elements functionally equivalent to those to be described for systems with 32-bit Intel CPUs. Interrupts generated by hardware devices are electrical signals and are handled in the first place by an interrupt controller, an integrated circuit that can sense a number of such signals and for each one generate a unique data pattern on the processor's data bus. This is necessary because the processor itself has only one input for sensing all these devices, and thus cannot differentiate which device needs service. PCs using Intel 32-bit processors are normally equipped with two such controller chips. Each can handle eight inputs, but one is a slave which feeds its output to one of the inputs of the master, so fifteen distinct external devices can be sensed by the combination, as shown in Fig. 4.33.

In the figure, interrupt signals arrive on the various *IRQ n* lines shown at the right. The connection to the CPU's INT pin tells the processor that an interrupt has occurred, the INTA (interrupt acknowledge) signal from the CPU causes the controller responsible for the interrupt to put data on the system data bus telling the processor which service routine to execute. The interrupt controller chips are programmed during system initialization, when ***main*** call ***intr–init***. The programming determines the output sent to the CPU for a signal received on each of the input lines, as well as various other parameters of the controller's operation. The data put on the bus is an 8-bit number, used to index into a table of up to 256 elements. The MINIX table has 56 elements. Of these, 35 are actually used; the others are reserved for use with future Intel processors or for future enhancements to MINIX. On 32-bit Intel processors this table contains interrupt gate descriptors, each of which is an 8-byte structure with several fields assembly language instruction. The only difference is that in the case of a hardware interrupt the *<nnn>* originates from a register in the interrupt controller chip, rather than from an instruction in program memory.

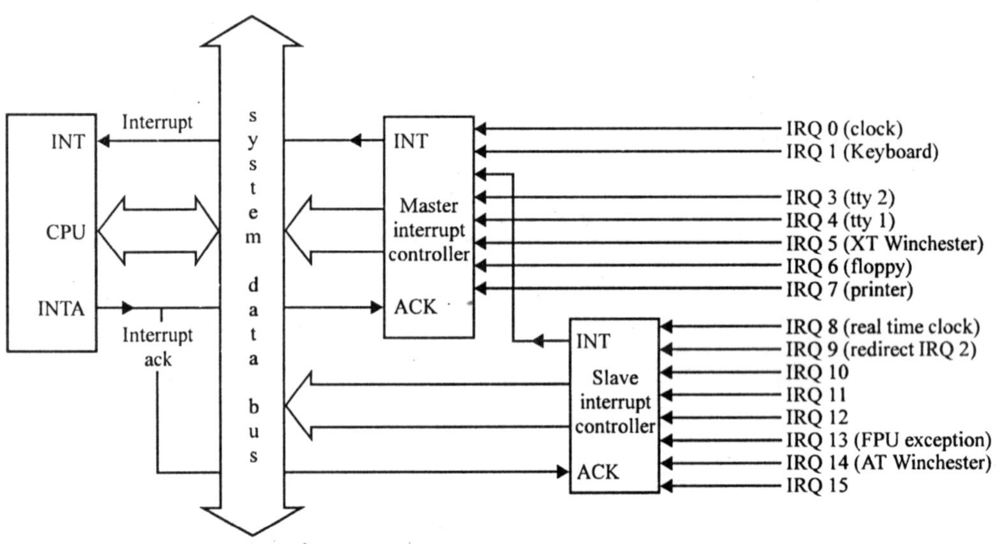

Fig. 4.33. Interrupt processing hardware on a 32-bit Intel PC.

The task-switching mechanism of a 32-bit Intel processor that is called into play in response to an interrupt is complex, and changing the program counter to execute another function is only a part of it. When the CPU receives an interrupt while running a process it sets up a new stack for use during the interrupt service. The location of this stack is determined by an entry in the **Task State**

Segment (TSS). There is one such structure for the entire system, initialized by *cstart's* call to *prot–init*, and modified as each process is started. The effect is that the new stack created by an interrupt always starts at the end of the *stackframe–s* structure within the process table entry of the interrupted process. The CPU automatically pushes several key registers onto this new stack, including those necessary to reinstate the interrupted process' own stack and restore its program counter. When the interrupt handler code starts running, it uses this area in the process table as its stack, and much of the information needed to return to the interrupted process will have already been stored. The interrupt handler pushes the contents of additional registers, filling the stackframe, and then switches to a stack provided by the kernel while it does whatever must be done to service the interrupt.

Termination of an interrupt service routine is done by switching the stack from the kernel stack back to a stackframe in the process table (but not necessarily the same one that was created by the last interrupt), explicitly popping the additional registers, and executing an iretd (return from interrupt) instruction. Iretd restores the state that existed before an interrupt, restoring the registers that were pushed by the hardware and switching back to a stack that was in use before an interrupt. Thus an interrupt stops a process, and completion of the interrupt service restarts a process, possibly a different one from the one that was most recently stopped. Unlike the simpler interrupt mechanisms that are the usual subject of assembly language programming texts, nothing is stored on the interrupted process' working stack during an interrupt. Furthermore, because the stack is created anew in a known location (determined by the TSS) after an interrupt, control of multiple processes is simplified. To start a different process all that is necessary is to point the stack pointer to another process' stackframe, pop the registers that were explicitly pushed, and execute an iretd instruction.

The privilege levels mentioned earlier control the different responses to interrupt received while a process is running and while kernel code (including interrupt service routines) is executing. The simpler mechanism is used when the privilege level of the interrupted code is the same as the privilege level of the code to be executed in response to the interrupt. It is only when the interrupted code is less privilege than the interrupt service code that the more elaborate mechanism, using the TSS and a new stack, is employed. The privilege level of a code segment is recorded in the code segment selector, and as this is one of the items stacked during an interrupt, it can be examined upon return from the interrupt to determine what the iretd instruction must do. Another service is provided by the hardware when a new stack is created to use while servicing an interrupt. The hardware checks to make sure the new stack is big enough for at least the minimum quantity of information that must be placed on it. This protects the more privileged kernel code from being accidentally (or maliciously) crashed by a user process making a system call with an inadequate stack. These mechanisms are built into the processor specifically for use in the implementation of operating systems that support multiple processes.

This behavior may be confusing if you are unfamiliar with the internal working of 32-bit Intel CPUs. Ordinarily we try to avoid describing such details, but understanding what happens when an interrupt occurs and when an iretd instruction is executed is essential to understanding how the kernel controls the transitions to and from the "running" state. The fact that the hardware handles much of the work makes life much easier for the programmer, and presumably makes the resulting system more efficient. All this help from the hardware does, however, make it hard to understand what is happening just by reading the software.

Only a tiny part of the MINIX kernel actually sees hardware interrupts. This code is in *mpx386.s*. There is an entry point for each interrupt. The source code at each entry point. *hwint00* to_hwint07, *looks like* a call to *hwint–master*, and the entry points–*hwint08* to *hwint15* look like calls to *hwint_slave*. Each entry point appears to pass a parameter in the call, indicating which device needs service. In fact, these are really not calls, but macros, and eight separate copies of the code defined by the macro definition of *hwint–master* are assembled, with only the *irq* parameters different. Similarly, eight copies of the *hwint–slave* macro are assembled. This may seem extravagant, but assembled code is very compact. The object code for each expanded macro occupies less than 40 bytes. In servicing an interrupt, speed is important, and doing it this way eliminates the overhead of executing code to load a parameter, call a subroutine, and retrieve the parameter.

We will continue the discussion of *hwint_master* as if it really were a single function, rather than a macro that is expanded in eight different places. Recall that before *hwint–master* begins to execute, the CPU has created a new stack in the interrupted process *stackframe–s,* within its process table slot, and that several key registers have already been saved there. The first action of *hwint–master* is to call *save*. This subroutine pushes all the other registers necessary to restart the interrupted process. *Save* could have been written inline as part of the macro to increase speed, but this would have more than doubled the size of the macro, and in any case *save* is needed for calls by other functions. As we shall see, *save* plays tricks with the stack. Upon returning to *hwint–master*, the kernel stack, not a stackframe in the process table, is in use. The next step is to manipulate the interrupt controller, to prevent it from receiving another interrupt from the source that generated the current interrupt. This operation masks the ability of the controller chip to respond to a particular input; the CPU's ability to respond to all interrupts is inhibited internally when it first receives the interrupt signal and has not yet been restored at this point.

The code resets the interrupt controller and then enables the CPU to again receive interrupts from other sources. Next, the number of the interrupts being serviced is used by the indirect call instruction index into a table of addresses of the device-specific low-level routines. We call these low-level routines, but they are written in C, and they typically perform operations like servicing an input device and transferring the data to a buffer where it can be accessed when the corresponding task has its next chance to run. A substantial amount of processing may happen before the return from this call.

We will see examples of low-level driver code in the next chapter. However, in order to understand what is happening here in *hwint_master,* we now mention that the low-level code may call *interrupt* (in *proc.c,* which we will discuss in the next section), and that *interrupt* transforms the interrupt into a message to the task that services the device that caused the interrupt. Furthermore, a call to *interrupt* invokes the scheduler and may select this task to run next. Upon returning from the call to the device-specific code, the processor's ability to respond to all interrupts is again disabled, by the cli instruction, and the interrupt controller is prepared to be able to respond to the particular device that caused the current interrupt when all interrupts are next re-enabled. Then *hwint_master* terminates with a ret instruction. It is not obvious that something tricky happens here. If a process was interrupted, the stack in use at this point is the kernel stack, and not the stack within a process table that was set up by the hardware before *hwint–master* was started. In this case, manipulation of the stack by *save* will have left the address of–*restart* on the kernel stack. This results in a task, server, or user process once again executing. It may not be, and in fact is unlikely to be, the same process as was executing originally. This depends upon whether the processing of the message created by the device-specific interrupt service routine caused a change in the process scheduling queues. This, then, is the heart of the mechanism which creates the illusion of multiple processes executing simultaneously.

Hwint–slave is very similar to *hwint–master,* except that it must re-enable both the master and slave controllers, since both of them are disabled by receipt of an interrupt by the slave. There are a few subtle aspects of assembly language to be seen here.

```
jmp     .+2
```

which specifies a jump whose target address is the immediately following instruction. This instruction is placed here solely to add a small delay. The authors of the original IBM PC BIOS considered a delay necessary between consecutive I/O instructions, and we are following their example, although it may not be necessary on all current IBM PC-compatible computers. This kind of fine tuning is one reason why programming hardware devices is considered an esoteric craft by some. This does not specify a number of bytes to jump over, as in the previous example. The *Of* here is not a hexadecimal number. This is the way the assembler used by the MINIX compiler specifies a **local label:** the *Of* means a jump **forward** to the next numeric label 0. Ordinary label names are not permitted to begin with numeric characters. Another interesting and possibly confusing point is that the same label occurs elsewhere in the same file, in *hwint–master*. The situation is even more complicated than it looks at first glance since these labels are within macros and the macros are expanded before the assembler sees this code. Thus there are actually sixteen 0: labels in the code seen by the assembler. The possible proliferation of labels declared within macros is, indeed, the reason why the assembly language provides local labels; when resolving a local label the assembler uses the nearest one that matches in the specified direction, and additional occurrences of a local label are ignored.

Now let us move on to look at *save*, which we have already mentioned several times. Its name describes one of its functions, which is to save the context of the interrupt process on the stack provided by the CPU, which is a stackframe within the process table. *Save* uses the variable–*k–reenter* to count and determine the level of nesting of interrupts. If a process was executing when the current interrupt occurred, the

```
mov     esp, k-stktop
```

instruction switches to the kernel stack, and the following instruction pushes the address of *_restart.* Otherwise, the kernel stack is already in use, and the address of *restart1* is pushed instead. In either case, with a possibly different stack in use from the one that was in effect upon entry, and with the return address in the routine that called it buried beneath the registers that have just been pushed, and ordinary return instruction is not adequate for returning to the caller. The

```
jmp     RETADR-P_STACKBASE(eax)
```

instructions that terminate the two exit point of *save,* use the address that was pushed when *save* was called.

The next procedure in *mpx386.s* is *–s–call,* which begins. Before looking at its internal detail, look at how it ends. There is no ret or jmp at its end. After disabling interrupts with the cli, execution continues at *_restart. –S–call* is the system call counterpart of the interrupt handling mechanism.

Control arrives at *–s–call* following a software interrupt, that is, execution of an int *nnn* instruction. Software interrupts are treated like hardware interrupts, except of course the index into the Interrupt Descriptor Table is encoded into the *nnn* part of an int *nnn* instruction, rather than being supplied by an interrupt controller chip. Thus, when s–call is entered, the CPU has already switched to a stack inside the process table (supplied by the Task State Segment), and several registers have already been pushed onto this stack. By falling through to *_restart*, the call to *_s_call* ultimately terminates with an iretd instruction, and, just as with a hardware interrupt, this instruction will start whatever process is pointed to by *proc_ptr* at that point. Figure 4.34 compares the handling of a hardware interrupt and a system call using the software interrupt mechanism.

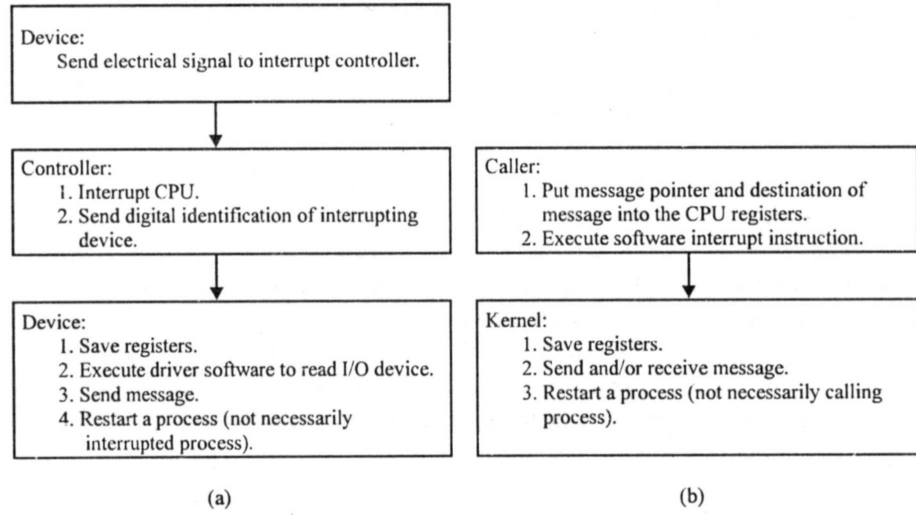

Fig.4.34. *(a) How a hardware interrupt is processed. (b) How a system call is made.*

Let us now look at sosem details of *_s_call.* The alternate label, *_p_s_call,* is a vestige of the 16-bit version of MINIX, which has separate routines for protected mode on real mode operation. In the 32-bit version all calls to either label end up here. A programmer invoking a MINIX system call writes a function call in C that looks like any other function call, whether to a locally defined function or to a routine in the C library. The library code supporting a system call sets up a message, loads the address of the message and the process id of the destination into CPU registers, and then invokes an int *SYS386_VECTOR* instruction. As described above, the result is that control passes to the start of *_s_call,* and several registers have already been pushed onto a stack inside the process table.

The first part of the *_s_call* code resembles an inline expansion of *save* and saves the additional registers that must be preserved. Just an in *save*, a

```
mov     esp, k_sktop
```

instruction then switches to the kernel stack, and interrupts are re-enabled. (The similarity of a software interrupt to a hardware interrupt extends to both, disabling all interrupts). Following this comes a call to *_sys_call,* which we will discuss in the next section. For now we just say that it causes a message to be delivered, and that this in turn causes the scheduler to run. Thus, when *_sys_call* returns, it is probable that *proc_ptr* will be pointing to a different process from the one that initiated the system call. Before execution falls through to *restart,* a clic instruction disables interrupts to protect the stackframe of the process that is about to be restarted.

We have seen that *_restart* is reached in several ways:

1. By a call from *main* when the system starts.
2. By a jump from *hwint_master* or *hwint_slave* after a hardware interrupt.
3. By falling through from *_s_call* after a system call.

In every case interrupts are disabled at this point. *_Restart* calls *unhold* if it detects that any unserviced interrupts have been held up because they arrived while other interrupts were being processed. This allows the other interrupts to be converted into messages before any process is restarted. This temporarily re-enables interrupts, but they are disabled again before *unhold* returns. The next process to run has been definitively chosen, and with interrupts disabled it cannot be changed. The process table was carefully constructed so it begins with a stack frame, and the instruction in this line,

```
mov esp, (_proc_ptr)
```

points the CPU's stack pointer register at the stack frame. The

```
lldt P_LDT_SEL(esp)
```

instruction then loads the processor's local descriptor table register from the stack frame. This prepares the processor to use the memory segments belonging to the next process to be run. The following instruction loads the address in the next process, process table entry that where the stack for the next interrupt will be set up, and the following instruction stores this address into the TSS. The first part of *_restart* is not necessary after an interrupt that occurs when kernel code, (including interrupt service code) is executing, since the kernel stack will be in use and termination of the interrupt service should allow the kernel code to continue. The label *restart 1* marks the point where execution resumes in this case. At this point *k_reenter* is decremented to record that one level of possibly nested interrupts has been disposed of, and the remaining instruction restore the processor to the state it was in when the next process executed last. The penultimate instruction modifies the stack pointer so the return address that was pushed when *save* was called is ignored. If the last interrupt occurred when a process was executing, the final instruction, iretd, completes the return to execution of whatever process is being allowed to run next, restoring its remaining registers, including its stack segment and stack pointer. If however, this encounter with the iretd came via *restart1,* the kernel stack in use is not a stackframe, but the kernel stack, and this is not a return t an interrupted process, but the completion of an interrupt that occurred while kernel code was executing. The CPU detects this when the code segment descriptor is popped from the stack during execution of the iretd, and the complete action of the iretd in this case is to retain the kernel stack in use.

There are a few more things to discuss in *mpx386.s.* In addition to hardware and software interrupts, various error conditions internal to the CPU can cause the initiation of an **exception.** Exceptions are not always bad. They can be used to stimulate the operating system to provide a service, such as providing more memory for a process to use, or swapping in a currently swapped-out memory page, although such services are not implemented in standard MINIX. But, when an exception occurs, it should not be ignored. Exceptions are handled by the same mechanism as interrupts, using descriptors in the interrupt descriptor table. These entries in the table point to the sixteen exception handler entry points, beginning with *_divide_ error* and ending with *_copr_error,* found near the end of *mpx386.s.* These all jump to *exception* or *erreception* depending upon whether the condition pushes an error code onto the stack or not. The handling here in the assembly code is similar to that we have already seen, registers are pushed and the C routine *_exception* (note the underscore) is called to handle the event. The consequences of exceptions vary. Some are ignored, some cause panics, and some result in sending signals to processes. We will examine *_exception* in a later section.

There is one other entry point that is handled like an interrupt, *_level0_call.* Its function will be discussed in the next section, when we discuss the code to which it jumps, *level0_func.* The entry point is here in *mpx386.s* with the interrupt and exception entry points because it too is invoked by execution of an int instruction. Like the exception routines, it calls *save,* and thus eventually the code that is jumped to here will terminate by a ret that leads to *_restart.* The last executable function in *mpx386.s* is *_idle_task.* This is a do nothing loop that is executed whenever there is no other process ready to run.

Finally, some data storage space is reserved at the end of the assembly language file. There are two different data segments defined here. The

```
.sect.rom
```

declaration ensures that this storage space is allocated at the very beginning of the kernel's data segment. The compiler puts a magic number here so *boot* can verify that the file it loads is a valid kernel image. *Boot* then overwrites the magic number and subsequent space with the *_sizes* array data, as described in the discussion of kernel data structures. Enough space is reserved here of a *_sizes* array with a total of sixteen entries, in case additional servers are added to MINIX.

Interprocess Communication in MINIX

Processes in MINIX communicate by messages, using the rendezvous principle. When a process does a SEND, the lowest layer of the kernel checks to see if the destination is waiting for a message from the sender (or from ANY sender). If so, the message is copied from the sender's buffer to the receiver's buffer, and both processes are marked as runnable. If the destination is not waiting for a message from the sender, the sender is marked as blocked and put onto a queue of processes waiting to send to the receiver.

When a process does a RECEIVE, the kernel checks to see if any process is queued trying to send to it. If so, the message is copied from the blocked sender to the receiver, and both are marked as runnable. If no process is queued trying to send to it, the receiver blocks until a message arrives.

The high-level code for interprocess communication is found in *proc.c.* The kernel's job is to translate either a hardware interrupt or a software interrupt into a message. The former are generated by hardware and the latter are the way a request for system services, that is, a system call, is communicated to the kernel. These cases are similar enough that they could have been handled by a single function, but it was more efficient to create two specialized functions.

First we will look at *interrupt.* It is called by the low-level interrupt service routine for a device after receipt of a hardware interrupt. *Interrupt's* function is to convert the interrupt into a message for the task that handles the interrupt in device, and typically very little processing is done before calling *interrupt.* For example, the entire low-level interrupt handler for the hard disk driver consists of just these three lines:

```
w_status = in_byte(w_wn->base + REG_STATUS); /* acknowledges interrupt */
interrupt(WINCHESTER);
return 1;
```

if it were not necessary to read an I/O port on the hard disk controller to obtain the status, the call to *interrupt* could have been in *mpx386.s* instead of *at_winic.c.* The first thing *interrupt* does is check if an interrupt was already being serviced when the current interrupt was received, by looking at the variable *k_reenter.* In this case the current interrupt is queued and *interrupt* returns. The current interrupt will be serviced later, when *unhold* is called. The next action is to check whether the task is waiting for an interrupt. If the task is not ready to receive, its *p_int_blocked* flag is set—we will see later that this makes it possible to recover that lost interrupt—and no message is sent. If this test is passed, the message is sent. Sending a message from *HARDWARE* to a task is simple, because the tasks and the kernel are compiled into the same file and can access the same data areas. The code sends the message, by filling in the destination task's message buffer source and type fields, resetting the destination's *RECEIVING* flag, and unblocking the task. Once the message is ready the destination task is scheduled to run. We will discuss scheduling in more detail in the next section. It is simple here, since messages originating from interrupts go only to tasks, and thus there is no need to determine which of the three process queues needs to be changed.

The next function in *proc.c* is *sys_call.* It has a similar function to *interrupt:* it converts a software interrupt (the int *SYS386_VECTOR* instruction by which a system call is initiated) into a message. But since there are a wider range of possible sources and destination in this case, and since the call may require either sending or receiving or both sending and receiving a message, *sys_call* has more work to do. As is often the case, this means the code for *sys_call* is short and simple, since it does most of its work by calling other procedures. The first such call is to *isoksrc_des,* a macro defined in *proc.h*), which incorporates yet another macro, *isokprocn,* also defined in *proc.h.* The effect is to check to make sure the process specified as the source or destination of the message is valid. A similar test, *isuserp* (also a macro defined in *proc.h),* is performed to make sure that if the call is from a user process it is asking to send a message and then receive a reply, the only kind of call permitted to user processes. Such errors are unlikely, but the tests are easily done, as ultimately they compile into code to perform comparisons of small integers. At this most basic level of the operating system testing for even the most unlikely errors is advisable. This code is likely to be executed many times each second during every second that the computer systems on which it runs is active.

Finally, if the call requires sending a message, *mini_send* is called, and if receiving a message is required, *mini_rec* is called. These functions are the heart of the normal message passing mechanism of MINIX and deserve careful study.

Mini_send has three parameters: the caller, the process to be sent to, and a pointer to the buffer where the message is. It performs a number of tests. First, it makes sure that user process tries to send messages only of FS or MM.

The parameter *caller_ptr* is tested with the macro *isuserp* to determine if the caller is a user process, and the parameter *dest* is tested with a similar function, *issysentn,* to determine if it is FS or MM. If the combination is not permitted *mini_send* terminates with an error.

Next a check is made to be sure the destination of the message is an active process, not an empty slot in the process table *mini_send* checks to see if the message falls entirely within the user's data segment, code segment, or the gap between them. If not, an error code is returned.

The next test is to check for a possible deadlock. It is a test to make sure the destination of the message is not trying to send a message back to the caller.

Here a check is made to see if the destination is blocked on a RECEIVE, as shown by the *RECEIVING* bit in the *p_flags* field of its process table entry. If it is waiting, then the next question is: "Who is it waiting for?" If it is waiting for the sender, or for ANY, *CopyMess* is executed to copy the message and the receiver is unblocked by resetting its *RECEIVING* bit. *CopyMess* is defined as a macro. It calls the assembly language routine *cp_mess* in *klib386.s*.

If, on the other hand, the receiver is not blocked, or is blocked but waiting for a message from someone else, the code is executed to block and queue the sender. All processes wanting to send to a given destination are strung together on a linked list, with the destination's *p_callerq* field pointing to the process table entry of the process at the head of the queue. The example of Fig 4.35 (a) shows what happens when process 3 is unable to send to process 0. If process 4 is subsequently also unable to send to process 0, we get the situation of Fig. 4.35 (b).

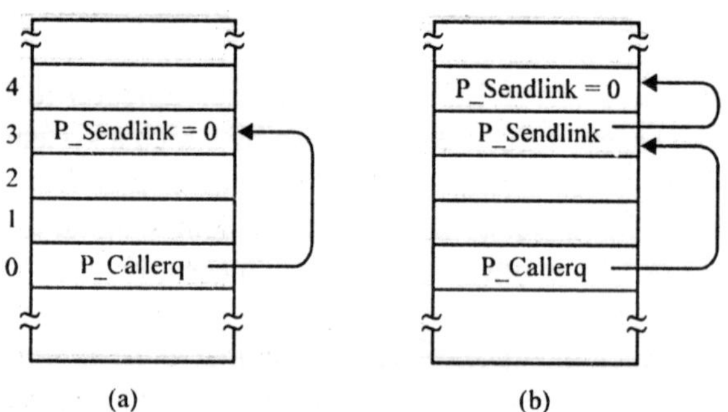

Fig.4.35. Queueing of processes trying to send to process 0.

Mini_rec is called by *sys_call* when its *function* parameter is *RECEIVES* or *BOTH.* The loop searches through all the processes queued waiting to send to the receiver to see if any are acceptable. If one is found, the message is copied from sender to receiver; then the sender is unblocked, made ready to run, and removed from the queue of processes trying to send to the receiver.

If no suitable sender is found, a check is made to see if the receiving process, *p_int_blocked* flag indicates that an interrupt for this destination was previously blocked. If so a message is constructed at this point—since messages from *HARDWARE* have no content other than *HARDWARE* in the source field and *HARD_INT* in the type field there is no need to call *CopyMess* in this case.

If a blocked interrupt is not found the process source and buffer address are saved in its process table entry, and it is marked as blocked with its *RECEIVING* bit set. The call to *unready* removes the receiver from the scheduler's queue of runnable processes. The call is conditional to avoid blocking the process just yet if there is another bit set in its *p_flags;* a signal may be pending, and the process should have another chance to run soon to deal with the signal.

The penultimate statement in *mini_rec* has to do with how the kernel-generated signals *SIGINT, SIGQUIT,* and *SIGALRM* are handled. When one of these occurs, a message is sent to the memory manager, if it is waiting for a message from ANY. If not, the signal is remembered in the kernel until the memory manager finally tries to receive from ANY. That is tested here, and, if necessary, *inform* is called to inform it of the pending signals.

Scheduling in MINIX

MINIX uses a multilevel scheduling algorithm that closely follows the structure shown in Fig. 4.36. In that figure we see I/O tasks in layer 2, server processes in layer 3, and user processes in layer 4. The scheduler maintains three queues of runnable process, one for each layer, as shown in Fig.4.36. The array *rdy_head* has one entry for each queue, with that entry pointing to the process at the head of the queue. Similarly, *rdy_tail* is an array whose entries point to the last process on each queue. Both of these arrays are defined with the *EXTERN* macro in *proc.h.*

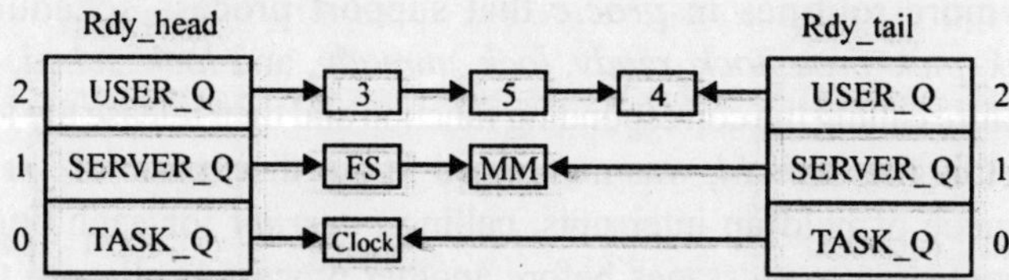

Fig.4.36. The scheduler maintains three queues, one per priority level.

Whenever a blocked process is awakened, it is appended to the end of its queue. The existence of the array *rdy_tail* makes adding a process to the end of a queue efficient. Whenever a running process becomes blocked, or a runnable process is killed by a signal, that process is removed from the scheduler's queues. Only runnable processes are queued.

Given the queue structures just described, the scheduling algorithm is simple: find the highest priority queue that is not empty and pick the process at the head of the queue. If all the queues are empty, the idle routine is run. In Fig. 4.36 *TASK_Q* has the highest priority. The scheduling code is in *proc.c*. The queue is chosen in *pick_proc*. This function's major job is to set *proc_ptr*. Any change to the queues that might affect the choice of which process to run next requires *pick_proc* to be called again. Whenever the current process blocks, *pick_proc* is called to reschedule the CPU.

Pick_proc is simple. There is a test for each queue. *TASK_Q* is tested first, and if a process on this queue is ready, *pick_proc* sets *proc_ptr* and returns immediately. Next, *SERVER_Q* is tested, and again, if a process is ready *pick_proc* sets *proc_ptr* and returns. If there is a ready process on the *USER_Q* queue, *bill_ptr* is changed to charge the user process for the CPU time it is about to be given. This assures that the last user process to run is charged for work done on its behalf by the system. If none of the queues have a ready task transfers billing to the *IDLE* process and schedules it. The process chosen to run is not removed from its queue merely because it has been selected.

The procedures *ready* and *unready* are called to enter a runnable process on its queue and remove a no-longer runnable process from its queue, respectively. *Ready* is called from both mini_*send* and *mini_rec*, as we have seen. It could also have been called from *interrupt*, but in the interest of speeding up interrupt processing its functional equivalent was written into *interrupt* as inline code. *Ready* manipulates one of the three process queues. It straightforwardly adds the process to the tail of the appropriate queue.

Unready also manipulates the queues. Normally, the process it removes is at the head of its queue, since a process must be running in order to block. In such a case *unready* calls *pick_proc* before returning, as, for example, a user process that is not running can also become unready if it is sent a signal, and if the process is not found at the head of one of the queues, a search is made through the *USER_Q* for it, and it is removed if found.

Although most scheduling decisions are made when a process blocks or unblocks, scheduling must also be done when the clock task notices that the current user process has exceeded its quantum. In this case the clock task calls *sched* to move the process at the head of *USER_Q* to the end of that queue. This algorithm results in running user processes in a straight round-robin fashion. The file system, memory manager, and I/O tasks are never put on the end of their queues because they have been running too long. They are trusted to work properly, and to block after having finished their work.

There are few more routines in *proc.c* that support process scheduling. Five of these, *lock_mini_send*, *lock_pick_proc*, *lock_ready*, *lock_unready*, and *lock_sched*, set a lock, using the variable *switching* before calling the corresponding function and then release the lock upon completion. The last function in this file, *unhold*, was mentioned in our discussion of *_restart* in *mpx386.s*. It loops through the queue of held-up interrupts, calling *interrupt* for each one, in order to get all pending interrupts converted to messages before another process is allowed to run.

Hardware-Dependent Kernel Support

There are several C functions that are very dependent upon the hardware. To facilitate porting MINIX to other systems these functions are segregated in the files to be discussed in this section, *exception.c*, *i8259.c*, and *protect.c*, rather than being included in the same files with the higher-level code they support

Exception.c contains the exception handler, *exception*, which is called (as *_exception*) by the assembly language part of the exception handling code in *mpx386.s*. Exceptions originating from user processes are converted to signals. Users are expected to make mistakes in their own programs, but an exception originating in the operating system indicates something is seriously wrong and causes a panic. The array *ex_data* determines the error message to be printed in case of panic, or the signal to be sent to a user process for each exception. Earlier Intel processors do not generate all the exceptions, and the third field in each entry indicates the minimum processor model that is capable of generating each one. This array provides an interesting summary of the evolution of the Intel family of processors upon which MINIX has been implemented.

The three functions in *i8259.c* are used during system initialization to initialize the Intel 8259 interrupt controller chips. *Intr_init* initializes the controllers. It writes data to several port locations. On a few lines a variable derived from the boot parameters is tested, for instance, the first port writes, to accommodate different computer models. The parameter *mine* is tested, and a value appropriate either for MINIX or for the BIOS ROM is written to the port. When leaving MINIX *intr_init* can be called to restore the BIOS vectors, allowing a graceful exit back to the boot monitor. *Mine* selects the mode to use. Fully understanding what is going on here would require study of the documentation for the

8259 integrated circuit, and thus we will not dwell on the details. We will point out that the *out_byte* call makes the master controller unresponsive to any input except from the slave, and the similar operation inhibits the response of the slave to all of its inputs. Also, the final line of the function preloads the address of *spurious_irq*, the next function in the file, into each slot in *irq_table*. This ensures that any interrupt generated before the real handlers are installed will do no harm.

The last function in *i8259.c* is *put_irq_handler*. At initialization each task that must respond to an interrupt calls this to put its own handler address into the interrupt table, overwriting the address of *spurious_irq*.

Protect.c contains routines related to protected mode operation of Intel processors. The **Global Descriptor Table** (GDT), **Local Descriptor Tables** (LDTs), and the **Interrupt Descriptor Table,** all located in memory, provide protected access to system resources. The GDT and IDT are pointed to by special registers within the CPU, and GDT entries point to LDTs. The GDT is available to all processes and holds segment descriptors for memory regions used by the operating system. There is normally one LDT for each process, holding segment descriptors for the memory regions used by the process. Descriptors are 8-byte structures with a number of components, but the most important parts of a segment descriptor are the fields that describe the base address and the limit of a memory region. The IDT is also composed of 8-byte descriptors, with the most important part being the address of the code to be executed when the corresponding interrupt is activated.

Prot_init is called by *start.c* to set up the GDT. The IBM PC BIOS requires that it be ordered in a certain way, and all the indices into it are defined in *protect.h*. Space for an LDT for each process is allocated in the process table. Each contains two descriptors, for a code segment and a data segment—recall we are discussing here segments as defined by the hardware; these are not the same as the segments managed by the operating system, which consider the hardware-defined data segment to be further divided into data and stack segments. The entries in the LDTs themselves are initialized when a process' memory map is changed (i.e., when an EXEC system call is made).

Another processor data structure that needs initialization is the **Task State Segment** (TSS). The structure is defined at the start of this file and provides space for storage of processor registers and other information that must be saved when a task switch is made. MINIX uses only the fields that define where a new stack is to be built when an interrupt occurs. The call to *init_dataseg* ensures that it can be located using the GDT.

To understand how MINIX works at the lowest level, perhaps the most important thing is to understand how exceptions, hardware interrupts, or int *<nnn>* instructions lead to the execution of the various pieces of code that has been written to service them. This is accomplished by means of the interrupt gate descriptor table. The array *gate_table*, is initialized by the compiler with the addresses of the routines that handle exception and hardware interrupts and then is used in the loop to initialize a large part of this table, using calls to the *init_gate* function. The remaining vectors, *SYS_VECTOR*, *SYS386_VECTOR*, and *LEVEL0_VECTOR*, require different privilege levels and are initialized following the loop.

There are good reasons for the way the data are structured in the descriptors, based on details of the hardware and the need to maintain compatibility between advanced processors and the 16-bit 286 processor. Fortunately, we can normally leave these details to Intel's processor designers. For the most part the C language allows us to avoid the details. However, in implementing a real operating system the details must be faced at some point. Figure 4.37 shows the internal structure of one kind of segment descriptor. Note that the base address, which C programs can refer to as a simple 32-bit unsigned integer, is split into three parts, two of which are separated by a number of 1-, 2-, and 4-bit quantities. The limit is a 20-bit quantity stored as separate 16-bit and 4-bit chunks. The limit is interpreted as either a number of bytes or a number of 4096-byte pages, based on the value of the *G* (granularity) bit. Other descriptors, such as those used to specify how interrupts are handled, have different, but equally complex structures.

Most of the other functions defined in *protect.c* are devoted to converting between variables used in C programs and the rather ugly forms these data take in the machine readable descriptors such as the one in Fig 4.37. *Init_codeseg* and *init_dataseg* are similar in operation and are used to convert the parameters passed to them into segment descriptors. They each, in turn, call the next function. This is where the messy details of the structure shown in Fig 4.37 are dealt with. *Init_codeseg* and *init_data_seg* are not used just at system initialization. In addition, they are also called by the system task whenever a new process is started up, in order to allocate the proper memory segments for the process to use. *Seg2phys* called only from *start.c* performs an operation which is the inverse of that of *sdesc*, extracting the base address of a segment from a segment descriptor. *Init_gate* performs a similar function to *init_codeseg* and *init_dataseg* in building entries for the interrupt descriptor table.

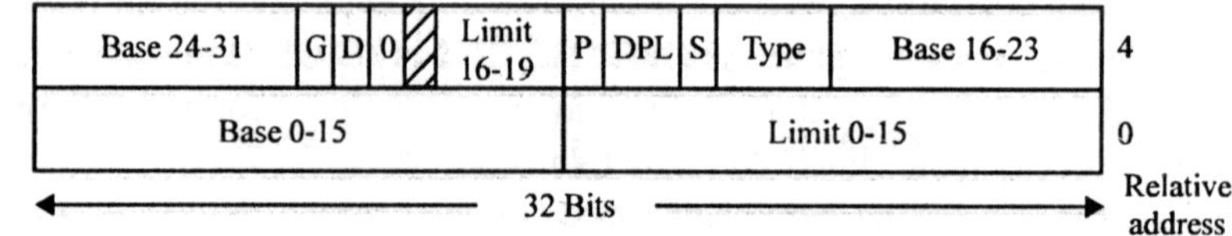

Fig. 4.37. The format of an Intel segment descriptor.

The final function in *protect.c*, *enable_iop* performs a dirty trick. We have pointed out in several places that one function of an operating system is to protect system resources, and one way MINIX does so is by using privilege levels to make certain kinds of instructions off limits to user programs. However, MINIX is also intended to be run on small systems, which are likely to have only one user or perhaps just a few trusted users. On such a system a user could very well want to write an application program that accesses I/O ports, for instance, for use in scientific data acquisition. The file system has a little secret built into it—when the files */dev/mem* or */dev/kmem* are opened, the memory task calls *enable_iop*, which changes the privilege level for I/O operations, allowing the current process to execute instructions which read and write I/O ports. The description of the purpose of the function is more complicated than the function itself, which just sets two bits in the word in the stack frame entry of the calling process that will be loaded into the CPU status register when the process is next executed. There is no need for another function to undo this, as it will apply only to the calling process.

Utilities and the Kernel Library

Finally, the kernel has a library of support functions written in assembly language that are included by compiling *klib.s* and a few utility programs, written in C, in the file *misc.c*. Let us first look at the assembly language files. *Klib.s*, is a short file similar to *mpx.s*, which selects the appropriate machine-specific version based upon the definition of *WORD_SIZE*. The code we will discuss is in *klib386.s*. This contains about two dozen utility routines that are in assembly code, either for efficiency or because they cannot be written in C at all.

_Monitor makes it possible to return to the boot monitor. From the point of view of the boot monitor all of MINIX is just as subroutine, and when MINIX is started, a return address to the monitor is left on the monitor's stack. *_Monitor* just has to restore the various segment selectors and the stack pointer that was saved when MINIX was started, and the return as from any other subroutine.

The next function, *_check_mem*, is used at startup time to determine the size of a block of memory. It performs a simple test on every sixteenth byte, using two patterns which test every bit with both "0" and "1"values.

Although *_phys_copy* (see below) could have been used for copying messages, *_cp_mess*, a faster specialized procedure, has been provided for that purpose. It is called by

cp_mess(source, src_clicks, src_offset, dest_clicks, dest_offset);

where *source* is the sender's process number, which is copied into the *m_source* field of the receiver's buffer. Both the source and destination addresses are specified by giving a click number, typically the base of the segment containing the buffer, and an offset from that click. This form of specifying the source and destination is more efficient than the 32-bit addresses used by *_phys_copy*.

Exit, * _exit*, and *_ _ _exit* are defined because some library routines that might be used in compiling MINIX make calls to the standard C function *exit*. An exit from kernel is not a meaningful concept; there is nowhere to go. The solution here is to enable interrupts and enter an endless loop. Eventually, an I/O operation or the clock will cause an interrupt and normal system operation will resume. The entry point for *_ _ _main* is another attempt to deal with a compiler action which, while it might make sense while compiling a user program, does not have any purpose in the kernel. It points to an assembly language ret (return from subroutine) instruction.

The next two short functions are very specific to Intel processors. *_Mem_rdw* returns a 16-bit word from anywhere in memory. The result is zero-extended into the 32-bit *eax* register. The *_reset* function resets the processor. It does this by loading the processor's interrupt descriptor table register with a null pointer and then executing a software interrupt. This has the same effect as a hardware reset.

The next two routines support the video display and are used by the console task. *_Mem_vid_copy* copies a string of words containing alternate character and attribute bytes from the kernel's memory region to the video display memory. *_Vid_vid_copy* copies a block within the video memory itself. This is somewhat more complicated, since the destination block may overlap the source block, and the direction of the move is important.

The last function in this file is *_level0*. It allows tasks to have the most privilege permission level, level zero, when necessary. It is used for such things as resetting the CPU or accessing the PC's ROM BIOS routines.

The C language utilities in *misc.c* are specialized. *Mem_init* is called only by *main*, when MINIX is first started. There can be two or three disjoint regions of memory on an IBM-PC compatible computer. The size of the lowest range, known to PC users as "ordinary" memory, and of the memory range that starts above the PC ROM area ("extended" memory) are reported by the BIOS to the boot monitor, which in turn passes the values as boot parameters, which are interpreted by *cstart* and written to *low_memsize* and *ext_memsize* at boot time. The third region is "shadow" memory, into which the BIOS ROM may be copied to provide an improvement in performance, since ROM memory is usually slower than writeable memory. Since MINIX does not normally use the BIOS, *mem_init* attempts to locate this memory and add it to the pool of memory available for its use. It does this calling *ckeck_mem* to test the memory region where this memory may sometimes be found.

The last two routines we will discuss in this chapter are *bad_assertion* and *bad_compare*. They are compiled only if the macro *DEBUG* is defined as *TRUE*. They support the macros in *assert.h*. Although they are not referenced in any of the code discussed in this text, they may be useful for debugging to the reader who wants to create a modified version of MINIX.

5

Real Storage

Storage Organization

Historically, main storage has been viewed as a relatively expensive resource. As such, it has demanded the attention of system designers who attempted to optimize main storage use. Although the cost of main storage has declined phenomenally in recent years, it is still relatively expensive compared to secondary storage. Also, today's applications demand ever more substantial quantities of main storage.

By *storage organization* we mean the manner in which the main storage is viewed. Do we place only a single user in the main storage, or do we place several users in it at the same time? If several user programs are in main storage at the same time, do we give each of them the same amount of space, or do we divide main storage into portions, called *partitions*, of different sizes? Do we partition the main storage in a rigid manner with partitions defined for extended periods of time, or do we provide for a more dynamic partitioning, allowing the computer system to adapt quickly to changes in the needs of user jobs? Do we require that user jobs be designed to run in a specific partition, or do we allow jobs to run anywhere they will fit? Do we require that each job be placed in one contiguous block of storage locations, or do we allow jobs to be parcelled up into separate blocks and placed in any available slots in main storage?

Storage Management

Regardless of what storage organization scheme we adopt for a particular system, we must decide what strategies to use to obtain optimal performance. *Storage management strategies* determine how a particular storage organization performs under various policies: When do we get a new program to place in the memory? Do we get it when the system specifically asks for it, or do we attempt to anticipate the system's request? Where in main storage do we place the next program to be run? Do we place programs as tightly as possible into available memory slots to minimize wasted space, or do we place programs quickly as possible to minimize execution time?

If a new program needs to be placed in main storage and if main storage is currently full, which of the other programs do we displace? Should we replace the oldest programs or should we replace those that are least frequently used, or those that are least recently used? Systems have been implemented using each of these storage management strategies.

Storage Hierarchy

In the 1950s and 1960s, main storage, usually magnetic core memory, was very expensive. A decision about how much main storage to place on a computer system was made carefully. An installation couldn't buy more than it could afford, but it had to buy enough to support the operating system and a given number of users. The goal was to buy the minimum amount that could adequately support the anticipated user loads within the economic constraints of the installation.

Programs and data need to be in main storage in order to be executed or referenced. Programs or data not needed immediately may be kept on secondary storage until needed and then brought into the main storage for execution or reference. Secondary storage media such as tape or disk are generally less costly than main storage and have much greater capacity. Main storage may generally be accessed much faster than secondary storage.

In systems with several levels of storage, a great deal of shuttling goes on in which programs and data are moved back and forth between the various levels. This shuttling consumes system resources such as CPU time that could otherwise be put to productive use.

In the 1960s it became clear that the *storage hierarchy* could be extended by one more level with dramatic improvements in performance and utilization. This additional level, the *cache* is a high-speed storage that is much faster than main storage. Cache storage is extremely expensive compared with main storage and therefore only relatively small caches are used. Figure 5.1 shows the relationship between cache, primary storage, and secondary storage.

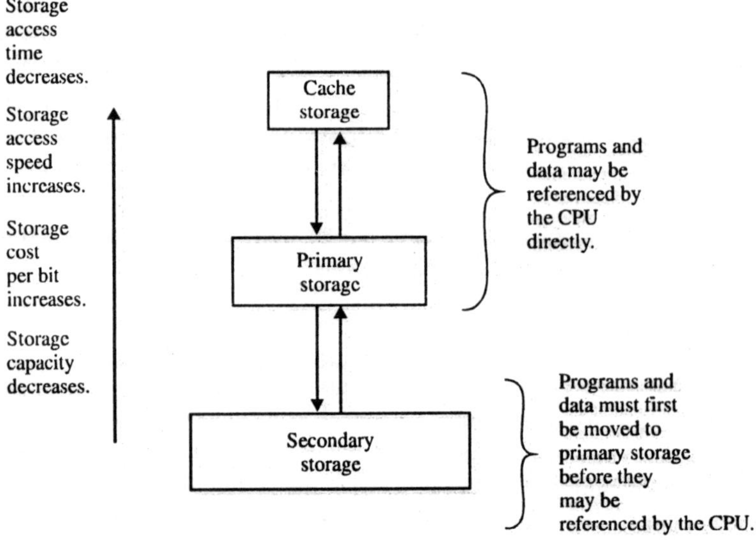

Fig. 5.1. Hierarchical storage organization.

Cache storage imposes one more level of shuttling on the system. Programs in the main storage are shuttled to the cache before being executed. In the cache, they may be executed much faster than in main storage. The hope of designers using the cache concept is that the overhead involved in shuttling programs back and forth will be much smaller than the performance increase obtained by the faster execution possible in the cache.

Storage Management Strategies

Expensive resources are managed intensively to achieve better use. Storage management strategies are geared to obtaining the best possible use of the main storage resource. Storage management strategies are divided into the following categories.

1. Fetch strategies
   (a) Demand fetch strategies
   (b) Anticipatory fetch strategies
2. Placement strategies
3. Replacement strategies

Fetch strategies are concerned with when to obtain the next piece of program or data for transfer to main storage from secondary storage. For many years, the conventional wisdom has been *demand fetch*, in which the next piece of program or data is brought in to the main storage when it is referenced by a running program. It was believed that since we cannot generally predict where program control will go next, the overhead involved in making guesses and anticipating the future would far exceed expected benefits. Today many researchers feel that *anticipatory fetching* will yield improved system performance.

Placement strategies are concerned with determining where in main storage to place an incoming program. In this chapter, we shall consider the *first-fit, best-fit*, and *worst-fit* storage placement strategies.

Replacement strategies are concerned with determining which piece of program or data to displace to make room for incoming programs.

Contiguous Vs. Noncontiguous Storage Allocation

The earliest computing systems required *contiguous storage allocation*—each program had to occupy a single contiguous block of storage locations. It wasn't until variable partition multiprogramming was attempted that it became clear noncontiguous storage allocation might be useful.

In *noncontiguous storage allocation*, a program is divided into several blocks or *segments* that may be placed throughout main storage in pieces not necessarily adjacent to one another. It is more difficult for an operating system to control noncontiguous storage allocation. The benefit is that if main storage has many small holes available instead of a single large hole, then the operating system can often load and execute a program that would otherwise need to wait.

Single User Contiguous Storage Allocation

The earliest computer systems allowed only a single person at a time to use the machine. All of the machine's resources were at the user's disposal. Billing for the use of the computer was straightforward—because the user had the entire machine, the user was charged for all of the resources whether or not the job used those resources. In fact, the normal billing mechanisms were based upon *wall clock time.* A user was given the machine for some time interval and was charged a flat hourly rate. Some of today's shared systems have far more complex billing algorithms.

Originally each user wrote all of the code necessary to implement a particular application, including the highly detailed machine level input/output instructions. Very quickly, the input/output coding needed to implement basic functions was consolidated into an *input/output control system (IOCS).* Users wishing to do input/output no longer had to code the instructions directly. Instead, they called ICOS routines to do the real work. This greatly simplified and speeded the coding process. The implementation of input/output control systems may have been the beginning of today's concept of operating systems. Figure 5.2 illustrates the storage organization for a typical *single user contiguous storage allocation system.*

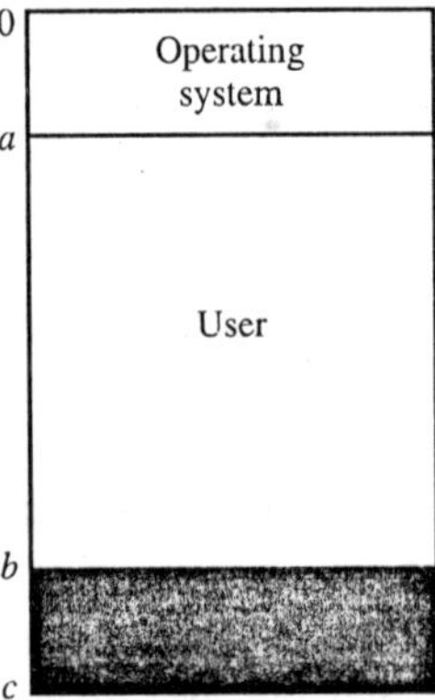

Fig. 5.2. *Single user contiguous storage allocation.*

Programs are limited in size to the amount of main storage, but it is possible to run programs larger than the main storage by using *overlays.* Figure 5.3 illustrates this concept. If a particular program section is not needed for the duration of the program's execution, then another section of program may be brought in from secondary storage to occupy the storage used by the program section that is no longer needed.

Overlay gives the programmer a way to extend limited main storage. But manual overlay requires careful and time-consuming planning. A program with a sophisticated overlay structure can be difficult to modify. As we will see in subsequent chapters, virtual storage systems have obviated the need for programmer-controlled overlays.

Protection in Single User Systems

In single user contiguous storage allocation systems, the user has complete control over all of main storage. Storage is divided into a portion holding operating system routines, a portion holding the user's program, and an unused portion. The question of protection is simple. How should the operating system be protected from destruction by the user's program?

If the user's program goes astray, it can destroy the operating system. If this is fatal and the user cannot proceed, then the user will know something is wrong, terminate execution, fix the problem, and retry the job. In these circumstances, the need for protecting the operating system is not apparent.

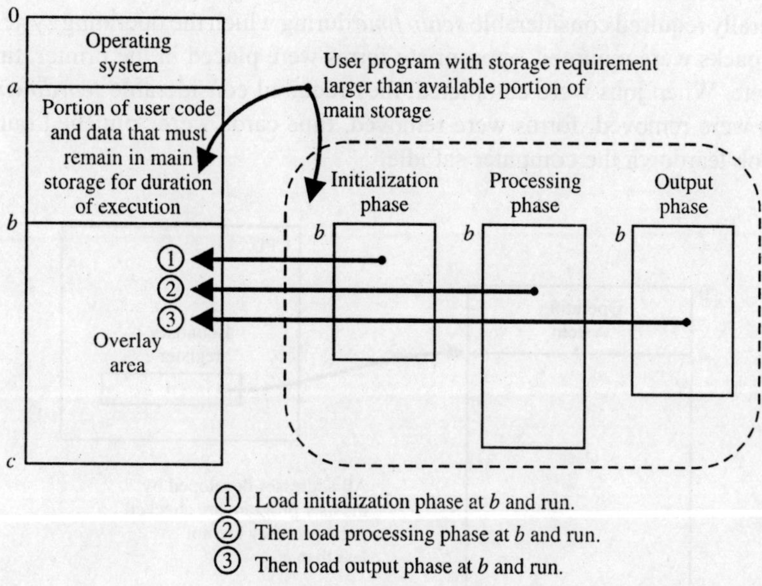

Fig. 5.3. A typical overlay structure.

But suppose the user destroys the operating system more "gently." For example, suppose certain input/output routines are accidentally changed. Then all output records might be truncated. The job could still run. If the results are not examined until it completes, then the machine resource will be wasted. Worse yet, the damage to the operating system might cause output to be produced that can not easily be determined to be inaccurate.

It surely is clear that the operating system should be protected from the user. Protection is implemented by the use of a *single boundary register* built into the CPU, as in Fig. 5.4. Each time a user program refers to a storage address, the boundary register is checked to be certain that the user is not about to destroy the operating system. The boundary register contains the highest address used by the operating system. If the user tries to enter the operating system, the instruction is intercepted and the job terminates with an appropriate error message.

Of course, the user needs to enter the operating system from time to time to obtain services such as input/output. This problem is solved by giving the user a specific instruction with which to request services from the operating system (i.e., *a supervisor call* instruction).The user wanting to read from tape will issue an instruction asking the operating system to do so in the user's behalf. The operating system will perform the desired function, and then return control to the user program.

As operating systems have become more complex, it has been necessary to implement far more sophisticated mechanisms to protect the operating system from the users and to protect the users from one another. We shall discuss these mechanisms in detail later.

Single Stream Batch Processing

Early single-user real storage systems were dedicated to one job for more than the job's execution time. Jobs generally required considerable *setup time* during which the operating system was loaded, tapes and disk packs were mounted, appropriate forms were placed in the printer, time cards were "punched in," etc. When jobs were completed, they required considerable *teardown time* as tapes and disk packs were removed, forms were removed, time cards were "punched out," etc. During job setup and job teardown the computer sat idle.

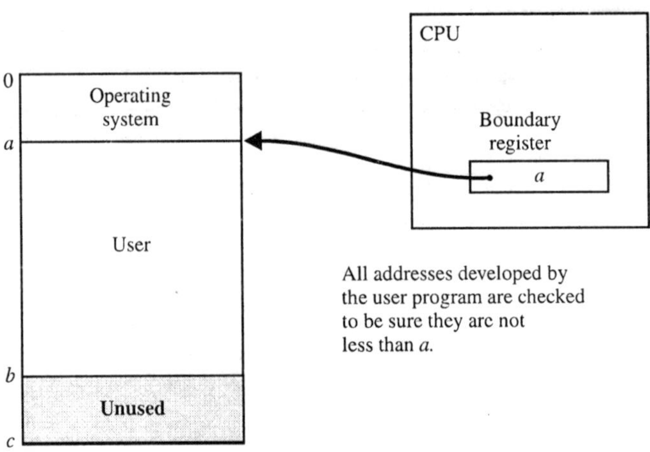

Fig. 5.4. Storage protection with single user contiguous storage allocation.

Designers realized that if they could automate *job-to-job transition,* then they could reduce considerably the amount of time wasted between jobs. This led to the development of *batch processing* systems. In *single stream batch processing*, jobs are grouped in *batches* by loading them consecutively onto tape or disk. A *job stream processor* reads the *job control language* statements, and facilitates the *setup* of the next job. It issues directives to the system operator, and performs many functions automatically that were previously performed manually. When the current job terminates, the job steam reader automatically reads in the control language statements for the next job, and performs appropriate *housekeeping* chores to facilitate the transition to the next job. Batch processing systems greatly improved the use of computer systems and helped demonstrate the real value of operating systems and *intensive resource management.* Single stream batch processing systems were the state of the art in the early 1960s.

Fixed Partition Multiprogramming

Even with batch processing operating systems, single user systems still waste a considerable amount of the computing resource. Figure 5.5 illustrates this situation. The program consumes the CPU resource until an input or output is needed. When the I/O request is issued, the job often cannot continue until the requested data is either sent or received. Input and output speeds are extremely slow compared with CPU speeds.

Designers saw that they could once again considerably increase the utilization of the CPU by intensive management. This time, they chose to implement *multiprogramming* systems, in which several users simultaneously compete for system resources. The job currently waiting for I/O will yield the CPU to another job ready to do calculations if, indeed, another job is waiting. Thus both input/output and CPU calculations can occur simultaneously. This greatly increases CPU utilization and system throughput.

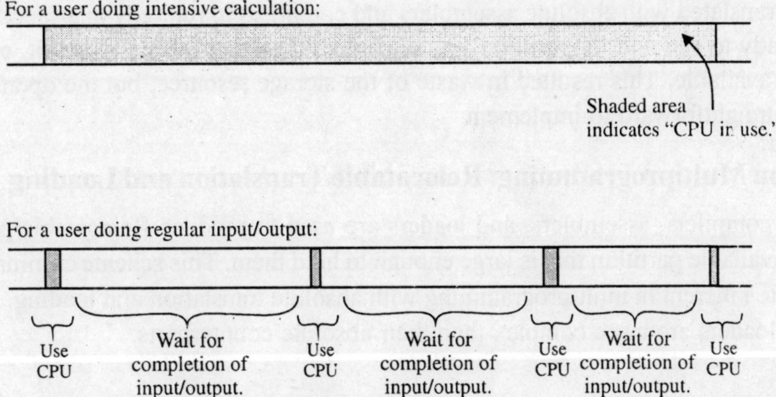

Fig. 5.5. CPU utilization on a single user system. Note: In many single user jobs, the length of the input/output waits is much larger relative to the length of periods of CPU utilization than is indicated in this diagram.

To make maximum advantage of multiprogramming, it is necessary for several jobs to reside in the computer's main storage at once. Thus when one job requests input/output, the CPU may be immediately switched to another, and may do calculations without delay. When this new job yields the CPU, another may be ready to use it.

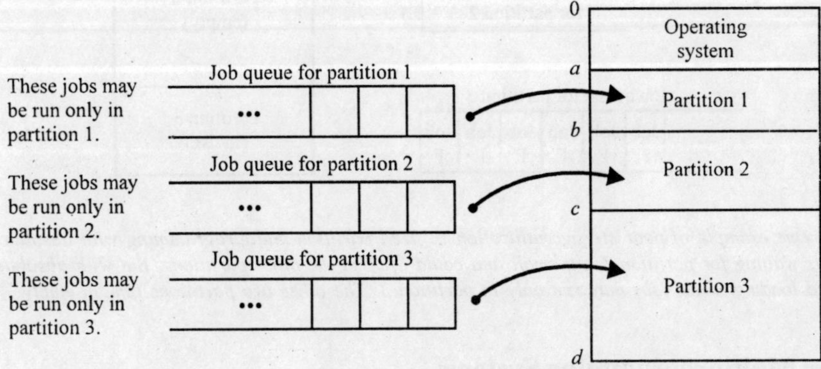

Fig. 5.6. Fixed partition multiprogramming with absolute translation and loading.

Multiprogramming normally requires considerably more storage than a single user system. However, the improved resource use for the CPU and the peripheral devices more than justifies the expense of additional storage. Many multiprogramming schemes have been implemented. We discuss these in the next several sections.

Fixed Partition Multiprogramming: Absolute Translation and Loading

The earliest multiprogramming systems used *fixed partition multiprogramming* in which main storage was divided into a number of fixed-size partitions. *Each* partition could hold a single job. The CPU was switched rapidly between users to create the illusion of simultaneity

Jobs were translated with absolute assemblers and compilers to run only in a specific partition. If a job was ready to run and its partition was occupied, then that job had to wait, even if other partitions were available. This resulted in waste of the storage resource, but the operating system was relatively straightforward to implement.

Fixed Partition Multiprogramming: Relocatable Translation and Loading

Relocating compilers, assemblers, and loaders are used to produce Relocatable program that can run in any available partition that is large enough to hold them. This scheme eliminates some of the storage waste inherent in multiprogramming with absolute translation and loading. Relocatable translators and loaders are more complex than their absolute counterparts.

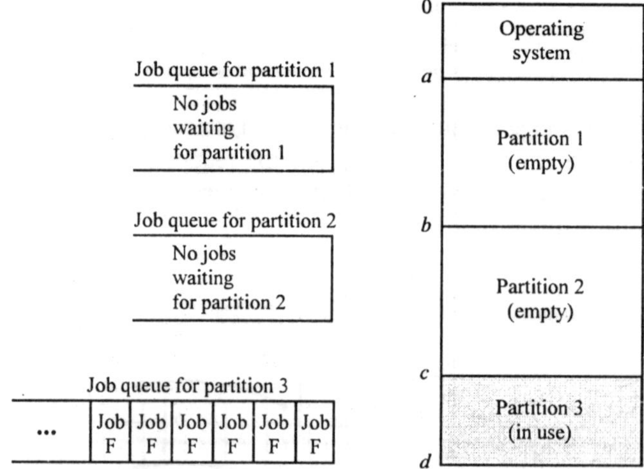

Fig.5.7. An extreme example of poor storage utilization in fixed partition multiprogramming with absolute translation and loading. Jobs waiting for partition 3 are small and could "fit" in the other partitions. But with absolute translation and loading, these jobs may run only in partition 3. The other two partitions remain empty.

Protection in Multiprogramming Systems

In contiguous allocation multiprogramming systems, protection is often implemented with several *boundary registers.* With two registers the low and high boundaries of a user partition can be delineated, or the low boundary (high boundary) and the length of the region can be indicated. The user needing to call upon the operating system uses a supervisor call instruction to do so. This allows the user to cross the boundary of the operating system and request its services without compromising operating system security.

Fragmentation in Fixed Partition Multiprogramming

Storage *fragmentation* occurs in every computer system regardless of its storage organization. In fixed partition multiprogramming systems, fragmentation occurs either because user jobs do not completely fill their designated partitions or because a partition remains unused if it is too small to hold a waiting job.

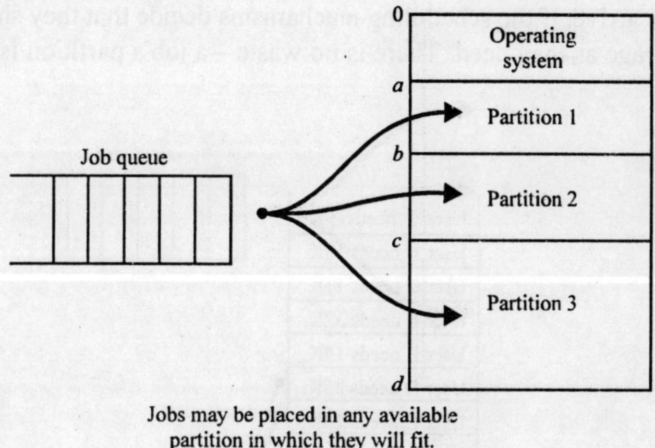

Fig. 5.8. Fixed partition multiprogramming with relocatable translation and loading.

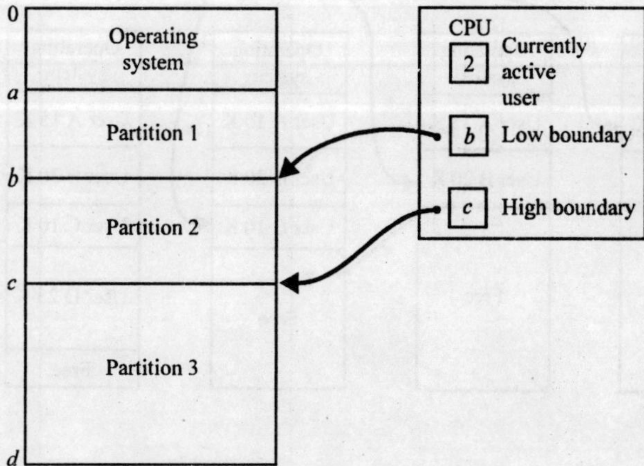

Fig. 5.9. Storage protection in contiguous allocation multiprogramming systems. While the user in partition 2 is active, all storage addresses developed by the running program are checked to be sure they fall between b and c.

Variable Partition Multiprogramming

Operating systems designers observing the problems with fixed partition multiprogramming decided that an obvious improvement would be to allow jobs to occupy as much space (short of the full real storage) as they needed. No fixed boundaries would be observed. Instead, jobs would be given as much storage as they required. This scheme is called variable partition multiprogramming. Initial partition assignment in *variable partition multiprogramming* is illustrated in Fig. 5.10.

We continue to discuss only *contiguous allocation schemes* here: a job must occupy adjacent storage locations. In variable partition multiprogramming, we make no assumptions about how large jobs will be (except that they must be no greater than the size of the computer's available main storage). As jobs arrive, if the scheduling mechanisms decide that they should proceed, they are given as much storage as they need. There is no waste—a job's partition is exactly the size of the job.

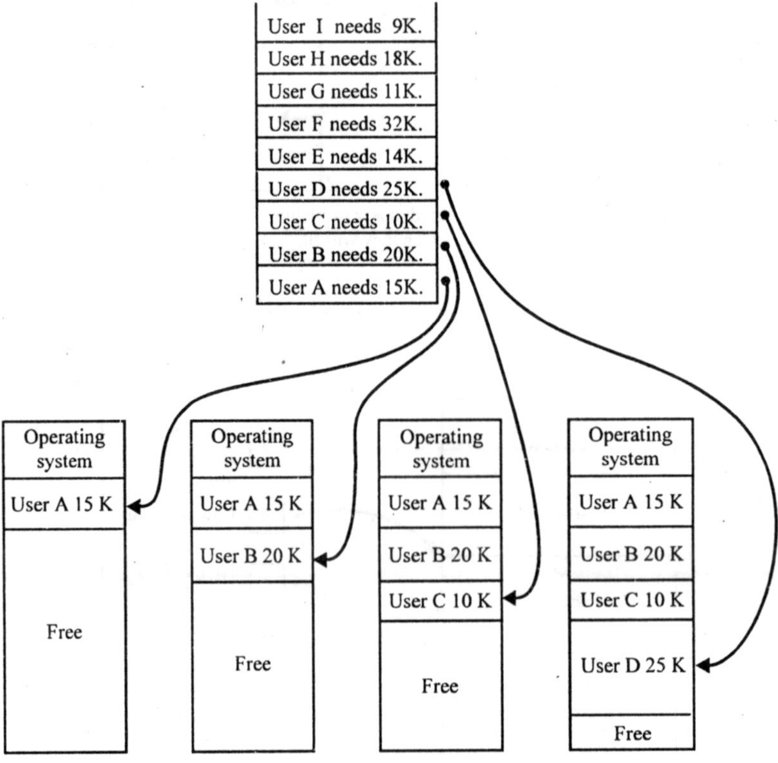

Fig. 5.10. Initial partition assignments in variable partition programming.

But every storage organization scheme involves some degree of waste. In variable partition multiprogramming, the waste does not become obvious until jobs start to finish and leave holes in the main storage as shown in Fig. 5.11 These holes can be used for other jobs, but even as this happens, the remaining holes get smaller eventually becoming too small to hold new jobs. So in variable partition multiprogramming waste does occur.

Coalescing Holes

When a job finishes in a variable partition multiprogramming system, we can check whether the storage being freed borders on other free storage areas (*holes*). If it does, then we may record in the *free storage list* either (1) an additional hole or (2) a single hole reflecting the merger of the existing hole and the new adjacent hole.

The process of merging adjacent holes to form a single larger hole is called *coalescing* and is illustrated in Fig. 5.12. By coalescing holes, we reclaim the largest possible contiguous blocks of storage.

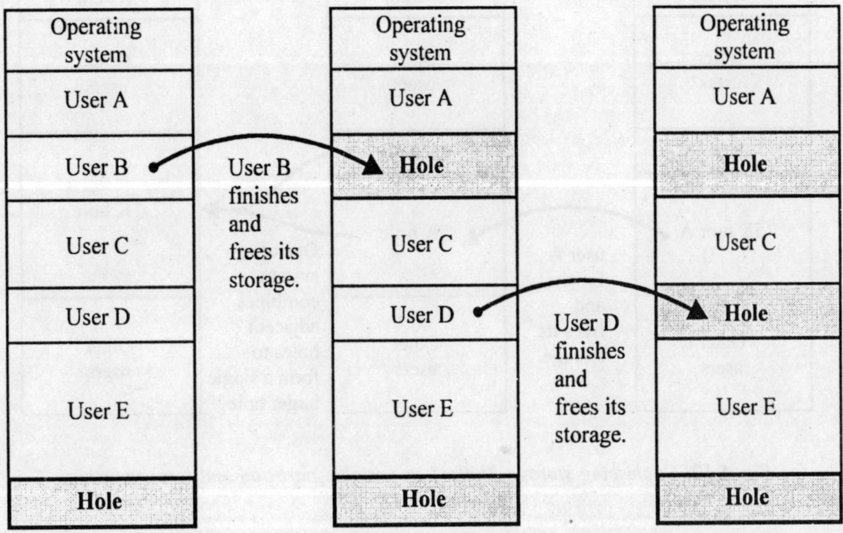

Fig. 5.11. Storage "holes" in variable partition multiprogramming.

Storage Compaction

Even as holes are coalesced, it is often the case that the separate holes distributed throughout the main storage constitute a significant amount of storage. Sometimes when a job requests a certain amount of main storage no individual hole is large enough to hold the job, even though the sum of all the holes is larger than the storage needed by the new job.

The technique of *storage compaction* involves moving all occupied area storage to one end or the other of main storage. This leaves a single large free storage hole instead of the numerous small holes common in variable partition multiprogramming. Now all of the available free storage is contiguous so that a waiting job can run if its memory requirement is met by the single hole that results from compaction. Sometimes, storage compaction is colorfully referred to as *burping the storage*. More conventionally, it is called *garbage collection*.

Compaction is not without drawbacks.

- It consumes system resources that could otherwise be used productively.
- The system must stop everything while it performs the compaction. This can result in erratic response times for interactive users and could be devastating in real-time systems.
- Compaction involves relocating the jobs that are in storage. This means that relocation information, ordinarily lost when a program is loaded, must now be maintained in readily accessible form.
- With a normal, rapidly changing job mix, it is necessary to compact frequently. The consumed system resources might not justify the benefit from compacting.

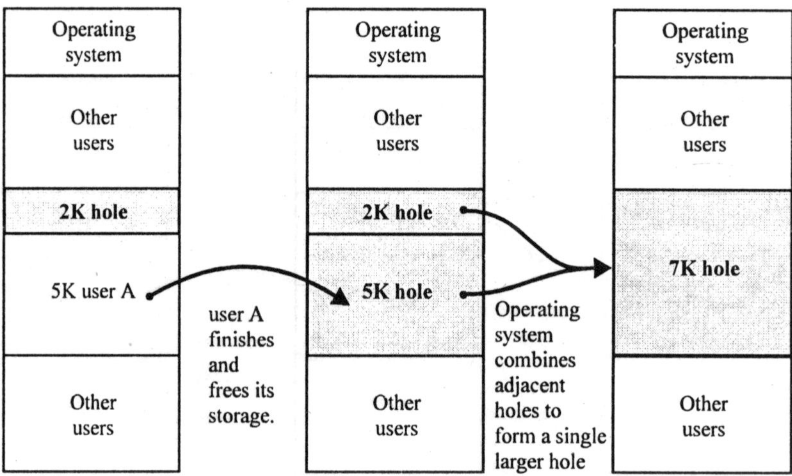

Fig. 5.12. Coalescing storage "holes" in variable partition multiprogramming.

Storage Placement Strategies

Storage placement strategies are used to determine where in the main storage to place incoming programs and data. Three strategies frequently discussed in the literature are illustrated in Fig. 5.14.

Best-fit strategy—An incoming job is placed in the hole in main storage in which it fits most tightly and leaves the smallest amount of unused space. To many people, best fit seems to be the most intuitively appealing strategy.

First-fit strategy—An incoming job is placed in the main storage in the first available hole large enough to hold it. First fit also has intuitive appeal in that it allows the placement decision to be made quickly.

Worst-fit strategy—At first, this appears to be a whimsical choice. After closer examination, worst fit also has strong intuitive appeal. Worst fit says to place a program in main storage in the hole in which it fits worst, i.e., the largest possible hole. The intuitive appeal is simple: after placing the program in this large hole, the remaining hole often is also large and is thus able to hold a relatively large new program.

A variation of first-fit, called the *next-fit strategy*, begins each search for an available hole at the point where the previous search ended. An exercise at the end of this chapter examines the next-fit strategy in detail.

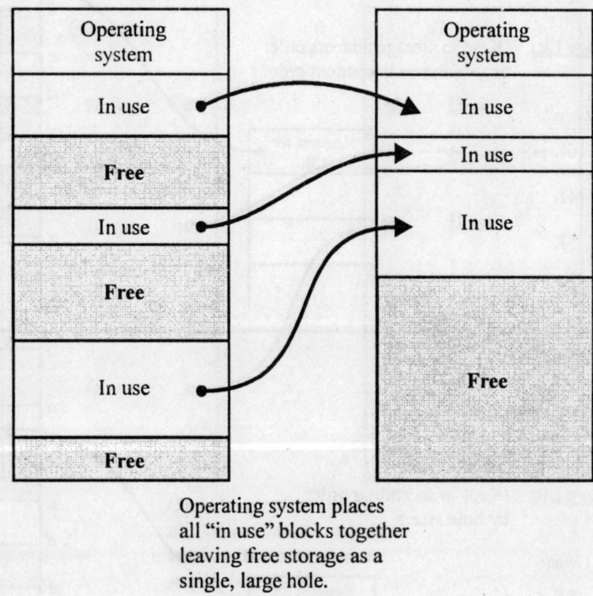

Fig. 5.13. Storage compaction in variable partition multiprogramming.

Multiprogramming With Storage Swapping

In each of the multiprogramming schemes discussed so far, user programs remain in main memory until completion. Another scheme, called *swapping*, does not have this requirement.

In some swapping systems, one job occupies the main storage at once. That job runs until it can no longer continue and then it relinquishes both the storage and the CPU to the next job. Thus the entire storage is dedicated to one job for a brief period, that job is then removed (i.e., *swapped out or rolled out*) and the next job is brought in (i.e., *swapped in or rolled in*). A job will normally be swapped in and out many times before it is completed.

Many early timesharing systems were implemented with this swapping technique. It was possible to guarantee reasonable response times for a few users but designers knew that better techniques would be needed to handle large numbers of users. The swapping systems of the early 1960s led to the paging systems in common use today. Paging is considered in detail in the next several chapters on virtual storage systems.

More sophisticated swapping systems have been developed that allow several user images to remain in main storage at once. In these systems, a user image is swapped out only when its storage is needed for an incoming user image. With a sufficient amount of storage, these systems greatly reduce the time spent swapping.

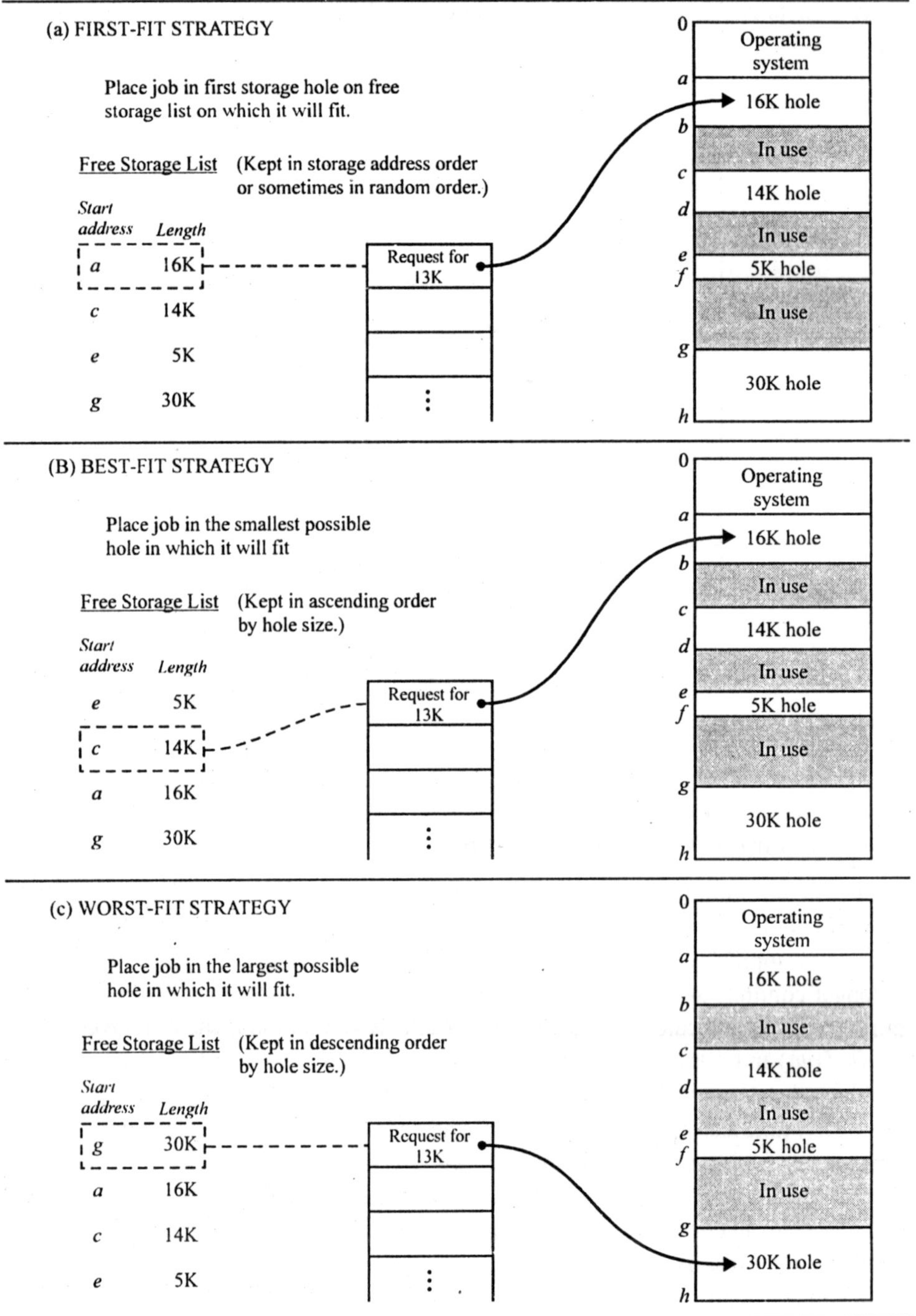

Fig. 5.14. First-fit, best-fit, and worst-fit storage placement strategies.

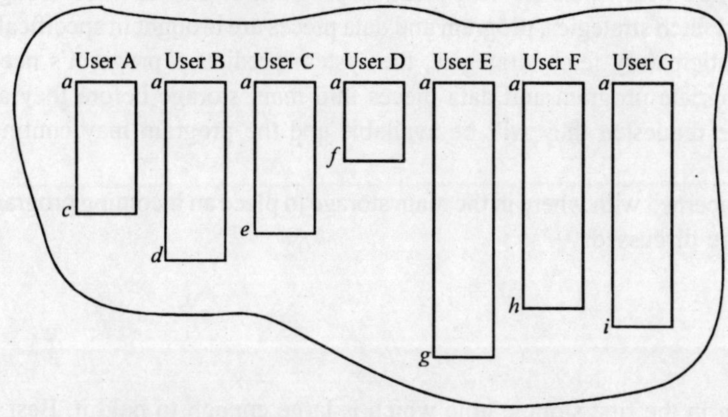

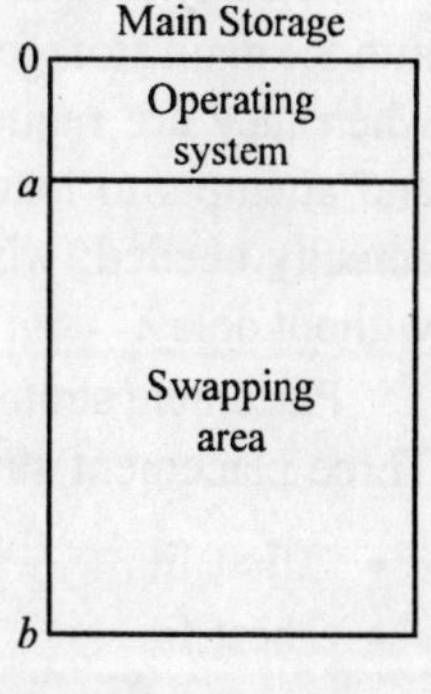

1. Only one user at a time is in main storage
2. That user runs until
   a) I/O is issued,
   b) time runout,
   c) voluntary termination.
3. Swapping area (main storage image) for that user is then copied to secondary storage (i.e., "swapped Out").
4. Main storage image for next user is read into the swapping area (i.e., "swapped in") and that user runs until it is eventually swapped out and the next user is swapped in, etc.
5. This scheme was common in early timesharing systems.

Fig. 5.15. Multiprogramming in a swapping system in whcih only a single user at a time is in main storage.

Summary

Historically, the organization and management of the computer's main storage has greatly affected operating systems evolution. Storage organization is the manner in which the main storage is viewed; in this chapter several popular storage organizations for real storage systems were discussed.

- single user systems
- fixed partition multiprogramming with absolute translation and loading
- fixed partition multiprogramming with relocatable translation and loading
- variable partition multiprogramming
- storage swapping systems

Storage management strategies seek to achieve the best possible use of and performance from the expensive main storage resource. Three types of storage management strategies were discussed.

- fetch strategies
- placement strategies
- replacement strategies

Fetch strategies are concerned with when the next piece of program or data is to be brought into the main storage. In demand fetch strategies, program and data pieces are brought in specifically when they are requested. In anticipatory fetch strategies, the system predicts a program's needs and attempts to load the appropriate program and data pieces into main storage before they are actually needed; when they are requested they will be available and the program may continue without delay.

Placement strategies are concerned with where in the main storage to place an incoming program. Three placement strategies were discussed.

- first fit
- best fit
- worst fit

First fit places the program in the first storage hole which is large enough to hold it. Best fit places the program in the "tightest" fitting hole, i.e., the smallest of the available storage holes large enough to hold it. Worst fit places the program or data piece in the larges available hole that will hold it. First fit is a low overhead strategy. Best fit is intuitively appealing to most people. Worst fit is appealing because it avoids creating small storage holes.

Computer storage systems have become hierarchical consisting of several levels of storage. Secondary storage is relatively inexpensive, but large. Primary storage is expensive but less abundant than secondary storage. Programs and data must be in primary storage to be used by the CPU. Programs and data not needed immediately may be kept on secondary storage, generally disk or drum. Cache storage is extremely expensive but offers high-speed execution of program instructions and referencing of data items.

Contiguous allocation systems require that an entire program occupy one block of adjacent storage locations in order to execute. Noncontiguous allocation systems allow programs and data to be separated into several smaller blocks that may be placed in any available free storage holes, even if these holes are not adjacent to one another. Virtual storage systems generally involve noncontiguous allocation and will be considered in the next several chapters.

The first computer systems were dedicated to one user at a time. These single user systems contained the earliest operating systems, generally input/output control systems to facilitate machine-level input/output programming. Protection was accomplished by a single boundary register that separated the user from the operating system. Single stream batch processing systems were developed to facilitate job-to-job transition and thus increase throughput.

Eventually, it became clear that several users could share a machine at once, but they had to be protected from one another. In fixed partition multiprogramming with absolute translation and loading, user programs are prepared to run in specific partitions. If the partition for a particular user program is unavailable, then that user has to wait, even if another sufficiently large partition goes unused. In fixed partition multiprogramming with relocatable translation and loading, a program can be loaded into any available partition that is large enough to hold it.

Protection is accomplished in contiguous allocation multiprogramming systems with two boundary registers that are part of the CPU. Every storage reference by a given program is checked to be sure that it is within the range of main storage addresses that program is allowed to access. The user wishing to enter the operating system to have input/output or other functions performed does so with the use of a supervisor call instruction. This instruction allows the user program to cross the operating system boundary to obtain certain services. After the operating system performs these services, it returns control to the user program.

Fixed partition multiprogramming system wastes a considerable amount of main storage when the user programs are much smaller than their designated partitions. In variable partition multiprogramming, a user program is assigned exactly as much storage as it needs (short of the main storage size). But as user programs finish in this scheme, many storage holes are left scattered throughout main storage.

Adjacent holes are coalesced to reclaim the largest possible contiguous blocks of main storage. Occasionally, a job arrives with a storage requirement larger than any available hole but smaller than the total of all free storage holes. In this case, storage may be compacted to create a hole sufficiently large to hold the program. In compaction, all user programs are relocated adjacent to one another at one end of storage so that a single large storage hole remains.

Once the fetch strategy determines that a new program should be brought into main storage, the placement strategy must decide where to put it. Sometimes, no storage hole is available and a program in main storage must be removed to make room. Storage replacement strategies decide which programs(s) to remove.

Multiprogramming may also be implemented via swapping with only a single user in main storage at once. The user program runs until it cannot continue. It is then swapped out of main storage, the next user is swapped in and this user runs until it cannot continue. The storage swapping technique is useful when main storage is limited. It was used in many early timesharing systems that supported relatively few users. More sophisticated storage swapping systems allow several programs to remain in storage at once.

6

Deadlocks

In a multiprogramming environment, several processes may compete for a finite number of resources. A process requests resources; if the resources are not available at that time, the process enters a wait state. Waiting processes may never again change state, because the resources they have requested are held by other waiting processes. This situation is called a **deadlock.**

Perhaps the best illustration of a deadlock can be drawn from a law passed by the Kansas legislature early in the 20th century. It said, in part: "When two trains approach each other at a crossing, both shall come to a full stop and neither shall start up again until the other has gone."

In this chapter, we describe methods that an operating system can use to prevent or deal with deadlocks. Most current operating systems do not provide deadlock-prevention facilities, but such features will probably be added soon. Deadlock problems can only become more common, given current trends, including larger numbers of processes, multithreaded programs, many more resources within a system, and the emphasis on long-lived file and database servers rather than batch systems.

System Model

A system consists of a finite number of resources to be distributed among a number of competing processes. The resources are partitioned into several types, each of which consists of some number of identical instances. Memory space, CPU cycles, files, and I/O devices (such as printers and tape drives) are examples of resource types. If a system has two CPU's then the resource type CPU has two instances. Similarly, the resource type *printer* may have five instances.

If a process requests an instance of a resource type, the allocation of *any* instance of the type will satisfy the request. If it will not, then the instances are not identical, and the resources type classes have not been defined properly. For example, a system may have two printers. These two printers may be defined to be in the same resources class if no one cares which printer prints which output. However, if one printer is on the ninth floor and the other is in the basement, then people on the ninth floor may not see both printers as equivalent, and separates resource classes may need to be defined for each printer.

A process must request a resource before using it, and must release the resource after using it. A process may request as many resources as it requires to carry out its designated task. Obviously, the number of resources requested may not exceed the total number of resources available in the system. In other words, a process cannot request three printers if the system has only two.

Under the normal mode of operation, a process may utilize a resource in only the following sequences:

1. **Request:** If the request cannot be granted immediately (for example, the resource is being used by another process), then the requesting process must wait until it can acquire the resource.
2. **Use:** The process can operate on the resource (for example, if the resource is a printer, the process can print on the printer).
3. **Release:** The process releases the resource.

The request and release of resources are system calls. Examples are the request and release device, open and close file, and allocate and free memory systems calls. Request and release of other resources can be accomplished through the *wait* and *signal* operations on semaphores. Therefore, for each use, the operating system checks to make sure that the using process has requested and been allocated the resource. A system table records whether each resource free or allocated, and, if a resource is allocated, to which process. If a process requests a resource that is currently allocated to another process, it can be added to a queue of processed waiting for this resource.

A set of processes is in a deadlock state when every process in the set is waiting for an event that can be caused only by another process in the set. The events with which we are mainly concerned here are resource acquisition and release. The resources may be either physical resources (for example, printers, tape drives, memory space, and CPU cycles) or logical resources (for example, files, semaphores, and monitors). However, other types of events may result in deadlocks.

To illustrate a deadlock state, we consider a system with three tape drives. Suppose each of three processes holds one of these tape drives. If each process now requests another tape drive, the three processes will be in a deadlock state. Each is waiting for the events "tape drive is released," which can be caused only by one of the other waiting processes. This example illustrates a deadlock involving the same resource type.

Deadlocks may also involve different resource types. For example, consider a system with one printer and one tape drive. Suppose that process P_i is holding the tape drive and process P_j is holding the printer. If P_i requests the printer and P_j requests the tape drive, a deadlock occurs.

A programmer who is developing multithreaded applications must pay particular attention to this problem: Multithreaded programs are good candidates for deadlock because multiple threads can compete for shared resources.

Deadlock Characterization

In a deadlock, processes never finish executing and system resources are tied up, preventing other jobs form starting. Before we discuss the various methods for dealing with the deadlock problem, we shall describe features that characterize deadlocks.

Necessary Conditions

A deadlock situation can arise if the following four conditions hold simultaneously in a system:

1. **Mutual exclusion:** At least one resource must be held in a nonsharable mode; that is, only one process at a time can use the resource. If another process requests that resource, the requesting process must be delayed until the resource has been released.

2. **Hold and wait:** A process must be holding at least one resource and waiting to acquire additional resources that are currently being held by other processes.
3. **No preemption:** Resources cannot be preempted; that is, resource can be released only voluntarily by the process holding it, after that process has complete its task.
4. **Circular wait:** A set $\{P_0, P_1, ..., P_n\}$ of waiting processes must exist such that P_0 is waiting for a resource that is held by P_1, P_1 is waiting for a resource that is held by $P_2, ..., P_{n-1}$ is waiting for a resource that is held by P_n, and P_n is waiting for a resource that is held by P_0.

We emphasize that all four conditions must hold for a deadlock to occur. The circular-wait condition implies the hold-and-wait condition, so the four conditions are not completely independent.

Resource-Allocation Graph

Deadlocks can be described more precisely in terms of a directed graph called a **system resource-allocation graph.** This graph consists of a set of vertices V and a set of edges E. The set of vertices V is partitioned into two different types of nodes $P = \{P_1, P_2, ..., P_n\}$, the set consisting of all the active processes in the system, and $R = \{R_1, R_2, ..., R_m\}$, the set consisting of all resource types in the system.

A directed edge from process P_i to resource type R_j is denoted by $P_i \rightarrow R_j$; it signifies that process P_i requested an instance of resource type R_j and is currently waiting for that resource. A directed edge from resource type R_j to process P_i is denoted by $R_j \rightarrow P_i$; it signifies that an instance of resource type R_j has been allocated to process P_j. A directed edge $P_i \rightarrow R_j$; is called a **request edge;** a directed edge $R_j \rightarrow P_i$; is called an **assignment edge.**

Pictorially, we represent each process P_i as a circle, and each resource type R_j as a square. Since resource type R_j may have more than one instance, we represent each such instance as a dot within the square. Note that a request edge points to only the square $R_{j,}$ whereas an assignment edge must also designate one of the dots in the square.

When process P_i requests an instance of resource type R_j, a request edge is inserted in the resource-allocation graph. When this request can be fulfilled, the request edge is *instantaneously* transformed to an assignment edge. When the process no longer needs access to the resource it releases the resource, and as a result the assignment edge is deleted.

The resource-allocation graph shown in Figure 6.1 depicts the following situation.

- The sets *P,R,* and *E:*
    - $P = \{P_1, P_2, P_3\}$
    - $R = \{R_1, R_2, R_3, R_4\}$
    - $E \rightarrow R_1, P_2 \rightarrow R_3, R_1 \rightarrow P_2, R_2 \rightarrow P_2, R_2 \rightarrow P_1, R_3 \rightarrow P_3\}$
- Resource instances:
    - One instance of resource type R_1
    - Two instances of resource type R_2
    - One instance of resource type R_3
    - Three instances of resource type R_4

- Process states:
  - Process P_1 is holding an instance of resource type R_2, and is waiting for an instance of resource type R_1.
  - Process P_2 is holding an instance of R_1 and R_2, and is waiting for an instance of resource type R_3.
  - Process P_3 is holding an instance of R_3.

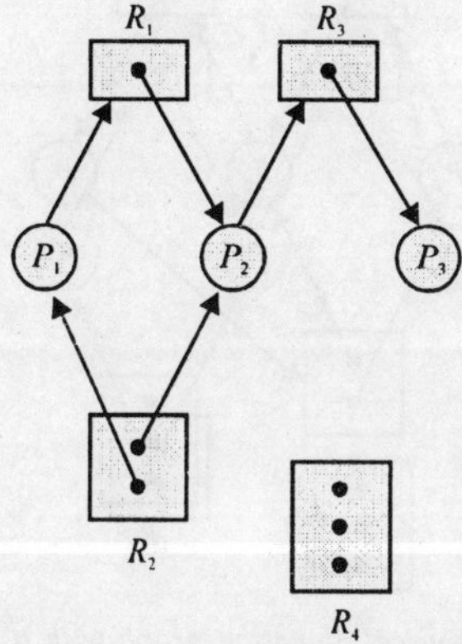

Fig. 6.1. Resource-allocation graph.

Given the definition of a resource-allocation graph, it can be shown that, if the graph contains no cycles, then no process in the system is deadlocked. If the graph does contain a cycle, then a deadlock may exist.

If each resource type has exactly one instance, then a cycle implies that a deadlock has occurred. If the cycle involves only a set of resource types, each of which has only a single instance, then a deadlock has occurred. Each process involved in the cycle is deadlocked. In this case, a cycle in the graph is both a necessary and a sufficient condition for the existence of deadlock.

If each resource type has several instances, then a cycle does not necessarily imply that a deadlock has occurred. In this case, a cycle in the graph is necessary but not a sufficient condition for the existence of deadlock.

Suppose that process P_3 requests an instance of resource type R_2. Since no resource instance is currently available, a request edge $P_3 \rightarrow R_2$ is added to the graph. At this point, two minimal cycles exist in the system:

$$P_1 \rightarrow R_1 \rightarrow P_2 \rightarrow R_3 \rightarrow P_3 \rightarrow R_2 \rightarrow P_1$$

$$P_2 \rightarrow R_3 \rightarrow P_3 \rightarrow R_2 \rightarrow P_2$$

Processes P_1, P_2, and P_3 are deadlocked. Process P_2 is waiting for the resource R_3, which is held by process P_3. Process P_3, on the other hand, is waiting for either process P_1 or process P_2 to release resource R_2. In addition, process P_1 is waiting for process P_2 to release resource R_1.

Now consider the resource-allocation graph in Figure 6.3. In this example, we also have a cycle

$$P_1 \rightarrow R_1 \rightarrow P_3 \rightarrow R_2 \rightarrow P_1$$

However, there is no deadlock. Observe that process P_4 may release its instance of resource type R_2. That resource can then be allocated to P_3, breaking the cycle.

In summary, if a resource-allocation graph does not have a cycle, then the system is *not* in a deadlock state. On the other hand, if there is a cycle, then the system may or may not be in a deadlock state. This observation is important when we deal with the deadlock problem.

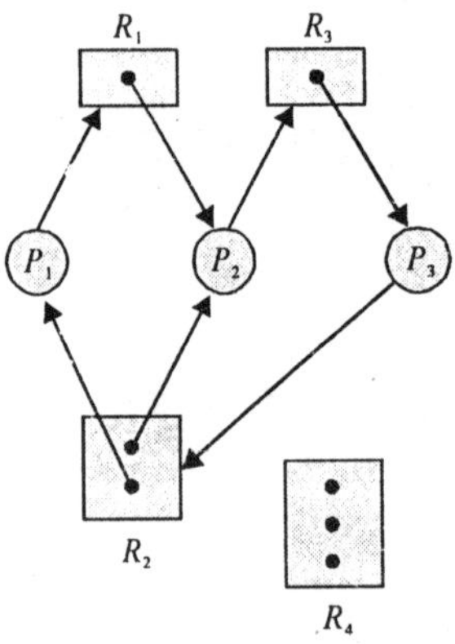

Fig. 6.2. Resource-allocation graph with a deadlock.

Methods for Handling Deadlocks

Principally, we can deal with the deadlocks problem is one of three ways:

- We can use a protocol to prevent or avoid deadlocks, ensuring that the system will *never* enter a deadlock state.
- We can allow the system to enter a deadlock state, detect it, and recover.
- We can ignore the problem altogether, and pretend that deadlocks never occur in the system. This solution is used by most operating systems, including UNIX.

We shall elaborate briefly on each method.

To ensure that deadlocks never occur, the system can use either a deadlock-prevention or a deadlocks-avoidance scheme. **Deadlock prevention** is a set of methods for ensuring that at least one of the necessary conditions cannot hold. These methods prevent deadlocks by constraining how requests for resources can be made.

Deadlock avoidance, on the other hand, requires that the operating system be given, in advance, additional information concerning which resources a process will request and use during its lifetime. With this additional knowledge, we can decide for each request, whether or not the process should wait. To decide whether the current request can be satisfied or must be delayed, the system must consider the resources currently available, the resources currently allocated to each process, and the future requests and releases of each process.

If a system does not employ either a deadlock-prevention or a deadlock-avoidance algorithm, then a deadlock situation may occur. In this environment, the system can provide an algorithm that examines the state of the system to determine whether a deadlock has occurred, and an algorithm to recover from the deadlock (if a deadlock has indeed occurred).

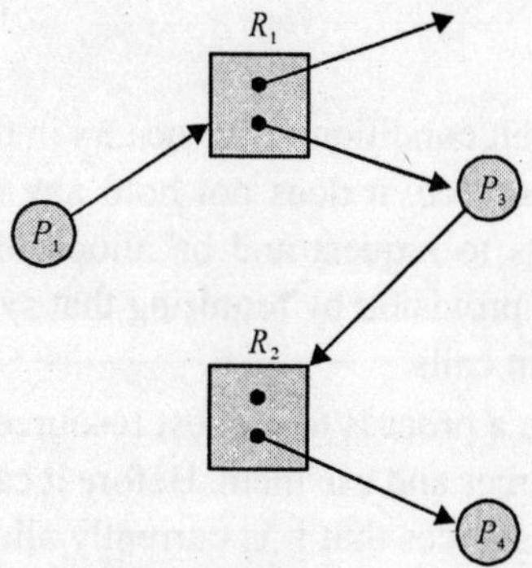

Fig. 6.3. Resource-allocation graph with a cycle but no deadlock.

If a system does not ensure that a deadlock will never occur, and also does not provide a mechanism for deadlock detection and recovery, then we may arrive at a situation where the system is in a deadlock state yet has no way of recognizing what has happened. In this case, the undetected deadlock will result in the deterioration of the system performance, because resources are being held by processes that cannot run, and because more and more processes, as they make requests for resources, enter a deadlock state. Eventually, the system will stop functioning and will need to be restarted manually.

Although this method does not seem to be a viable approach to the deadlock problem, it is nevertheless used in some operating systems. In many systems, deadlocks occur infrequently (say, once per year); thus, this method is cheaper than the costly deadlock-prevention, deadlock-avoidance, or deadlock-detection and recovery methods that must be used constantly. Also, in some circumstances, the system is in a frozen state but not in a deadlock state. As an example, consider a real-time process running at the highest priority (or any process running on a non-preemptive scheduler) and never returning control to the operating systems. Thus, systems must have manual recovery methods for non-deadlock conditions, and may simply use those techniques for deadlock recovery.

Prevention and Deadlock

For a deadlock to occur, each of the four necessary conditions must hold. By ensuring that at least one of these conditions cannot hold, we can *prevent* the occurrence of a deadlock. Let us elaborate on this approach by examining each of the four necessary conditions separately.

Mutual Exclusion

The mutual-exclusion condition must hold for nonsharable resources. For example, a printer cannot be simultaneously shared by several processes. Sharable resources, on the other hand, do not require mutually exclusive access, and thus cannot be involved in a deadlock. Read-only files are a good example of a sharable resource. If several processes attempt to open a read-only file at the same time, they can be granted simultaneous access to the file. A process never needs to wait for a sharable resource. In general, however, we cannot prevent deadlocks by denying the mutual-exclusion condition: Some resources are intrinsically nonsharable.

Hold and Wait

To ensure that the hold-and wait condition never occurs in the system, we must guarantee that, whenever a process requests a resource, it does not hold any other resources. One protocol that can be used requires each process to request and be allocated all its resources before it begins execution. We can implement this provision by requiring that system calls requesting resources for a process, precede all other system calls.

An alternative protocol allows a process to request resources only when the process has none. A process may request some resources and use them. Before it can request any additional resources, however, it must release all the resources that it is currently allocated.

To illustrate the difference between these two protocols, we consider a process that copies data from a tape drive to a disk file, sorts the disk file, and then prints the results to a printer. If all resources must be requested at the beginning of the process, then the process must initially request the tape drive, disk file, and printer. It will hold the printer for its entire execution, even though it needs the printer only at the end.

The second method allows the process to request initially only the tape drive and disk file. It copies from the tape drive to the disk, then releases both the tape drive and the disk file. The process must then again request the disk file and the printer. After copying the disk file to the printer, it release these two resources and terminates.

These protocols have two main disadvantages. First, **resource** utilization may be low, since many of the resources may be allocated but unused for a long period. In the example given, for instance, we can release the tape drive and disk file, and then again request the disk file and printer, only if we can be sure that our data will remain on the disk file. If we cannot be assured that they will, then we must request all resources at the beginning for both protocols.

Second, starvation is possible. A process that needs several popular resources may have to wait indefinitely, because at least one of the resources that it needs is always allocated to some other process.

No Preemption

The third necessary condition is that there be no preemption of resources that have already been allocated. To ensure that this condition does not hold, we can use the following protocol. If a process is holding some resources and requests another resource that cannot be immediately allocated to it (that is, the process must wait), then all resources currently being held are preempted. In other words, these resources are implicitly released. The preempted resources are added to the list of resources for which the process is waiting. The process will be restarted only when it can regain its old resources, as well as the new ones that it is requesting.

Alternatively, if a process requests some resources, we first check whether they are available. If they are, we allocate them. If they are not available, we check whether they are allocated to some other process that is waiting for additional resources. If so, we preempt the desired resources from the waiting process and allocate them to the requesting process. If the resources are not either available or held by a waiting process, the requesting process must wait. While it is waiting, some of its resources may be pre empted, but only if another process requests them. A process can be restarted only when it is allocated the new resources it is requesting and recovers any resources that were pre empted while it was waiting.

This protocol is often applied to resources whose state can be easily saved and restored later, such as CPU registers and memory space. It cannot generally be applied to such resources as printers and tape drives.

Circular Wait

The fourth and final condition for deadlocks is the circular-wait condition. One way to ensure that this condition never holds is to impose a total ordering of all resource types, and to require that each process requests resources in an increasing order of enumeration.

Let $R = \{R_1, R_2, \ldots, R_m)$ be the set of resource types. We assign to each resource type a unique integer number, which allows us to compare two resources and to determine whether one precedes another in our ordering. Formally, we define a one-to-one function $F: R \rightarrow N$, where N is the set of natural numbers. For example, if the set of resource types R includes tape drives, disk drives, and printers, then the function F might be defined as follows:

$$F(\text{tape drive}) = 1,$$
$$F(\text{disk drive}) = 5,$$
$$F(\text{printer}) = 12.$$

We can now consider the following protocol to prevent deadlocks: Each process can request resources only in an increasing order of enumeration. That is, a process can initially request any number of instances of a resource type, say R_i. After that, the process can request instances of resource type R_j if and only if $F(R_j) > F(R_i)$. If several instances of the same resource type are needed, a *single* request for all of them must be issued. For example, using the function defined previously, a process that wants to use the tape drive and printer at the same time must first request the tape drive and then request the printer.

Alternatively, we can require that, whenever a process requests an instance of resource type R_j, it has released any resources R_i such that $F(R_i) \geq F(R_j)$.

If these two protocols are used, then the circular-wait condition cannot hold. We can demonstrate this fact by assuming that a circular wait exists (proof by contradiction). Let the set of processes involved in the circular wait be $\{P_0, P_1, \ldots, P_n\}$, where P_i is waiting for a resource R_i, which is held by process P_{i+1}. (Modulo arithmetic is used on the indexes, so that P_n is waiting for a resource R_n held by P_0.) Then, since process P_{i+1} is holding resource R_j while requesting resource R_{i+1}, we must have $F(R_i) < F(R_{i+1})$, for all i, But this condition means that $F(R_0) < F(R_1) < \ldots < F(R_n) < F(R_0)$. By transitivity, $F(R_0) < F(R_0)$, which is impossible. Therefore, there can be no circular wait.

Note that the function F should be defined according to the normal order of usage of the resources in a system. For example, since the tape drive is usually needed before the printer, it would be reasonable to define $F(\text{tape drive}) < F(\text{printer})$.

Avoidance of Deadlock

Deadlock-prevention algorithms, prevent deadlocks by restraining how request can be made. The restraints ensure that at least one of the necessary conditions for deadlock cannot occur, and, hence, that deadlocks cannot hold. Possible side effects of preventing deadlocks by this method, however, are bow device utilization and reduced system throughput.

An alternative method for avoiding deadlocks is to require additional information about how resources are to be requested. For example, in a system with one tape drive and one printer, we might be told that process *P* will request first the tape drive, and later the printer, before releasing both resources. Process *Q*, on the other hand, will request first the printer, and then the tape drive. With this knowledge of the complete sequence of requests and releases for each process, we can decide for each request whether or not the process should wait. Each request requires that the systems consider the resources currently available, the resources currently allocated to each process, and the future requests and releases of each process, to decide whether the current request can be satisfied or must wait to avoid a possible future deadlock.

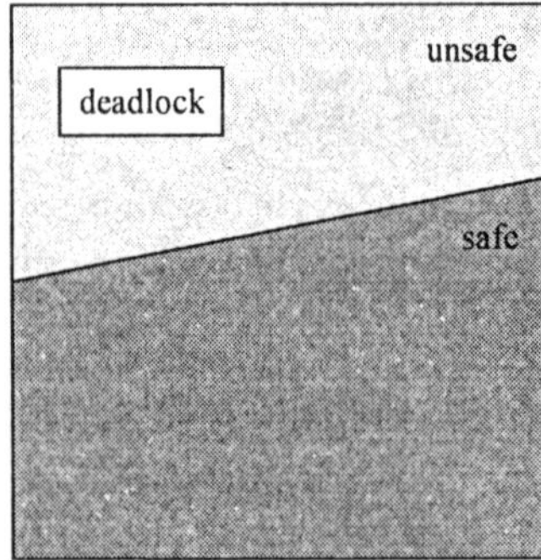

Fig. 6.4. Safe, unsafe, and deadlock state spaces.

The various algorithms differ in the amount and type of information required. The simplest and most useful model requires that each process declare the *maximum number* of resources of each type that it may need. Given a priority information about the maximum number of resources of each type that may be requested for each process, it is possible to construct an algorithm that ensures that the system will never enter a deadlock state. This algorithm defines the **deadlock-avoidance** approach. A deadlock-avoidance algorithm dynamically examines the resource-allocation state to ensure that a circular-wait condition can never exist. The resource-allocation *state* is defined by the number of available and allocated resources, and the maximum demands of the processes.

Safe State

A state is *safe* if the systsem can allocate resources to each process (up to its maximum) in some order and still avoid a deadlock. More formally, a system is in a safe state only if there exists a **safe sequence.** A sequence of processes $<P_1, P_2, ..., P_n>$ is a safe sequence for the current allocation state if, for each P_i, the resources that P_i can still request can be satisfied by the currently available resources plus the resources held by all the P_j, with $j < i$. In this situation, if the resources that process P_i needs are not immediately available, then P_i can wait until all P_j have finished. When they have finished, P_i can obtain all of its needed resources, complete its designated task, return its allocated resources, and terminate. When P_i terminates, P_{i+1} can obtain its needed resources, and so on. If no such sequence exists, then the system state is said to be *unsafe*.

A safe state is not a deadlock state. Conversely, a deadlock state is an unsafe state. Not all unsafe states are deadlocks, however. An unsafe state *may* lead to a deadlock. As long as the state is safe, the operating system can avoid unsafe (and deadlock) states. In an unsafe state, the operating system cannot prevent processes form requesting resources such that a deadlock occurs: The behaviour of the processes controls unsafe states.

To illustrate, we consider a system with 12 magnetic tape drives and 3 processes: P_0, P_1, and P_2. Process P_0 requires 10 tape drives, process P_1 may need as may as 4, and process P_2 may need up to 9 tape drives. Suppose that, at time t_0, process P_0 is holding 5 tape drives, process P_1 is holding 2, and process P_2 is holding 2 tape drives. (Thus, there are 3 free tape drives.)

	Maximum Needs	Current Needs
P_0	10	5
P_1	4	2
P_2	9	2

At time t_0, the system is in a safe state. The sequence $<P_1, P_0, P_2>$ satisfies the safety condition, since process P_1 can immediately be allocated all its tape drives and then return them (the system will then have 5 available tape drives), then process P_0 can get all its tape drives and return them (the system will then have 10 available tape drives), and finally process P_2 could get all its tape drives and return them (the system will then have all 12 tape drives available).

A system may go from a safe state to an unsafe state. Suppose that, at time t_1, process P_2 requests and is allocated 1 more tape drive. The system is no longer in a safe state. At this point, only process P_1 can be allocated all its tape drives. When it returns them, the system will have only 4 available tape drives. Since process P_0 is allocated 5 tape drives, but has a maximum of 10, it may then request 5 more tape drives. Since they are unavailable, process P_0 must wait. Similarly, process P_2 may request an additional 6 tape drives and have to wait, resulting in a deadlock.

Our mistake was in granting the request from process P_2 for 1 more tape drive. If we had made P_2 wait until either of the other processes had finished and released its resources, then we could have avoided the deadlock.

Given the concept of a safe state, we can define avoidance algorithms that ensures that the system will never deadlock. The idea is simply to ensure that the system will always remain in a safe state. Initially, the system is in a safe state. Whenever a process requests a resource that is currently available, the system must decide whether the resource can be allocated immediately or whether the process must wait. The request is granted only if the allocation leaves the system in a safe state.

In this scheme, if a process requests a resource that is currently available, it may still have to wait. Thus, resource utilization may be lower than it would be without a deadlock-avoidance algorithm.

Graph Algorithm of Resource Allocation

If we have a resource-allocation system with only one instance of each resource type, a variant of the resource-allocation graph can be used for deadlock avoidance.

In addition to the request and assignment edges, we introduce a new type of edge, called a **claim edge.** A claim edge $P_i \rightarrow R_j$ indicates that process P_i may request resources R_j at some time in the future. This edge resembles a request edge in direction, but is represented by a dashed line. When process P_i requests resource R_j, the claim edge $P_i \rightarrow R_j$ is converted to a request edge. Similarly, when a resource R_j is released by P_i, the assignment edge $R_j \rightarrow P_i$ is reconverted to a claim edge $P_i \rightarrow R_j$. We note that the resources must be claimed a priori in the system. That is, before process P_i starts executing, all its claim edges must already appear in the resource-allocation graph. We can relax this condition by allowing a claim edge $P_i \rightarrow R_j$ to be added to the graph only if all the edges associated with process P_i are claim edges.

Suppose that process P_i requests resources R_j. The request can be granted only if converting the request edge $P_i \rightarrow R_j$ to an assignment edge $R_j \rightarrow P_i$ does not result in the formation of a cycle in the resource-allocation graph. Note that we check for safety by using a cycle-detection algorithm. An algorithm for detecting a cycle in this graph requires an order of n^2 operations, where n is the number of processes in the system.

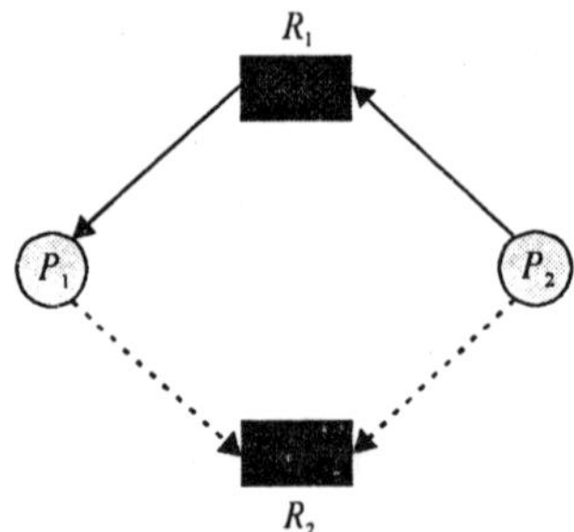

Fig. 6.5. Resource-allocation graph for deadlock avoidance.

If no cycle exists, then the allocation of the resource will leave the system in a safe state. If a cycle is found, then the allocation will put the system in an unsafe state. Therefore, process P_i will have to wait for its requests to be satisfied.

To illustrate this algorithm, we consider the resource-allocation graph. Suppose that p_2 requests R_2. Although R_2 is currently free, we cannot allocate it to p_2, since this action will create a cycle in the graph. A cycle indicates that the system is in an unsafe state. If P_1 requests R_2, and P_2 requests R_1, then a deadlock will occur.

Banker's Algorithm

The resource-allocation graph algorithm is not applicable to a resource-allocation system with multiple instances of each resource type. The deadlock-avoidance algorithm that we describe next is applicable to such a system, but is less efficient than the resource-allocation graph scheme. This algorithm is commonly known as the *banker's algorithm.* The name was chosen because this algorithm could be used in a banking system to ensure that the bank never allocates it's available cash such that it can no longer satisfy the needs of all its customers.

When a new process enters the system, it must declare the maximum number of instances of each resource type that it may need. This number may not exceed the total number of resources in the system. When a user requests a set of resources, the system must determine whether the allocation of these resources will leave the system in a safe state. If it will, the resources are allocated; otherwise, the process must wait until some other process releases enough resources.

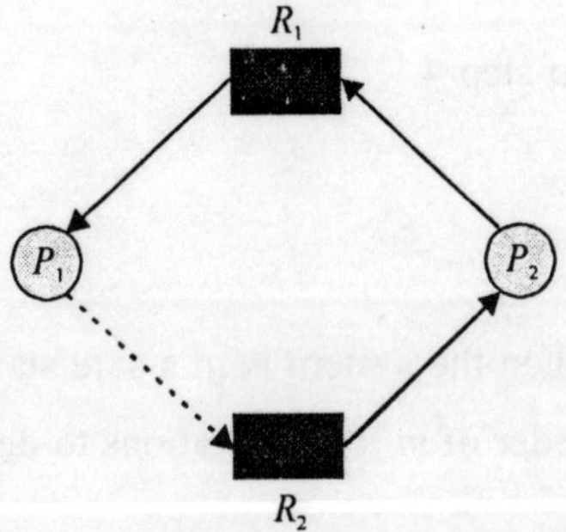

Fig. 6.6. An unsafe state in a resource-allocation graph.

Several data structures must be maintained to implement the banker's algorithm. These data structures encode the state of the resource-allocation systems. Let n be the number of processes in the system and m be the number of resource types. We need the following data structures:

- **Available:** A vector of length m indicates the number of available resources of each type. If *Available* $[j] = k$, there are k instances of resource type R_j available.
- **Max:** An $n \times m$ matrix defines the maximum demand of each process. If *Max* $[i,j] = k$, then process P_i may request at most k instances of resource type R_j.
- **Allocation:** An $n \times m$ matrix defines the number of resources of each type currently allocated to each process. If *Allocation* $[i,j] = k$, then process P_i is currently allocated k instances of resource type R_j.
- **Need:** An $n \times m$ matrix indicates the remaining resource need of each process. If *Need* $[i,j] = k$, then process P_i may need k more instances of resource type R_j to complete its task. Note that *Need* $[i,j]$ = *Max* $[i,j]$ — *Allocation* $[i,j]$.

These data structures vary over time in both size and value.

To simplify the presentation of the banker's algorithm, let us establish some notation. Let X and Y be vectors of length n. We say that $X \le Y$ if and only if $X[i] \le Y[i]$ for all $i = 1,2, \ldots, n$. For example, if $X = (1,7,3,2)$ and $Y = (0,3,2,1)$, then $Y \le X$, $Y < X$ if $Y \le X$ and $Y \ne X$.

We can treat each row in the matrices *Allocation* and *Need* as vectors and refer to them as $Allocation_i$ and $Need_i$, respectively. The vector $Allocation_i$ specifies the resources currently allocated to process P_i; the vector $Need_i$ specifies the additional resources that process P_i may still request to complete its task.

Safety Algorithm

The algorithm for finding out whether or not a system is in a safe state can be described as follows:

1. Let *Work* and *Finish* be vectors of length m and n, respectively. Initialize *Work* := *Available* and *Finish*[i] := *false* for $i = 1,2, \ldots, n$.
2. Find an i such that both

   a. *Finish*[i] = *false*

   b. $Need_i \leq Work$.

   If no such i exists, go to step 4.
3. $Work := Work + Allocation_i$

   Finish[i] := *true*

   Go to step 2.
4. If *Finish*[i] = *true* for all i, then the system is in a safe state.

This algorithm may require an order of $m \times n^2$ operations to decide whether a state is safe.

Resource-Request Algorithm

Let $Request_i$ be the request vector for process p_i. If $Request_i\,[j] = k$, then process P_i wants k instances of resource type R_j. When a request for resources is made by process P_i, the following actions are taken:

1. If $Request_i \leq Need_i$, go to step 2. Otherwise, raise an error condition, since the process has exceeded its maximum claim.
2. If $Request_i \leq Available$, go to step 3. Otherwise, P_i must wait, since the resources are not available.
3. Have the system pretend to have allocated the requested resources to process P_i by modifying that state as follows:

$$Available := Available - Request_i;$$

$$Allocation_i := Allocation - Request_i;$$

$$Need_i := Need_i - Request_i;$$

If the resulting resource-allocation state is safe, the transaction is completed and process P_i is allocated its resources. However, if the new state is unsafe, then P_i must wait for Request_i and the old resource-allocation state is restored.

An Illustrative Example

Consider a system with five processes P_0 through P_4 and three resource types *A, B, C*. Resource type *A* has 10 instances, resource type *B* has 5 instances, and resource type *C has 7 instances. Suppose that, at time* T_0, the following snapshot of the system has been taken:

	Allocation	*Max*	*Available*
	A B C	*A B C*	*A B C*
P_0	010	753	332
P_1	200	322	
P_2	302	902	
P_3	211	222	
P_4	002	433	

The content of the matrix *Need* is defined to be *Max — Allocation* and is

	Need
	A B C
P_0	743
P_1	122
P_2	600
P_3	011
P_4	431

We claim that the system is currently in a safe state. Indeed, the sequence $<P_1, P_3, P_4, P_2, P_0>$ satisfies the safety criteria. Suppose now that process P_1 requests one additional instance of resource type *A* and two instances of resource type *C*, so $Request_1 = (1,0,2)$. To decide whether this request can be immediately granted, we first check that $Request_1 \leq Available$ (that is, $(1,0,2) \leq (3,3,2)$), which is true. We then pretend that this request has been fulfilled, and we arrive at the following new state.

	Allocation	*Max*	*Available*
	A B C	*A B C*	*A B C*
P_0	010	743	230
P_1	302	020	
P_2	302	600	
P_3	211	011	
P_4	002	431	

We must determine whether this new system state is safe. To do so, we execute our safety algorithm and find that the sequence $<P_1, P_3, P_4, P_0, P_2>$ satisfies our safety requirement. Hence, we can immediately grant the request of process P_1.

You should be able to see, however, that when the system is in this state, a request for (3,3,0) by P_4 cannot be granted, since the resources are not available. A request for (0,2,0) by P_0 cannot be granted, even though the resources are available, since the resulting state is unsafe.

Deadlock Detection

If a systems does not employ either a deadlock-prevention or a deadlock-avoidance algorithm, then a deadlock situation may occur. In this environment, the system must provide.

- An algorithm that examines the state of the system to determine whether a deadlock has occurred
- An algorithm to recover from the deadlock

In the following discussion, we elaborate on these two requirements as they pertain to systems with only a single instance of each resource type, as well as to systems with several instances of each resources type. At this point, however, let us note that a detection-and-recovery scheme requires overhead that includes not only the run-time costs of maintaining the necessary information and executing the detection algorithm, but also the potential losses inherent in recovering from a deadlock.

Single Instance of Each Resource Type

If all resources have only a single instance, then we can define a deadlock-detection algorithm that uses a variant of the resource-allocation graph, called a *wait-for* graph. We obtain this graph from the resource-allocation graph by removing the nodes of type resource and collapsing the appropriate edges.

More precisely, an edge from P_i to P_j in a wait-for graph implies that process P_i is waiting for process P_j to release a resource that P_i needs. An edge $P_i \rightarrow P_j$ exists in a wait-for graph if and only if the corresponding resource-allocation graph contains two edges $P_i \rightarrow R_q$ and $R_q \rightarrow P_j$ for some resource R_q. We present a resource-allocation graph and the corresponding wait-for graph.

As before, a deadlock exists in the system if and only if the wait-for graph contains a cycle. To detect deadlocks, the system needs to *maintain* the wait-for graph and periodically to *invoke an algorithm* that searches for a cycle in the graph.

An algorithm to detect a cycle in a graph requires an order of n^2 operations, where n is the number of vertices in the graph.

Several Instances of a Resource Type

The wait-for graph scheme is not applicable to a resource-allocation system with multiple instance of each resource type. The deadlock-detection algorithm that we describe next is applicable to such a system. The algorithm employs several times-varying data structures that are similar to those used in the banker's algorithm.

- **Available:** A vector of length m indicates the number of available resources of each type.
- **Allocation:** An $n \times m$ matrix defines the number of resources of each type currently allocated to each process.
- **Request:** An $n \times m$ matrix indicates the current request of each process. If *Request*$[i,j]$ $= k$, then process P_i is requesting k more instances of resource type R_j.

The $\leq$ relation between two vectors is defined in earlier topics. To simplify notation, we shall again treat the rows in the matrices *Allocation* and *Request* as vectors, and shall refer to them as

$Allocation_i$ and $Request_i$, respectively. The detection algorithm described here simply investigates every possible allocation sequence for the processes that remain to be completed.

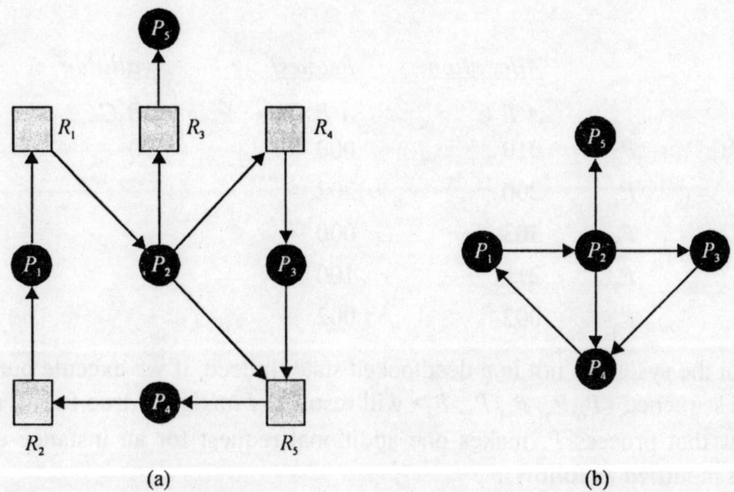

Fig. 6.7. (a) Resource-allocation graph. (b) Corresponding wait-for graph.

1. Let *Work* and *Finish* be vectors of length *m* and *n*, respectively. Initialize *Work* := *Available*. For $i = 1, 2, \ldots, n$, if $Allocation_i \neq 0$, then *Finish*[*i*] := *false* otherwise, *Finish*[*i*] := *true*.
2. Find an index *i* such that both

   a. *Finish*[*i*] = *false*

   b. $Request_i \leq Work$.

   If no such *i* exists, go to step 4.
3. $Work := Work + Allocation_i$
   Finish[*i*] := *true*
   go to step 2.
4. If *Finish*[*i*] = false, for some *i*, $1 \leq i \leq n$, then the system is in a deadlock state. Moreover, if *Finish*[*i*] = *false*, then process P_i is deadlocked.

This algorithm requires an order of $m \times n^2$ operations to detect whether the system is in a deadlocked state.

You may wonder why we reclaim the resources of process P_i (in step 3) as soon as we determine that $Request_i \leq Work$ (in step 2b). We know that P_i is currently *not* involved in a deadlock (since $Request_i \leq Work$). Thus, we take an optimistic attitude, and assume that P_i will require no more resources to complete its task; it will thus soon return all currently allocated resources to the system. If our assumption is incorrect, a deadlock may occur later. That deadlock will be detected the next time such that the deadlock-detection algorithm in invoked.

To illustrate this algorithm, we consider a system with five processes P_0 through P_4 and three resource types *A, B, C*. Resource type *A* has 7 instances, resource, type *B* has 2 instances, and resource type *C* has 6 instances. Suppose that, at time T_0, we have the following resource-allocation state:

	Allocation	*Request*	*Available*
	A B C	*A B C*	*A B C*
P_0	010	000	000
P_1	200	202	
P_2	303	000	
P_3	211	100	
P_4	002	002	

We claim that the system is not in a deadlocked state. Indeed, if we execute our algorithm, we will find that the sequence $<P_0, P_2, P_3, P_1, P_4>$ will result in *Finish*[*i*] = true for all *i*.

Suppose now that process P_2 makes one additional request for an instance of type *C*. The *Request* matrix is modified as follows:

	Request
	A B C
P_0	000
P_1	202
P_2	001
P_3	100
P_4	002

We claim that the system is now deadlocked. Although we can reclaim the resources held by process P_0, the number of available resources is not sufficient to fulfill the requests of the other processes. Thus, a deadlock exists, consisting of processes P_1, P_2, P_3, and P_4.

Detection-Algorithm Usage

When should we invoke the detection algorithm? The answer depends on two factors:

1. How *often* is a deadlock likely to occur?
2. How *many* processes will be affected by deadlock when it happens?

If deadlocks occur frequently, then the detection algorithm should be invoked frequently. Resources allocated to deadlocked processes will be idle until the deadlock can be broken. In addition, the number of processes involved in the deadlock cycle may grow.

Deadlocks occur only when some process makes a request that cannot be granted immediately. This request may be the final request that completes a chain of waiting processes. In the extreme, we could invoke the deadlock-detection algorithm every time a request for allocation cannot be granted immediately. In this case, we can identify not only the set of processes that is deadlocked, but also the specific process that "caused" the deadlock. (In reality, each of the deadlocked processes is a link in the cycle in the resource graph, so all of them, jointly, caused the deadlock.) If there are many different resource types, one request may cause many cycles in the resource graph, each cycle completed by the most recent request and "caused" by the one identifiable process.

Of course, invoking the deadlock-detection algorithm for every request may incur a considerable overhead in computation time. A less expensive alternative is simply to invoke the algorithm at less frequent intervals—for example, one per hour, or whenever CPU utilization drops below 40 percent. (A deadlock eventually cripples system throughout and will cause CPU utilization to drop.) If the detection algorithm is invoked at arbitrary points in time, there may be many cycles in the resource graph. We would generally not be able to tell which of the many deadlocked processes "caused" the deadlock.

Recovery from Deadlock

When a detection algorithm determines that a deadlock exists, several alternatives exist. One possibility is to inform the operator that a deadlock has occurred, and to let the operator deal with the deadlock manually. The other possibility is to let the system *recover* from the deadlock automatically. There are two options for breaking a deadlock. One solution is simply to abort one or more processes to break the circular wait. The second option is to pre empt some resources from one or more of the deadlocked processes.

Process Termination

To eliminate deadlocks by aborting a process, we use one of the two methods. In both methods, the system reclaims all resources allocated to the terminated processes.

- **Abort all deadlocked processes:** This method clearly will break the deadlock cycle, but at a great expense; these processes may have computed for a long time, and the results of these partial computations must be discarded and probably recomputed later.
- **Abort one process at a time until the deadlock cycle is eliminated:** This method incurs considerable overhead, since, after each process is aborted, a deadlock-detection algorithm must be invoked to determine whether any processes are still deadlocked.

Aborting a process may not be easy. If the process was in the midst of updating a file, terminating it will leave that file in an incorrect state. Similarly, if the process was in the midst of printing data on the printer, the system must reset the printer to a correct state before printing the next job.

If the partial termination method is used, then, given a set of deadlocked processes, we must determine which process (or processes) should be terminated in an attempt to break the deadlock. Thus determination is a policy decision, similar to CPU-scheduling problems. The question is basically an economic one; we should abort those processes the termination of which will incur the minimum cost. Unfortunately, the term *minimum cost* is not a precise one. Many factors may determine which process is chosen, including:

1. What the priority of the process is?
2. How long the process has computed, and how much longer the process will compute before completing its designated task?
3. How many and what type of resources the process has used (for example, whether the resources are simple to pre empt)?
4. How may more resources the process needs in order to complete?
5. How many processes will need to be terminated?
6. Whether the process is interactive or batch?

Resource Preemption

To eliminate deadlocks using resource pre emption, we successively pre empt some resources from processes and give these resources to other processes until the deadlock cycle is broken.

If pre emption is required to deal with deadlocks, then three issues need to be addressed:

1. **Selecting a victim:** Which resources and which processes are to be pre empted? As in process termination, we must determine the order of pre emption to minimize cost. Cost factors may include such parameters as the number of resources a deadlock process is holding, and the amount of time a deadlocked process has thus far consumed during its execution.
2. **Rollback:** If we pre empt a resource from a process, what should be done with that process? Clearly, it cannot continue with it's normal execution; it is missing some needed resource. We must roll back the process to some safe state, and restart it from that state.

   Since, in general, it is difficult to determine what a safe state is, the simplest solution is a total rollback: Abort the process and then restart it. However, it is more effective to roll back the process only as far as necessary to break the deadlock. On the other hand, this method requires the system to keep more information about the state of all the running processes.
3. **Starvation:** How do we ensure that starvation will not occur? That is, how can we guarantee that resources will not always be pre empted from the same process?

   In a system where victim selection is based primarily on cost factors, it may happen that the same process is always picked as a victim. As a result, this process never completes its designated task, a *starvation* situation that needs to be dealt with in any practical system. Clearly, we must ensure that a process can be picked as a victim only a (small) finite number of times. The most common solution is to include the number of rollbacks in the cost factor.

Summary

A deadlock state occurs when two or more processes are waiting indefinitely for an event that can be caused only by one of the waiting processes. Principally, there are three methods for dealing with deadlocks:

- Use some protocol to prevent or avoid deadlocks, ensuring that the system will never enter a deadlock state.
- Allow the systems to enter deadlock state, detect it, and then recover.
- Ignore the problem all together, and pretend that deadlocks never occur in the system. This solution is the one used by most operating systems, including UNIX.

A deadlock situation may occur if and only if four necessary conditions hold simultaneously in the system: mutual exclusion, hold and wait, no pre emption, and circular wait. To prevent deadlocks, we ensure that at least one of the necessary conditions never holds.

Another method for avoiding deadlock that is less stringent than the prevention algorithms is to have a priority information on how each process will be utilizing the resources. The banker's algorithm, for example, needs to know the maximum number of each resource class that may be requested by each process. Using this information, we can define a deadlock-avoidance algorithm.

If a system does not employ a protocol to ensure that deadlocks will never occur, then a detection-and-recovery scheme must be employed. A deadlock-detection algorithm must be invoked to determine whether a deadlock has occurred. If a deadlock is detected, the system must recover either by terminating some of the deadlocked processes, or by pre empting resources from some of the deadlocked processes.

In a system that selects victims for rollback primarily on the basis of cost factors, starvation may occur. As a result, the selected process never completes its designated task.

Storage Management

The main purpose of a computer system is to execute programs. These programs, together with the data they access, must be in main memory (at least partially) during execution.

To improve both the utilization of the CPU and the speed of its response to users, the computer must keep several processes in memory. Many memory-management schemes exist, reflecting various approaches, and the effectiveness of each algorithm depends on the situation. Selection of a memory-management scheme for a system depends on many factors, especially on the *hardware* design of the system. Each algorithm requires its own hardware support.

Since main memory is usually too small to accommodate all the data and programs permanently, the computer system uses disks as the primary on-lines storage medium of information (both programs and data). The file system provides the mechanism for on-line storage of and access to both data and programs residing on the disks. A file is a collection of related information defined by its creator. The files are mapped; by the operating system onto physical devices. Files are normally organized into directories to ease their use.

7

Memory Management

We showed how the CPU can be shared by a set of processes. As a result of CPU scheduling, we can improve both the utilization of the CPU and the speed of the computer's response to it's users. To realize this increase in performance, however, we must keep several processes in memory; that is, we must *share* memory.

In this chapter, we discuss various ways to manage memory. The memory-management algorithms vary from a primitive base-machine approach to paging and segmentation strategies. Each approach has its own advantages and disadvantages. Selection of a memory-management method for a specific system depends on many factors, especially on the *hardware* design of the system. As we shall see, many algorithms require hardware support, although recent designs have closely integrated the hardware and operating system.

Background

Memory is central to the operation of a modern computer system. Memory consists of a large array of words or bytes, each with its own address. The CPU fetches instructions from memory according to the value of the program counter. These instructions may cause additional loading from and storing to specific memory addresses.

A typical instruction-execution cycle, for example, first fetches an instruction from memory. The instruction is then decoded and may cause operands to be fetched from memory. After the instruction has been executed on the operands, results may be stored back in memory. The memory unit sees only a stream of memory addresses; it does not know how they are generated (by the instruction counter, indexing, indirection, literal addresses, and so on) or what they are for (instructions or data). Accordingly, we can ignore *how* a memory address is generated by a program. We are interested in only the sequence of memory addresses generated by the running program.

Address Binding

Usually, a program resides on a disk as a binary executable file. The program must be brought into memory and placed within a process for it to be executed. Depending on the memory management in use, the process may be moved between disk and memory during its execution. The collection of processes on the disk that is waiting to be brought into memory for execution forms the input queue.

The normal procedure is to select one of the processes in the input queue and to load that process into memory. As the process is executed, it accesses instructions and data from memory. Eventually, the process terminates, and its memory space is declared available.

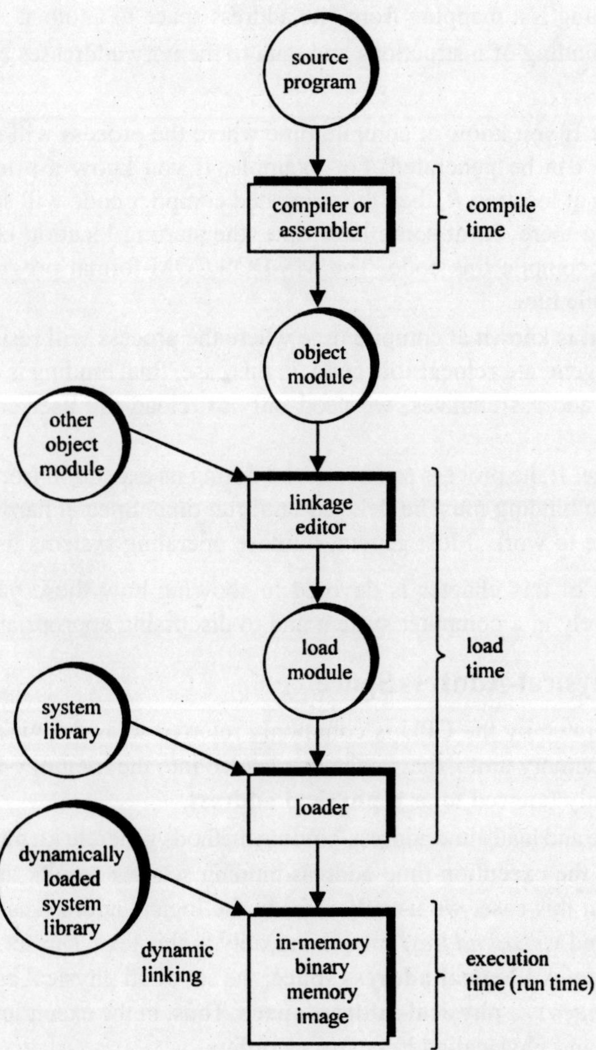

Fig. 7.1. Multistep processing of a user program.

Most systems allow a user process to reside in any part of the physical memory. Thus, although the address space of the computer starts at 00000, the first address of the user process does not need to be 00000. This arrangement affects the addresses that the user program can use. In most cases, a user program will go through several steps—some of which may be optional—before being executed. Addresses may be represented in different ways during these steps. Addresses in the source program are generally symbolic (such as *count*). A compiler will typically bind these symbolic addresses to relocatable addresses (such as "14 bytes from the beginning of this module"). The linkage editor or loader will in turn bind these relocatable addresses to absolute addresses (such as 74014). Each binding is a mapping from one address space to another.

Classically, the binding of instructions and data to memory addresses can be done at any step along the way:

- **Compile time:** If you know at compile time where the process will reside in memory, then **absolute code** can be generated. For example, if you know a priori that a user process resides starting at location *R*, then the generated compiler code will start at that location and extend up from there. If, at some later time, the starting location changes, then it will be necessary to recompile this code. The MS-DOS.COM-format programs are absolute code bound at compile time.
- **Load time:** If it is known at compile time where the process will reside in memory, then the compiler must generate **relocatable code**. In this case, final binding is delayed until load time. If the starting address changes, we need only to reload the user code to incorporate this changed value.
- **Execution time:** If the process can be moved during its execution from one memory segment to another, then binding must be delayed until run time. Special hardware must be available for this scheme to work. Most general-purpose operating systems use this method.

A major portion of this chapter is devoted to showing how these various bindings can be implemented effectively in a computer system and to discussing appropriate hardware support.

Logical-versus Physical-Address Space

An address generated by the CPU is commonly referred to as a **logical address**, whereas an address seen by the memory unit—that is, the one loaded into the **memory-address register** of the memory-–is commonly referred to as a **physical address**.

The compile-time and load-time address-binding methods generate identical logical and physical addresses. However, the execution-time address-binding scheme results the differing logical and physical addresses. In this case, we usually refer to the logical address as a **virtual address**. We use *logical address* and *virtual address* interchangeably in this text. The set of all logical addresses generated by a program is a **logical-address space**; the set of all physical addresses corresponding to these logical addresses is a **physical-address space**. Thus, in the execution-time address-binding scheme, the logical- and physical-address spaces differ.

The run-time mapping from virtual to physical addresses is done by a hardware device called the **memory-management unit (MMU)**. We can choose from among many different methods to accomplish such a mapping. For the time being, we illustrate this mapping with a simple MMU scheme, which is a generalization of the base-register scheme. This method requires hardware support slightly different from the hardware configuration. The base register is now called a **relocation register**. The value in the relocation register is *added* to every address generated by a user process at the time it is sent to memory. For example, if the base is at 14000, then an attempt by the user to address location 0 is dynamically relocated to location 14000; an access to location 346 is mapped to location 14346. The MS-DOS operating system running on the Intel 80x86 family of processors uses four relocation registers when loading and running processes.

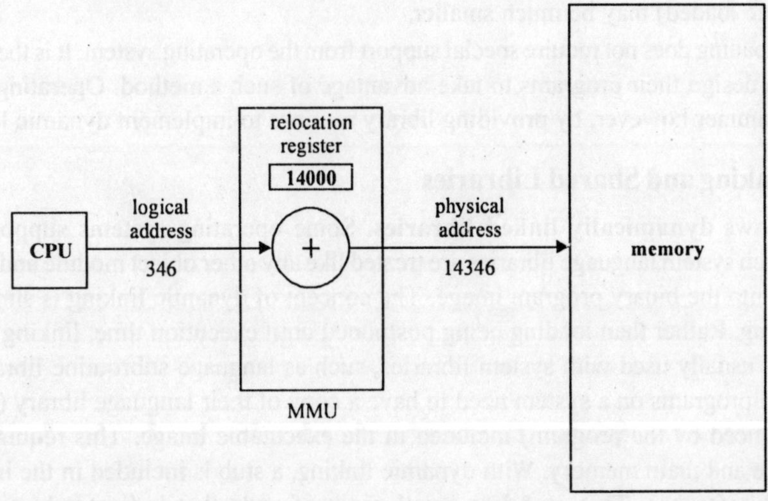

Fig. 7.2. Dynamic relocation using a relocation register.

The user program never sees the *real* physical addresses. The program can create a pointer to location 346, store it in memory, manipulate it, compare it to other addresses—all as the number 346. Only when it is used as a memory address (in an indirect load or store, perhaps) is it relocated relative to the base register. The user program deals with *logical* addresses. The memory-mapping hardware converts logical addresses into physical addresses. The final location of a referenced memory address is not determined until the reference is made.

We now have two different types of addresses: logical addresses (in the range 0 to *max*) and physical addresses (in the range $R + 0$ to $R + max$ for a base value R). The user generates only logical addresses and thinks that the process runs in locations 0 to *max*. The user program supplies logical addresses; these logical addresses must be mapped to physical addresses before they are used.

The concept of a *logical-address space* that is bound to a separate *physical address space* is central to proper memory management.

Dynamic Loading

In our discussion so far, the entire program and data of a process must be in physical memory for the process to execute. The size of a process is limited to the size of physical memory. To obtain better memory-space utilization, we can use **dynamic loading**. With dynamic loading, a routine is not loaded until it is called. All routines are kept on disk in a relocatable load format. The main program is loaded into memory and is executed. When a routine needs to call another routine, the calling routine first checks to see whether the other routine has been loaded. If not, the relocatable linking loader is called to load the desired routine into memory and to update the program's address tables to reflect this change. Then, control is passed to the newly loaded routine.

The advantage of dynamic loading is that an unused routine is never loaded. This method is particularly useful when large amounts of code are needed to handle infrequently occurring cases, such as error routines. In this case, although the total program size may be large, the portion that is used (and hence loaded) may be much smaller.

Dynamic loading does not require special support from the operating system. It is the responsibility of the users to design their programs to take advantage of such a method. Operating systems may help the programmer however, by providing library routines to implement dynamic loading.

Dynamic Linking and Shared Libraries

It also shows **dynamically linked libraries**. Some operating systems support only **static linking**, in which system language libraries are treated like any other object module and are combined by the loader into the binary program image. The concept of dynamic linking is similar to that of dynamic loading. Rather than loading being postponed until execution time, linking is postponed. This feature is usually used with system libraries, such as language subroutine libraries. Without this facility, all programs on a system need to have a copy of their language library (or at least the routines referenced by the program) included in the executable image. This requirement wastes both disk space and main memory. With dynamic linking, a stub is included in the image for each library-routine reference. This *stub* is a small piece of code that indicates how to locate the appropriate memory-resident library routine, or how to load the library if the routine is not already present.

When this stub is executed, it checks to see whether the needed routine is already in memory. If not, the program loads the routine into memory. Either way, the stub replaces itself with the address of the routine, and executes the routine. Thus, the next time that code segment is reached, the library routine is executed directly, incurring no cost for dynamic linking. Under this scheme, all processes that use a language library execute only one copy of the library code.

This feature can be extended to library updates (such as bug fixes). A library may be replaced by a new version, and all programs that reference the library will automatically use the new version. Without dynamic linking, all such programs would need to be relinked to gain access to the new library. So that programs will not accidentally execute new, incompatible versions of libraries, version information is included in both the program and the library. More than one version of a library may be loaded into memory, and each program uses its version information to decide which copy of the library to use. Minor changes retain the same version number, whereas major changes increment the version number. Thus, only programs that are compiled with the new library version are affected by the incompatible changes incorporated in it. Other programs linked before the new library was installed will continue using the older library. This system is also known as **shared libraries**.

Unlike dynamic loading, dynamic linking generally requires help from the operating system. If the processes in memory are protected from one another then the operating system is the only entity that can be checked to see whether the needed routine is in another process memory space, or that can allow multiple processes to access the same memory addresses.

Overlays

To enable a process to be larger than the amount of memory allocated to it, we can use **overlays**. The idea of overlays is to keep in memory only those instructions and data that are needed at any given time. When other instructions are needed, they are loaded into space occupied previously by instructions that are no longer needed.

As an example, consider a two-pass assembler. During pass 1, it constructs a symbol table; then, during pass 2, it generates machine-language code. We may be able to partition such an assembler into pass 1 code, pass 2 code, the symbol table, and common support routines used by both pass 1 and pass 2. Assume that the sizes of these components are as follows:

Pass 1	70 KB
Pass 2	80 KB
Symbol table	20 KB
Common routines	30 KB

To load everything at once, we would require 200 KB of memory. If only 150 KB is available, we cannot run our process. However, notice that pass 1 and pass 2 do not need to be in memory at the same time. We thus define two overlays: Overlay *A* is the symbol table, common routines, and pass 1, and overlay *B* is the symbol table, common routines, and pass 2.

We add an overlay driver (10 KB) and start with overlay *A* in memory. When we finish pass 1, we jump to the overlay driver, which reads overlay *B* into memory, overwriting overlay *A*, and then transfer control to pass 2. Overlay *A* needs only 120 KB, whereas overlay *B* needs 130 KB. We can now run our assembler in the 150 KB of memory. It will load somewhat faster because fewer data need to be transferred before execution starts. However, it will run somewhat slower, due to the extra I/O to read the code for overlay *B* over the code for overlay *A*.

The code for overlay *A* and the code for overlay *B* are kept on disk as absolute memory images, and are read by the overlay driver as needed. Special relocation and linking algorithms are needed to construct the overlays.

As in dynamic loading, overlays do not require any special support from the operating system. They can be implemented completely by the user with simple file structures, reading from the files into memory and then jumping to that memory and executing the newly read instructions. The operating system notices only that there is more I/O than usual.

The programmer, on the other hand, must design and program the overlay structure properly. This task can be a major undertaking, requiring complete knowledge of the structure of the program, its code, and its data structures. Because the program is, by definition, large—small programs do not need to be overlaid—obtaining a sufficient understanding of the program may be difficult. For these reasons, the use of overlays is currently limited to microcomputer and other systems that have limited amounts of physical memory and that lack hardware support for more advanced techniques. Some micro computer compilers provide the programmer with support for overlays to make the task easier. Automatic techniques to run large programs in limited amounts of physical memory are certainly preferable.

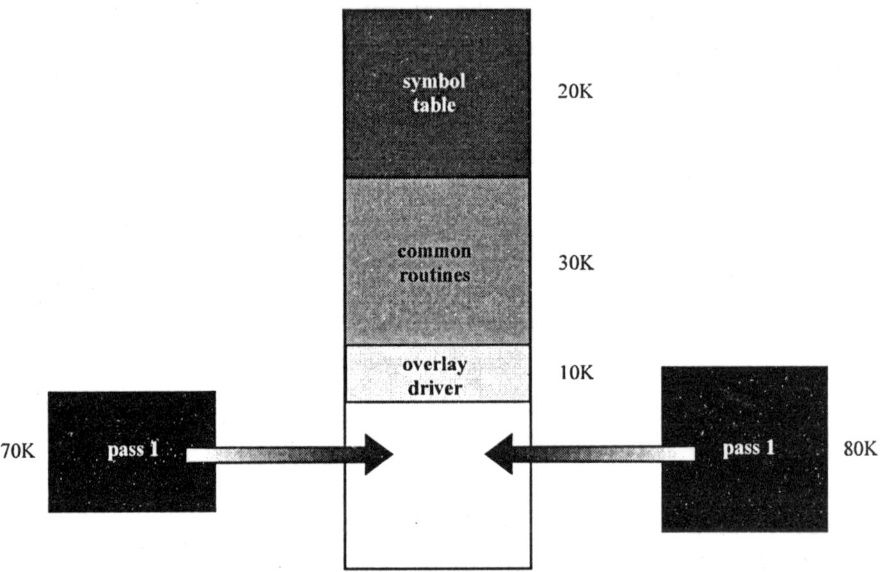

Fig. 7.3. Overlays for a two-pass assembler.

Swapping

A process, however, can be **swapped** temporarily out of memory to a **backing store**, and then brought back into memory for continued execution. For example, assume a multiprogramming environment with a round-robin CPU-scheduling algorithm. When a quantum expires, the memory manager will start to swap out the process that just finished, and to swap in another process to the memory space that has been freed. In the meantime, the CPU scheduler will allocate a time slice to some other process in memory. When each process finishes its quantum, it will be swapped with another process. Ideally, the memory manager can swap processes fast enough that some processes will be in memory, ready to execute, when the CPU scheduler wants to reschedule the CPU. The quantum must also be sufficiently large that reasonable amounts of comprising are done between swaps.

A variant of this swapping policy is used for priority-based scheduling algorithms. If a higher-priority process arrives and wants service, the memory manager can swap out the lower-priority process so that it can load and execute the higher-priority process. When the higher-priority process finishes, the lower-priority process can be swapped back in and continued. This variant of swapping is sometimes called **roll out**, **roll in**.

Normally a process that is swapped out will be swapped back into the same memory space that it occupied previously. This restriction is dictated by the method of address binding. If binding is done at assembly or load time, then the process cannot be moved to different locations. If execution-time binding is being used, then a process can be swapped into a different memory space, because the physical addresses are computed during execution time.

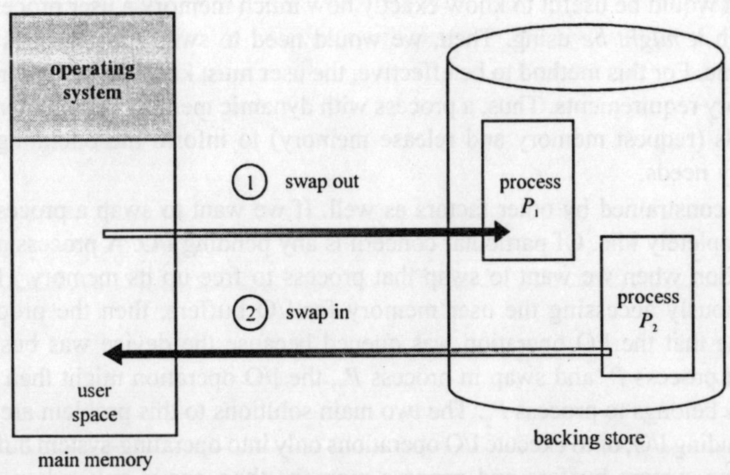

Fig. 7.4. Swapping of two processes using a disk as a backing store.

Swapping requires a backing store. The backing store is commonly a fast disk. It must be large enough to accommodate copies of all memory images for all users, and it must provide direct access to these memory images. The system maintains a **ready queue** consisting of all processes whose memory images are on the backing store or in memory and are ready to run. Whenever the CPU scheduler decides to execute a process, it calls the dispatcher. The dispatcher checks to see whether the next process in the queue is in memory. If not, and there is no free memory region, the dispatcher swaps out a process currently in memory and swaps in the desired process. It then reloads registers as normal and transfers control to the selected process.

The context-switch time in such a swapping system is fairly high. To get an idea of the context-switch time, let us assume that the user process is of size 1 MB and the backing store is a standard hard disk with a transfer rate of 5 MB per second. The actual transfer of the 1 MB process to or from memory takes.

1000 KB/5000 KB per second	=	1/5 second
	=	200 milliseconds.

Assuming that no head seeks are necessary and an average latency of 8 milliseconds, the swap time takes 208 milliseconds. Since we must both swap out and swap in, the total swap time is then about 416 milliseconds

For efficient CPU utilization, we want our execution time for each process to be long relative to the swap time. Thus, in a round-robin CPU-scheduling algorithm, for example, the time quantum should be substantially larger than 0.416 seconds.

Notice that the major part of the swap time is transfer time. The total transfer time is directly proportional to the *amount* of the memory swapped. If we have a computer system with 128 MB of main memory and a resident operating system taking 5 MB, the maximum size of the user process is 123 MB. However, many user processes may be much smaller than this size—say, 1 MB. A 1 MB process could be swapped out in 208 milliseconds, compared to the 24.6 seconds for swapping 123 MB. Therefore, it would be useful to know exactly how much memory a user process *is* using, not simply how much it *might be* using. Then, we would need to swap only what is actually used, reducing swap time. For this method to be effective, the user must keep the system informed of any changes in memory requirements. Thus, a process with dynamic memory requirements will need to issue system calls (request memory and release memory) to inform the operating system of its changing memory needs.

Swapping is constrained by other factors as well. If we want to swap a process, we must be sure that it is completely idle. Of particular concern is any pending I/O. A process may be waiting for an I/O operation when we want to swap that process to free up its memory. However, if the I/O is asynchronously accessing the user memory for I/O buffers, then the process cannot be swapped. Assume that the I/O operation was queued because the device was busy. Then, if we were to swap out process P_1 and swap in process P_2, the I/O operation might then attempt to use memory that now belongs to process P_2. The two main solutions to this problem are never to swap a process with pending I/O, or to execute I/O operations only into operating-system buffers. Transfers between operating-system buffers and process memory then occur only when the process is swapped in.

The assumption that swapping requires few, if any, head seeks needs further explanation. Generally, swap space is allocated as a chunk of disk, separate from the file system, so that its use is as fast as possible.

Currently, standard swapping is used in few systems. It requires too much swapping time and provides too little execution time to be a reasonable memory-management solution. Modified versions of swapping, however, are found on many systems.

A modification of swapping is used in many versions of UNIX. Swapping was normally disabled, but would start if many processes were running and were using a threshold amount of memory. Swapping would again be halted if the load on the system were reduced.

Early PCs lacked sophisticated hardware (or operating systems that take advantage of the hardware) to implement more advanced memory management methods, but they were used to run multiple large processes by a modified version of swapping. A prime example is the Microsoft Windows 3.1 operating system, which supports concurrent execution of processes in memory. If a new process is loaded and there is insufficient main memory, an old process is swapped to disk. This operating system, however, does not provide full swapping, because the user, rather than the scheduler, decides when it is time to pre empt one process for another. Any swapped-out process remains swapped out (and not executing) until the user selects that process to run.

Contiguous Memory Allocation

The main memory must accommodate both the operating system and the various user processes. We therefore need to allocate different parts of the main memory in the most efficient way possible. This section will explain one common method, contiguous memory allocation.

The memory is usually divided into two partitions: one for the resident operating system, and one for the user processes. We may place the operating system in either low memory or high memory. The major factor affecting this decision is the location of the interrupt vector. Since the interrupt vector is often in low memory, programmers usually place the operating system in low memory as well. Thus, in this text, we shall discuss only the situation where the operating system resides in low memory. The development of the other situation is similar.

We usually want several user processes to reside in memory at the same time. We therefore need to consider how to allocate available memory to the processes that are in the input queue waiting to be brought into memory. In this contiguous memory allocation, each process is contained in a single contiguous section of memory.

Memory Protection

Before discussing memory allocation, we must discuss the issue of memory protection—protecting the operating system from user processes, and protecting user processes from one another. We can provide this protection by using a relocation register with a limit register. The relocation register contains the value of the smallest physical address; the limit register contains the range of logical addresses (for example, relocation = 100040 and limit = 74600). With relocation and limit registers, each logical address must be less than the limit register; the MMU maps the logical address *dynamically* by adding the value in the relocation register. This mapped address is sent to memory.

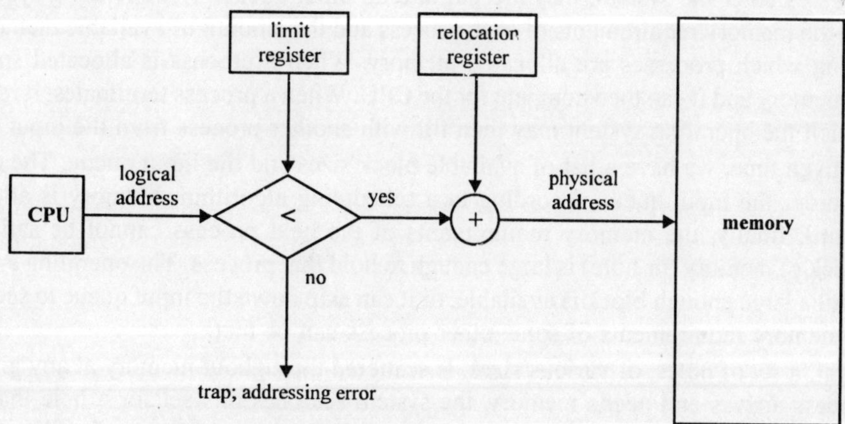

Fig. 7.5. Hardware support for relocation and limit registers.

When the CPU scheduler selects a process for execution, the dispatcher loads the relocation and limit registers with the correct values as part of the context switch. Because every address generated by the CPU is checked against these registers, we can protect both the operating system and the other users' programs and data from being modified by this running process.

The relocation-register scheme provides an effective way to allow the operating-system size to change dynamically. This flexibility is desirable in many situations. For example, the operating system contains code and buffer space for device drivers. If a device driver (or other operating-system service) is not commonly used, we do not want to keep the code and data in memory, as we might be able to use that space for other purposes. Such code is sometimes called **transient** operating-system code; it comes and goes as needed. Thus, using this code changes the size of the operating system during program execution.

Memory Allocation

Now we are ready to turn to memory allocation. One of the simplest methods for memory allocation is to divide memory into several fixed-sized **partitions**. Each partition may contain exactly one process. Thus, the degree of multiprogramming is bound by the number of partitions. In this **multi-partition method**, when a partition is free, a process is selected from the input queue and is loaded into the free partition. When the process terminates, the partition becomes available for another process. This method was originally used by the IBM OS/360 operating system (called MFT); it is no longer in use. The method described next is a generalization of the fixed-partition scheme (called MVT); it is used primarily in a batch environment. Many of the ideas presented here are also applicable to a time-sharing environment in which pure segmentation is used for memory management.

The operating system keeps a table indicating which parts of memory are available and which are occupied. Initially, all memory is available for user processes, and is considered as one large block of available memory, a **hole**. When a process arrives and needs memory, we search for a hole large enough for this process. If we find one, we allocate only as much memory as is needed, keeping the rest available to satisfy future requests.

As processes enter the system, they are put into an input queue. The operating system takes into account the memory requirements of each process and the amount of available memory space in determining which processes are allocated memory. When a process is allocated space, it is loaded into memory and it can then compete for the CPU. When a process terminates, it releases its memory, which the operating system may then fill with another process from the input queue.

At any given time, we have a list of available block sizes and the input queue. The operating system can order the input queue according to a scheduling algorithm. Memory is allocated to processes until, finally, the memory requirements of the next process cannot be satisfied; no available block of memory (or hole) is large enough to hold that process. The operating system can then wait until a large enough block is available, or it can skip down the input queue to see whether the smaller memory requirements of some other process can be met.

In general, a *set* of holes, of various sizes, is scattered throughout memory at any given time. When a process arrives and needs memory, the system searches this set for a hole that is large enough for this process. If the hole is too large, it is split into two: One part is allocated to the arriving process; the other is returned to the set of holes. When a process terminates, it releases its block of memory, which is then placed back in the set of holes. If the new hole is adjacent to other holes, these adjacent holes are merged to form one larger hole. At this point, the system may need to check whether there are processes waiting for memory and whether this newly freed and recombined memory could satisfy the demands of any of these waiting processes.

The procedure is a particular instance of the general **dynamic storage-allocation problem,** which is how to satisfy a request of size *n* from a list of free holes. There are many solutions to this problem. The set of holes is searched to determine which hole is best to allocate. The **first-fit, best-fit**, and **worst-fit** strategies are the most common ones used to select a free hole from the set of available holes.

- *First fit*: Allocate the *first* hole that is big enough. Searching can start either at the beginning of the set of holes or where the previous first-fit search ended. We can stop searching as soon as we find a free hole that is large enough.

- *Best fit*: Allocate the *smallest* hole that is big enough. We must search the entire list, unless the list is kept ordered by size. This strategy produces the smallest leftover hole.
- *Worst fit*: Allocate the *largest* hole. Again, we must search the entire list, unless it is sorted by size. This strategy produces the largest leftover hole, which may be more useful than the smaller leftover hole from a best-fit approach.

Simulations have shown that both first fit and best are better than worst fit in terms of decreasing both time and storage utilization. Neither first fit nor best fit is clearly better in terms of storage utilization, but first fit is generally faster.

These algorithms, however, suffer from **external fragmentation**. As processes are loaded and removed from memory, the free memory space is broken into little pieces. External fragmentation exists when enough total memory space exists to satisfy a request, but it is not contiguous; storage is fragmented into a large number of small holes. This fragmentation problem can be severe. In the worst case, we could have a block of free (or wasted) memory between every two processes. If all this memory were in one big free block, we might be able to run several more processes.

The selection of the first-fit versus best-fit strategies can affect the amount of fragmentation. (First fit is better for some systems, whereas best fit is better for others.) Another factor is which end of a free block is allocated. (Which is the leftover piece—the one on the top, or the one on the bottom?) No matter which algorithm is used, external fragmentation will be a problem.

Depending on the total amount of memory storage and the average process size, external fragmentation may be a minor or a major problem. Statistical analysis of first fit, for instance, reveals that, even with some optimization, given N allocated blocks, another $0.5N$ blocks will be lost due to fragmentation. That is, one-third of memory may be unusable! This property is known as the 50-**percent rule**.

Fragmentation

Memory fragmentation can be internal as well as external. Consider a multiple-partition allocation scheme with a hole of 18,464 bytes. Suppose that the next process requests 18,462 bytes. If we allocate exactly the requested block, we are left with a hole of 2 bytes. The overhead to keep track of this hole will be substantially larger than the hole itself. The general approach is to break the physical memory into fixed-sized blocks, and allocate memory in unit of block sizes. With this approach, the memory allocated to a process may be slightly larger than the requested memory. The difference between these two numbers is **internal fragmentation**—memory that is internal to a partition but is not being used.

One solution to the problem of external fragmentation is **compaction**. The goal is to shuffle the memory contents to place all free memory together in one large block. Compaction is not always possible. If relocation is static and is done at assembly or load time, compaction cannot be done; compaction is possible *only* if relocation is dynamic, and is done at execution time. If addresses are relocated dynamically, relocation requires only moving the program and data, and then changing the base register to reflect the new base address. When compaction is possible, we must determine its cost. The simplest compaction algorithm is simply to move all processes toward one end of memory; all holes move in the other direction, producing one large hole of available memory. This scheme can be expensive.

Another possible solution to the external-fragmentation problem is to permit the logical-address space of a process to be noncontiguous, thus allowing a process to be allocated physical memory wherever the latter is available. Two complementary techniques achieve this solution: paging (Section 9.4) and segmentation (Section 9.5). These techniques can also be combined (Section 9.6).

Paging

Paging is a memory-management scheme that permits the physical-address space of a process to be noncontiguous. Paging avoids the considerable problem of fitting the varying-sized memory chunks onto the backing store, from which most of the previous memory-management schemes suffered. When some code fragments or data residing in main memory need to be swapped out, space must be found on the backing store. The fragmentation problems discussed in connection with main memory are also prevalent with backing store, except that access is much slower, so compaction is impossible. Because of its advantages over the previous methods, paging in its various forms is commonly used in most operating systems.

Traditionally, support for paging has been handled by hardware. However, recent designs have implemented paging by closely integrating the hardware and operating system, especially on 64-bit microprocessors.

8

Virtual Memory

FIFO Page Replacement

The simplest page-replacement algorithm is a FIFO algorithm. A FIFO replacement algorithm associates with each page the time when that page was brought into memory. When a page must be replaced, the oldest page is chosen. Notice that it is not strictly necessary to record the time when a page is brought in. We can create a FIFO queue to hold all pages in memory. We replace the page at the head of the queue. When a page is brought into memory, we insert it at the tail of the queue.

For our example reference string, our three frames are initially empty. The first three references (7, 0, 1) cause page faults, and are brought into these empty frames. The next reference (2) replaces page 7, because page 7 was brought in first. Since 0 is the next reference and 0 is already in memory, we have no fault for this reference. The first reference to 3 results in page 0 being replaced, since it was the first of the three pages in memory (0, 1, and 2) to be brought in. Because of this replacement, the next reference, to 0, will fault. Page 1 is then replaced by page 0. This process continues as shown in Figure 8.1. Every time a fault occurs, we show which pages are in our three frames. There are 15 faults altogether.

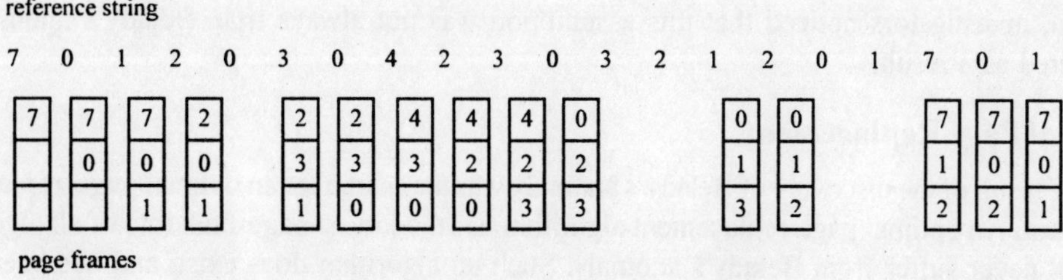

Fig. 8.1. FIFO page-replacement algorithm.

The FIFO page-replacement algorithm is easy to understand and program. However, its performance is not always good. The page replaced may be an initialization module that was used a long time ago and is no longer needed. On the other hand, it could contain a heavily used variable that was initialized early and is in constant use.

Notice that, even if we select for replacement a page that is in active use, everything still works correctly. After we page out an active page to bring in a new one, a fault occurs almost immediately to retrieve the active page. Some other page will need to be replaced to bring the active page back into memory. Thus, a bad replacement choice increases the page-fault rate and slows process execution, but does not cause incorrect execution.

To illustrate the problems that are possible with a FIFO page-replacement algorithm, we consider the reference string

1, 2, 3, 4, 1, 2, 5, 1, 2, 3, 4, 5.

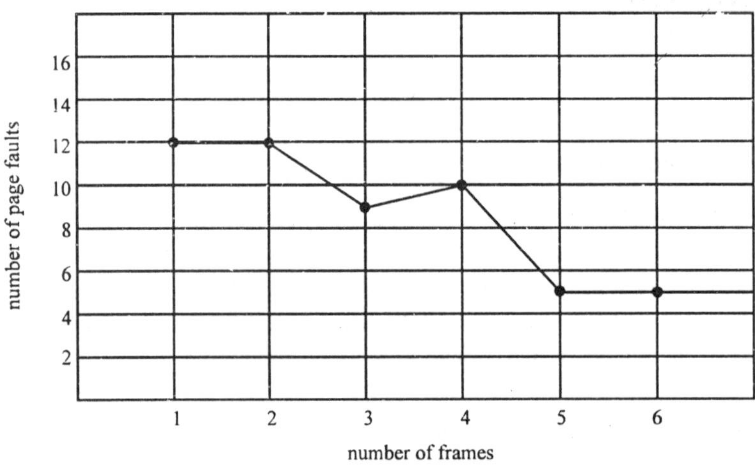

Fig. 8.2. Page-fault curve for FIFO replacement on a reference string.

Figure 8.2 shows the curve of page faults versus the number of available frames. We notice that the number of faults for four frames (10) is *greater* than the number of faults for three frames (nine)! This most unexpected result is known as **Belady's anomaly:** For some page-replacement algorithms, the page-fault rate may *increase* as the number of allocated frames increases. We would expect that giving more memory to a process would improve its performance. In some early research, investigators noticed that this assumption was not always true. Belady's anomaly was discovered as a result.

Optimal Page Replacement

One result of the discovery of Belady's anomaly was the search for an optimal **page-replacement algorithm.** An optimal page-replacement algorithm has the lowest page-fault rate of all algorithms, and will never suffer from Belady's anomaly. Such an algorithm does exist, and has been called OPT or MIN. It is simply

Replace the page that will not be used
for the longest period of time

Use of this page-replacement algorithm guarantees the lowest possible page-fault rate for a fixed number of frames.

For example, on our sample reference string, the optimal page-replacement algorithm would yield nine page faults, as shown in Figure 8.3. The first three references cause faults that fill the three empty frames. The reference to page 2 replaces page 7, because 7 will not be used until reference 18, whereas page 0 will be used at 5, and page 1 at 14. The reference to page 3 replaces page 1, as page 1 will be the last of the three pages in memory to be referenced again. With only nine page faults, optimal replacement is much better than a FIFO algorithm, which had 15 faults. (If we ignore the first three, which all algorithms must suffer, then optimal replacement is twice as good as FIFO replacement). In fact, no replacement algorithm can process this reference string in three frames with less than nine faults.

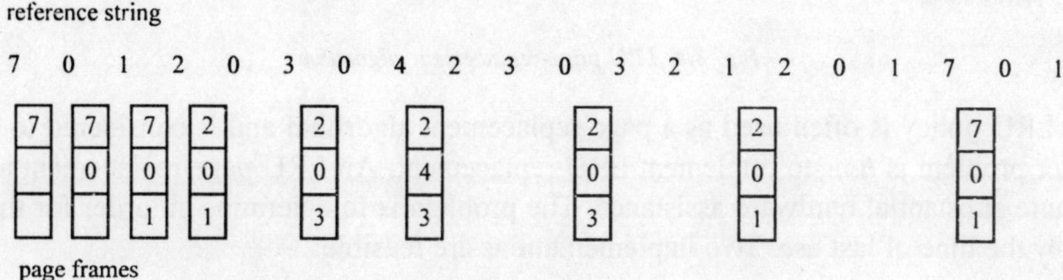

Fig. 8.3. Optimal page-replacement algorithm.

Unfortunately, the optimal page-replacement algorithm is difficult to implement, because it requires future knowledge of the reference string. As a result, the optimal algorithm is used mainly for comparison studies. For instance, it may be useful to know that, although a new algorithm is not optimal, it is within 12.3 percent of optimal at worst, and within 4.7 percent on average.

LRU Page Replacement

If the optimal algorithm is not feasible, perhaps an approximation to the optimal algorithm is possible. The key distinction between the FIFO and OPT algorithms (other than looking backward or forward in time) is that the FIFO algorithm uses the time when a page was brought into memory; the OPT algorithm uses the time when a page is to be *used.* IF we use the recent past as an approximation of the near future, then we will replace the page that *has not been used* for the longest period of time. This approach is the **least-recently-used (LRU)** algorithm.

LRU replacement associates with each page the time of that page's last use. When a page must be replaced, LRU chooses that page that has not been used for the longest period of time. This strategy is the optimal page-replacement algorithm looking backward in time, rather than forward. (Strangely, if we let S^R be the reverse of a reference string S, then the page-fault rate for the OPT algorithm on S is the same as the page-fault rate for the OPT algorithm on S^R. Similarly, the page-fault rate for the LRU algorithm on S is the same as the page-fault rate for the LRU algorithm on S^R.)

The result of applying LRU replacement to our example reference string. The LRU algorithm produces 12 faults. Notice that the first five faults are the same as the optimal replacement. When the reference to page 4 occurs, however, LRU replacement sees that, of the three frames in memory, page 2 was used least recently. The most recently used page is page 0, and just before that page 3 was used. Thus, the LRU algorithm replaces page 2, not knowing that page 2 is about to be used. When it then faults for page 2, the LRU algorithm replaces page 3 since, of the three pages in memory {0, 3, 4}, page 3 is the least recently used. Despite these problems, LRU replacement with 12 faults is still much better than FIFO replacement with 15.

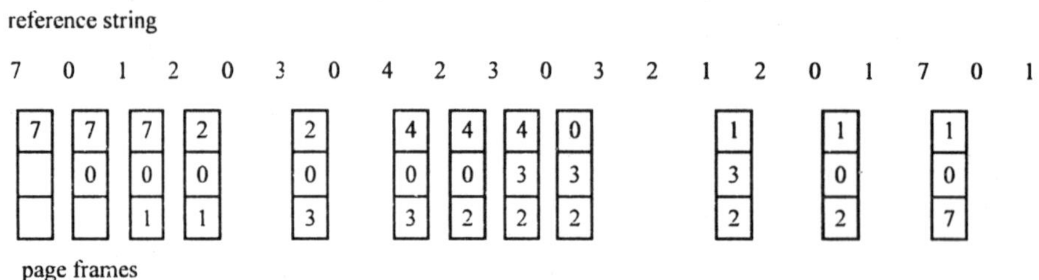

Fig. 8.4. LRU page-replacement algorithm

The LRU policy is often used as a page-replacement algorithm and is considered to be good. The major problem is *how* to implement LRU replacement. An LRU page-replacement algorithm may require substantial hardware assistance. The problem is to determine an order for the frames defined by the time of last use. Two implementations are feasible:

- **Counters:** In the simplest case, we associate with each page-table entry a time-of-use field, and add to the CPU a logical clock or counter. The clock is incremented for every memory reference. Whenever a reference to a page is made, the contents of the clock register are copied to the time-of-use field in the page-table entry for that page. In this way, we always have the "time" of the last reference to each page. We replace the page with the smallest time value. This scheme requires a search of the page table to find the LRU page, and a write to memory (to the time-of-use field in the page table) for each memory access. The times must also be maintained when page tables are changed (due to CPU scheduling). Overflow of the clock must be considered.
- **Stack:** Another approach to implementing LRU replacement is to keep a stack of page numbers. Whenever a page is referenced, it is removed from the stack and put on the top. In this way, the top of the stack is always the most recently used page and the bottom is the LRU page. Because entries must be removed from the middle of the stack, it is best implemented by a doubly linked list, with a head and tail pointer. Removing a page and putting it on the top of the stack then requires changing six pointers at worst. Each update is a little more expensive, but there is no search for a replacement; the tail pointer points to the bottom of the stack, which is the LRU page. This approach is particularly appropriate for software or microcode implementations of LRU replacement.

Neither optimal replacement nor LRU replacement suffers from Belady's anomaly. There is a class of page-replacement algorithms, called **stack algorithms,** that can never exhibit Belady's anomaly. A stack algorithm is an algorithm for which it can be shown that the set of pages in memory for n frames is always a *subset* of the set of pages that would be in memory with $n + 1$ frames. For LRU replacement, the set of pages in memory would be the n most recently referenced pages. If the number of frames is increased, these n pages will still be the most recently referenced and so will still be in memory.

Note that neither implementation of LRU would be conceivable without hardware assistance beyond the standard TLB registers. The updating of the clock fields or stack must be done for *every* memory reference. If we were to use an interrupt for every reference, to allow software to update such data structures, it would slow every memory reference by a factor of at least ten, hence slowing every user process by a factor of ten. Few systems could tolerate that level of overhead for memory management.

LRU Approximation Page Replacement

Few computer systems provide sufficient hardware support for true LRU page replacement. Some systems provide no hardware support, and other page-replacement algorithms (such as a FIFO algorithm) must be used. Many systems provide some help, however, in the form of a **reference bit.** The reference bit for a page is set, by the hardware, whenever that page is referenced (either a read or a write to any byte in the page). Reference bits are associated with each entry in the page table.

Initially, all bits are cleared (to 0) by the operating system. As a user process executes, the bit associated with each page referenced is set (to 1) by the hardware. After some time, we can determine which pages have been used and which have not been used by examining the reference bits. We do not know the *order* of use, but we know which pages were used and which were not used. This partial ordering information leads to many page-replacement algorithms that approximate LRU replacement.

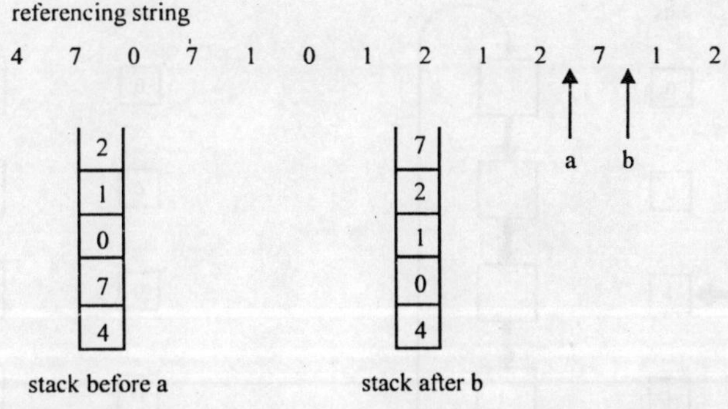

Fig. 8.5. Use of a stack to record the most recent page references.

Additional-Reference-Bits Algorithm

We can gain additional ordering information by recording the reference bits at regular intervals. We can keep an 8-bit byte for each page in a table in memory. At regular intervals (say, every 100 milliseconds), a timer interrupt transfers control to the operating system. The operating system shifts the reference bit for each page into the high-order bit of its 8-bit byte, shifting the other bits right 1 bit, discarding the low-order bit. These 8-bit shift registers contain the history of page use for the last eight time periods. If the shift register contains 00000000, then the page has not been used for eight time periods; a page that is used at least once each period would have a shift register value of 11111111.

A page with a history register value of 11000100 has been used more recently than has one with 01110111. If we interpret these 8-bit bytes as unsigned integers, the page with the lowest number is the LRU page, and it can be replaced. Notice that the numbers are not guaranteed to be unique, however. We can either replace (swap out) all pages with the smallest value, or use a FIFO selection among them.

The number of bits of history can be varied, of course, and would be selected (depending on the hardware available) to make the updating as fast as possible. In the extreme case, the number can be reduced to zero, leaving only the reference bit itself. This algorithm is called the **second-chance page-replacement algorithm.**

Second-Chance Algorithm

The basic algorithm of second-chance replacement is a FIFO replacement algorithm. When a page has been selected, however, we inspect its reference bit. If the value is 0, we proceed to replace this page. If the reference bit is set to 1, however, we give that page a second chance and move on to select the next FIFO page. When a page gets a second chance, its reference bit is cleared and its arrival time is reset to the current time. Thus, a page that is given a second chance will not be replaced until all other pages are replaced (or given second chances). In addition, if a page is used often enough to keep its reference bit set, it will never be replaced.

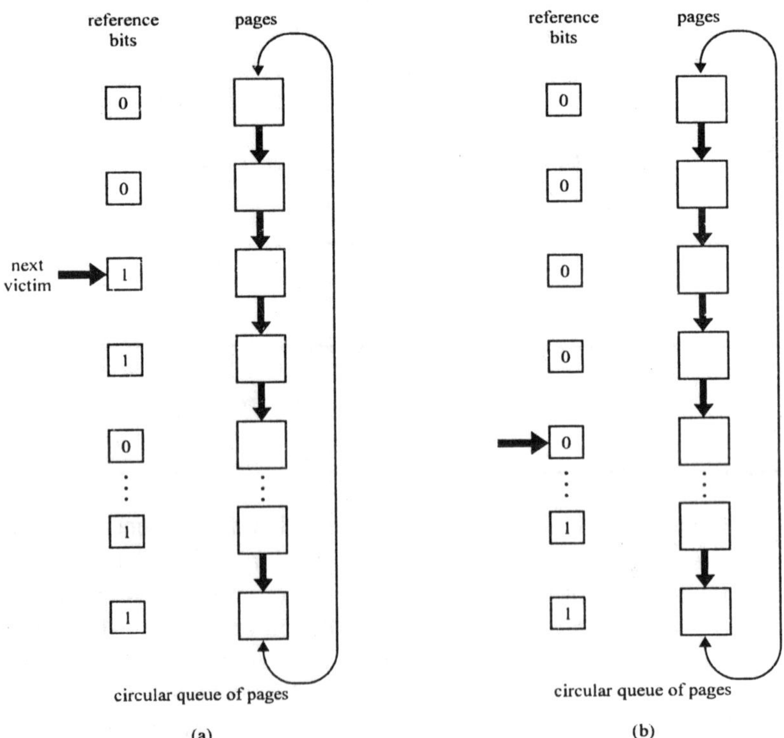

Fig. 8.6. Second-chance (clock) page-replacement algorithm.

One way to implement the second-chance (sometimes referred to as the *clock*) algorithm is as a circular queue. A pointer indicates which page is to be replaced next. When a frame is needed, the pointer advances until it finds a page with a 0 reference bit. As it advances, it clears the reference bits. Once a victim page is found, the page is replaced, and the new page is inserted in the circular queue in that position. Notice that, in the worst case, when all bits are set, the pointer cycles through the whole queue, giving each page a second chance. It clears all the reference bits before selecting the next page for replacement. Second-chance replacement degenerates to FIFO replacement if all bits are set.

Enhanced Second-Chance Algorithm

We can enhance the second-chance algorithm by considering both the reference bit and the modify bit as an ordered pair. With these two bits, we have the following four possible classes:

1. (0, 0) neither recently used nor modified—best page to replace
2. (0, 1) not recently used but modified—not quite as good, because the page will need to be written out before replacement
3. (1, 0) recently used but clean—it probably will be used again soon
4. (1, 1) recently used and modified—it probably will be used again soon, and the page will be needed to be written out to disk before it can be replaced.

When page replacement is called for, each page is in one of these four classes. We use the same scheme as the clock algorithm, but instead of examining whether the page to which we are pointing has the reference bit set to 1, we examine the class to which that page belongs. We replace the first page encountered in the lowest non-empty class. Notice that we may have to scan the circular queue several times before we find a page to be replaced.

This algorithm is used in the Macintosh virtual-memory-management scheme. The major difference between this algorithm and the simpler clock algorithm is that here we give preference to those pages that have been modified to reduce the number of I/Os required.

Counting-Based Page Replacement

There are many other algorithms that can be used for page replacement. For example, we could keep a counter of the number of references that have been made to each page, and develop the following two schemes:–

- The **least frequently used (LFU) page-replacement algorithm** requires that the page with the smallest count be replaced. The reason for this selection is that an actively used page should have a large reference count. This algorithm suffers from the situation in which a page is used heavily during the initial phase of a process, but then is never used again. Since it was used heavily, it has a large count and remains in memory even though it is no longer needed. One solution is to shift the counts right by 1 bit at regular intervals, forming an exponentially decaying average usage count.
- The **most frequently used (MFU) page-replacement algorithm** is based on the argument that the page with the smallest count was probably just brought in and has yet to be used.

As you might expect, neither MFU nor LFU replacement is common. The implementation of these algorithms is expensive, and they do not approximate OPT replacement well.

Page-Buffering Algorithm

Other procedures are often used in addition to a specific page-replacement algorithm. For example, systems commonly keep a pool of free frames. When a page fault occurs, a victim frame is chosen as before. However, the desired page is read into a free frame from the pool before the victim is written out. This procedure allows the process to restart as soon as possible, without waiting for the victim page to be written out. When the victim is later written out, its frame is added to the free-frame pool.

An expansion of this idea is to maintain a list of modified pages. Whenever the paging device is idle, a modified page is selected and is written to the disk. Its modify bit is then reset. This scheme increases the probability that a page will be clean when it is selected for replacement, and will not need to be written out.

Another modification is to keep a pool of free frames, but to remember which page was in each frame. Since the frame contents are not modified when a frame is written to the disk, the old page can be reused directly from the free-frame pool if it is needed before that frame is reused. No I/O is needed in this case. When a page fault occurs, we first check whether the desired page is in the free-frame pool. If it is not, we must select a free frame and read into it.

This technique is used in the VAX/VMS system, with a FIFO replacement algorithm. When the FIFO replacement algorithm mistakenly replaces a page that is still in active use, that page is quickly retrieved from the free-frame buffer, and no I/O is necessary. The free-frame buffer provides protection against the relatively poor, but simple, FIFO replacement algorithm. This method is necessary because the early versions of the VAX did not implement the reference bit correctly.

Allocation of Frames

How do we allocate the fixed amount of free memory among the various processes? If we have 93 free frames and two processes, how many frames does each process get?

The simplest case of virtual memory is the single-user system. Consider a single-user system with 128 KB memory composed of pages of size 1 KB. Thus, there are 128 frames. The operating system may take 35 KB, leaving 93 frames for the user process. Under pure demand paging, all 93 frames would initially be put on the free-frame list. When a user process started execution, it would generate a sequence of page faults. The first 93 page faults would all get free-frames from the free-frame list. When the free-frame list was exhausted, a page-replacement algorithm would be used to select one of the 93 in-memory pages to be replaced with the ninety-fourth, and so on. When the process terminated, the 93 frames would once again be placed on the free-frame list.

There are many variations on this simple strategy. We can require that the operating system allocate all its buffer and table space from the free-frame list. When this space is not in use by the operating system, it can be used to support user paging. We can try to keep three free frames reserved on the free-frame list at all times. Thus, when a page fault occurs, there is a free frame available to page into. While the page swap is taking place, a replacement can be selected, which is then written to the disk as the user process continues to execute.

Other variants are also possible, but the basic strategy is clear: The user process is allocated any free frame.

A different problem arises when demand paging is combined with multi-programming. Multiprogramming puts two (or more) processes in memory at the same time.

Minimum Number of Frames

Our strategies for the allocations of frames are constrained in various ways. We cannot allocate more than the total number of available frames (unless there is page sharing). We must also allocate at least a minimum number of frames. Obviously, as the number of frames allocated to each process decreases, the page-fault-rate increases, slowing process execution.

Besides the undesirable performance properties of allocating only a few frames, there is a minimum number of frames that must be allocated. This minimum number is defined by the instruction-set architecture. Remember that, when a page fault occurs before an executing instruction is complete, the instruction must be restarted. Consequently, we must have enough frames to hold all the different pages that any single instruction can reference.

For example, consider a machine in which all memory-reference instructions have only one memory address. Thus, we need at least one frame for the instruction and one frame for the memory reference. In addition, if one-level indirect addressing is allowed (for example, a load instruction on page 16 can refer to an address on page 0, which is an indirect reference to page 23), then paging requires at least three frames per process. Think about what might happen if a process had only two frames.

The minimum number of frames is defined by the given computer architecture. For example, the move instruction for the PDP-11 is more than one word for some addressing modes, and thus the instruction itself may straddle two pages. In addition, each of its two operands may be indirect references, for a total of six frames. The worst case for the IBM 370 is probably the MVC instruction. Since the instruction is storage to storage, it takes 6 bytes and can straddle two pages. The block of characters to move and the area to be moved to can each also straddle two pages. This situation would require six frames. (Actually, the worst case occurs when the MVC instruction is the operand of an EXECUTE instruction that straddles a page boundary; in this case, we need eight frames.)

The worst-case scenario occurs in computer architectures that allow multiple levels of indirection (for example, each 16-bit word could contain a 15-bit address plus a 1-bit indirect indicator). Theoretically, a simple load instruction could reference an indirect address that could reference an indirect address (on another page) that could also reference an indirect address (on yet another page), and so on, until every page in virtual memory had been touched. Thus, in the worst case, the entire virtual memory must be in physical memory. To overcome this difficulty, we must place a limit on the levels of indirection (for example, limit an instruction to at most 16 levels of indirection). When the first indirection occurs, a counter is set to 16; the counter is then decremented for each successive indirection for this instruction. If the counter is decremented to 0, a trap occurs (excessive indirection). This limitation reduces the maximum number of memory references per instruction to 17, requiring the same number of frames.

The minimum number of frames per process is defined by the architecture, whereas the maximum number is defined by the amount of available physical memory. In between, we are still left with significant choice in frame allocation.

Allocation Algorithms

The easiest way to split m frames among n processes is to give everyone an equal share, m/n frames. For instance, if there are 93 frames and five processes, each process will get 18 frames. The leftover three frames could be used as a free-frame buffer pool. This scheme is called **equal allocation.**

An alternative is to recognize that various processes will need differing amounts of memory. Consider a system with a 1 KB frame size. If a small student process of 10KB and an interactive database 127 KB are the only two processes running in a system with 62 free frames, it does not make much sense to give each process 31 frames. The student process does not need more than ten frames, so the other 21 are strictly wasted.

To solve this problem, we can use **proportional allocation.** We allocate available memory to each process according to its size. Let the size of the virtual memory for process p_i be s_i, and define

$$S = \Sigma s_i$$

Then, if the total number of available frames is m, we allocate a_i frames to process p_i, where a_i is approximately

$$a_i = s_i / S \times m.$$

Of course, we must adjust each a_i to be an integer that is greater than the minimum number of frames required by the instruction set, with a sum not exceeding m.

For proportional allocation, we would split 62 frames between two processes, one of 10 pages and one of 127 pages, by allocating 4 frames and 57 frames, respectively, since

$$10/137 \times 62 \approx 4$$

$$127/137 \times 62 \approx 57$$

In this way, both processes share the available frames according to their "needs," rather than equally.

In both equal and proportional allocation, of course, the allocation to each process may vary according to the multiprogramming level. If the multiprogramming level is increased, each process will lose some frames to provide the memory needed for the new process. On the other hand, if the multiprogramming level decreases, the frames that had been allocated to the departed process can now be spread over the remaining processes.

Notice that, with either equal or proportional allocation, a high-priority process is treated the same as a low-priority process. By its definition, however, we may want to give the high-priority process more memory to speed its execution, to the detriment if low-priority processes.

One approach is to use a proportional allocation scheme where the ratio of frames depends not on the relative sizes of processes, but rather on the priorities of processes, or on a combination of size and priority.

Global Versus Local Allocation

Another important factor in the way frames are allocated to the various processes is page replacement. With multiple processes competing for frames, we can classify page-replacement algorithms into two broad categories: **global replacement** and **local replacement.** Global replacement allows a process to select a replacement frame from the set of all frames, even if that frame is currently allocated to some other process; one process can take a frame from another. Local replacement requires that each process select from only its own set of allocated frames.

For example, consider an allocation scheme where we allow high-priority processes to select frames from low-priority processes for replacement. A process can select a replacement from among its own frames or the frames of any lower-priority process. This approach allows a high-priority process to increase its frame allocation at the expense of the low-priority process.

With a local replacement strategy, the number of frames allocated to a process does not change. With global replacement, a process may happen to select only frames allocated to other processes, thus increasing the number of frames allocated to it (assuming that other processes do not choose its frames for replacement).

One problem with a global replacement algorithm is that a process cannot control its own page-fault rate. The set of pages in memory for a process depends not only on the paging behavior of that process, but also on the paging behavior of other processes. Therefore, the same process may perform quite differently (taking 0.5 seconds for one execution and 10.3 seconds for the next execution) due to totally external circumstances. Such is not the case with a local replacement algorithm. Under local replacement the set of pages in memory for a process is affected by the paging behaviour of only that process. For its part, local replacement might hinder a process by not making available to it other, less used pages of memory. Thus, global replacement generally results in greater system throughput, and is therefore the more common method.

Thrashing

If the number of frames allocated to a low-priority process falls below the minimum number required by the computer architecture, we must suspend that process' execution. We should then page out its remaining pages, freeing all its allocated frames. This provision introduces a swap-in, swap-out level of intermediate CPU scheduling.

In fact, look at any process that does not have "enough" frames. Although it is technically possible to reduce the number of allocated frames to the minimum, there is some (larger) number of pages in active use. If the process does not have this number of frames, it will quickly page fault. At this point, it must replace some page. However, since all its pages are in active use, it must replace a page that will be needed again right away. Consequently, it quickly faults again, and again, and again. The process continues to fault, replacing pages for which it then faults and brings back in right away.

This high paging activity is called **thrashing.** A process is thrashing if it is spending more time paging than executing.

Cause of Thrashing

Thrashing results in severe performance problems. Consider the following scenario, which is based on the actual behaviour of early paging systems.

The operating system monitors CPU utilisation. If CPU utilisation is too low, we increase the degree of multiprogramming by introducing a new process to the system. A global page-replacement algorithm is used; it replaces pages with no regard to the process to which they belong. Now suppose that a process enters a new phase in its execution and needs more frames. It starts faulting and taking frames away from other processes. These processes need those pages, however, and so they also fault, taking frames from other processes. These faulting processes must use the paging device to swap pages in and out. As they queue up for the paging device, the ready queue empties. As processes wait for the paging device, CPU utilisation decreases.

The CPU scheduler sees the decreasing CPU utilisation, and *increases* the degree of multiprogramming as a result. The new process tries to get started by taking frames from running processes, causing more page faults, and a longer queue for the paging device. As a result, CPU utilisation drops even further, and the CPU scheduler tries to increase the degree of multiprogramming even more. Thrashing has occurred and system throughput plunges. The page-fault rate increases tremendously. As a result, the effective memory access time increases. No work is getting done, because the processes are spending all their time paging.

This phenomenon is illustrated in Figure 8.7, in which CPU utilisation is plotted against the degree of multiprogramming. As the degree of multiprogramming increases, CPU utilisation also increases, although more slowly, until a maximum is reached. If the degree of multiprogramming is increased even further, thrashing sets in and CPU utilisation drops sharply. At this point, to increase CPU utilisation and stop thrashing, we must *decrease* the degree of multiprogramming.

We can limit the effects of thrashing by using a **local replacement algorithm** (or **priority replacement algorithm**). With local replacement, if one process starts thrashing, it cannot steal frames from another process and cause the latter to thrash also. Pages are replaced with regard to the process of which they are a part. However, if processes are thrashing, they will be in the queue for the paging device most of the time. The average service time for a page fault will increase, due to the longer average queue for the paging device. Thus, the effective access time will increase even for a process that is not thrashing.

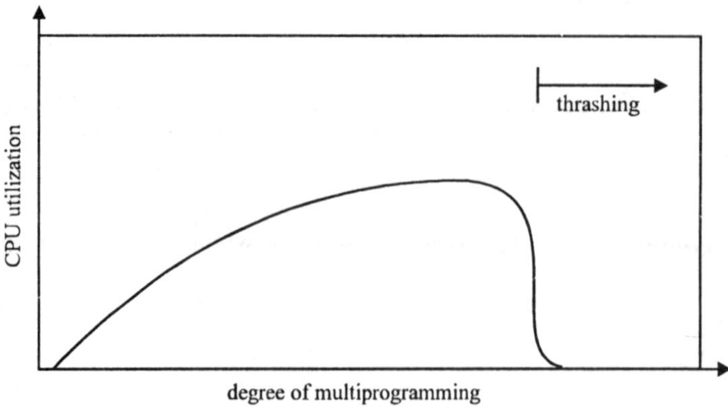

Fig. 8.7. Thrashing.

To prevent thrashing, we must provide a process as many frames as it needs. But how do we know how many frames it "needs"? There are several techniques. The working-set strategy starts by looking at how many frames a process is actually using. This approach defines the **locality model** of process execution.

The locality model states that, as a process executes, it moves from locality to locality. A locality is a set of pages that are actively used together. A program is generally composed of several different localities, which may overlap.

For example, when a subroutine is called, it defines a new locality. In this locality, memory references are made to the instructions of the subroutine, its local variables, and a subset of the global variables. When the subroutine is exited, the process leaves this locality, since the local variables and instructions of the subroutine are no longer in active use. We may return to this locality later. Thus, we see that localities are defined by the program structure and its data structures. The locality model states that all programs will exhibit this basic memory reference structure. Note that the locality model is the unstated principle behind the caching discussions so far in this book. If accesses to any types of data were random rather than patterned, caching would be useless.

Suppose that we allocate enough frames to a process to accommodate its current locality. It will fault for the pages in its locality until all these pages are in memory; then, it will not fault again until it changes localities. If we allocate fewer frames than the size of the current locality, the process will thrash, since it cannot keep in memory all the pages that it is actively using.

Working-Set Model

The **working-set model** is based on the assumption of locality. This model uses a parameter, Δ, to define the **working-set window.** The idea is to examine the most recent Δ page references. The set of pages in the most recent Δ page references is the **working set.** If a page is in active use, it will be in the working set. If it is no longer being used, it will drop from the working set Δ time units after its last reference. Thus, the working set is an approximation of the program's locality.

For example, given the sequence of memory references shown in Figure 8.8, if $\Delta = 10$ memory references, then the working set at time t_1 is {1, 2, 5, 6, 7}. By time t_2, the working set has changed to {3,4}.

The accuracy of the working set depends on the selection of Δ. If Δ is too small, it will not encompass the entire locality; if Δ is too large, it may overlap several localities. In the extreme, if Δ is infinite, the working set is the set of pages touched during the process execution.

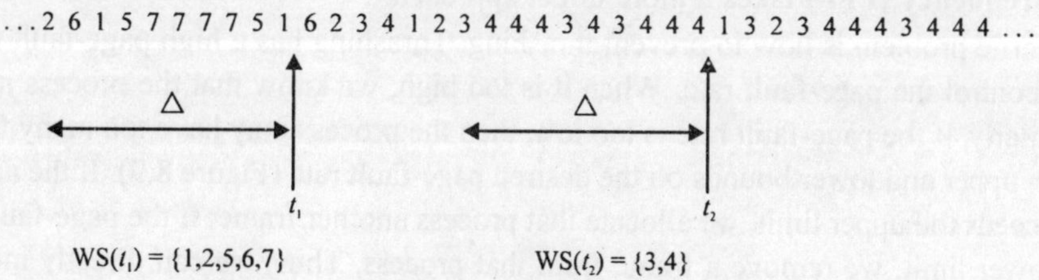

Fig. 8.8. Working-set model.

The most important property of the working set is its size. If we compute the working-set size, WSS_i, for each process in the system, we can then consider

$$D = \sum WSS_i$$

where D is the total demand for frames. Each process is actively using the pages in its working set. Thus, process i needs WSS_i frames. If the total demand is greater than the total number of available frames ($D > m$), thrashing will occur, because some processes will not have enough frames.

Use of the working-set model is then simple. The operating system monitors the working set of each process and allocates to that working set enough frames to provide it with its working-set size. If there are enough extra frames, another process can be initiated. If the sum of the working-set sizes increases, exceeding the total number of available frames, the operating system selects a process to suspend. The process' pages are written out and its frames are reallocated to other processes. The suspended process can be restarted later.

This working-set strategy prevents thrashing while keeping the degree of multiprogramming as high as possible. Thus, it optimizes CPU utilization.

The difficulty with the working-set model is keeping track of the working set. The working-set window is a moving window. At each memory reference, a new reference appears at one end and the oldest reference drops off the other end. A page is in the working set if it is referenced anywhere in the working-set window. We can approximate the working-set model with a fixed interval timer interrupt and a reference bit.

For example, assume $\triangle$ is 10,000 references and we can cause a timer interrupt every 5,000 references. When we get a timer interrupt, we copy and clear the reference-bit values for each page. Thus, if a page fault occurs, we can examine the current reference bit and 2 in-memory bits to determine whether a page was used within the last 10,000 to 15,000 references. If it was used, at least 1 of these bits will be on. If it has not been used, these bits will be off. Those pages with at least 1 bit on will be considered to be in the working set. Note that this arrangement is not entirely accurate, because we cannot tell where, within an interval of 5,000, a reference occurred. We can reduce the uncertainty by increasing the number of out history bits and the frequency of interrupts (for example, 10 bits and interrupts every 1,000 references). However, the cost to service these more frequent interrupts will be correspondingly higher.

Page-Fault Frequency

The working-set model is successful, and knowledge of the working set can be useful for prepaging (Section 10.8.1), but it seems a clumsy way to control thrashing. A strategy that uses the **page-fault frequency (PFF)** takes a more direct approach.

The specific problem is how to prevent thrashing. Thrashing has a high page-fault rate. Thus, we want to control the page-fault rate. When it is too high, we know that the process needs more frames. Similarly, if the page-fault rate is too low, then the process may have too many frames. We can establish upper and lower bounds on the desired page-fault rate (Figure 8.9). If the actual page-fault rate exceeds the upper limit, we allocate that process another frame; if the page-fault rate falls below the lower limit, we remove a frame from that process. Thus, we can directly measure and control the page-fault rate to prevent thrashing.

As with the working-set strategy, we may have to suspend a process. If the page-fault rate increases and no free frames are available, we must select some process and suspend it. The freed frames are then distributed to process with high page-fault rates.

Examples of Operating-System

In this section we describe how Windows NT and Solaris 2 implement virtual memory.

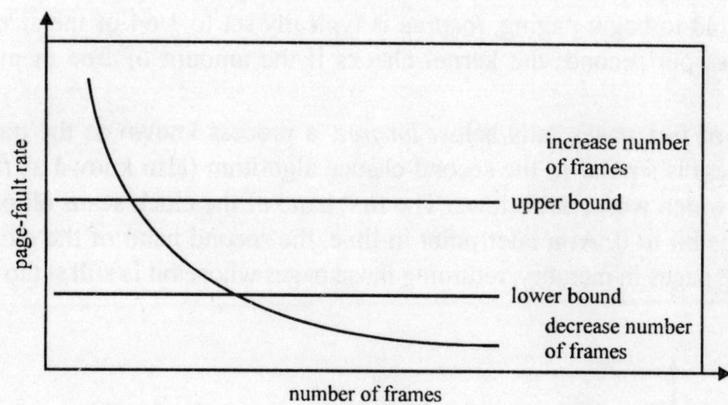

Fig. 8.9. Page-fault frequency.

Window NT

Windows NT implements virtual memory using demand paging with clustering. Clustering handles page faults by bringing in not only the faulting page, but also multiple pages surrounding the faulting page. When a process is first created, it is assigned a working-set minimum and maximum. The **working-set minimum** is the minimum number of pages the process is guaranteed to have in memory. If sufficient memory is available, a process may be assigned as many pages as its **working-set maximum.** (In some circumstances, a process may be allowed to exceed its working-set maximum.) The virtual-memory manager maintains a list of free page frames. Associated with this list is a threshold value that is used to indicate whether there is sufficient free memory available or not. If a page fault occurs for a process that is below its working-set maximum, the virtual-memory manager allocates a page from this list of free pages. If a process is at its working-set maximum and it incurs a page fault, it must select a page for replacement using a local page-replacement policy. When the amount of free memory falls below the threshold, the virtual-memory manager uses a tactic known as **automatic working-set trimming** to restore the value above the threshold. Automatic working-set trimming works by evaluating the number of pages allocated to processes. If a process has been allocated more pages than its working-set minimum, the virtual-memory manager removes pages until the process reaches its working-set minimum. A process that is at its working-set minimum may be allocated pages from the free page frame list once sufficient free memory is available.

The algorithm used to determine which page to remove from a working set depends upon the type of processor the operating system is running on. On single-processor ×86 systems, Windows NT uses a variation of the *clock* algorithm. On Alpha and multiprocessor ×86 systems, clearing the reference bit may require invalidating the entry in the translation look-aside buffer on other processors. Rather than involving this overhead, Windows NT uses a variation on the FIFO algorithm.

Solaris 2

When a thread incurs a page fault, the kernel assigns a page to the faulting thread from the list of free pages it maintains. Therefore, it is imperative that the kernel maintain sufficient amount of free memory available. Associated with this list of free pages is a parameter—*lotsfree*—which represents a threshold to begin paging, *lotsfree* is typically set to 1/64 of the size of the physical memory. Four times per second, the kernel checks if the amount of free memory is less than *lotsfree.*

If the number of free pages falls below *lotsfree,* a process known as the **pageout** starts up. This **pageout** process is similar to the second-chance algorithm (also known as the **two-handed-clock algorithm),** which works as follows. The first hand of the clock scans all pages in memory, setting the reference bit to 0. At a later point in time, the second hand of the clock examines the reference bit for the pages in memory, returning those pages whose bit is still set to 0 to the free list.

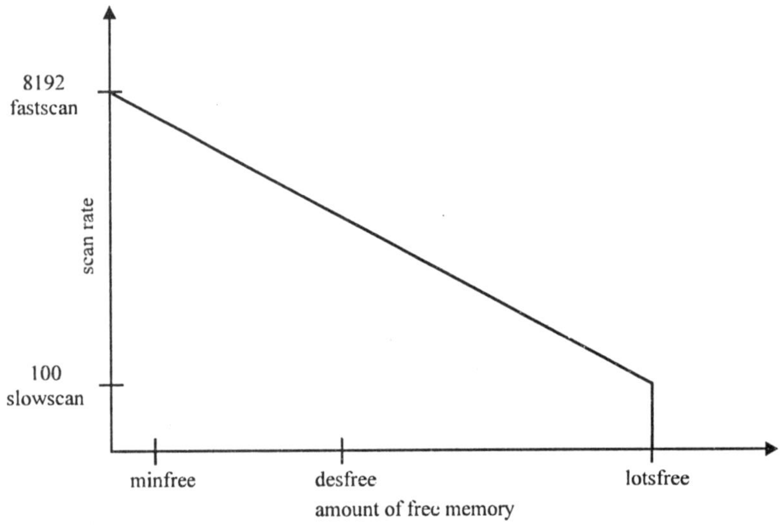

Fig. 8.10. *Solaris 2 page scanner.*

The **pageout** algorithm uses several parameters to control the rate at which pages are scanned (Known as the *scanrate*). The scanrate is expressed in pages per second and ranges from *slowscan* to *fastscan.* When free memory falls below *lotsfree,* scanning occurs at *slowscan* pages per second and progresses to *fastscan* depending upon the amount of free memory available. The default value of *slowscan* is 100 pages per second, *fastscan* is typically set to (*TotalPhysicalPages*)/2 pages per second with a maximum of 8,192 pages per second. This is shown in Figure 8.10 (with *fastscan* set to the maximum).

The distance (in pages) between the hands of the clock is determined by a system parameter *handspread.* The amount of time between the front hand clearing a bit and the back hand investigating its value depends upon the *scanrate* and the *handspread.* If *scanrate* is 100 pages per second and *handspread* is 1,024 pages, 10 seconds can pass between the time a bit is set by the front hand and checked by the backhand. However, because of the demands placed on the memory system, a *scanrate* of several thousand is not uncommon. This means that the amount of time between checking and investigating a bit is often a few seconds.

As described above, the **pageout** process checks memory four times per second. However, if free memory falls below *desfree* **pageout** will run 100 times per second with the intention of keeping at least *desfree* free memory available. If the **pageout** process is unable to keep the amount of free memory for a 30-second average at *desfree*, the kernel begins swapping processes, thereby freeing all pages allocated to the process. In general, the kernel looks for processes that have been idle for long periods of time. Last if the system is unable to maintain the amount of free memory at *minfree,* the **pageout** process is called for every request for a new page.

Recent releases of the Solaris 2 kernel have provided enhancements to the paging algorithm. One such enhancement is recognizing pages from shared libraries. Pages belonging to libraries that are being shared by several processes—even if they are eligible to be claimed by the scanner—are skipped during the page-scanning process. Another enhancement concerns distinguishing pages that have been allocated to processes from pages allocated to regular files. This is known as **priority paging.**

Other Considerations for Paging System

The selections of a replacement algorithm and allocation policy are the major decisions that we make for a paging system. There are many other considerations as well.

Prepaging

An obvious property of a pure demand-paging system is the large number of page faults that occur when a process is started. This situation is a result of trying to get the initial locality into memory. The same situation may arise at other times. For instance, when a swapped-out process is restarted, all its pages are on the disk and each must be brought in by its own page fault. **Prepaging** is an attempt to prevent this high level of initial paging. The strategy is to bring into memory at one time all the pages that will be needed.

In a system using the working-set model, for example, we keep with each process a list of the pages in its working set. If we must suspend a process (due to an I/O wait or a lack of free frames), we remember the working set for that process. When the process is to be resumed (I/O completion or enough free frames), we automatically bring back into memory its entire working set before restarting the process.

Prepaging may be an advantage in some cases. The question is simply whether the cost of using prepaging is less than the cost of servicing the corresponding page faults. It may well be the case that many of the pages brought back into memory by prepaging are not used.

Assume that *s* pages are prepaged and a fraction α of these s pages is actually used ($0 \leq \alpha \leq 1$). The question is whether the cost of the $s * \alpha$ saved page faults is greater or less than the cost of prepaging $s * (1 - \alpha)$ unnecessary pages. If α is close to zero, prepaging loses; if α is close to one, prepaging wins.

Page Size

The designers of an operating system for an existing machine seldom have a choice concerning the page size. However, when new machines are being designed, a decision regarding the best page size must be made. As you might expect, there is no single best page size. Rather, there is a set of factors that support various sizes. Page sizes are invariably powers of 2, generally ranging from 4,096 (2^{12}) to 4,194,304 (2^{22}) bytes.

How do we select a page size? One concern is the size of the page table. For of a given virtual-memory space, decreasing the page size increases the number of pages, and hence the size of the page table. For a virtual memory of 4 MB (2^{22}), there would be 4,096 pages of 1,024 bytes, but only 512 pages of 8,192 bytes. Because each active process must have its own copy of the page table, a large page size is desirable.

On the other hand, memory is better utilized with smaller pages. If a process is allocated memory starting at location 00000, and continuing until it has as much as it needs, it probably will not end exactly on a page boundary. Thus, a part of the final page must be allocated (because pages are the units of allocation) but is unused (internal fragmentation). Assuming independence of process size and page size, we would expect that, on the average, one-half of the final page of each process will be wasted. This loss would be only 256 bytes for a page of 512 bytes, for but would be 4,096 bytes for a page of 8,192 bytes. To minimize internal fragmentation, we need a small page size.

Another problem is the time required to read or write a page. I/O time is composed of seek, latency and transfer times. Transfer time is proportional to the amount transferred (that is, the page size)— a fact that would seem to argue for a small page size. Remember from Chapter 2, however, that latency and seek time normally dwarf transfer time. At a transfer rate of 2 MB per second, it takes only 0.2 milliseconds to transfer 512 bytes. Latency, on the other hand, is perhaps 8 milliseconds and seek time 20 milliseconds. Of the total I/O time (28.2 milliseconds), therefore, 1 percent is attributable to the actual transfer. Doubling the page size increases I/O time to only 28.4 milliseconds. It takes 28.4 milliseconds to read a single page of 1,024 bytes, but 56.4 milliseconds to read the same amount as two pages of 512 bytes each. Thus, a desire to minimize I/O time argues for a larger page size.

With a smaller page size, however, total I/O should be reduced, since locality will be improved. A smaller page size allows each page to match program locality more accurately. For example, consider a process of size 200 KB, of which only one-half (100 KB) are actually used in an execution. If we have only one large page, we must bring in the entire page, a total of 200 KB transferred and allocated. If we had pages of only 1 byte, then we could bring in only the 100 KB that are actually used, resulting in only 100 KB being transferred and allocated. With a smaller page size, we have better **resolution,** allowing us to isolate only the memory that is actually needed. With a larger page size, we must allocate and transfer not only what is needed, but also anything else that happens to be in the page, whether it is needed or not. Thus, a smaller page size should result in less I/O and less total allocated memory.

On the other hand, did you notice that with a page size of 1 byte, we would have a page fault for *each* byte? A process of 200 KB, using only one-half of that memory, would generate only one page fault with a page size of 200 kb, but 102,400 page faults for a page size of 1 byte. Each page fault generates the large amount of overhead needed for processing the interrupt, saving registers, replacing a page, queueing for the paging device, and updating tables. To minimize the number of page faults, we need to have a large page size.

There are other factors to consider (such as the relationship between page size and sector size on the paging device). The problem has no best answer. Some factors (internal fragmentation, locality) argue for a small page size, whereas others (table size, I/O time) argue for a large page size. However, the historical trend is toward larger page sizes. Indeed, the first edition of **Operating Systems Concepts** (1983) used 4,096 bytes as the upper bound on page sizes, and this value was the most common page size in 1990. However, modern systems may now use page sizes that are much larger than this. We explore this in the following section.

TLB Reach

We introduced the **hit ratio** of the TLB. Recall the hit ratio for the TLB refers to the percentage of virtual address translations that are resolved in the TLB rather than the page table. Clearly, the hit ratio is related to the number of entries in the TLB and the way to increase the hit ratio is by increasing the number of entries in the TLB. This however, does not come cheaply, as the associative memory used to construct the TLB is both expensive and power-hungry.

Related to the hit ratio is a similar metric: the **TLB reach.** The TLB reach refers to the amount of memory accessible from the TLB and is simply the number of entries multiplied by the page size. Ideally, the working set for a process is stored in the TLB. If not, the process will spend a considerable amount of time resolving memory references in the page table rather than TLB. If we double the number of entries in the TLB, we double the TLB reach. However, for some memory-intensive applications this may still prove sufficient for storing the working set.

Another approach for increasing the TLB reach is by either increasing the size of the page or providing multiple page size. If we increase the page size—say from 8 KB to 32 KB—we quadruple the TLB reach. However, this may lead to an increase in fragmentation for some applications that do not require such a large page size in 32KB. Alternatively, an operating system may provide several different page sizes. For example, the UltraSparc II supports 8 KB, 64 KB, 512 KB, and 4 MB page sizes. Of these available page sizes, Solaris 2 uses both 8 KB and 4 MB page sizes. And with a 64-entry TLB, the TLB reach for Solaris 2 ranges from 512 KB with KB pages to 256 MB 4 MB pages. For the majority of applications, the 8 KB page size is sufficient, although Solaris 2 maps the first 4 MB of kernel code and data with two 4 MB pages. Solaris 2 also allows applications—such as databases—to take advantage of the large 4 MB page size as well.

However, providing support for multiple pages requires the operating system—not hardware—to manage the TLB. For example, one of the fields in a TLB entry must indicate the size of the page frame corresponding to the TLB entry. Managing the TLB in software and not hardware comes at a cost in performance. However, the increased hit ratio and TLB reach offsets the performance costs. Indeed, recent trends indicate a move towards software-managed TLBS and operating system support for multiple page sizes. The UltraSparc, MIPS, and Alpha architectures employ software-managed TLBS. The PowerPC and Pentium manage the TLB in hardware.

Inverted Page Table

The concept of an inverted page table was introduced. The purpose of this form of page management was to reduce the amount of physical memory that is needed to track virtual-to-physical address translations. We accomplish this savings by creating a table that has one entry per physical memory page, indexed by the pair <process-id, page-number>.

Because they keep information about which virtual–memory page is stored in each physical frame, inverted page tables reduce the amount of physical memory needed to store this information. However the inverted page table no longer contains complete information about the logical address space of a process, and that information is required if reference page is not currently in memory. Demand paging requires this information to process page faults. For this information to be available, an external page table (one per process) must be kept. Each such table looks like the traditional per-process page table, containing information on where each virtual page is located.

But do external page tables negate the utility of inverted page tables? Since these tables are referenced only when a page fault occurs, they do not need to be available quickly. Instead, they are themselves paged in and out of memory as necessary. Unfortunately, a page fault may now result in the virtual-memory manager causing another page fault as it pages in the external page table it needs to locate the virtual page on the backing store. This special case requires careful handling in the kernel and a delay in the page-lookup processing.

Program Structure

Demand paging is designed to be transparent to the user program. In many cases, the user is completely unaware of the paged nature of memory. In other cases, however, system performance can be improved if the user (or compiler) has an awareness of the underlying demand paging.

Let's look at a contrived but informative example. Assume that pages are 128 words in size. Consider a Java program whose function is to initialize to 0 each element of a 128 by 128 array. The following code is typical;

```
int A [] [] = new int [128] [128];

for ( int j = 0; j < A. length; j++)
    for (int i = 0; i < A.length; i++)
        A [i] [j] = 0;
```

Notice that the array is stored row major. That is, the array is stored A [0] [0], A [0] [1], ..., A [0] [127], A [1] [0], A [1] [1], ..., A [127] [127]. For pages of 128 words, each row takes one page. Thus, the preceding code zeros one word in each page, then another word in each page, and so on. If the operating system allocates less than 128 frames to the entire program, then its execution will result in 128 × 128 = 16,384 page faults. Changing the code to

```
int A [] [] = new int [128] [128];

for ( int i = 0; i < A. length; i++)
    for (int j = 0; j < A.length; j++)
        A [i] [j] = 0;
```

on the other hand, zeros all the words on one page before starting the next page, reducing the number of page faults to 128.

Careful selection of data structures and programming structures can increase locality and hence lower the page-fault rate and the number of pages in the working set. A stack has good locality; since access is always made to the top. A hash table, on the other hand, is designed to scatter references, producing bad locality. Of course, locality of reference is just one measure of the efficiency of the use of a data structure. Other heavily weighted factors include search speed, total number of memory references, and total number of pages touched.

At a later stage, the compiler and loader can have a significant effect on paging. Separating code and data and generating re-entrant code means that code pages can be read only and hence will never be modified. Clean pages do not have to be paged out to be replaced. The loader can avoid placing routines across page boundaries, keeping each routine completely in one page. Routines that call each other many times can be packed into the same page. This packaging is a variant of the bin-packing problem of operations research: Try to pack the variable-sized load segments into the fixed-sized pages so that interpage references are minimized. Such an approach is particularly useful for large page sizes.

The choice of programming language can affect paging as well. For example, C and C++ use pointers frequently, and pointers tend to randomize access to memory, thereby potentially diminishing a process locality. Some studies have shown that object-oriented programs also tend to have a poor locality of reference. Contrast these languages with Java, which does not provide pointers. Java programs will have better locality of references than C or C++ programs in a virtual-memory system.

I/O Interlock

When demand paging is used, we sometimes need to allow some of the pages to be locked in memory. One such situation occurs when I/O is done to or from user (virtual) memory. I/O is often implemented by a separate I/O processor. For example, a magnetic-tape controller is generally given the number of bytes to transfer and a memory address for the buffer. When the transfer is complete, the CPU is interrupted.

We must be sure the following sequence of events does not occur. A process issues an I/O request, and is put in a queue for that I/O device. Meanwhile, the CPU is given to other processes. These processes cause page faults, and, using a global replacement algorithm, one of them replaces the page containing the memory buffer for the waiting process. The pages are paged out. Some time later, when the I/O request advances to the head of the device queue, the I/O occurs to the specified address. However, this frame is now being used for a different page belonging to another process.

There are two common solutions to this problem. One solution is never to execute I/O to user memory. Instead, data are always copied between system memory and user memory. I/O takes place only between system memory and the I/O device. To write a block on tape, we first copy the block to system memory, and then write it to tape.

This extra copying may result in unacceptably high overhead. Another solution is to allow pages to be locked into memory. A lock bit is associated with every frame. If the frame is locked, it cannot be selected for replacement. Under this approach, to write a block on tape, we lock into memory the pages containing the block. The system can then continue as usual. Locked pages cannot be replaced. When the I/O is complete, the pages are unlocked.

Frequently, some or all of the operating-system kernel is locked into memory. Most operating system cannot tolerate a page fault caused by the kernel. Consider the result of the page-replacement routine causing a page fault.

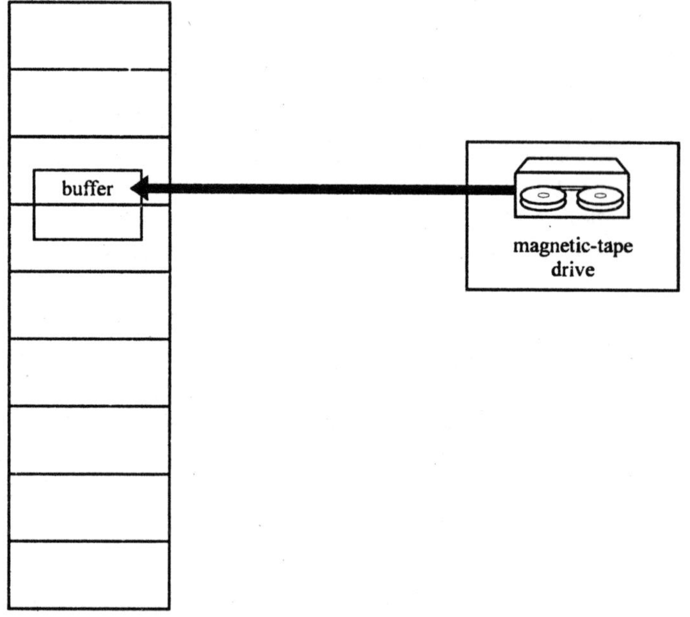

Fig. 8.11. The reason why frames used for I/O must be in memory.

Another use for a lock bit involves normal page replacement. Consider the following sequence of events. A low-priority process faults. Selecting a replacement frame, the paging system reads the necessary page into memory. Ready to continue, the low-priority process enters the ready queue and waits for the CPU. Since it is a low-priority process, it may not be selected by the CPU scheduler for a while. While the low-priority process waits, a high-priority process faults. Looking for a replacement , the paging system sees a page that is in memory but has not been referenced or modified: It is the page that the low-priority process just brought in. This page looks like a perfect replacement: It is clean and will not need to be written out, and it apparently has not been used for a long time.

Whether the high-priority process should be able to replace the low-priority process is a policy decision. After all, we are simply delaying the low-priority process for the benefit of the high-priority process. On the other hand, we are wasting the effort spent to bring in the page of the low-priority process. If we decide to prevent replacing a newly brought-in page until it can be used at least once, then we can use the lock bit to implement this mechanism. When a page is selected for replacement, its lock bit is turned on; it remains on until the faulting process is again dispatched.

Using a lock bit can be dangerous, however: The lock bit may get turned on but never turned off. Should this situation occur (due to a bug in the operating system, for example), the locked frame becomes unusable. The Macintosh Operating System provides a page-locking mechanism because it is a single user system, and the over use of locking would hurt only the user doing the locking. Multiuser systems must be less trusting of users. For instance, Solaris 2 allows locking "hints," but it is free to disregard these hints if the free-frame pool becomes too small or if an individual process requests that too many pages be locked in memory.

Real-Time Processing

The discussions in this chapter have concentrated on providing the best overall utilization of a computer system by optimizing the use of memory. By using memory for active data and moving inactive data to disk, we increase overall system throughput. However, individual processes may suffer as a result, because they now may take additional page faults during their execution.

Consider a real-time process or thread. Such a process expects to gain control of the CPU, and to run to completion with a minimum of delays. Virtual memory is the antithesis of real-time computing, because it can introduce unexpected long-term delays in the execution of a process while pages are brought into memory, Therefore, real-time systems almost never have virtual memory.

In the case of Solaris 2, the developers at Sun Microsystems wanted to allow both time-sharing and real-time computing within a system. To solve the page-fault problem, Solaris 2 allows a process to tell it which pages are important to that process. In addition to allowing "hints" on page use, the operating system allows privileged users to require pages to be locked into memory. If abused, this mechanism could lock all other processes out of the system. It is necessary to allow real-time processes to have bounded and low-dispatch latency.

Summary

It is desirable to be able to execute a process whose logical address space is larger than the available physical address space. The programmer can make such a process executable by restructuring it using overlays, but doing so is generally a difficult programming task. Virtual memory is a technique to allow a large logical address space to be mapped onto a smaller physical memory. Virtual memory allows extremely large process to be run, and also allows the degree of multiprogramming to be raised, increasing CPU utilization. Further, it frees application programmers from worrying about memory availability.

Pure demand paging never brings in a page until that page is referenced. The first reference causes a page fault to the operating-system resident monitor. The operating system consults an internal table to determine where the page is located on the backing store. It then finds a free frame and reads the page in from the backing store. The page table is updated to reflect this change, and the instruction that caused the page fault is restarted. This approach allows a process to run even though its entire memory image is not in main memory at once. As long as the page-fault rate is reasonably low, performance is acceptable.

We can use demand paging to reduce the number of frames allocated to a process. This arrangement can increase the degree of multiprogramming (allowing more processes to be available for execution at one time) and—in theory, at least—the CPU utilization of the system. It also allows processes to be run even though their memory requirements exceed the total available physical memory. Such processes run in virtual memory.

If total memory requirements exceed the physical memory, then it may be necessary to replace pages from memory to free frames for new pages. Various page-replacement algorithms are used. FIFO page replacement is easy to program, but suffers from Belady's anomaly. Optimal page replacement requires future knowledge. LRU replacement is an approximation of optimal, but even it may be difficult to implement. Most page-replacement algorithms, such as the second-chance algorithm, are approximations of LRU replacement.

In addition to a page-replacement algorithm, a frame-allocation policy is needed. Allocation can be fixed, suggesting local page replacement, or dynamic, suggesting global replacement. The working-set model assumes that processes execute in localities. The working set is the set of pages in the current locality. Accordingly, each process should be allocated enough frames for its current working set.

If a process does not have enough memory for its working set, it will thrash. Providing enough frames to each process to avoid thrashing may require process swapping and scheduling.

In addition to requiring that we solve the major problems of page replacement and frame allocation, the proper design of a paging system requires that we consider page size, I/O, locking, prepaging, process creation, program structure, thrashing, and other topics. Virtual memory can be thought of as one level of a hierarchy of storage levels in a computer system. Each level has its own access time, size, and cost parameters. A full example of a hybrid, functional virtual-memory system is presented in the Mach chapter, which is available on our web site (http://www.bell-labs.com/topic/bookd/os-book).

9

Virtual Storage Organization

Evolution of Storage Organizations

Figure 9.1 shows how storage organizations have evolved from real storage systems dedicated to a single user, to virtual storage systems combining the techniques of paging and segmentation. Real storage organizations were discussed in the previous chapter. Because virtual storage is far more complex, the discussion has been split into two chapters. In this chapter, the various virtual storage organizations are examined.

Virtual Storage: Basic Concepts

The key to the virtual storage concept is disassociating the addresses referenced in a running process from the addressed available in primary storage.

Real | Real | Virtual

Single user dedicated systems

Real storage multiprogramming systems

Virtual storage multiprogramming systems

Fixed partition multiprogramming

Variable partition multiprogramming

Pure paging

Pure segmentation

Combined paging segmentation

Absolute

Relocatable

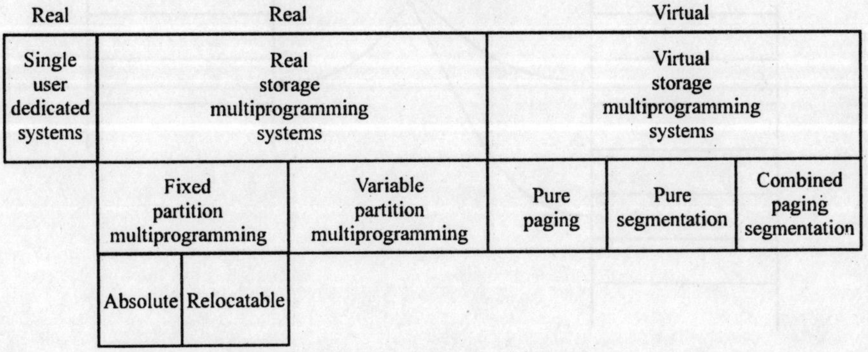

Fig. 9.1. Evolution of Storage organizations.

The addresses referenced by a running process are called *virtual addresses*. The addresses available in primary storage are called *real addresses*. The range of virtual addresses a running process may reference is called that process's *virtual address space, V*. The range of real addresses available on a particular compute system is called that computer's *real address space. R*. The number of addressed in V is denoted $|V|$, and the number of addressed in R is denoted $|R|$. In actual implemented virtual storage systems it is normally the case that $| V | >> | R |$, although systems have been built in which $| V | < | R |$.

Even though processed reference only virtual addresses, they must actually run in real storage. *Thus virtual addresses must be mapped into real addressed as a process executes*. This must be done quickly, or else the performance of the computer system would degrade to intolerable levels, thus eliminating many gains from using the virtual storage concept in the first place.

Various means have been developed for associating virtual addressed with real addressed. *Dynamic address translation (DAT)* mechanisms convert virtual addressed to real addresses as a process executed. All these systems exhibit the property that the addresses contiguous in a process's virtual address space need not be contiguous in real storage—this is called *artificial contiguity*. Thus the user is freed from concern about where procedures and data are positioned in real storage. The user is able to write programs in the most natural manner, considering details of algorithm efficiency and program structure, but ignoring details of the underlying hardware structure. The compute is (or can be) viewed in a logical sense as an implementor of algorithms rather than in a physical sense as a device with unique characteristics, some of which may impede the program development process.

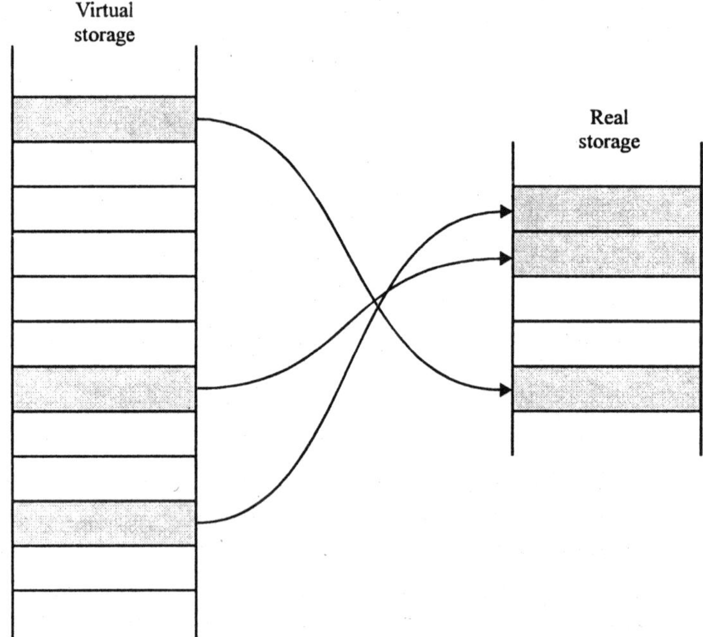

Fig. 9.2. Item mapping from virtual address space to real address space.

Multilevel Storage Organization

If we are to permit a user's virtual address space to be larger than the real address space, and certainly if we are to multiprogram a system effectively with many users sharing the real storage resource, we must provide a means for retaining programs and data in a large auxiliary storage. This is normally accomplished by using a two-level storage scheme (Fig. 9.4) The first level is the real storage in which processes execute and in which data must reside in order to be reference by a running process. The second level consists of large capacity storage media such as disks or drums capable of holding the programs and data that cannot all fit into the limited real storage at once. This second level of storage is generally called *auxiliary, secondary*, or *backing storage*, when a process is to be run, its code and data are brought to the main storage. The details of how this is done will be explained thoroughly in this and the next chapter.

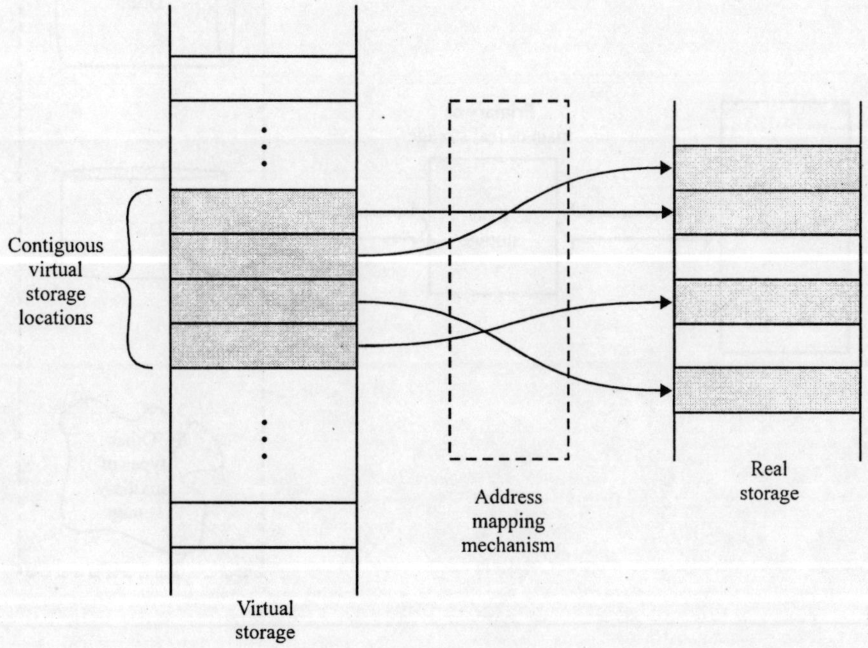

Fig. 9.3. *Artificial contiguity. Items that are contiguous in virtual storage are mapped to items in real storage that are not necessarily contiguous.*

Because the real storage is shared among many processes, and because each process may have a virtual address space much larger than real storage, only a small portion of each process's programs and data may be maintained in real storage at a time. Figure 9.5 illustrates a two-level storage system in which items from various user's virtual storages have been placed in the real storage.

Block Mapping

The dynamic address translation mechanism must maintain *address translation maps* illustrating which virtual storage locations are currently in real storage, and where they are. If this mapping were performed on a word-by-word or byte-by-byte basis, i.e., if a mapping entry were provided for every entry in V, then the mapping information would be so voluminous that it would require as much or more real storage than the processes themselves need. A method is needed to reduce the amount of mapping information in order to make implementation of virtual storage worthwhile.

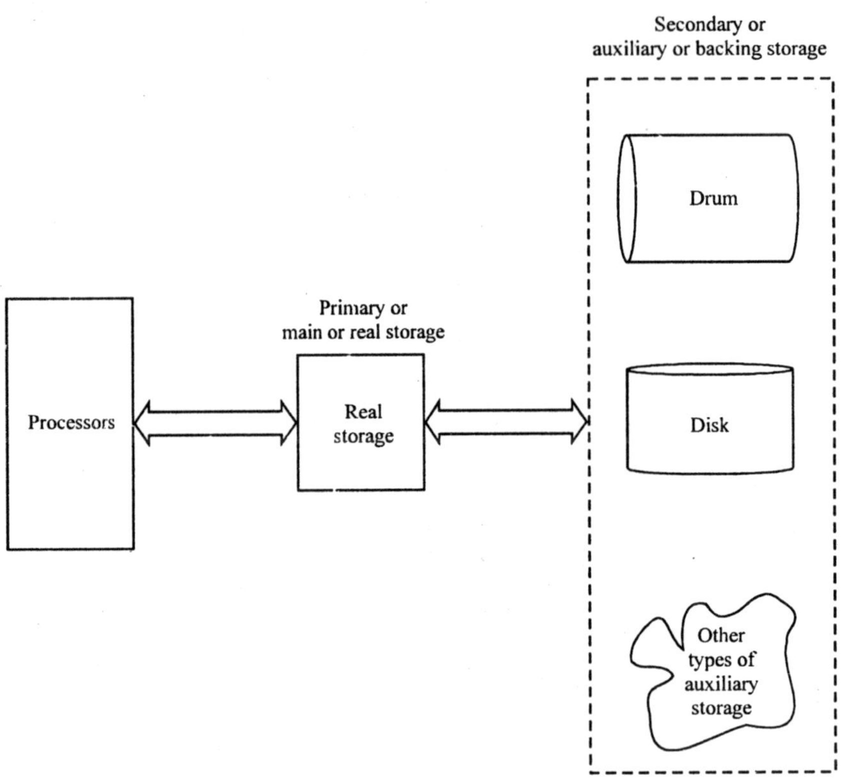

Fig. 9.4. *Two-level storage.*

We simply cannot afford to map addressed individually. Therefore, information is grouped into *blocks*, and the system keeps track of where in real storage the various virtual storage blocks have been placed. The larger the block size, the smaller the fraction of real storage that must be devoted to storing mapping information.

Making blocks large lowers the storage overhead of the mapping mechanism. But large blocks take longer to transfer between secondary and primary storage, and consume more real storage, possibly limiting the number of processes that can share the real storage.

There is some question as to whether the blocks should all be the same size, or of different sizes. When blocks are the same size, they are called *pages* and the associated virtual storage organization is called *paging*. When the blocks may be of different sizes, they are called *segments*, and the associated virtual storage organization is called *segmentation*. Some systems combine the two techniques, implementing segments as variable-sized entities composed of fixed-sized pages.

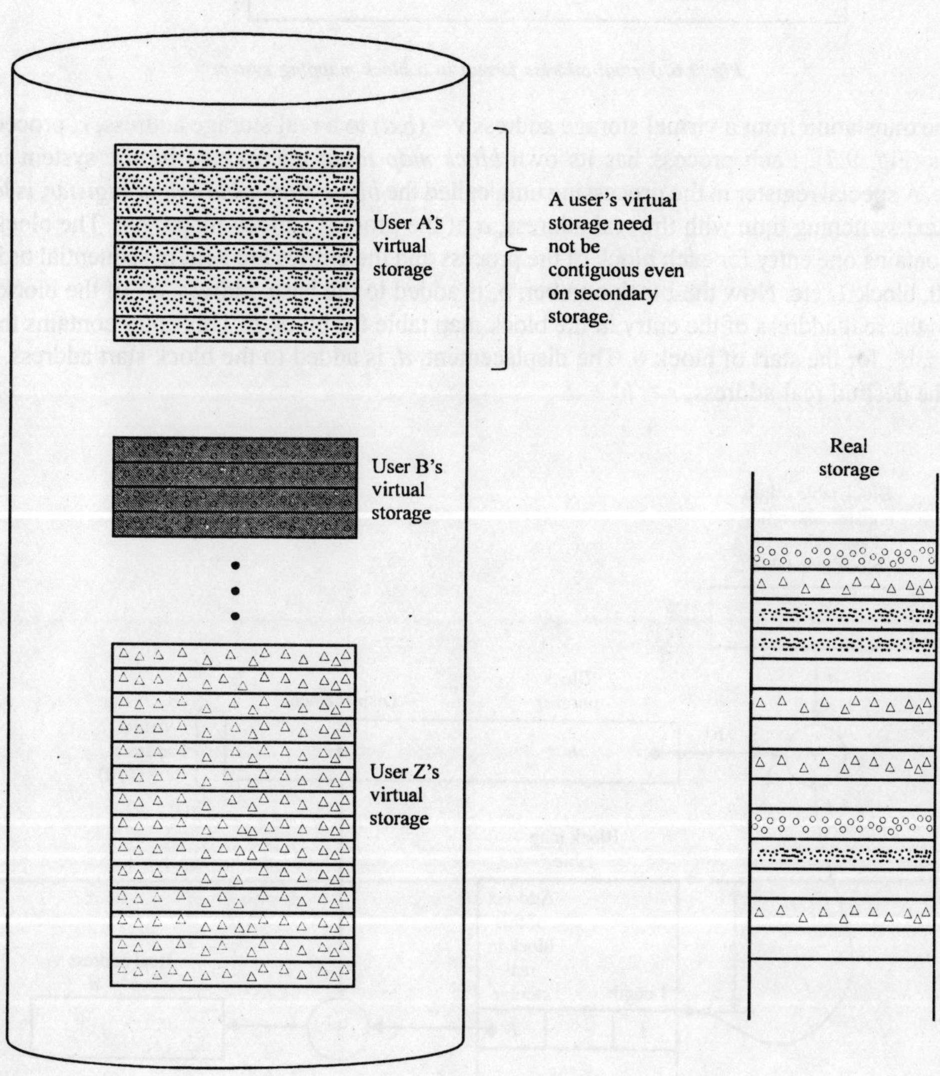

Fig. 9.5. A small portion of each user's programs and data may normally be maintained in primary storage once.

Addressed in a block mapping system are *two-dimensional.* To refer to a particular item, a program specifies the block in which the item resides, and the *displacement* of the item from the start of the block (Fig. 9.6) A virtual address, *v*, is denoted by an ordered pair (*b,d*) where *b* is the block number in which the referenced item resides, and *d* is the displacement from the start of the block.

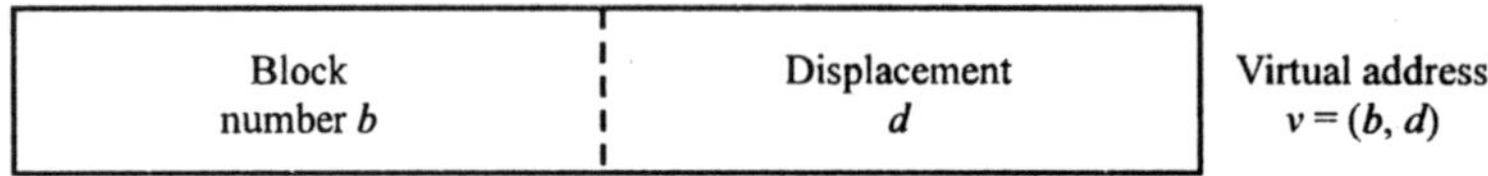

Fig. 9.6. Virtual address format in a block mapping system.

The translation from a virtual storage address $v = (b,d)$ to a real storage address, r, proceeds as follows (Fig. 9.7). Each process has its own *block map table* maintained by the system in real storage. A special register in the processing unit, called the *block map table origin register*, is loaded at context switching time with the real address, a of the process's block map table. The block map table contains one entry for each block of the process and the entries are kept in sequential order for block 0, block 1, etc. Now the block number, b, is added to the base address, a , of the block table to form the real address of the entry in the block map table for block b. This entry contains the real address, b', for the start of block b. The displacement, d, is added to the block start address, b', to form the desired real address, $r = b' + d$.

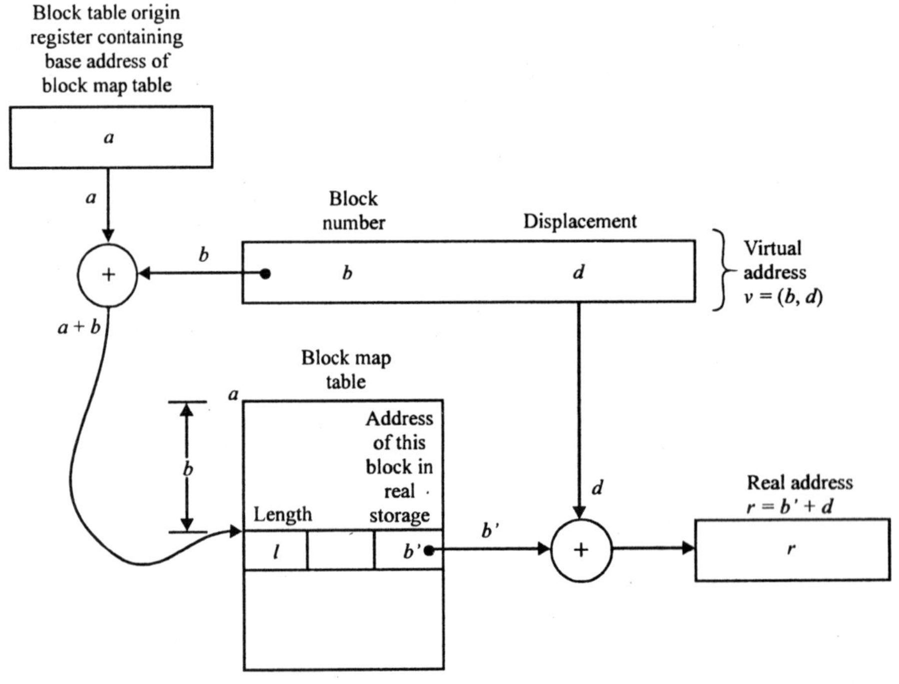

Fig. 9.7. Virtual address translation with block mapping.

The block mapping techniques employed in segmentation, paging, and combined paging/segmentation systems are all similar to the mapping shown in Fig. 9.7.

It is important to note that block mapping is performed dynamically as a process runs. If not implemented efficiently, its overhead could cause performance degradation that would negate much of the benefit of using virtual storage. For example, the two additions indicated in Fig 9.7 must be much faster than conventional machine language add instructions. These additions are performed automatically within the execution of each machine language instruction for each virtual address referenced; if the additions look as long as machine language adds, then the computer might run at only a small fraction of the speed at which a real storage computer would execute. Also, the block mapping table is normally placed in special high-speed storage to dramatically decrease the time it takes to retrieve block-mapping entries.

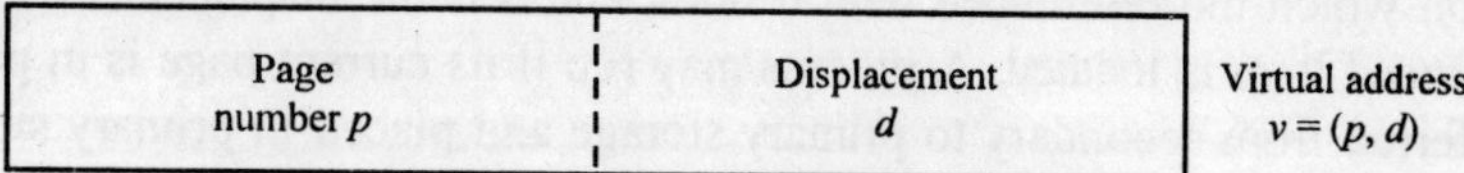

Fig. 9.8. Virtual address format in a pure paging system.

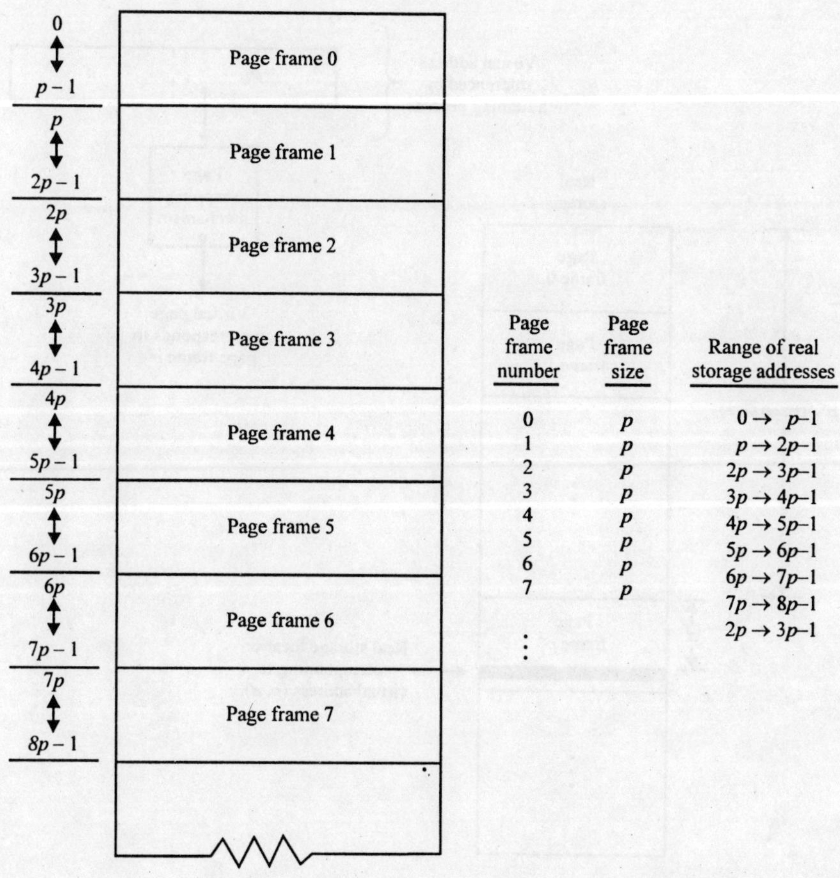

Fig. 9.9. Real storage divided into page frames.

Paging: Basic Concepts

Recalling the complexity of managing variable-sized blocks under variable partition multiprogramming, let us begin by considering fixed-size block mapping, i.e., paging. In this section we consider *pure paging* as distinguished from paging in a system with combined segmentation and paging.

A virtual address in a paging system is an ordered pair (p,d) where p is the page number in virtual storage on which the referenced item resides, and d is the displacement within page p at which the referenced item is located. A process may run if its current page is in primary storage. Pages are transferred from secondary to primary storage and placed in primary storage in blocks called *page frames* that are the same size as the incoming pages. Page frames begin at real storage addresses that are integral multiples of the fixed page size. An incoming page may be placed in any available page frame.

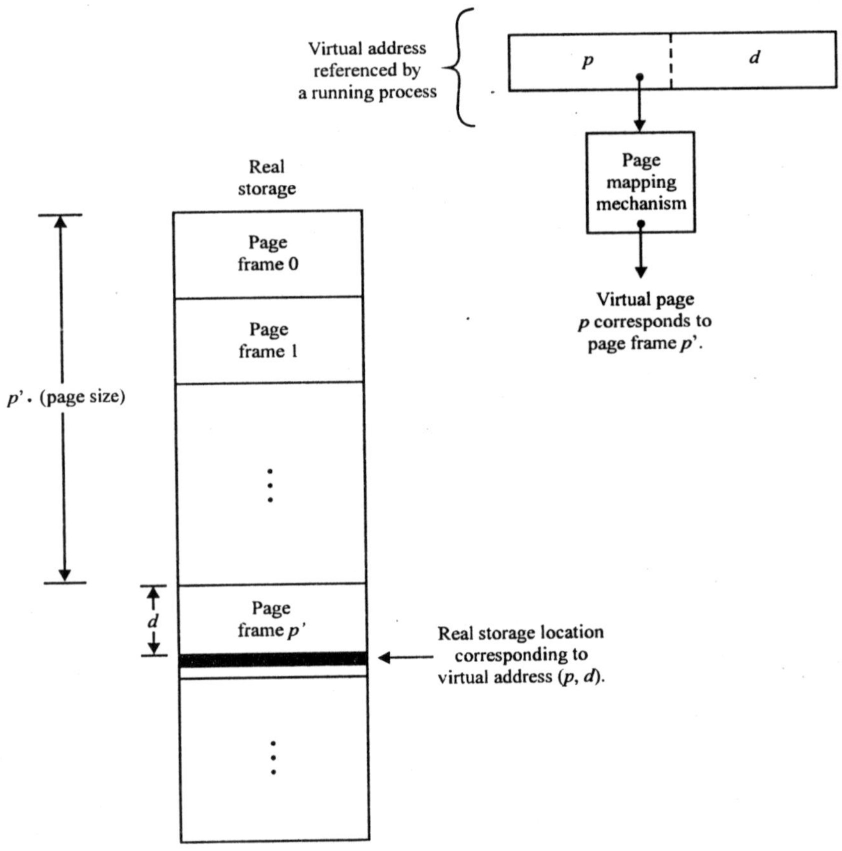

Fig. 9.10. Correspondence between virtual storage addresses and real storage addresses in a paging system.

Dynamic address translation under paging proceeds as follows. A running process references a virtual storage address $v = (p,d)$. A page mapping mechanism, Fig. 9.10 looks up page p in a *page map table*, and determines that page p is in page frame p'. The real storage address is then formed by concatenating p' and d.

Now consider this process in more detail. In particular, because not every page of the process is ordinarily in primary storage at the same time, the page map table must indicate whether or not the referenced page is in primary storage; if it is, where it is; and if it isn't, where it may be found in secondary storage. Figure 9.11 shows a typical page map table entry. A page residence bit, r, is set to 0 if the page is not in primary storage and set to 1 if the page is in primary storage. If the page is not in primary storage, then s is its secondary storage address. If the page is in primary storage, then p' is its page frame number. Note that p' is not an actual primary storage address; the primary storage address at which page frame p' begins is the product of p' and the fixed page size (assuming page frames are numbered 0, 1, 2, etc.)

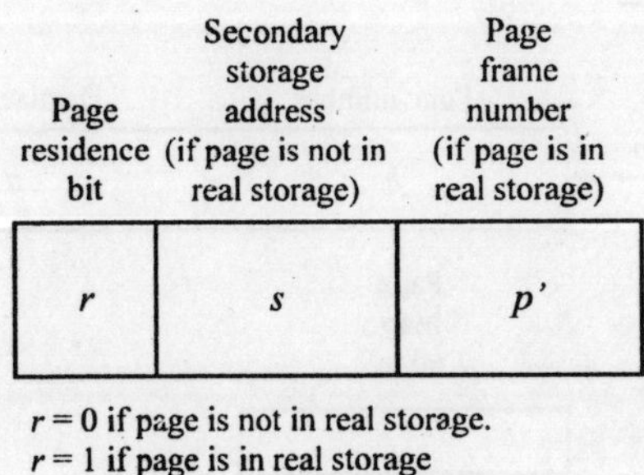

Fig. 9.11. A page map table entry.

Paging Address Translation by Direct Mapping

In this and the next several section, we consider several techniques for performing page mapping. First we consider *direct mapping* as illustrated in Fig. 9.12.

A running process references virtual address $v = (p,d)$. Before a process begins running, the operating system loads (at context switching time) the primary storage address of the page map table into the *page map table origin register*. The base address, b, of the page map table is added to the page number, p, to form the address in primary storage, $b + p$, of the entry in the page map table for page p. This entry indicates that page frame p' corresponds to virtual page p. Then p' is concatenated with the displacement, d, to form real address, r. This is said to be an example of *direct mapping* because the page map table contains an entry for every page in this process's virtual storage. If the process has n pages in its virtual storage, then the direct mapped page map table for the process contains entries successively for page 0, page 1, page 2, ..., page $n - 1$. Direct mapping is much like accessing an array location via subscripting; any entry in the table can be directly located with a single access to the table.

The virtual address being translated and the base address of the page map table are both kept in high-speed registers in the control processor, so the operations involving them can be performed quickly within a single instruction execution cycle. But the direct mapped page map table, which can be quite large, is ordinarily kept in primary storage. Consequently, the reference to the page map table requires one complete primary storage cycle. Because the primary storage cycle time ordinarily represents the largest part of an instruction execution cycle, and because we require an additional primary storage execution cycle for page mapping, then the use of direct mapping page address translation can cause the computer system to run programs at about half speed! This is intolerable. Therefore, to achieve faster translation, many of today's systems implement the complete direct mapped page map table in very high-speed cache storage. This has been made more feasible because of the steady decline in the cost of cache memory due to advances in memory technology.

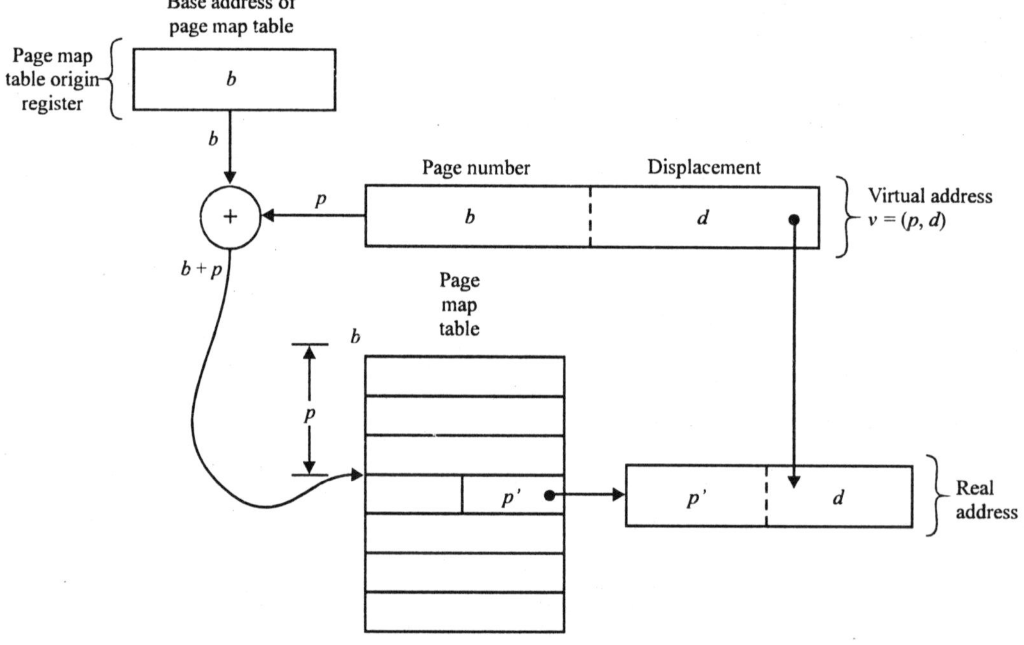

Fig. 9.12. Paging address translation by direct mapping.

Paging Address Translation by Associative Mapping

One way of speeding dynamic address translation is to place the entire page map table into a content-addressed (rather than location-addressed) *associative storage* which has a cycle time perhaps an order or magnitude faster than primary storage. Figure 9.13 illustrates how dynamic address translation proceeds with pure *associative mapping*. A running program refers to virtual address $v = (p,d)$. Every entry in the associative storage is searched simultaneously for page p. It returns p' as the page frame corresponding to page p, and p' is concatenated with d, forming the real address, r. Note that the arrows into the associative map actually enter every cell of the map. This indicates that every cell of the associative storage is searched simultaneously for a match on p. This is what makes associative storage prohibitively expensive even compared to cache, so pure associative mapping is not used; we show it here in case the economics of associative mapping become more favorable.

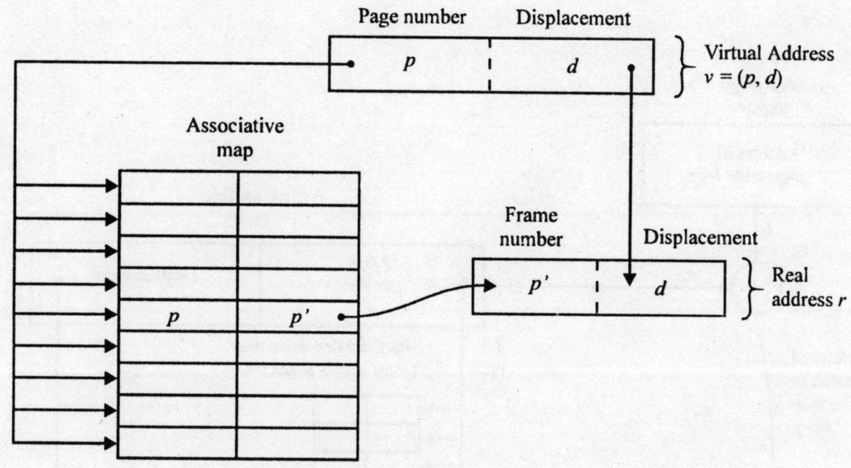

Fig. 9.13. Paging address translation with pure associative mapping.

Paging Address Translation with Combined Associative/Direct Mapping

Much of the discussion to this point has dealt with the computer hardware it takes to implement virtual storage efficiently. The hardware view presented has been a logical one rather a than physical one. We are concerned not with the precise structure of the devices but with their functional organization and relative speeds. This view of hardware is typical of that which the operating systems designer must have, especially in development environments in which hardware designs may be modified.

Improvements in hardware over the last three decades have come at a much more dramatic pace than improvements in software. It has actually come to the point that designers are often reluctant to commit themselves to a particular hardware technology because they expect a better technology will soon be available. Operating systems designers generally have little choice in these matters because they must implement operating systems with existing technologies. They must also deal with the realities and economics of today's hardware. Currently, cache and associative storage are far more expensive than direct access primary storage. This leads some designers to a compromise page mapping mechanism.

An associative storage capable of holding only a small percentage of the complete page map table for a process is used (this is sometimes called a *translation lookaside buffer*). The page entries maintained in this map corresponds to the most recently referenced pages only, using the heuristic that a page referenced recently in the past is likely to be referenced again in the near future.

Dynamic address transiation proceeds as follows. A running program references virtual address $v = (p,d)$. The address translation mechanism first tires to find page p in the partial associative page map. If p is there, then the associative map return p' as the frame number corresponding to virtual page p, and p' is concatenated with the displacement d to form the real address r that corresponds to virtual address $v = (p,d)$.

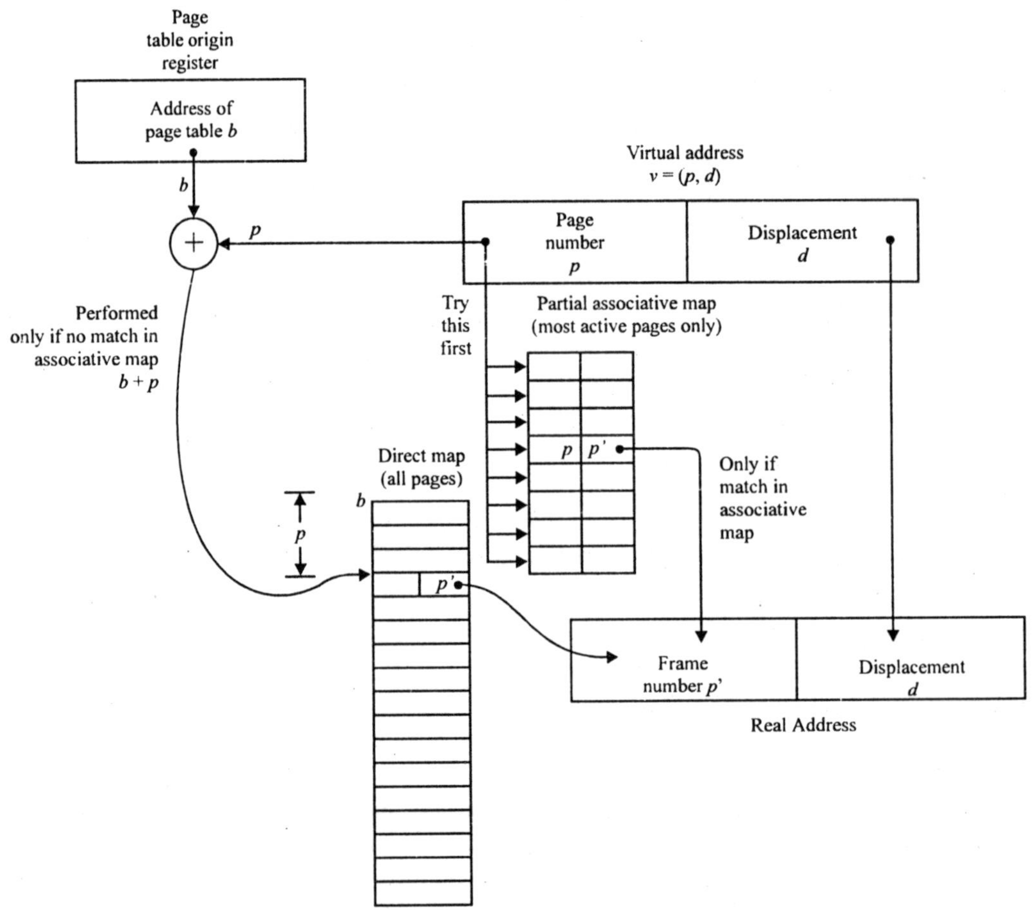

Fig. 9.14. Paging address translation with combined associative/direct mapping.

If there is no match for page p in the partial associative page map, a conventional direct map in primary storage is referenced. The address, b, in the page table origin register is added to p to locate the appropriate entry for page p in the direct-mapped page map table in primary storage. The table indicates that p' is the page frame corresponding to virtual page p, and p' is concatenated with the displacement, d, to form the real address r corresponding to virtual address $v = (p,d)$. Now that p has been located in frame p', the partial associative map is updated to contain this information; the hardware replaces the entry for the least recently-used page. Now references (in the near future) to page p will be translated quickly through the partial associative page map.

The partial associative page map does not need to be large to achieve good performance. In fact, systems using this technique with only eight or sixteen associative storage registers often achieve 90 per cent or more of the performance possible with a complete associative map, which on today's systems might require hundreds, or even thousands, of times as many entries. This also occurs because of the phenomenon of locality.

Using a combined associative/direct mapping mechanism is an engineering decision based on the relative economics and capabilities of existing hardware technologies. Therefore, it is important for operating systems students and developers to be aware of emerging hardware technologies.

Sharing in a Paging System

In multiprogrammed computer systems, especially in timesharing systems, it is common for many users to be executing the same programs. If individual copies of these programs were given to each user, much of primary storage would be wasted. The obvious solution is to share those pages that can be shared.

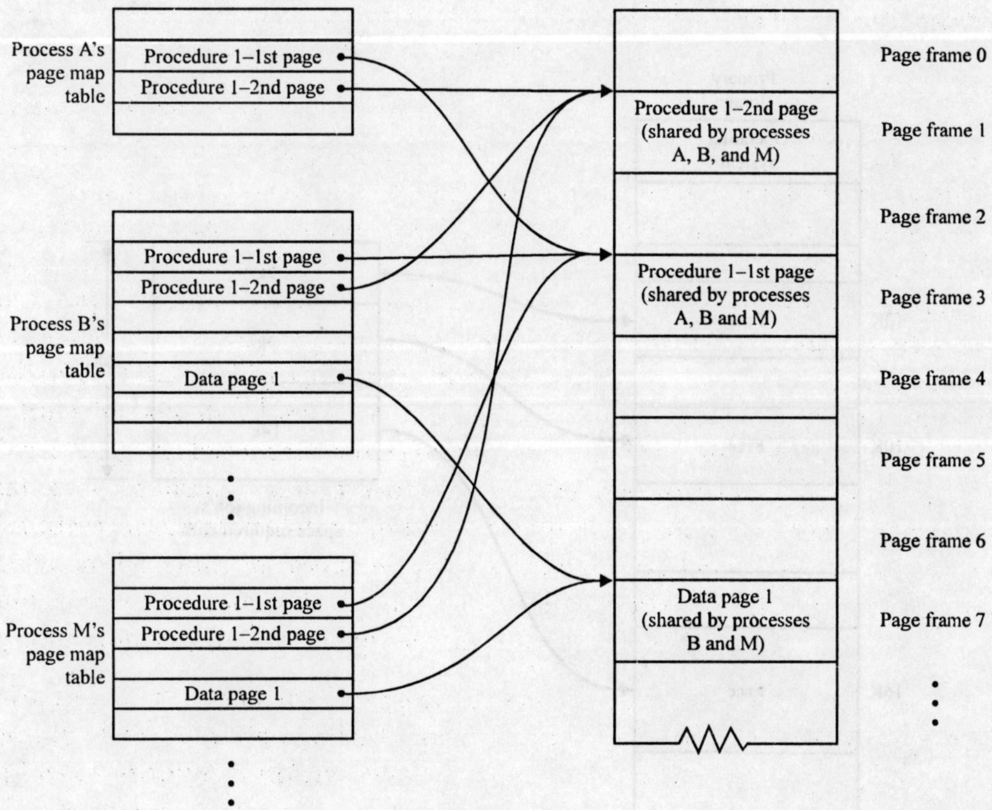

Fig. 9.15. Sharing a pure paging system.

Sharing must be carefully controlled to prevent one process form modifying data that another process is accessing. In most of today's systems that implement sharing, programs are divided into separate procedure and data areas. Nonmodifiable procedures are called *pure procedures* or *reentrant procedures*. Modifiable data clearly cannot be shard without careful concurrency control. Nonmodifiable data (such as fixed tabular information, for example) can be shared. Modifiable procedures cannot be shared (although someone might envision an esoteric example where doing this with some form of concurrency control would make sense).

All this discussion points to the need to identify each page as either sharable or nonsharable. Once each process's pages have been categorized in this fashion, then sharing in pure paging systems is implemented as in Fig. 9.15. By having page map table entries of different processes point to the same page frame, that page frame is shared among those processes. Sharing reduces the amount of primary storage needed for a group of processes to run efficiently, and can make it possible for a given system to support more users. In the next chapter, the issues of how sharing affects virtual storage management will be considered.

Note in Fig. 9.15 that we have placed the entries for the pages of shared procedures in the same positions in each page map. Is this mandatory? This question is left to the exercises.

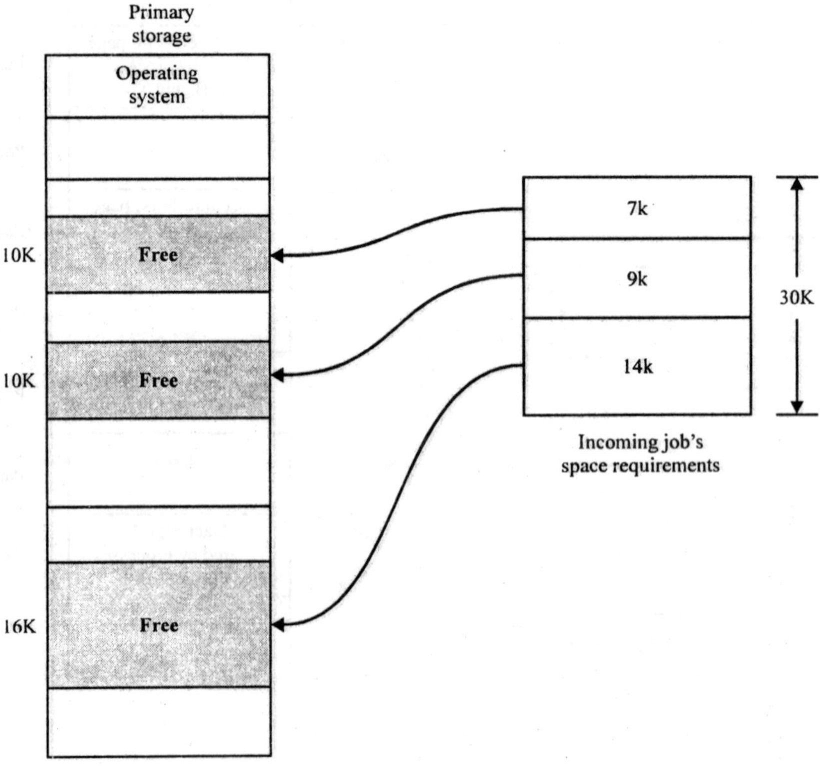

Fig. 9.16. Noncontiguous storage allocation in a real storage segmentation system.

Segmentation

In real storage *segmentation* systems, this restriction is removed and a program (and its data) are allowed to occupy many separate blocks of real storage. The blocks themselves need not be the same size and must still consist of contiguous locations, but the separate blocks need not be adjacent to one another.

This introduces several interesting problem. For example, the problem of protecting each user from destruction by other users now becomes more complex. A pair of bounds registers no longer suffices. Similarly, it becomes more difficult to limit the range of access of any given program. One scheme for implementing storage protection in segmentation systems is the use of *storage protection keys* as shown in Fig. 9.17.

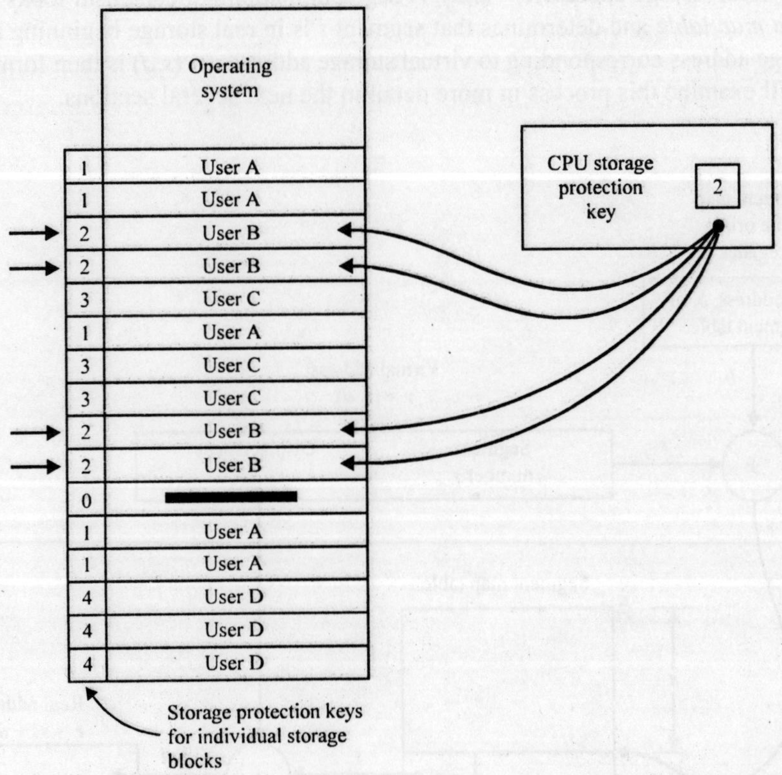

Fig. 9.17. Storage protection with keys in noncontiguous storage allocation multiprogramming systems. While the storage protection key in CPU is 2, corresponding to User B, User B's program may refer only to other blocks of storage with the same storage protection key of 2. These keys are strictly under the control of the operating system and can be manipulated only by priviledged instructions.

In a virtual storage segmentation system, a virtual address is an ordered pair $v = (s,d)$ where s is the segment number in virtual storage in which the referenced item resides, and d is the displacement within segment s at which the referenced item is located. A process may run only if its current segment (as a minimum) is in primary storage. Segments are transferred from secondary to primary storage as complete units. All the locations within a segment are placed in contiguous locations in primary storage. An incoming segment may be placed in any available area in primary storage large enough to hold the segment. The placement strategies for segmentation identical to those used in variable partition multiprogramming with first fit and best fit being most common.

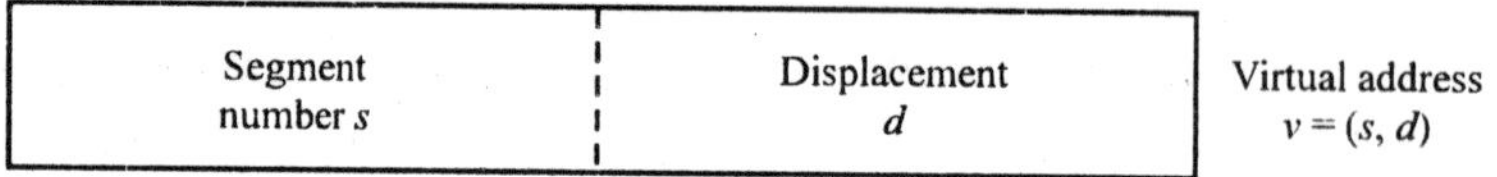

Fig. 9.18. Virtual address format in a pure segmentation system.

Dynamic address translation under segmentation proceeds as follows. A running process references a virtual storage address $v = (s,d)$. A segment mapping mechanism looks up segment s in the *segment map table* and determines that segment s is in real storage beginning at location s'. The real storage address corresponding to virtual storage address $v = (s,d)$ is then formed by adding s' to d. We will examine this process in more detail in the next several sections.

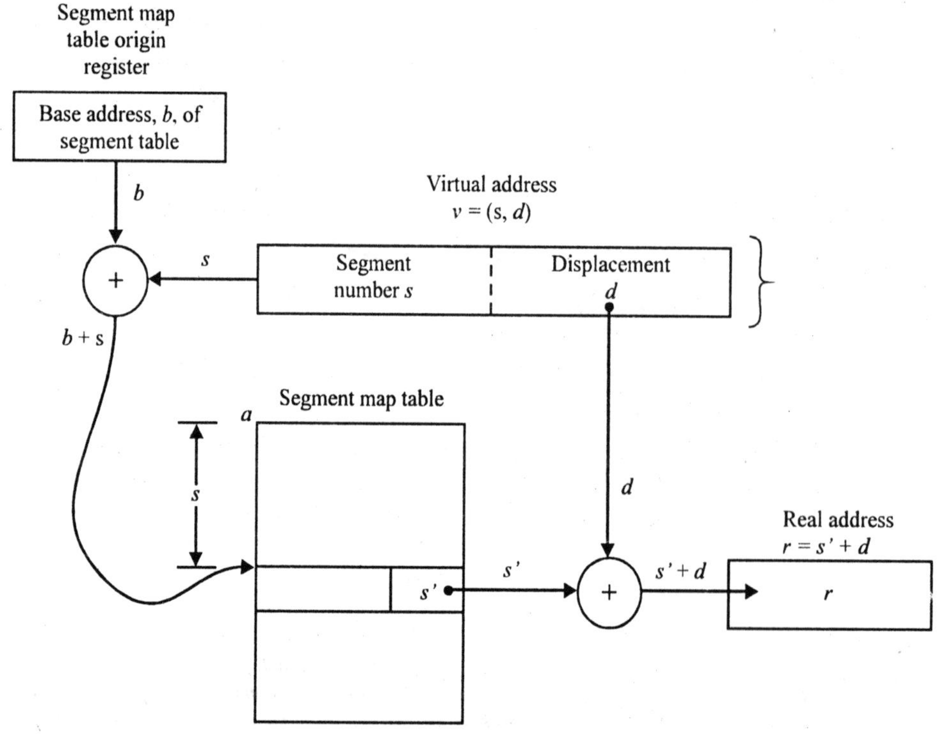

Fig. 9.19. Virtual address translation in a pure segmentation system.

Access Control in Segmentation Systems

It is unwise to give each process unlimited access to every segment in the system. In fact, one of the attractions of segmentation systems is the careful access control that is possible. This is provided by giving each process certain access rights to each segment and by, in fact, completely denying access to many segments.

Figure 9.20 lists the most common access control types in use in today's systems. If a process has *real access* to a segment, then the process may obtain any item of information contained in that segment. The process may make a complete copy of the segment if it so desires.

Type of access	Abbreviation	Explanation
Read	R	This segment may be used.
Write	W	This segment may be modified.
Execute	E	This segment may be executed.
Append	A	This segment may have information added to it at its end.

Fig. 9.20. *Access control types.*

If a process is given *write access* to a segment, then the process may modify any of the contents of the segment, and may place additional information in the segment. The process may destroy all the information in the segment if it so desires.

A prococess given *execute access* to a segment may run that segment as a program. Execute access to a data segment is normally denied.

A Process given *append access* to a segment may write additional information at the end of the segment, but may not modify existing information.

In a system with these four access control types, by either allowing or denying each type it is possible to create sixteen different *access control modes*. Some of these are interesting, while others do not make sense. For simplicity, consider the eight different combinations or read, write, and execute access shown in Fig. 9.21.

In mode 0, no access is permitted to the segment. This is useful in security schemes in which the segment is not to be accessed by a particular process.

In mode 1, a process is given *execute only access* to the segment. This mode is useful when a process is to be allowed to use a program contained in the segment, but may not copy or modify it.

	Read	Write	Execute	Explanation	Application
Mode 0	No	Yes	No	No access permitted	Security
Mode 1	No	No	Yes	Execute only	A program made available to users who cannot modify it or copy to, but who can run it.
Mode 2	No	Yes	No	Write only	These possibilities are not useful; it doesn't make sense to grant write access while denying read access
Mode 3	No	Yes	Yes	Write/execute but cannot be read	
Mode 4	Yes	No	Yes	Read only	Information retrieval
Mode 5	Yes	No	Yes	Read/execute	A program can be copied or execute but cannot be modified.
Mode 6	Yes	Yes	No	Read/write but no execution	Protects data from an erroneous attempt to execute it.
Mode 7	Yes	Yes	No	Unrestricted access	This access is granted to trusted users.

Fig. 9.21. Combining read, write, and execute access to yield useful protection modes.

Modes 2 and 3 are not useful—it does not make sense to give a process the right to modify a segment without also giving it the right to read the segment.

Mode 4 allows a process *read only access* to a segment. This is useful in information retrieval applications in which a process is to have access to information, but may not modify it.

Mode 5 allows a process *read/execute access* to a segment. This is useful in situation in which a process is allowed to use the program contained in the segment, but may not modify the original copy. The process may, however, make its own copy of the segment which it may then modify.

Mode 6 allows a process *real/write access* to a segment. This is useful when the segment is data that may be read or written by the process but that must be protected from accidental execution (since the segment is not a program).

Mode 7 allows a *process unrestricted access* to a segment. This is useful for allowing a process completed access to its own segments, and for giving it most-trusted status to access other user's segments.

The simple access control mechanism described in this section is the basis of segment protection in many implemented systems.

Segmented Address Translation by Direct Mapping

Just as in paged systems, there are many strategies for implementing segmented address translation. It can be done by direct mapping, by associative mapping, or by combined direct/associative mapping. It can be done with cache storages large enough to hold the entire segment map table, or it can be done with partial associative storages large enough to hold entries for the most recently referenced segments. In this section, we consider segmented address translation using direct mapping with the complete segment map table maintained in a fast access cache storage. A typical segment map table entry is shown in detail in Fig. 9.22.

Segment residence bit	Secondary storage address (if not in real storage)	Segment length	Protection bits				Base address of segment (if segment is in storage)
r	a	l	R	W	E	A	s'

$r = 0$ if segment is not in primary storage
$r = 1$ if segment is in primary storage

Protection bits: (1–yes, 0–no)

R – read access
W – write access
E – execute access
A – append access

Fig. 9.22. Segment map table entry.

First, we consider the case in which the address translation proceeds normally, and then we consider several problems that may arise. A running process references virtual address $v = (s,d)$. The segment number, s, is added to the base address, b, in the segment map table origin register to form the real storage address, $b + s$, of the entry for segment s in the segment map table. The segment map table contains the primary storage address, s', at which the segment begins. The displacement, d, is added to s' forming the real address, $r = s' + d$, corresponding to virtual address $v = (s.d)$.

Figure 9.22 shows a typical segment map table entry in detail. A residence bit, r indicates whether or not that segment is currently in primary storage. If the segment is in primary storage, then s' is the primary storage address at which the segment begins. If the segment is not in primary storage, then a is the secondary storage address from which the segment must be retrieved before the process may proceed. All references to the segment are checked against the segment length, l, to be sure that they fall within the range of the segment. Each reference to the segment is also checked against the protection bits to determine if the operation being attempted is allowed. Now, during dynamic address translation, once the segment map table entry for segment s has been located, first r is examined to be sure the segment is in primary storage. If the segment is not in primary storage, then *a missing segment fault* is generated, causing the operating system to gain control and load the referenced segment from secondary storage address *a*. Once the segment is loaded, address translation proceeds with checking that the displacement, *d* is less than or equal to the segment length, *l*. If it is not, then a *segment overflow* exception is generated, causing the operating system to get control and terminate execution of this process. If the displacement is within the range of the segment, then the protection bits are checked to be sure that the operation being attempted is allowed. If it is, then finally the base address, *s'*, of the segment in primary storage is added to the displacement, *d*, to form the real storage address $r = s' + d$ corresponding to virtual storage address $v = (s,d)$. If the operation being attempted is not allowed, then a *segment protection exception* is generated, causing the operating system to get control and terminate execution of this process.

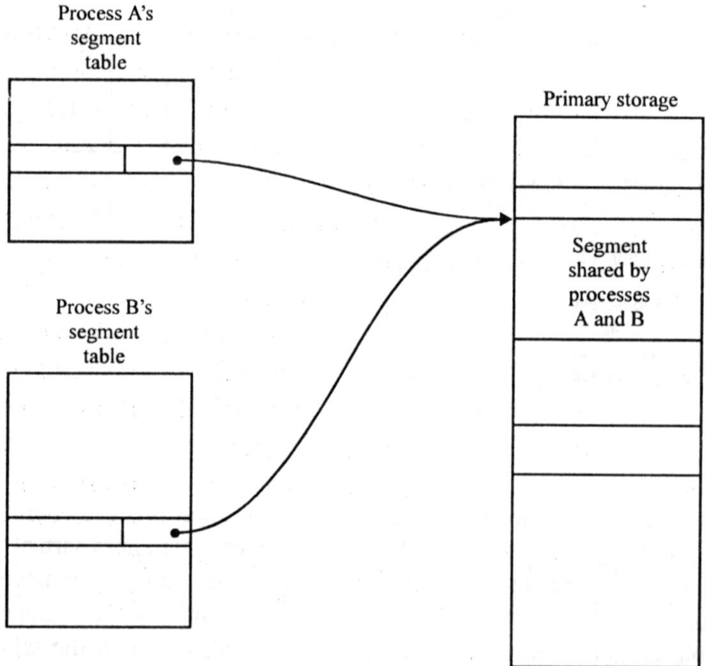

Fig. 9.23. Sharing in a pure segmentation system.

Sharing in a Segmentation System

One of the advantages of segmentation over paging is that segmentation is a logical rather than a physical concept. In their most general form, segments are not arbitrarily constrained to a certain size. Instead, they are allowed to be (within reasonable limits) as large (or as small) as they need to be. A segment corresponding to an array is as large as the array. A segment corresponding to a dynamic data structure may grow and shrink as the data structure itself grows and shrinks. A segment corresponding to procedural code generated by a compiler is as large as it needs to be to hold the code.

Sharing segments is quite straightforward when compared to sharing in a pure paging system. If an array in a pure paging system is three and one-half pages long, then instead of having simple entries that indicated "share this array," we must now have separate entries for each of the pages on which the array resides. Handling the partial page can be awkward. The situation is even worse with a dynamic data structure. When a dynamic data structure grows into a new page, the sharing indications must be adjusted at execution time. In a segmentation system, once the segment is declared as shared, data structures may grow and shrink without changing the logical fact that they reside on shared segments.

Paging/Segmentation Systems

Both segmentation and paging offer significant advantages as virtual storage organizations. Beginning with systems constructed in the mid-1960s, in particular Multics and **IBM**'s TSS, many computer systems have been built that combine paging and segmentation. These systems offer the advantages of both virtual storage organization techniques. Segments are usually multiples of pages in size, all the pages of a segment need not be in primary storage at once, and virtual storage pages that are contiguous in virtual storage need not be contiguous in real storage. Addressing is three dimensional with a virtual storage address, v, being an ordered triple $v = (s,p,d)$ where s is the segment number, p is the page number within the segment, and d is the displacement within the page at which the desired item is located.

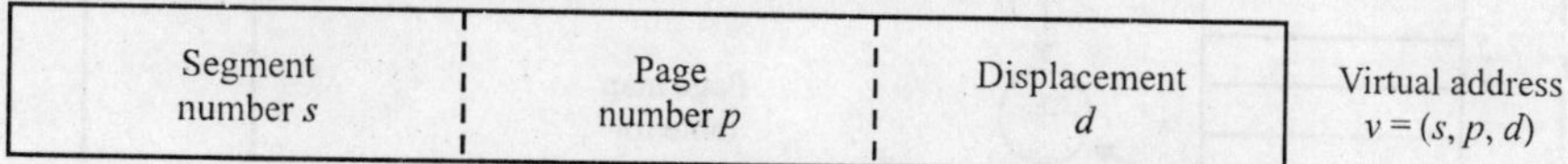

Fig. 9.24. Virtual address format in a paged and segmented system.

Dynamic Address Translation in Paging/Segmentation Systems

Now consider the dynamic address translation of virtual addresses to real addresses in a paging/segmentation system using combined associative/direct mapping as illustrated a Fig. 9.25.

A running process references virtual address $v = (s,p,d)$. The most recently referenced pages have entries in partial associative storage. An associative search is performed to attempt to locate (s,p) in the associative storage. If (s,p) is found, then the page fame, p', at which page p of segments s resides in primary storage, is concatenated to the displacement, d, to form the real storage address, r, corresponding to virtual address $v = (s,p,d)$, and the address translation is complete.

Normally, most address translation requests are satisfied by this associative storage search. When a request is not satisfied by searching the associative storage, a complete direct mapping occurs as follows. The base address, b, of the segment map table (in primary storage) is added to the segment number, s, to form the address, $b + s$, of the entry in the segment map table for segment s in primary storage. The segment map table entry indicates the base address, s', of the page table (in primary storage) for segment s. The page number, p, is added to s' to form the address, $p + s'$, of the entry in the page table for page p of segment s. This table yields the fact that p' is the page frame number corresponding to virtual page p. The frame number, p', is concatenated with the displacement, d, to form the real address, r, corresponding to virtual address $v = (s,p,d.)$.

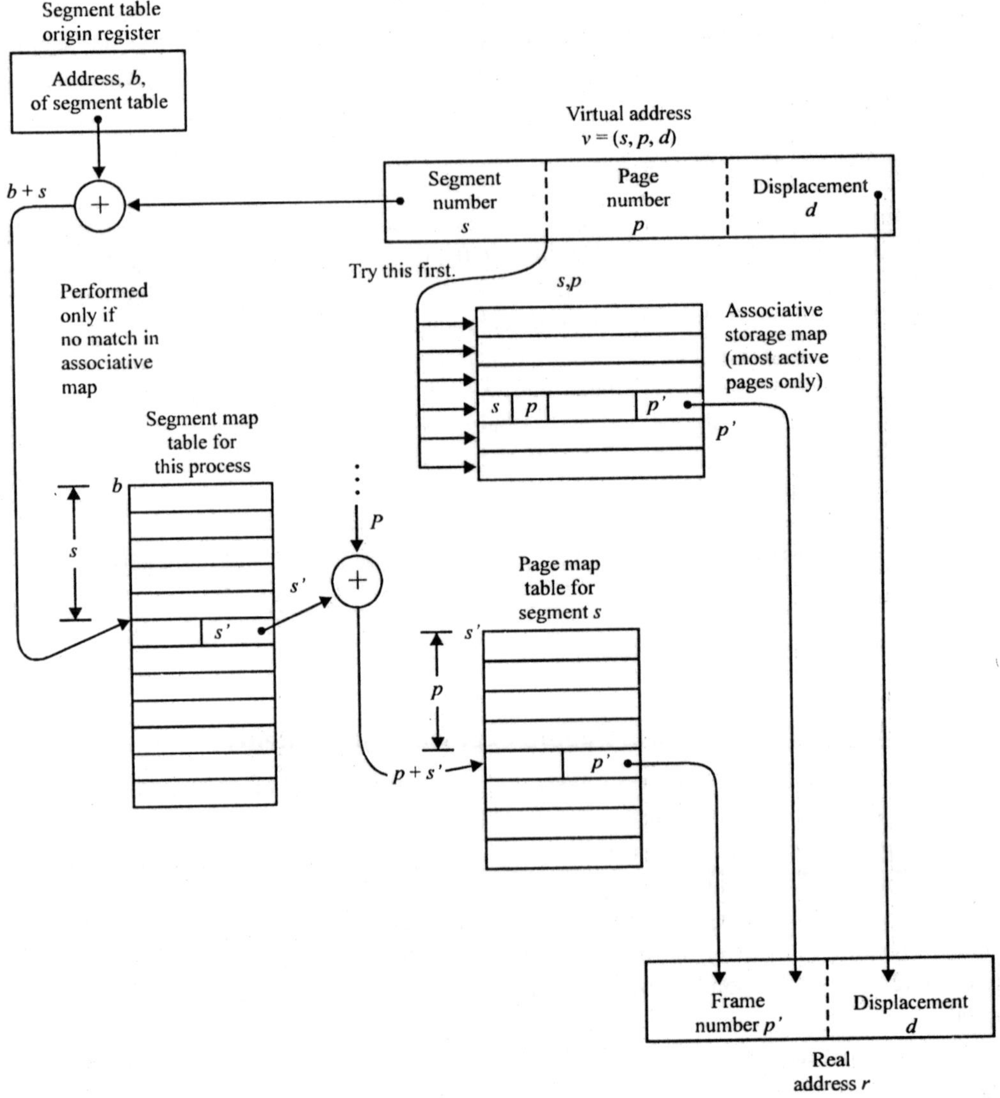

Fig. 9.25. Virtual address translation with combined associative/direct mapping paged and segmented system.

This translation process has, of course, assumed that every piece of information is exactly where it's supposed to be. But there are many steps along the way where the translation process may fail. The segment map table search may indicate that segment *s* is not in primary storage, thus generating a *missing segment fault* and causing the operating system to locate the segment on secondary storage, create a page table for the segment, and load the appropriate page into primary storage, possibly replacing an existing page of this or some other process. If the segment is in primary storage, then the reference to the page map table may indicate that the desired page is not in primary storage. This would generate a *missing page fault*, causing the operating system to gain control, locate the page on secondary storage, and load the page (again, possibly replacing another page). Just as in pure segmentation, a virtual storage address may be past the end of a segment, thus generating a *segment overflow exception*. Or the protection bits may indicate that the operation to be performed on the referenced virtual address is not allowed, thus generating a *segment protection exception*. The operating system must handle all these eventualities.

The associative storage (or similarly, a high-speed cache storage) is critical to the efficient operation of this dynamic address translation mechanism. If a purely direct mapping mechanism were used with the complete map maintained in primary storage, the range virtual storage reference would require a storage cycle to access the segment map tale, a second storage cycle to reference the page map table, and a third storage cycle to reference the desired item in real storage, thus every reference to an item would involve three storage cycle, and the computer system would run only at approximately one-third its normal speed, with two-thirds of its time being spend tin address translation! It is interesting that with only eight or sixteen associative registers, many systems achieve operating speeds of 90 per cent and higher of the full processing speed of their control processors.

Figure 9.26 indicates the detailed table structure required by paged/segmented systems. At the top level is a *process table* containing an entry for every process known to the system. The process table entry for a given process points to that process's segment map table. Each entry of a process's segment map table points to the page map table for the associated segment, and each entry in a page map table points either to the page frame in which that page resides or to the secondary storage address at which the page may be found. In a system with a large number of processes, segments, and pages, this table structure can consume a significant portion of primary storage. The trade-off here is that address translation proceeds more quickly at execution time if all the tables are in primary storage, but with more tables in primary storage, the system supports fewer processes, and thus productivity declines. Operating systems designers must evaluate many such trade-offs to achieve the delicate balance needed for a system to run efficiently and to provide responsible service to its users.

Sharing in a Paging/Segmentation System

In a paging/segmentation system the advantages of segment sharing become important. Sharing is implemented by having entries in segment map tables for different processes point to the same page map table, as is indicated in Fig. 9.27.

Sharing, whether it be in pages systems, segmented systems, or paged/segmented systems, requires careful management by the operating system. In particular, the reader should consider what would happen if an incoming page were to replace a page shared by many processes.

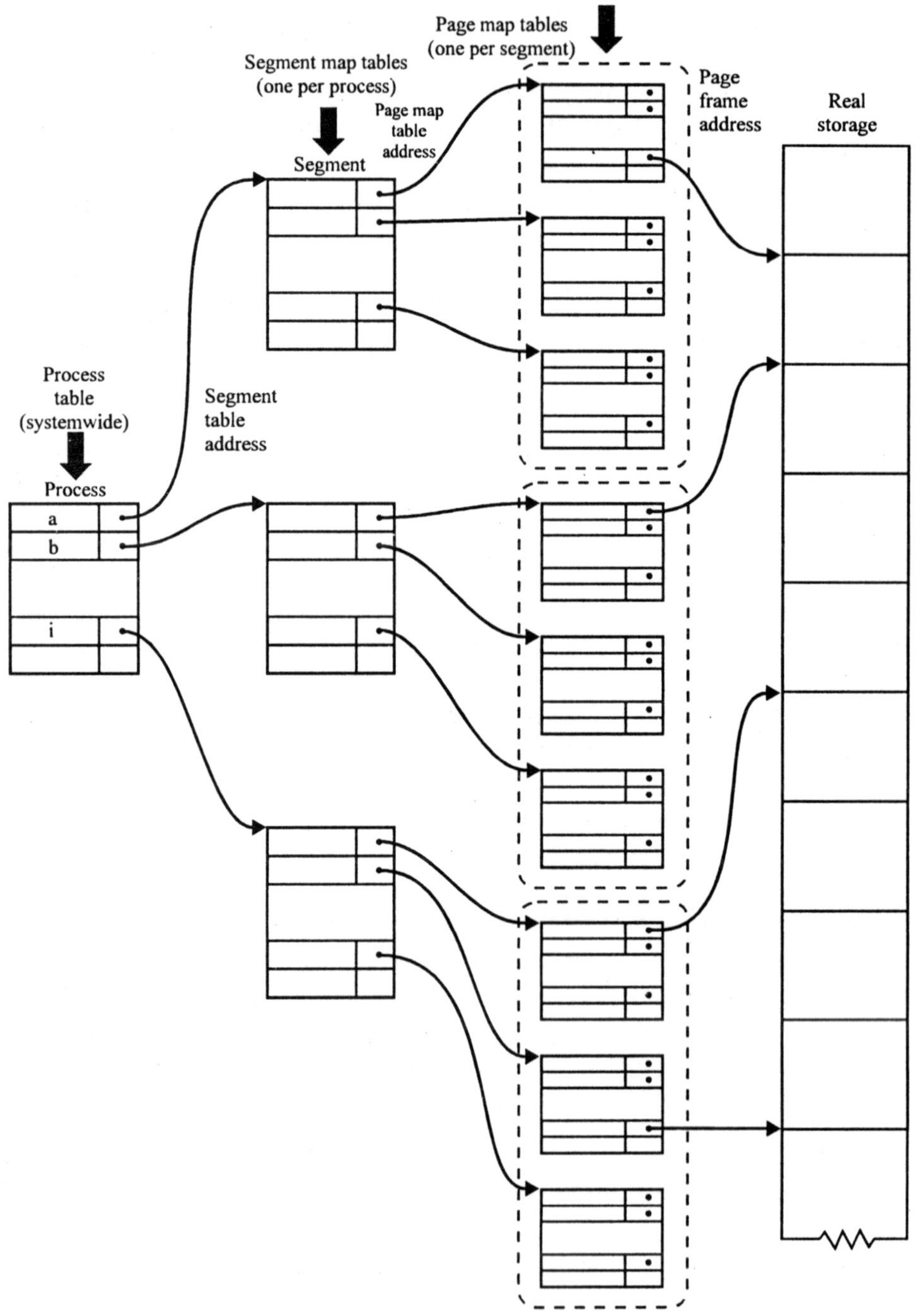

Fig. 9.26. Table structure for a paged and segmented system.

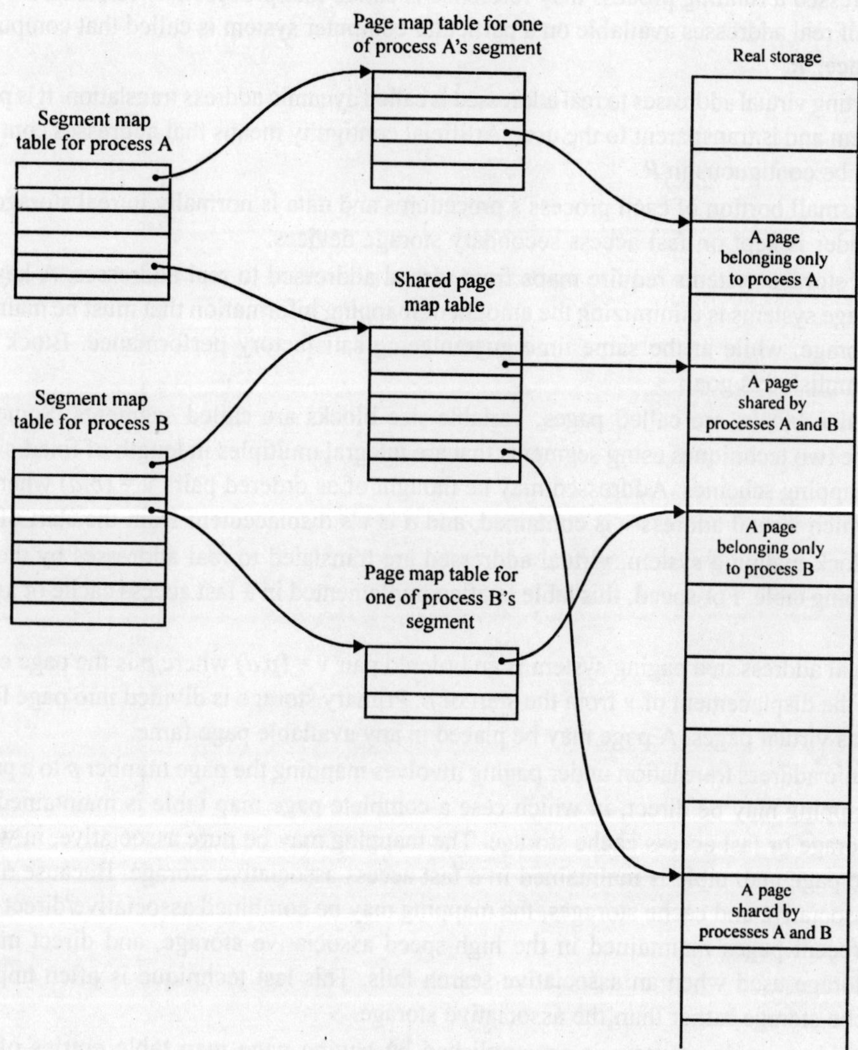

Fig. 9.27. Two processes sharing a segment in a paged and segmented system.

Summary

The two most common methods of implementing virtual storage are paging and segmentation. Virtual addresses are normally selected from a much larger set of addresses than is available in primary storage.

The key to the virtual storage concept is disassociating the virtual addressed referenced in a running process from the addresses available in primary storage, real addresses. The range of virtual addressed a running process may reference is called that process's virtual address space, V. The range of real addresses available on a particular computer system is called that computer's real address space, *R*.

Converting virtual addresses to real addressed is called dynamic address translation. It is performed by the system and is transparent to the user. Artificial contiguity means that addresses contiguous in V need not be contiguous in *R*.

Only a small portion of each process's procedures and data is normally in real storage at once. The remainder is kept on fast access secondary storage devices.

Virtual storage systems require maps from virtual addressed to real addresses. A key issue in virtual storage systems is minimizing the amount of mapping information that must be maintained in primary storage, while at the same time guaranteeing satisfactory performance. Block mapping helps accomplish this goal.

Fixed-size blocks are called pages; variable-size blocks are called segments. Some systems combine the two techniques using segments that are integral multiples in length of fixed-size pages. In block mapping schemes. Addressed may be thought of as ordered pairs $v = (b,d)$ where b is the block in which virtual address v is contained, and d is v's displacement from the start of block b.

In a block mapping system, virtual addressed are translated to real addresses by the use of a block mapping table. For speed, this table is often implemented in a fast access cache or associative storage.

A virtual address in a paging system is an ordered pair $v = (p,d)$ where p is the page containing v, and d is the displacement of v from the start of p. Primary storage is divided into page frames the same size as virtual pages. A page may be placed in any available page fame.

Dynamic address translation under paging involves mapping the page number p to a page frame p'. The mapping may be direct, in which case a complete page map table is maintained in either primary storage or fast access cache storage. The mapping may be pure associative, in which case a complete page map table is maintained in a fast access associative storage. Because of the high costs of associative and cache storages, the mapping may be combined associative/direct with only the most recent pages maintained in the high-speed associative storage, and direct mapping in primary storage used when an associative search fails. This last technique is often implemented with a cache storage rather than the associative storage.

Sharing in a paging system is accomplished by having page map table entries of different processes point to the same page frame. Sharing in this manner is awkward because processes really share logical entities like procedures and data, which can often occupy several pages and grow and shrink as a process executes.

Segmentation uses variable-size blocks. Each block, within reasonable limits, is as large as it needs to be to hold a logical entity such as a procedure or a data structure. A process's segments need not all be in primary storage at once, nor must they be contiguous in primary storage. A process may run if its current segment (as a minimum) is in primary storage.

A virtual address in a segmentation system is an ordered pair $v = (s,d)$, where s is the segment in which v resides and d is v's displacement within s. Dynamic address translation can be performed with essentially the same types of direct, associative, and combined direct/associative mapping performed in paging systems. Because segments vary in length, this displacement *d* must be checked to see that it is within the range of the segment.

Protection in segmentation systems is more natural than in paging systems because logical rather than physical entities are being protected. Processes are given various combinations of read, write, execute, and append access to various segments, sharing is also more natural in a segmentation system. The segment table entries of different processes are made to point to the shared segment.

Many systems employ both paging and segmentation. A virtual address in a paging/segmentation system is an ordered triple $v = (s,p,d)$ with s the segment in which v resides, p the page within s that contains v, and d the displacement of v within p. Dynamic address translation is complex in such systems with segment map table entries pointing to page map tables, and page map table entries pointing to page frames. A fast access associative storage or cache storage is almost always used in such systems to prevent the dynamic address translation from causing serious performance degradation.

Sharing in a paging/segmentation system is accomplished by having entries in different segment map tables point to the page map table of the shared segment.

Virtual Storage Management Strategies

The chapter on real storage discussed fetch, placement, and replacement storage management strategies. These are reconsidered here in the context of virtual storage systems.

- Fetch strategies—These are concerned with when a page or segment should be brought from secondary to primary storage. Demand fetch strategies wait for a page or segment to be referenced by a running process before bringing the page or segment to primary storage. Anticipatory fetch schemes attempt to determine in advance what pages or segments will be referenced by a process. If the likelihood of reference is high and if space is available, then the page or segment will be brought to primary storage before it is explicitly referenced.
- Placement strategies—These are concerned with where in primary storage to place an incoming page or segment. *Paging systems trivialize the placement decision because an incoming page may be placed in any available page frame.* Segmentation systems require placement strategies like those we discussed in the context of variable partition multiprogramming systems.
- Replacement strategies—These are concerned with deciding which page or segment to displace to make room for an incoming page or segment when primary storage is already fully committed.

Page Replacement Strategies

It is common in paging systems for all page frames to be in use. In this case operating system storage management routines must decide which page in primary storage to displace to make room for an incoming page (Ah71). We consider each of the following page replacement strategies.

- The Principle of Optimality
- Random page replacement
- First-in-first-out

- Least-recently-used
- Least-frequently-used
- Not-used-recently
- Second chance
- Clock
- Working set
- Page fault frequency

The Principle of Optimality

The *Principle of Optimality* states that to obtain optimum performance the page to replace is the one that will not be used again for the furthest time into the future. It is possible to demonstrate the optimality of this strategy, but of course the strategy is not realizable sine we cannot predict the future. This optimal replacement strategy is called *OPT or MIN.*

Thus to achieve good performance we attempt to approach the Principle of Optimality by using page replacement techniques that approximate optimal page replacement.

Random Page Replacement

If we seek a low overhead page replacement strategy that does not discriminate against particular users, one simple technique to choose is *random page replacement.* All pages in main storage thus have an equal likelihood of being selected for replacement. This strategy could select may page for replacement, including the next page to be referenced (which is, of course, the worst page to replace). Random page replacement decisions can be made quickly, and with any significant number of page frames to choose from would actually have only a small probability of replacing a page likely to be referenced again almost immediately. Because of its hit-or-miss approach, however, this scheme is rarely used.

First-In-First-Out (FIFO) Page Replacement

In *First-in first-out (FIFO) page replacement*, we time-stamp each page as it enters primary storage. When a page needs to be place, we choose the one that has been in storage the longest. The intuitive appeal of this strategy seems reasonable; namely that this page has had its chance and it's time to give another page a chance. Unfortunately, first-in-first-out is likely to replace heavily used pages because the reason a page has been in primary storage for a long time may be that it is in constant use. For example, on large timesharing systems it is common for many users to share a copy of a text editor as they enter and correct programs. First-in-first-out page replacement on such a system might choose a heavily used editor page to replace. This would certainly be a poor choice. This page would be recalled to main storage almost immediately. First-in-first-out page replacement can also be implemented with a simple FIFO queue; as each page arrives, it is placed at the tail of the queue and pages are replaced from the head of the queue.

FIFO Anomaly

It would seem reasonable that the more page frames allocated to a process, the fewer page faults the process would experience. Belady, Nelson, and Shedler (Be69b) discovered that under

FIFO page replacement, certain page reference patterns actually cause more page faults when the number of page frames allocated to a process is increased. This phenomenon is called the *FIFO Anomaly or Belady's Anomaly.*

Consider Fig. 9.28. The leftmost column indicates the page reference pattern of a process. The first table shows how this page reference pattern cause pages to be located into storage and replaced under FIFO when three page frames are allocated to the process. The second table shows how this process behaves in these same circumstances, but instead with four page frames allocated to it. To the left of each table we indicate whether the new page reference caused a page fault or not. When the process runs in four pages, it actually experiences one more page fault than when it runs in three pages, an observation certainly contrary to intuition.

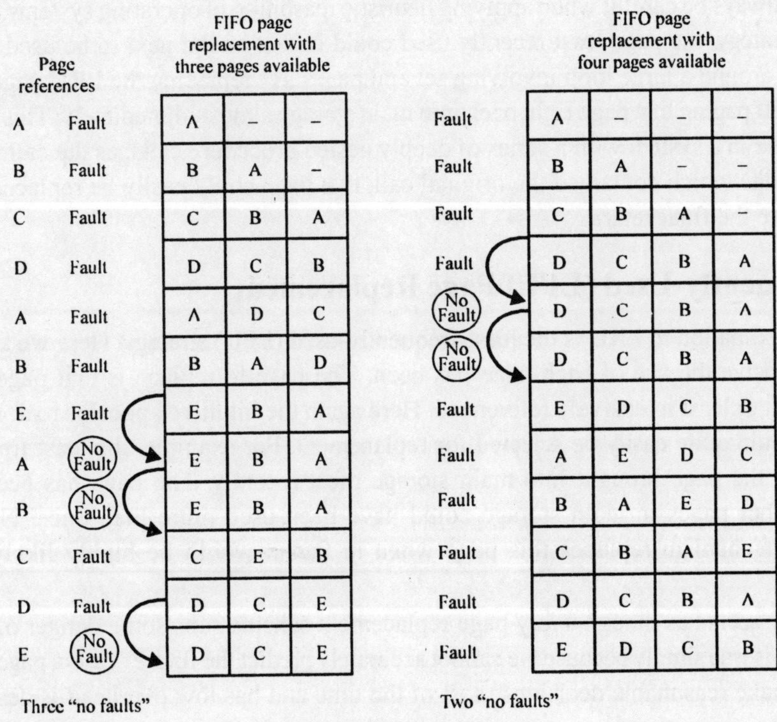

Fig. 9.28. The FIFO Anomaly.

The FIFO Anomaly is considered to be more of a curiosity than an important result. Perhaps its real significance to the operating systems student is to serve as a warning that operating systems are complex entities that sometimes defy intuition.

Least-Recently-Used (LRU) Page Replacement

This strategy selects that page for replacement that has not been used for the longest time. Here we rely on the locality heuristic that the recent past is a good indicator of the near future. LRU requires that each page be time-stamped whenever it is referenced. This could require substantial overhead, and thus the LRU strategy, although appealing, is not often implemented in current systems. Instead, lower overhead strategies that approximate LRU are used.

LRU can be implemented with a list structure containing one entry for each occupied page frame. Each time a page frame is referenced, the entry for that page is placed at the head of the list. Older entries migrate toward the tail of the list. When a page must be replaced to make room for an incoming page, the entry at the tail of the list is selected, the corresponding page frame is freed (possibly requiring a modified page to be written to secondary storage), the incoming page is placed in that page frame, and the entry for that page frame is placed at the head of the list because that page is now the one that has been most recently used. This scheme would faithfully implement LRU, but it, too, incurs substantial overhead.

We must always be careful when applying heuristic reasoning in operating systems. For example, in the LRU strategy, the page least recently used could in fact be the next to be used as a program cycles its way around a large loop involving several pages. By replacing the LRU page, this system would find itself paging that page right back into main storage almost immediately. This phenomenon could also occur in a system with a series of deeply nested procedure calls; as the called procedures return to the page which contained the original call, that page could easily be replaced as the LRU page just before the final return.

Least-Frequently-Used (LFU) Page Replacement

One approximation to LRU is the least-frequently-used (LFU) strategy. Here we are concerned with how intensive the sue of each page has been. The page to replace is that page that is least frequently used or least intensively referenced. Here again the intuitive appeal is real. However, the wrong page could quite easily be selected for replacement. For example, the least frequently used page could be the page brought into main storage most recently. The page has been used once whereas all other pages in main storage could have been used more than once. Now the page replacement mechanism replaces this page when in fact it would be highly likely to be used immediately.

It certainly seems as though every page replacement scheme runs some danger of making bad decisions. This is true simply because we cannot accurately predict the future. Thus a page replacement strategy that make reasonable decisions most of the time and has low overhead is desired.

Not-Used-Recently (NUR) Page Replacement

One popular scheme for approximating LRU with little overhead is not-used-recently (NUR). Pages not used recently are not likely to be used in the near future and they may be replaced with incoming pages.

Because is desirable to replace a page that has not been changed while in primary storage, the NUR strategy is implemented with the addition of two hardware bits per page. These are

(a) *referenced bit* = 0 if the page has not been referenced
= 1 if the page has been referenced

(b) *modified bit* = 0 if the page has not been modified
= 1 if the page has been modified

The modified bit is often called the *dirty bit*. The NUR strategy works as follows. Initially, the referenced bits of all pages are set to 0. As a reference to a particular page occurs, the referenced bit of that page is set to 1. Initially, the modified bits on all pages are 0. Whenever a page is modified, its modified bit is set to 1. When a page is to be replaced, we first try to find a page which has not been referenced (because we're approximating LRU). Otherwise we have no choice but to replace a referenced page. If a page has not been referenced, we check to see whether or not it has been modified. If it has not been modified, we replace it on the basis that there is less overhead involved than in replacing a modified page that must be written back to secondary storage. Otherwise we must replace a modified page.

Of course, main storage will be actively referenced in a multiple ucer system, and sooner or latter most or all the referenced bits will be set on. We then lose our ability to distinguish the most desirable pages to replace. One technique that has been widely implemented to avoid this problem is to periodically set all the referenced bits to 0 to get a fresh start, and then to allows referenced bits to be set to 1 again under normal referencing patterns. Unfortunately, this makes even active pages vulnerable to replacement, but only for a brief moment after the bits are reset. Active pages will have their referenced bits set to 1 again almost immediately.

The NUR scheme as described above results in the existence of four groups of pages

Group 1	unreferenced	unmodified
Group 2	unreferenced	modified
Group 3	referenced	unmodified
Group 4	referenced	modified

The pages in the lowest numbered groups should be replaced first, and those in the highest numbered groups should be replaced last. Pages within a group are selected randomly for replacement. Not that Group 2 seems to describe an unrealistic situation. Namely pages that have been modified but not referenced. Actually, this is a simple consequence of the periodic resetting of the referenced bits (but not of the modified bits), and is perfectly reasonable.

Schemes like NUR can be implemented on machines like the VAX that lack a hardware referenced bit (Bb81), and even on machines that lack a hardware modified bit. The referenced and modified bits are normally implemented in hardware and set automatically as part of the execution of each machine instruction. Each of these bits can be simulated by "tapping into" an operating system's fault handlers and exception handlers as follows: The referenced bit can be simulated by a corresponding software bit and by setting each entry in the page table to indicate that the page is not present; referencing a page causes a page fault and give control to the page fault handler which then sets the referenced bit on, and resumes normal processing. The modified bit is simulated simply by marking each page as readonly; when an attempt is made to modify the page, an accessing exception occurs, and the exception handler gains control, sets the (software-controlled) modified bit on, and changes the access control on that page to read/write. Of course, the mechanism that implements the modified bit must still protect genuine readonly pages from being modified so the operating system must keep track of which pages are truly readonly and which are truly read/write.

Modifications to FIFO; Clock Page Replacement and Second Chance Page Replacement

The clear weakness of the FIFO strategy, is that it may choose to replace a heavily used page that has been in memory for a long item. This possibility can be avoided by replacing only those pages whose referenced bits are off.

The *second chance* variation of FIFO examines the referenced bit of the oldest page; if this bit is off, the page is immediately selected for replacement. If the referenced bit is on, it is set off and the page is moved to the tail of the FIFO list and treated essentially as a new arrival; this page gradually moves to the head of the list from which it will be selected for replacement only if its referenced bit is still off. This essentially gives the page a second chance to remain in primary storage if indeed its referenced bit is turned on before the page reaches the head of the list. Active pages will repeatedly have their referenced bits set on, move to the head of the list have their referenced buts set off, and move to the tail of the list, thus remaining in primary storage. Obviously, a modified page must be copied to secondary storage (pushed) before it can be replaced; so when its referenced bit is set off, the page remains "temporarily unreplaceable" until the push is completed. If this page is referenced before it is replaced, then it is recaptured, thus saving an expensive page-in operation from secondary storage.

Locality

Central to most storage management strategies is the concept of locality—that *processes tend to reference storage in nonuniform, highly localized patterns.*

Locality manifests itself in both time and space. *Temporal locality* is locality over time. For example, if the weather is sunny at 3 p.m., then there is a good chance (but certainly no guarantee) that the weather was sunny at 2:30 p.m., and will be sunny at 3.:30 p.m. *spatial locality* means that nearby items tend to be similar. Again, considering the weather, if it's sunny in one town, then it's likely (but not guaranteed) to be sunny in nearby towns.

Locality is also observed in operating systems environments, particularly in the area of storage management. It is an empirical (observed) property rather than a theoretical one. It is never guaranteed but is often highly likely. For example, in paging systems, we observe that processed tend to favor certain subsets of their pages, and that these pages often tend to be adjacent to one another in a process's virtual address space. This doesn't mean that a process won't make a reference to a new page—if this were the case, then processes could not start running in the first place. It does mean that a process will tend to concentrate its references in a time interval to a particular subset of its pages.

Actually, locality is quite reasonable in computer systems, when one considers the way program are written and data is organized. In particular,

1. Temporal locality—means that storage locations referenced recently are likely to be referenced in the near future. Supporting this observation are

(a) looping,
(b) subroutines,
(c) stacks, and
(d) variables used for counting and totaling

2. Spatial locality—means that storage references tend to be clustered so that once a location is referenced, it is highly likely that nearby locations will be referenced. Supporting this observation are
(a) array traversals,
(b) sequential code execution, and
(c) the tendency of programmers to place related variable definitions near one another.

Perhaps the most significant consequence of storage reference locality is that a program can run efficiently as long as its favored subset of pages is in primary storage. Denning formulated the *working set theory of program behavior* based upon observations of locality. We discuss Denning's working set theory in the next section.

Many studies have been performed that illustrate the phenomenon of locality. Figure 9.29 shows a graph of a process's storage reference pattern across its pages. The darkened areas show which storage areas were referenced during consecutive time intervals. The figure vividly illustrates how this process tends to favor a subset of its pages during certain execution intervals.

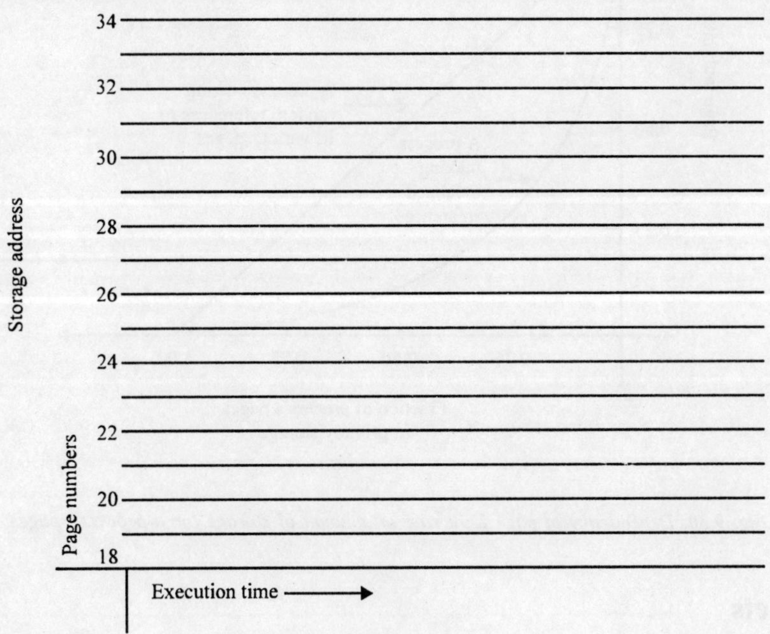

Fig. 9.29. Storage reference pattern exhibiting locality.

Figure 9.30 also supports the existence of the phenomenon of locality. It shows how a process's page fault rate depends on the amount of primary storage available for its pages. The straight line shows how this relationship would appear if processes exhibited random reference patterns uniformly distributed over their various page. The curved line shows how most processes actually behave when observed in operation. As the number of page frame available to a process is reduced, there is some interval over which it does not dramatically affect the page fault rate. But at a certain point when the number of page frames is further reduced, the number of page faults experienced by the running process rises dramatically. What is being observed here is that as long as the favored subset of the process's pages remains in primary storage, the page fault rate does not change much. But as soon as pages in the favored subset are removed from storage, the process's paging activity greatly increases as it constantly references and recalls these pages to primary storage. All of this supports Denning's working set concept, which is considered in the next section. (Note that this discussion also applies to the establishment of working sets in cache memories as well.)

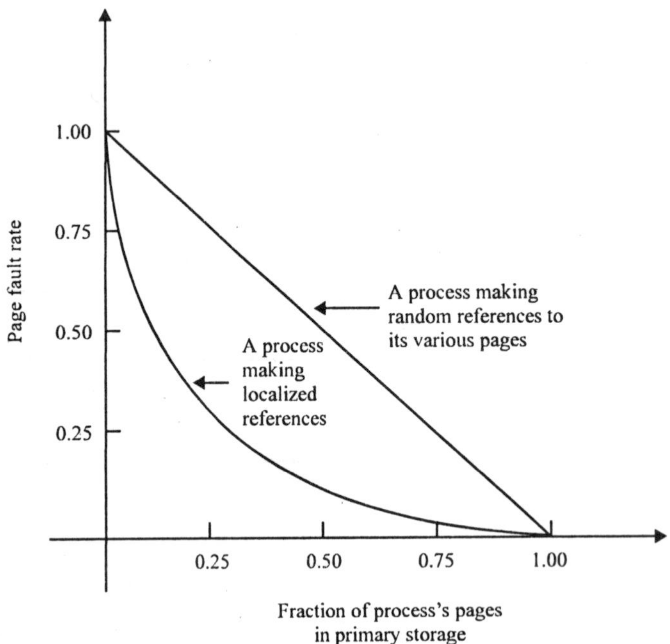

Fig. 9.30. Dependency of page fault rate on amount of storage for a process's pages.

Working Sets

Denning developed view of program paging activity called the *working set theory of program behavior.* Informally, a working set is a collection of pages a process is actively referencing. Denning maintained that for a program to run efficiently, its working set of pages must be maintained in primary storage. Otherwise, excessive paging activity called *thrashing* (De68b) might occur as the program repeatedly request pages from secondary storage. One popular rule of thumb is that thrashing may be avoided by giving processes enough page frames to hold half their virtual space. Unfortunately, rules like this often result in excessively conservative virtual storage management, ultimately limiting the number of processed that may effectively share primary storage.

A *working set storage management policy* seeks to maintain the working sets of active programs in primary storage. The decision to add a new process to the active set of processes (i.e., to increase the level of multiprogramming) is based on whether sufficient space is available in primary storage to accommodate the working set of pages of the new process. This decision, especially in the case of freshly initiated processes, is often made by the use of heuristics because it is impossible for the system to know in advance how large a given process's set will be.

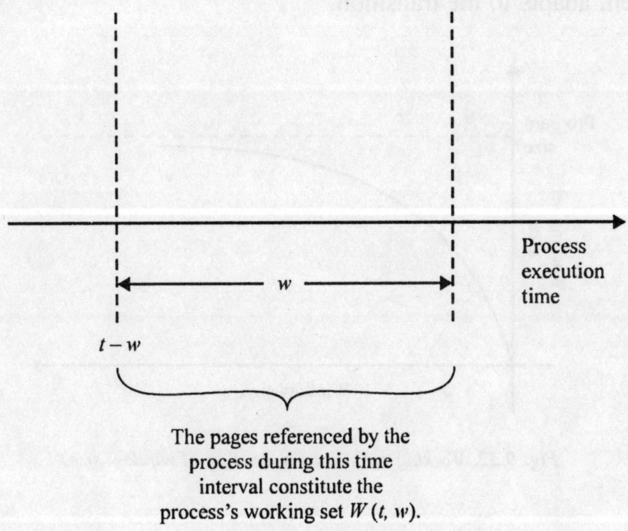

Fig. 9.31. One definition of a process's working set of pages.

The working set of pages of a process, $W(t,w)$ at time t, is the set of pages referenced by the process during the process time interval $t - w$ to t. Process time is the time during which a process has the CPU. The variable w is called the *working set window size*, and the determination of just how large w should be is critical to the effective operation of a working set storage management strategy. Figure 9.32 illustrates how working set size increases as w increases. This is a consequence of the mathematical definition of working set, and is not an indication of empirically observable working set sizes. *The real working set of a process is the set of pages that must be in primary storage for a process to execute efficiently.*

Working sets change as a process executes. Sometimes pages are added or deleted. Sometimes dramatic changes occur when the process enters a phase of execution requiring a completely different working set. Thus any assumptions about the size and content of a process's initial working set do not necessarily apply to the subsequent working sets the process will accumulate. This complicates precise storage management under a working set strategy.

Figure 9.33 shows how a process running under a working set storage management strategy might use primary storage. First, as the process demand pages in its working set one page at a time, the process gradually receives enough storage to hold its working set. At this point, its storage use stabilized as it actively references the pages in its first working set. Eventually, the process will make a transition to the next working set, as indicated by the curved line from first working set to second working set. Initially, the curved line rises above the number of pages in the first working because the process is rapidly demand paging in its new working set. The system has no way of knowing whether this process is expanding its working set or changing working sets. Once the process stabilizes in its next working set, the system sees fewer page references in the window and reduces the primary storage allocation of the process of the number of pages in its second working set. Each time a transition between working sets occurs, this rising and then falling curved line shows how the system adapts to the transition.

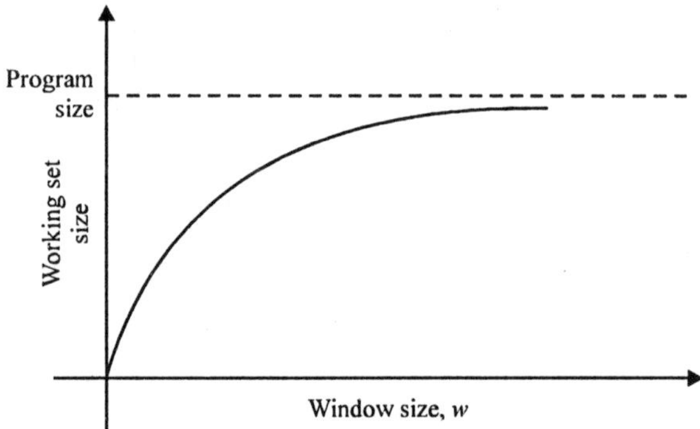

Fig. 9.32. Working set size as a function of window size.

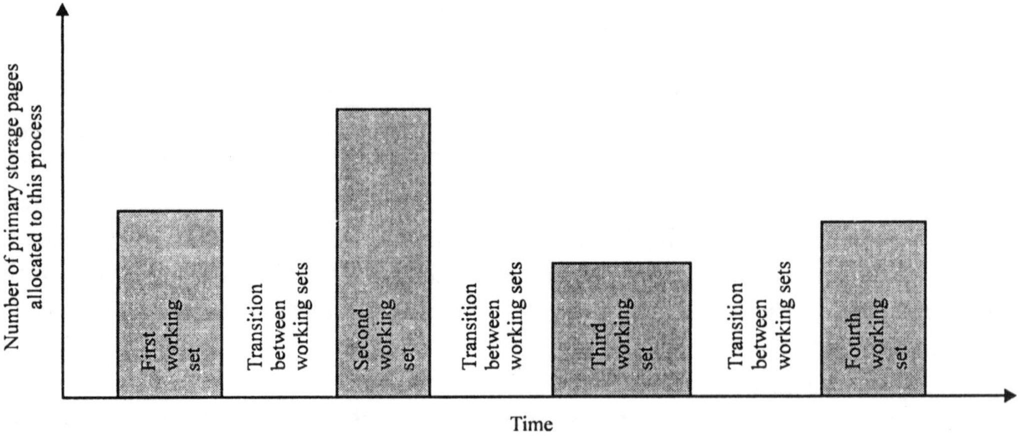

Fig. 9.33. Primary storage allocation under working set storage management.

The figure illustrates one of the difficulties with a working set storage management strategy, namely that *working sets are transient, and a process's next working set may differ substantially from its current working set.* A storage management strategy must carefully consider this fact in order to prevent overcommitment of primary storage, and consequent thrashing.

Page Fault Frequency Page Replacement

One measure of how well a process executes in a paging environment is its page fault rate. Processes that fault constantly may be thrashing because they have too few page frames and cannot maintain their working sets in primary storage. Processes that almost never fault, may in fact have too many page frames and thus they may be impeding the progress of other processes on the system. Ideally, processed should operate at some point intermediate to these extremes. *The page fault frequency (PFF) algorithm* adjusts a *process's resident page set*, i.e., those of its pages which are currently in memory, based on the frequency at which the process is faulting (or alternatively, based on the time between page faults, called the *interfault time*).

PFF observes the time between the last and the current page faults. If that time is larger than an upper threshold value, then all pages unreferenced in that interval are released. If the time is less than a lower threshold values, the incoming page becomes a member of the process's resident page set.

The beauty of PFF is that is adjusts a process's resident page set dynamically in response to the changing behavior of the process. If a process is switching to a larger working set, then it will fault frequently and PFF will give it more page frames. Once the new working set is accumulated, the page fault rate will settle down and PFF will either maintain the resident page set or even reduce it.

Clearly, the key to the proper and efficient operation of PFF is maintaining the thresholds at appropriate values.

An advantage of PFF over working ser page replacement is that it adjust the resident page set only after each page fault, whereas a working set mechanism must operate after each storage reference.

Demand Paging

It is the conventional wisdom that a process's pages should be loaded on demand. No page should be brought from secondary to primary storage until it is explicitly referenced by a running process. There are several reasons for the appeal of this strategy.

- Computability results, specifically the *halting problem*, tell us that the path of execution of a program will take cannot be accurately predicted. Therefore, any attempt to preload pages in anticipation of their use might result in the wrong page being loaded.
- Demand paging guarantees that the only pages brought to main storage are those actually needed by processes.
- The overhead involved in deciding which pages to bring to main storage is minimal. Anticipatory page fetch strategies might require substantial execution time overhead.

Demand paging is not without its problems, as indicated in Fig. 9.34. A process must accumulate its pages one at a time. As each new page is referenced, the process must wait while the new page is transferred to primary storage. Depending on how many pages of this process are already in primary storage, these waits become increasingly costly as greater amounts of storage are occupied by waiting processes. The figure illustrates the concept of a *space-time product* often used in operating systems to assess a process's storage usage. The space-time product correspond to the area under the "curve" in the figure. It reflects both the amount of storage a process uses, and how long it is used. *Reducing the space-time product of a process's page waits is an important goal of storage management strategies.*

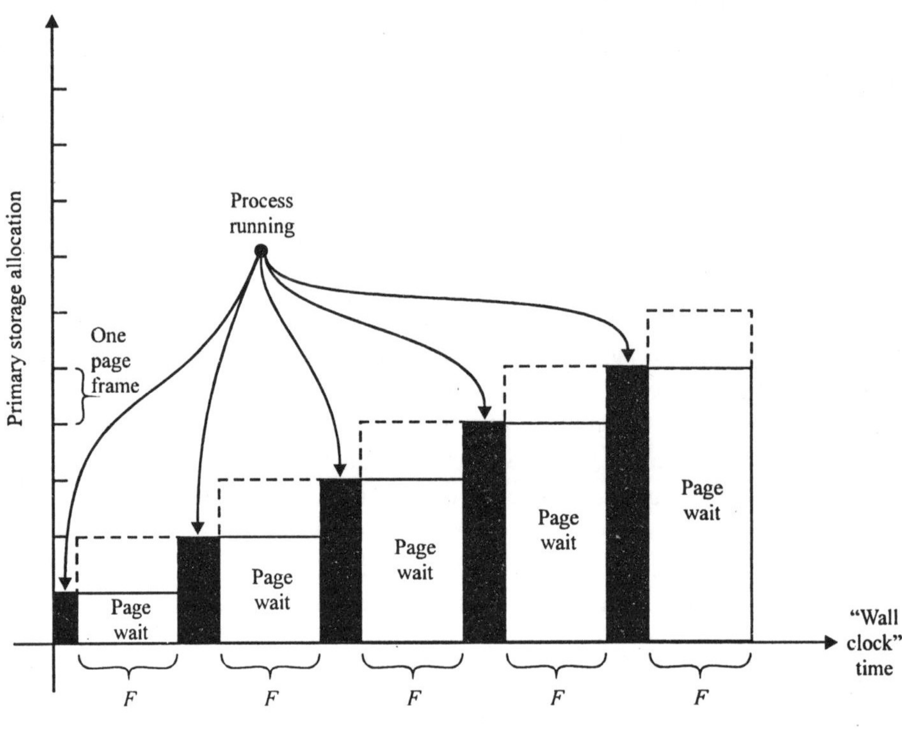

Fig. 9.34. Space-time product under demand paging.

Anticipatory Paging

A central theme in resource management is that *the relative value of a resource influences just how intensively the resource should be managed.* Hardware cost have been decreasing dramatically. The relative value of machine time to people time has been considerably reduced. Now operating systems designers are concerned with methods of reducing the amount of time people must wait for result from a computer. *Anticipatory paging* is one technique that holds promise. Anticipatory paging is sometimes called prepaging.

In anticipatory paging, the operating system attempts to predict the pages a process will need, and them preloads these pages when space is available. If correct decisions are made, the total run time of the process can be reduced considerably. While the process runs with its current pages, the system loads new pages that will be available when the process requests them.

Some operating systems, such as VAX/VMS, take advantage of spatial locality by paging in clusters of contiguous pages; the page being directly referenced is demand paged while the other pages in the cluster are essentially being prepaged.

Anticipatory paging offers the following advantages.

- If correct decisions can be made in a large majority of the cases, the running time of a process will be reduced considerably. Therefore, its worth trying to develop anticipatory paging mechanisms even though they cannot be 100 per cent accurate.
- Accurate decisions can be made in many cases, if this decision making can be implemented with relatively low overhead, then the execution of a given process can be considerably speeded without adversely affecting other active processes.
- With computer hardware becoming more economical, the consequences of a bad decision are less serious. We can buy extra main storage to support the accumulation of the excess pages an anticipatory mechanism would bring to main storage.

Page Release

Under working set storage management, programs tell us what pages they want to use by explicit reference. Programs that no longer require specific pages should have those pages passed from their working sets. There is usually a period of time during which the pages no longer needed remain in main storage.

When it becomes clear that a page will no longer be needed, a user could issue a *voluntary page release* command to free the page frame. This would eliminate the delay period caused by letting the process gradually pass the page from its working set.

Voluntary page release could eliminate waste and speed program execution. But most users of today's computer systems don't even know what a page is, and these users should not be asked to make system-level decisions. The incorporation of page release commands into user programs might considerably slow applications development.

The real hope in this area is for compilers and operating systems to detect page release situations automatically, and much sooner than is possible under working set strategies.

Page Size

In paging systems, real storage is normally divided into fixed-size page frames. How large should these page frames be? How large should a page be? Should all the pages in a system be the same size, or should several different page sizes be used? If several sizes are used, should the larger page sizes be integral multiples of the smaller page sizes?

These questions require judgment and a careful understanding of the hardware, software, and intended applications for a particular system. There are no universal answers. There is no pressing need for all computer systems to have the same page size, or a single page size for that matter.

What considerations determine whether a page should be large or small? Several are summarized here.

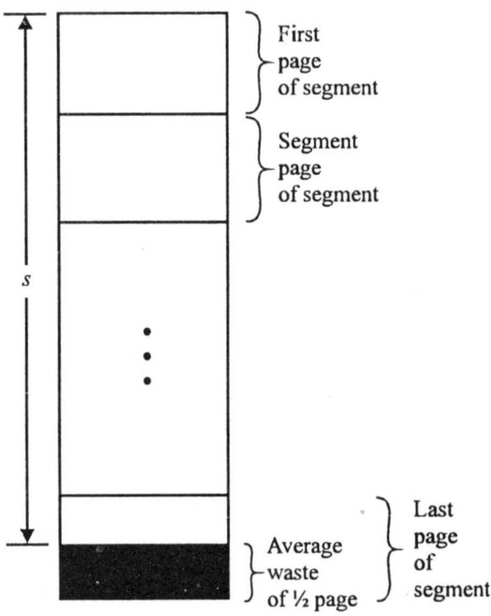

Fig. 9.35. Internal fragmentation in a paged system.

The smaller the page size, the more pages and page frames there are and the larger the page tables need to be. On systems in which pages tables occupy primary storage, this points to the need for larger pages. The waste of storage due to excessively large tables is called *table fragmentation.* We not here that this argument is less valid today with the availability of very large and economical memories.

With large page sizes, large amounts of information that ultimately may not be referenced are paged into primary storage. This points to the need for smaller pages.

Manufacturer	Model	Page size	Unit
Honeywell	Multics	1024	36-bit word
IBM	370/168	1024 or 512	32-bit word
DEC	PDP - 10 PDP - 20	512	32-bit word
DEC	VAX 8800	512	8-bit byte
Intel	80386	4096	8-bit byte

Fig. 9.36. Some common page sizes.

Because I/O transfers from disk are relatively time-consuming, we wish to minimize the number of transfers a program will experience as it runs. This seems to point to the need for large page sizes.

Programs tend to exhibit the property of locality of reference, and these localities tend to be small. Thus a smaller page size would help a program establish a tighter working set, i.e., the working set pages maintained in real storage would contain more intensively referenced items.

Because procedure and data units rarely comprise an integral number of pages, paging systems experience internal fragmentation, as illustrated in Fig. 9.38. A segment of length *s* is just as likely to have its last page nearly full as nearly empty, and thus, on the average, there is one-half page of internal fragmentation (with the restriction that a page may not contain portions of more than one segment). The smaller the page size, the less the internal fragmentation.

Many results in the literature, both theoretical and empirical, point to the need for small pages. Figure 19.36 shows the page sizes used in several historically popular and important computers. Note the relatively small page size chosen for the VAX 8800. Also, note the popularity of approximately 4K-character page sizes. As computer memories continue to increase in size and decrease in cost, and as applications that use more memory proliferate, it is likely that the meaning of "small page size" may be recast in the context of more powerful machines. Indeed, page sizes of 32K and even 1Mb could eventually be considered "small."

Program Behavior Under Paging

Paging is a valuable concept, and it will probably continue to be integrated into computer systems for the next several decades. Many studies have been performed examining the behavior of processes in paging environments.

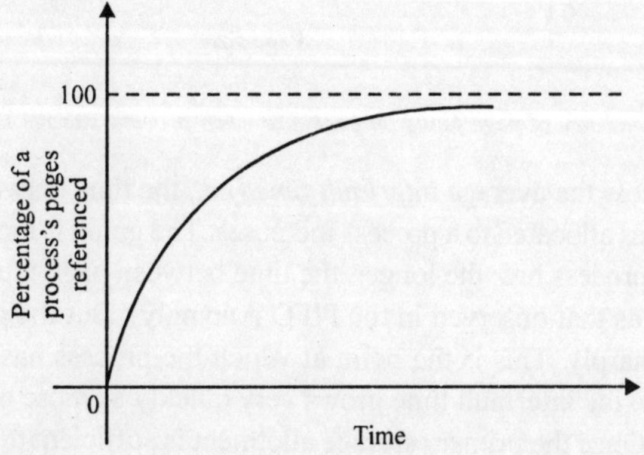

Fig. 9.37. Percentage of a process's pages referenced with time.

Figure 9.37 shows the percentage of a typical process's pages referenced from the time the process begins execution. The initial sharp upward slope indicates that a process tends to reference a significant portion of its pages immediately after it begins execution. With time, the slope diminished, and the graphs asymphotically approaches 100 per cent. Certainly some processed reference 100 per cent of their pages, but the graph is drawn to reflect that many processes may execute for a long time without referencing 100 per cent of their pages. This is often the case when certain error processing routines are rarely invoked.

Figure 9.38 indicates the effects of varying the page size when the amount of primary storage is held constant. The graph shows that the number of page faults experienced by a running process tends to increase as the page size increases. This occurs because as page size increases more procedures and data that will not be referenced are brought into a fixed size primary storage. Thus there is a decrease in the percentage of a process's limited primary storage occupied by procedures and data that will be referenced. Because the referencing pattern of the process is essentially independent of the amount of primary storage allocated, more page faults are generated to bring the required procedures and data into primary storage throughout the process's execution. The dotted portion of the graph indicates that as the page size approaches the size of the entire process, the number of page faults rapidly falls to zero.

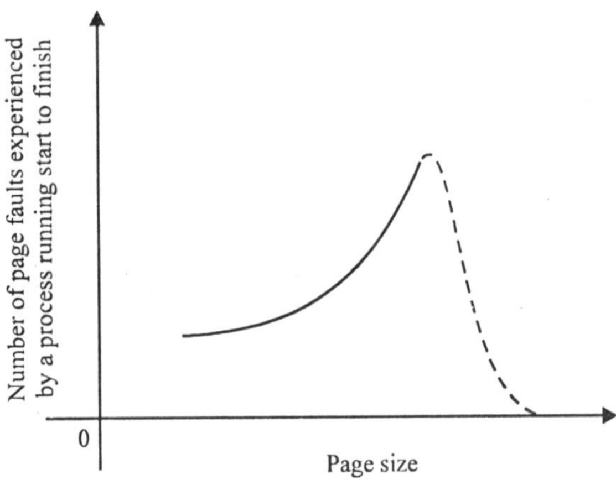

Fig. 9.38. Dependency of page faults on page size when primary storage is held constant.

Figure 9.39 shows how the average *interfault time* (i.e., the time between page faults) varies as the number of page frames allocated to a process increases. The graph is monotonically increasing—the more page frames a process has, the longer, the time between page faults (subject, of course, to eccentric behavior such as that observed in the FIFO Anomaly). But the graph bends at one point, and its slope declined sharply. This is the point at which the process has its entire working set in primary storage. Initially, the interfault time grows very quickly as more of the working set may be kept in primary storage. Once the primary storage allotment is sufficient to hold the working set, the curve bends sharply indicating that the effect of allocating additional page frames on increasing the interfault time is not as great. The key is to get the working set into primary storage, Franklin, Graham, and Gupta have observed anomalous situations in which increasing the size of the working set window, and hence the size of the working set, actually decreases the interfault time. But this kind of behavior is rare.

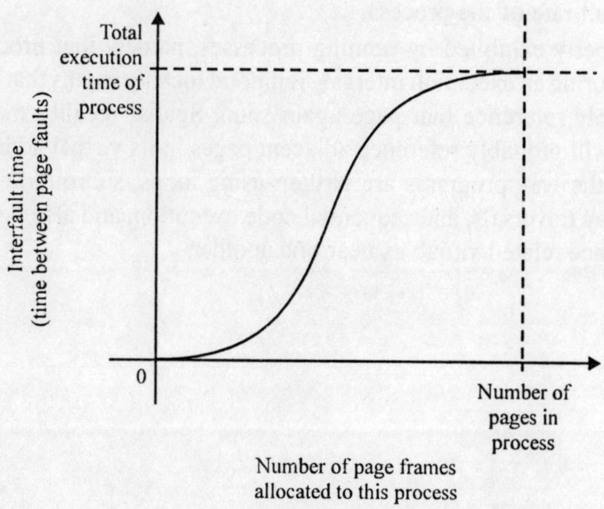

Fig. 9.39. *Dependency of interfault time on the number of page frames allocated to a process.*

Summary

Virtual storage management strategies are divided into three categories. Fetch strategies are concerned with when to bring the next page or segment to primary storage. Demand fetch does so upon explicit reference; anticipatory fetch does so in advance when it is likely that a page or segment will soon be referenced. Placement strategies are concerned with where in primary storage to place the incoming page or segment. Replacement strategies are concerned with which page or segment to replace to make room for an incoming page or segment when primary storage is fully committed.

Some of the page replacement strategies discussed in this chapter are

- Principle of Optimality—replaces the page which will not be used until the furthest time into the future.
- Random—pages are selected at random.
- FIFO—the page in primary storage the longest is selected (we also discussed the second chance and the clock variations of FIFO).
- LRU—the least-recently-used page is selected.
- LFU—the least-frequently-used page is selected.
- NUR—an inexpensive and efficient approximation of LRU that replaces a page not used-recently.
- Workingset—replaces a page if it is not in the favored subset of a process's pages.
- Page fault frequency—adjusts the size of a process's resident set of pages in response to changes in the process's page fault rate.

The FIFO Anomaly occurs when increasing the number of page frames available to a process increases the page fault rate of the process.

Locality is a property exhibited by running processes, namely that processes tend to favor a subset of their pages during an execution interval. Temporal locality means that if a process references a page, it will probably reference that page again soon. Spatial locality means that if a process references a page, it will probably reference adjacent pages in its virtual address space. Locality is expected because of the way programs are written using loops, subroutines, stack, counting and totaling variables, array traversals, and sequential code execution, and also because of the tendency of programmers to place related variables near one another.